Della Innocenti

Della
Innocenti

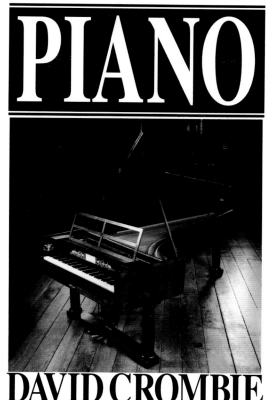

PIANO

DAVID CROMBIE

PIANO
BY DAVID CROMBIE

GPI BOOKS
AN IMPRINT OF MILLER FREEMAN BOOKS, SAN FRANCISCO

PUBLISHED IN THE UK BY BALAFON BOOKS, AN IMPRINT OF OUTLINE PRESS LTD,
115J CLEVELAND STREET, LONDON W1P 5PN, ENGLAND.

FIRST AMERICAN EDITION 1995
PUBLISHED IN THE UNITED STATES BY MILLER FREEMAN BOOKS,
600 HARRISON STREET, SAN FRANCISCO, CA 94107
PUBLISHERS OF *KEYBOARD* MAGAZINE
A MEMBER OF THE UNITED NEWSPAPERS GROUP

ISBN 0-87930-372-7
LIBRARY OF CONGRESS CATALOG NUMBER 95-77072

95 96 97 98 99 5 4 3 2 1
PRINTED IN HONG KONG

THE AUTHOR EXTENDS SPECIAL THANKS FOR CONSIDERABLE HELP IN THE PREPARATION OF THIS BOOK TO:
RICHARD AND KATRINA BURNETT (FINCHCOCKS, GOUDHURST, KENT, UK); BILL DOW (FINCHCOCKS, GOUDHURST,
KENT, UK); STEFAN G. JAKUBOWSKI (BÖSENDORFER, LONDON, UK); MICHAEL LATCHAM (HAAGS
GEMEENTEMUSEUM, THE HAGUE, NETHERLANDS); JEFF PRETT (STEINWAY & SONS, LONDON, UK); MICHAEL RYDER
(THE MUSICAL MUSEUM, BRENTFORD, UK); HENRY Z. STEINWAY (STEINWAY & SONS, NEW YORK, US);
ROGER D. WILLSON (WHELPDALE MAXWELL & CODD, LONDON, UK).

CREATIVE DIRECTOR: NIGEL OSBORNE
DESIGN: SALLY STOCKWELL
ILLUSTRATIONS: MARION APPLETON
PICTURE RESEARCH: DAVID CROMBIE
EDITORIAL DIRECTOR: TONY BACON
EDITOR: JOHN MORRISH
EDITORIAL ASSISTANCE: PETER BARBER

THE MAJORITY OF COMMISSIONED PHOTOGRAPHY IS BY NIGEL BRADLEY (VISUEL 7). ADDITIONAL COMMISSIONED
PHOTOGRAPHS ARE BY WILL TAYLOR (VISUEL 7), MIKI SLINGSBY AND THE AUTHOR.

TYPESETTING BY KEVIN DODD & MICHAEL CUSHING AT TYPE TECHNIQUE, LONDON W1
PRINT & ORIGINATION BY REGENT PUBLISHING SERVICES

C O N T E N T S

EARLY STRINGED INSTRUMENTS 4

INTRODUCTION OF THE KEYS 6

CLAVICHORDS, SPINETS, VIRGINALS AND HARPSICHORDS 8

CRISTOFORI 11

THE SECOND WAVE 15

THE RISE OF THE SQUARE PIANO 18

THE FALL OF THE SQUARE PIANO 20

THE EARLY PORTABLE PIANO 22

THE EARLY VIENNESE PIANO 24

THE EVOLUTION OF THE VIENNESE PIANO 26

THE GRAND PIANO IN ENGLAND 28

THE EVOLUTION OF THE GRAND PIANO 30

FROM STRENGTH TO STRENGTH 32

PIANOS AND PEOPLE 35

UPRIGHT GRANDS AND UPRIGHT SQUARES 39

THE EARLY UPRIGHT PIANO 42

THE EVOLUTION OF THE UPRIGHT PIANO 44

THE GREAT EXHIBITIONS 46

A PERIOD OF CONSOLIDATION 48

VARIATIONS ON A THEME 50

THE BARREL PIANO 52

THE PIANO PLAYER AND PLAYER PIANO 54

THE REPRODUCING PIANO AND OTHER AUTOMATIC INSTRUMENTS 56

THE MODERN GRAND PIANO 59

THE ART-CASE PIANO 63

THE ART-CASE PIANO: INTO THE MODERN ERA 66

KEYBOARD VARIATIONS 68

ALL SHAPES AND SIZES 70

ON THE MOVE 72

THE EARLY ELECTRIC PIANO 74

FROM ELECTRIC TO ELECTRONIC 76

RECENT TIMES 78

THE MODERN UPRIGHT PIANO 80

20TH CENTURY INSTRUMENTS OF SIGNIFICANCE 83

HOW A PIANO WORKS 87

PIANO HOUSES 96

PIANOS ON RECORD 104

GLOSSARY 105

INDEX 108

ACKNOWLEDGEMENTS 112

To some the piano is a piece of furniture, to others a musical instrument. Pianos are often taken for granted, and yet they are the most complex mechanical device found in any home, with a typical instrument containing over 10,000 parts.

Unlike other keyboard instruments such as harpsichords and organs, pianos are truly expressive. The player is able to articulate every note, and the piano has become increasingly popular because of this capability. Keyboard players can express themselves on the piano whether they are interpreting the works of the great composers, rousing the sound of a jazz group, or playing at the heart of a blues or pop performance.

Throughout its 300-year existence the piano has had a history as varied as the eras through which it has lived, and while it continues to mutate and develop in parallel with evolving technological, artistic and aesthetic demands, the piano remains quite unchallenged as the greatest of all musical instruments.

The piano's sound source is simple: vibrating strings. And while many instruments such as guitars, harps, violins and clavichords also derive their sound from vibrating strings, they differ in the way that their strings are made to vibrate. There are three main ways in which a string can be set into vibration. It can be plucked, like a guitar; it can be bowed, like a violin; or it can be struck, like a piano. In the case of the piano, small hammers hit the strings and bounce off, allowing the strings to vibrate freely. This ability contributes to the unique sound of the piano. Other keyboard instruments do vibrate strings by hitting them, but the clavichord, for example, does so with brass 'tangents' that remain in contact with the strings.

An early term for the piano was 'pianoforte', which comes from the Italian piano, soft, and forte, loud. The combination of the two words emphasizes the piano's potential to produce loud or soft tones depending on how hard its keys are struck. During the 18th and 19th centuries instrument manufacturers often called their square or grand pianos 'forte-pianos'. In Spain the term fuerte-piano was used to describe all pianos, and in some countries fortepiano is still used. It is most often used today to refer to an early piano, typically one that was built

DULCIMER

before 1850, or an instrument of particular historical importance or note. Modern recordings of early pianos use the word fortepiano to indicate that the recording was made with an early instrument rather than with a modern piano. The term fortepiano may still be heard today in piano stores and showrooms where the aim may be to impress, but in general the instrument's full name is shortened to the much more familiar 'piano'.

The history of the piano can be traced back to the earliest of stringed instruments, the zither, which existed during the Bronze Age, around 3000BC, in Africa and south-east Asia. A zither has a string or strings stretched between two 'bridges', and the string is plucked or struck. The ground zither, for example, consisted of a hole dug in the earth. A string was stretched over this cavity, and when the string was struck or plucked it vibrated and caused the air in the hollow to resonate and thus amplify the vibration. Many different types of zither evolved. The stick or bar zither was one of the earliest and consisted of a stick of wood with a string tied to both ends: tension in the string was applied by bending the stick. Frets could be formed as part of the stick to facilitate simple tunings. The sound of the vibrating strings was amplified by attaching some form of resonant chamber, such as a hollowed gourd (a large fruit), or by the player pressing the instrument to his or her body and using that as a resonant cavity.

Board zithers had a raised, slightly arched top with bridges at either end. The strings ran over the bridges and through holes along the length of the instrument and then ran back again to anchor points. This top surface formed part of a soundbox which amplified the sound. As demand increased for more strings, raft zithers emerged. These consisted of a series of single-strung 'tube' zithers bound together, resembling a raft. Again, a gourd was widely used as a resonant chamber to amplify the sound. In the Far East the long zither had been developed over thousands of years. The long zither came both fretted and unfretted, with a long, arched soundboard across which were stretched strings, often made of silk and up to 25 in number. The best known form of this type of zither today is the Japanese koto, the tunings of which are determined by moveable bridges.

The monochord, sometimes referred to as the manichordian or manichord, was not so much a musical as a scientific instrument. It evolved from the zither, and had a long, hollow, oblong soundbox across which was stretched a string supported by two fixed bridge pieces. A third bridge piece could be slid along the string to divide it into two separate speaking lengths, and the string was plucked. Along the top of the monochord was a scale to enable the relative lengths of each half of the string to be measured. The monochord was used by Greek philosophers and in particular Pythagoras as an experimental apparatus for investigating musical principles. Pythagoras lived in the sixth century BC and attempted to prove that all the laws of music are based on simple mathematical ratios. The monochord was an ideal device for visualizing the mathematical relationship that exists between notes. The instrument was still being used in the Middle Ages, and Guido of Arezzo, the leading musical theorist of the 11th century, is known to have used one to show how the structure of the Church's plainsong was based on eight tones. In addition to being used for scientific purposes, the monochord often provided a reference pitch for choral works, songs of worship and pipe organs. As more strings were gradually added the monochord became what we now call the polychord.

MONOCHORD

The zither, monochord and polychord, with strings stretched between two bridge pieces and amplified by a soundboard, represent early, simple incarnations of the assembly of string, frame and soundboard that is at the heart of the piano's sound-producing mechanism. The next instrumental development, which would also eventually find its way into the piano, concerned the way in which strings were made to vibrate. The psaltery appeared in medieval times and was like a board zither, trapezoidal in shape to accommodate the different length strings. Its soundboard (the top of the soundbox) to which the bridges were mounted was flat, and it had gut strings, which were struck. The psaltery could either be worn, by means of a strap around the player's neck; placed in the player's lap; placed on a table; or held in one hand and played with the other. Many are seen in works of art of the time. The psaltery was often highly decorated itself, and elaborate paintings are sometimes to be found on the inside of the casework. The psaltery's trapezoidal shape is found in many subsequent stringed instruments such as the spinet and harpsichord.

KOTO

The zither did not reach central Europe until around the 11th century. The quanum, or qanum, had plucked strings, and was a trapezoidal psaltery, held vertically. It was introduced to Spain by travelers to the Middle East and North Africa, and by the 12th century the quanum had reached much of non-Moorish Europe. The dulcimer (probably from the Latin dulcis, sweet, and melos, song) was similar to the psaltery but was the first instrument with strings that were specifically designed to be hit. Its strings are made of metal and struck with two small, padded hammers, and the dulcimer is still used today as a folk instrument in many countries. With the addition of a keyboard the piano, in concept at least, was not so very far away.

Early keyboard instruments *were played using the hands – and in some extreme cases the fists – rather than the fingers. One of the earliest known examples of a keyboard instrument was the hydraulis, or water organ, used in ancient Greece around the 3rd century BC. In fact this used wooden sliders rather than pivoted keys, and had a reservoir of air kept under compression by a head of water. Each of the organ's pipes had a valve which was opened when the slider was pushed in, allowing air to flow from the wind-chest through the pipe.*

The hurdy-gurdy (also known as the organistrum, symphonie or armonie) was probably the earliest stringed instrument to use a keyboard. References are made to the organistrum as far back as the 10th century. The hurdy-gurdy looks like a type of fretted zither, but in fact it originated in the violin family of instruments. Instead of using a conventional bow to excite the strings as with a violin, the hurdy-gurdy has a rosined wheel positioned to press against the strings. As the wheel is turned, usually by means of a hand-operated crank, the strings are set into vibration. The string's length is determined by a simple and primitive keyboard mechanism that moves a small anvil to press a string on to the fretboard and the note sounds for as long as the handle is turned.

In the late 15th century, Leonardo da Vinci designed a stringed musical instrument developed from the organistrum which used a keyboard and could sustain the vibration of the string as long as required. The plans for his 'viola organista' showed a revolving wheel bowing a string. The sound would continue as long as the key was pressed, which kept the turning wheel in contact with the string. Unfortunately there is no evidence that such an instrument was ever made.

GEIGENWERCK

It was not until the 10th and 11th centuries that small two-octave organs began to appear in western Europe. The pipes of these organs were activated by sliders, each with a handle to enable the player to push and pull these 'keys' in and out. The identical handles had to be marked with identifying letters, and the instrument's two-octave keyboard compass was found to be sufficient at the time.

The valve mechanism evolved to use pivoted keys, but as there was a direct link between key and pipe, the physical width of the keys was determined by the width of the pipes, resulting in keys up to three inches wide. Keyboards used on organs up to the 13th century were originally without sharps and flats, and started on a C note. Gradually a white Bflat note was incorporated to allow music written in the scale of G – notably plainsong melodies – to be transposed into C. But by the end of the 13th century most keyboards featured a raised Bflat note positioned between the normal A and B notes.

By the beginning of the 14th century organ keyboards had grown to a compass of up to three octaves, and chromatic keys (sharps and flats) were introduced. The lower chromatic keys were in fact seldom used, primarily because the instruments were still used for plainsong.

SHORT AND BROKEN
BASS OCTAVE

Consequently organ makers didn't waste money incorporating expensive pipes that weren't going to be used. As a result only the Bflat note was required in the bass, and the 'short bass octave' was developed, and later used on other keyboard instruments such as harpsichords.

With the C short bass octave, the keys that would normally be assigned to F♯ and G♯ were used as D and E, with the bottom note (normally an E) tuned to C. The notes available in order of rising pitch were: C, D, E, F, G, A, Bflat, c, c♯ and so on. This short octave is indicated by C/E (C in the E position). The G short bass octave is configured in a similar way, indicated by GG/BB (GG in the BB position). [For an explanation of keyboard-position terms such as c, GG, BB etc, see KEYBOARD REFERENCE *in* the Glossary at the rear of the book.] In the early 17th century the short and broken octave was introduced. In the case of the C scale, the F♯ and G♯ accidental keys were split so that the front half of the key played D or E and the rear half F♯ or G♯. The scale ran: C, D, E, F, F♯, G, G♯, A, Bflat, B, c and so on.

The geigenwerck was an instrument that set its strings into vibration by using a stroking action, and as such can also be considered to have evolved from the organistrum. The instrument was documented in musicologist Michael Praetorius's famous book Theatrum Instrumentorum of 1620. The geigenwerck was built like a harpsichord, with a chromatic keyboard, but instead of plucking the strings to make them vibrate it used a set of rotating wheels with cloth covers or rosined edges. These were positioned to cover the entire compass of the instrument, and were kept in rotation by a treadle mechanism. When a key was depressed the corresponding string was pushed against one of the rotating wheels and the string was set in vibration. The note would continue to sound until the key was released or the wheel ceased to rotate.

An important person in the evolution of the piano was Pantaleon Hebenstreit. Born in Eisleben, Germany, in 1667, he later became a famous dulcimer player, wielding the instrument's hammers with a degree of showmanship that made Hebenstreit a celebrity across Europe. The dulcimer was unlike the harpsichord, the primary keyboard instrument of the time, in that it could produce a wide dynamic range, from very soft to loud. As with any stringed instrument, the tone produced by a string can be varied by striking the string at a different point. A good dulcimer player would therefore have had considerable control over both the volume and tone of each individual note played, and could introduce their own expression into any piece of music. That is exactly what made Hebenstreit famous.

Such was Hebenstreit's fame as a dulcimer virtuoso that he set about redesigning the instrument to suit his talents. He greatly enlarged the instrument so that it was more than nine feet long, four times the usual size. He increased its range by providing 180 strings, and added an extra soundboard. In order to give himself a yet wider tonal spectrum he developed double-faced hammers, where each face was covered with different material so that he could choose between a hard and a soft impact upon the strings. Louis XIV of France saw Hebenstreit's new dulcimer in Paris in 1705 and said that in honor of its designer it should be called a pantaleon. The instrument incorporated a dynamic range unusual at the time, but the skills required to play it meant that few could master it, and its complexity and size meant that still fewer were attracted to own one. Consequently the pantaleon was a shortlived instrument. But its influence was considerable in the story of the development of the pianoforte, and it is an important link between the world of keyed and non-keyed stringed instruments.

The keyed monochord or polychord had evolved in the 15th century and subsequently became known as the clavichord (this and the related keyboard instruments such as spinets, virginals and harpsichords are covered on pages 8 to 10). The compass of the keyboard had itself grown in the 16th century to four-and-a-half octaves, often using the short bass octave. By 1700, harpsichord manufacturers were using keyboards of five octaves, typically from F to f^3, and as the piano became increasingly popular, keyboard dimensions grew steadily. In the mid 1790s, six-octave instruments began to appear, and in the 1860s the first commercially available seven-octave instruments were being built. Today's piano keyboards are typically of 88 notes (seven-and-a-third octaves), ranging from AAA to c^5.

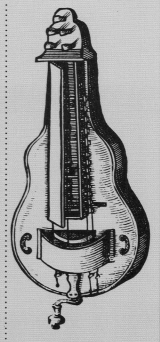

HURDY-GURDY

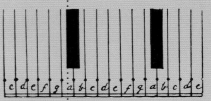

EARLY KEYBOARD WITH B FLAT KEY

GEORG FRIEDRICH SCHMAHL, Ulm, Germany, 1807, fretted clavichord

CASEWORK:	Spruce, painted dark red
COMPASS:	4½ octaves C - f³
REGISTER:	Bichord 8 ft+4 ft (C-c); bichord 8 ft (c♯-f³)
INSCRIPTION:	Georg Friedrich Schmahl / Orgel-und Instrumentenmacher / in Ulm Ao 1807 No. 53
DIMENSIONS (INS.):	54½ (W) x 16 (D) x 6 (Height of case)

This illustration (below) shows the clavichord's action. A metal wedge (the tangent) is attached to the end of each key. When the key is played the tangent

rises and strikes the string. The tangent is in effect the moveable bridge of the monochord and polychord, but in addition to dividing the string it also sets it into vibration. The tangent remains in contact with the string until the key is released. In order to stop both portions of the string sounding at the same time, the non-speaking end of the string is damped with felt. The string sounds as long as the key is held.

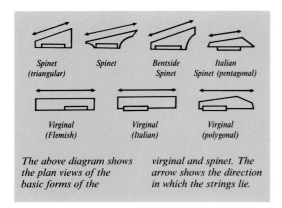

Spinet (triangular)   Spinet   Bentside Spinet   Italian Spinet (pentagonal)

Virginal (Flemish)   Virginal (Italian)   Virginal (polygonal)

The above diagram shows the plan views of the basic forms of the virginal and spinet. The arrow shows the direction in which the strings lie.

A mid-18th century oil painting by Martin Meytens, depicting an Italian family of musicians. The picture is focused on Christina Antonia Somis, who is playing a small octave spinet, while her brother Lorenzo and father Francesco accompany her on violin and cello respectively.

JOSEPH MAHOON, London, 1742, bentside spinet

CASEWORK:	Walnut veneer
COMPASS:	5 octaves; GG-g³
REGISTER:	1 x 8 ft
INSCRIPTION:	Joseph Mahoon London
DIMENSIONS (INS.):	74 (W-oblique) x 25 (D) x 8¼ (Height of case)

This is a small domestic instrument with strings running obliquely to the keyboard. The typical harpsichord shape can be clearly seen, but with the shorter strings it has been skewed to make it smaller, producing this shape. The keyboard features black accidentals with white inserts running along them. These have subsequently become known as 'skunk's tail' keys. In Germany this type of instrument is known as a Querspinett, and first appeared around 1660. The design, with its oblique stringing, was later adapted for small pianos.

CLAVICHORDS, SPINETS, VIRGINALS AND HARPSICHORDS

The clavichord and the harpsichord family both owe their origins to the development of keyed versions of the polychord and the psaltery at the beginning of the 13th century. It took another two centuries before the clavichord and harpsichord arrived.

Both instruments were to play a decisive part in ensuring the widespread availability and acceptability of keyboard instruments. As with any advance in musical technology these new keyboards had important consequences in terms of composition and performance.

Both the clavichord and harpsichord family appeared first at the beginning of the 15th century. The opportunities that these new instruments brought were to prove enormously influential in shaping the future of music.

THE CLAVICHORD

The first reports of the clavichord's existence are from 1404. The instrument is generally rectangular in shape, with the strings running parallel to the keyboard.

The action mechanism, although simple, gives the player considerable control. The harder the key is struck, the greater the force with which the anvil strikes the string and the louder the note. And when the note is held, the player is able to increase and decrease the pressure on the string. This raises and lowers its pitch slightly, producing a vibrato effect known as 'bebung'.

The early clavichords were what is known as 'fretted', that is to say several keys (as many as four) could strike a single string or pair of strings at different places to produce the correct pitch. Later, 'unfretted' instruments appeared, with one or more strings

per note. By the early 17th century, this had been taken a stage further by tuning the two or three strings assigned to each note to different octaves to produce an harmonically richer, and slightly louder, voicing. At the same time the instrument grew to accommodate longer strings and a larger soundboard.

The clavichord was really only suited to domestic use or small gatherings. Its relatively low cost, however, and its musicality gave it great popularity in central Europe, especially Germany.

PLUCKED STRINGS

Spinets, virginals and harpsichords all belong to the same basic family, in which strings are activated by a plucking action. The harpsichord is the largest of the instruments and the only one suitable for ensemble or concert work.

The spinet comes in various shapes, including the wing-shaped version known as the bentside spinet. It is diagonally strung, with its tuning pins located just above and behind the keyboard. The virginal is normally rectangular in shape. Its strings and keyboard both run parallel to the long side of the casework.

The lid of this virginal case is decorated with a painting of fantasy architecture set against a background of an unfinished landscape.

The outer case, which is an integral part of the instrument, affording it a degree of protection when not in use, is finely decorated with imitation marble inlay.

The front panel of the outer casing is hinged, revealing the keyboard, but when the virginal was to be played it would be removed from the outer case, allowing more sound to emerge.

accommodate the much longer strings it was necessary to run the string perpendicular to the keyboard (parallel to the keys). In some instances, to save space, the strings would run vertically, producing what is known as a 'clavicytherium'.

'Stops', operated by levers, were used to introduce various effects, the most enduring being the 'forte' stop, which lifts the dampers away from the keys, and the 'piano' stop, which leaves the dampers sitting on the strings when plucked.

Later two and three strings per note were introduced to generate more volume, and these were often tuned an octave apart (8 ft and 4 ft, sometimes 16 ft) in order to give greater variation in tone. By the end of the 18th century some manufacturers were using up to five strings per note (quintuple-chord). Originally the harpsichord used a single keyboard and was single strung. A second manual started to appear in the 17th century and then a third.

The harpsichord, unlike the little clavichord, was unable to provide dynamic control of each note. The demand for a truly 'loud and soft' harpsichord became irresistible.

SASSMANN, Hückeswagen, Germany, 1994, harpsichord, after Henri Hemsch c1756

CASEWORK:	*Limetree or Poplar*
COMPASS:	*FF-e³*
REGISTER:	*Manual I - 8 ft, 4 ft*
	Manual II - 8 ft buff stop, coupler
INSCRIPTION:	*SASSMANN*
DIMENSIONS (INS.):	*94½ (L) x 36 (W) x 11 (Height of case)*

Some parts of the original harpsichord by Henri Hemsch have been lost over the years, but this modern reproduction is thought to be accurate. Hemsch was born in Cologne in 1700, but moved to Paris to work initially under Antoine Vatter, adopting the French style, which is both visually (and mechanically) different from that of the Flemish harpsichord below. Hemsch, Vatter, and Taskin (another emigré), all produced high quality French-style instruments in Paris.

ADLAM & BURNETT, Goudhurst/Welbeck, UK, 1982, double manual harpsichord after Ruckers 1638.

CASEWORK:	*Poplar*
COMPASS:	*GG/BB-d³ (short and broken bottom octave)*
REGISTER:	*2 x 8 ft; 1 x 4 ft*
INSCRIPTION:	*ADLAM BURNETT FECERUNT*
DIMENSIONS (INS.):	*89½ (L) x 32½ (W) x 11 (Height of case)*

This superb reconstruction is based on the double manual harpsichord of Andreas Ruckers, who lived and worked in Antwerp. The Ruckers family made harpsichords and virginals of the finest quality from c1580 to 1680. Their designs were copied by many harpsichord makers in France and England in both the 18th century and in recent times. This instrument, in keeping with the original, features a short and broken bottom octave which effectively extends the compass of each keyboard to 4-2/3 octaves. Harpsichords tended to be more highly decorated than did the subsequent pianos. The interior of this instrument is embellished with printed papers, and the soundboard is painted, both common forms of adornment for the period.

SHUDI-BROADWOOD, London, 1770, harpsichord

SERIAL NO:	*625*
CASEWORK:	*Burr walnut with mahogany crossbanding*
COMPASS:	*2 x 5½ octaves; CC-f³*
MODIFIERS:	*Venetian swell*
INSCRIPTION:	*Burkat Shudi and Johannes Broadwood / No. 625 Londini fecerunt 1770*
DIMENSIONS (INS.):	*95 (L) x 60 (W) x 13 (Height of case)*

This harpsichord was one of the first to feature the new Venetian swell (patented the previous year). This gave the player a degree of control over the overall volume of the instrument. However, it didn't address the need to be able to control the volume of individual notes. Originally from Switzerland, Burkat Shudi moved to England in 1728, where he became one of the great harpsichord makers.

KEY DATES

1700	First documented evidence of Bartolomeo Cristofori's piano experiments, in the inventory of musical instruments belonging to Prince Ferdinand.
c1709	Cristofori publicly reveals his pianoforte, which uses a hammer mechanism instead of the plucked string action of the harpsichord.
1711	Maffei documents Cristofori's invention in the *Giornale dei letterati d'Italia*.
1713	Prince Ferdinand dies and Cristofori becomes curator of his instrument collection, which includes a *Geigenwerck*.
c1716	Gottlieb Schröter, a keyboard teacher, produces two piano actions (one up-striking, the other down-striking) for adapting a traditional harpsichord to hammers.
1720	Production of Cristofori's earliest surviving piano.
c1722	Bartolomeo Cristofori develops 'una corda' mechanism. This enables the player to move the action so that the hammer strikes just one string for each note.
1726	Cristofori produces his last piano.
c1728	Gottfried Silbermann, a clavichord maker, produces two refinements on the 'harpsichord with hammers' theme but neither achieves success.
1731	Cristofori dies

BARTOLOMEO CRISTOFORI, Florence, 1722, grand piano

CASEWORK:	*Poplar and cypress*
COMPASS:	*4 octaves; C–c³*
ACTION:	*Cristofori jack with check and escapement*
STRINGS:	*Bichord*
MODIFIERS:	*1 hand stop: keyboard shift to una corda*
INSCRIPTION:	*BARTHOLOMAEVS DE CHRISTOPHORIS PATAVINVS INVENTOR FACIEBAT FLORENTIAE MDCCXXII*
DIMENSIONS (INS.):	*89 (L) x 32 (W) x 8½ (Depth of case)*

Two Cristofori instruments from 1722 survive: this piano, now in the Museo degli Strumenti Musicali in Rome, and a harpsichord in Leipzig. Both have a four-octave compass with the strings tuned in unison. This piano is the smallest of the surviving instruments. Like the 1726 instrument, it features an inverted pin block with the tuning pins driven right through. The strings are attached to the lower ends, whch leaves more room for the action and also leads to increased tuning stability, as the action of the hammer is towards the nut rather than away from it. This can be seen in the photographs showing the action (far right).

None of Cristofori's pianos had pedals, but he did eventually develop an 'una corda' stop which moved the hammers so that they struck just one string of each pair

CRISTOFORI

The first instrument that we would recognize today as a piano was the work of one man. Bartolomeo Cristofori was the keeper of instruments in the Florentine court. He built a tiny number of pianos, but all brilliantly solved the technical problems involved in creating an instrument in which strings are struck by hammers. Sadly, little interest was shown in his invention, at least initially. Cristofori reverted to making other stringed instruments. Nevertheless the surviving pianos shown here demonstrate the vision and mechanical ingenuity that has indisputably established Cristofori as the father of the pianoforte.

At the end of the 17th century, three types of keyboard instrument were in general use: organs, harpsichords (including virginals and spinets) and clavichords.

None of these gave the player a satisfactory way of controlling dynamics. In other words, it was impossible to control individually the volume of each note played. This made it difficult to introduce expression to the music.

There were various ineffective solutions. The organist could change stops to give the instrument a more powerful sound. The harpsichord player could introduce extra sets of strings to make the instrument louder. The clavichord player was able to take some advantage of the instrument's limited degree of dynamic response, but it was such a quiet instrument anyway that playing it more softly wasn't of practical use. The only effective way that composers could draw expression from these instruments was by actually writing in more notes when emphasis was required.

This was a time of great experimentation in music. Violinists were introducing expression into their repertoire and this was reflected elsewhere in musical taste. The new music was fresher,

This piano utilizes an inverted pin block, whereby the tuning pins pass right through the pin block and the strings are wound to their underside.

By raising the level of the stringing, Cristofori was able to accommodate a larger soundboard than typically found on the harpsichord.

Few recordings of Cristofori's pianos are available. However, the CD **Historische Tasteninstrumente aus dem Musikinstrumenten-Museum der Universität Leipzig**, 1995, features Walter Heinz Bernstein playing Giuseppe Paladini's **Divertimento in G major** on the 1726 Cristofori piano.

The soundboard is not attached directly to the case of the instrument, which helps to reduce the forces of compression acting on it.

This is the oldest surviving piano in the world. It is still in playable condition, and remains in use today. However, it has undergone some restoration in its three centuries of existence. Work was carried out to the keyboard in the 18th century, and a major restoration in 1938 saw, among other things, the soundboard and ribbing replaced. Apart from these works, the instrument is as Cristofori built it.

BARTOLOMEO CRISTOFORI, Florence, 1720, grand piano

CASEWORK:	Poplar, cypress soundboard
COMPASS:	4½ octaves; C – f³
ACTION:	Cristofori jack action, with check and escapement
STRINGS:	Bichord
MODIFIERS:	1 hand stop; knob on left hand key block
INSCRIPTION:	BARTHOLOMAEVS DE CHRISTOPHORIS PATAVINVS INVENTOR FACIEBAT FLORENTIAE MDCCXX
DIMENSIONS (INS.):	90 (L) x 37½ (W) x 9¼ (Height of case)

The piano, now housed at the Metropolitan Museum of Art in New York, is the oldest surviving piano in the world, although it was restored in 1938 and includes some parts that are not original. Like the other Cristofori pianos, it has a tone that is warm yet bright in the bass but becoming duller towards the treble. There is little sustain in the upper octaves. The speaking length of the bottom C is 74 in, compared to 4½ in for the top f³, and thus a single gauge of string can be accommodated. This piano originally belonged to the Medici family.

The legs and casework Cristofori used were in keeping with the style of the Italian harpsichords of the day.

❋ For information on recordings on this instrument, see Pianos on Record, p104.

SASSMANN, Hückeswagen, Germany, Virginal, after Couchet 1650

CASEWORK:	*Poplar*
COMPASS:	*4 octaves; E/C - c³ (short bottom octave)*
REGISTER:	*1 x 8 ft*
INSCRIPTION:	*SASSMANN*
DIMENSIONS (INS.):	*67 (W) x 20 (D) x 10 (Height of case)*

Jan Couchet was a nephew of Johannes Ruckers, and he too lived and worked in Antwerp, spending some 17 years of his life in the employ of the Ruckers family. This modern copy of his 1650 virginal illustrates clearly the typical styling of the Flemish instrument as opposed to that of the Italian virginal shown to the right. The virginal was widely used for chamber music in the 17th century, and several paintings by the Dutch masters feature this type of instrument.

JS Bach: Clavierbüchlein für Anna Magdalena Bach, Nicholas McGegan, harpsichord and clavichord. *This selection of pieces by Bach, for his second wife Anna Magdalena, beautifully ilustrates the way in which the harpsichord and clavichord were used at the beginning of the 17th century.*

Virginals are typically rectangular in shape, with strings running parallel to the keyboard. Italian virginals and spinets, however, usually have keyboards that project from their cases, as here, and are often not so regular in shape, the corners being 'cut off' to produce a polygonal appearance.

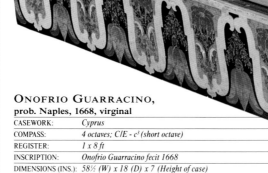

ONOFRIO GUARRACINO, prob. Naples, 1668, virginal

CASEWORK:	*Cyprus*
COMPASS:	*4 octaves; C/E - c³ (short octave)*
REGISTER:	*1 x 8 ft*
INSCRIPTION:	*Onofrio Guarracino fecit 1668*
DIMENSIONS (INS.):	*58½ (W) x 18 (D) x 7 (Height of case)*

This beautiful Italian virginal was probably made in Guarracino's Naples workshop. The inscription gives it an authenticated date of 1668. Italian virginals, or spinetti tavola as they are known in Italy, typically featured keyboards that projected from the case. They also rarely have stands or lids. Most have an outer case, from which the instrument is removed for playing. As a result, this instrument has survived for more than 300 years in excellent condition.

The basic action mechanism for the harpsichord, spinet and virginal centers around the jack, a small strip of wood that rests on the far end of the key. At the top of the jack is a small damper that sits on top of the string. Beneath the string is a plectrum of quill or cow hide, mounted on a tongue pivoted to the jack.

As the key is depressed, the jack rises, lifting the damper and causing the plectrum to pluck the string. The action mechanism and key of the harpsichord are now completely free of the string. The string will vibrate until it loses all the energy imparted to it or until the key is released.

The tongue to which the plectrum is mounted is pivoted so that when the key is released and the jack falls back, it allows the plectrum to slide past the string and back to its initial rest position. At the same time, the damper returns to sit on the string and mute any remaining vibrations.

SPINETS AND VIRGINALS

Many different kinds of spinet have been developed over the years. The 'octave spinet', for instance, used a set of 4 ft strings,

that is strings pitched an octave higher than normal.

The 'bentside spinet' was a wing-shaped instrument dating from the 1680s , with strings running obliquely to the keyboard. A smaller version, pitched an octave higher was known as the 'bentside octave spinet'.

Double manual spinets and double manual octave spinets were also made, as were spinets fitted with a pedalboard. There are also 'hybrid' virginals, for instance the octave virginal and the double manual virginal.

HARPSICHORDS

The clavichords, spinets and virginals were generally too quiet for concert or ensemble use. To get more volume, the strings needed to be thicker, longer and tauter. A larger soundboard was also required. The harpsichord, being much larger than its cousins, was consequently a far more powerful instrument.

The harpsichord enjoyed great popularity until the early 19th century, when the piano began to dominate.

Early harpsichords were essentially large spinets. However, to

KEY DATES

1397	First documented reference to a 'Clavicembalum' (harpsichord).
1404	First documented reference to a 'Clavicordium' (clavichord).
1425	First appearance of a harpsichord, depicted in a altarpiece carving at Minden Cathedral, Germany.
1460	First documented reference to a virginal.
c1490	Date of manufacture of what is believed to be the earliest surviving stringed keyboard instrument, a 'clavicytherium' or upright harpsichord.
1521	Date of production of earliest surviving harpsichord, made by Hieronymus Bononiensis (Italy)
1523	Date of production of earliest surviving spinet, made by Franciscus de Portalupis, Italy
1631	Date of production of earliest surviving bentside spinet, made by Girolamo Zenti
1689	Bartolomeo Cristofori, subsequently inventor of the pianoforte, builds his first harpsichord
c1700	Cristofori produces his first pianoforte, which uses a hammer mechanism instead of the plucked string action of the harpsichord.
c1736	First spinet made in America by Johann Clemm
c1810	Harpsichords no longer produced in significant numbers
c1812	Clavichords no longer produced in significant numbers

The two upper doors of this piano are hinged at the top and at the point where the curved edge meets the vertical. The doors are beautifully decorated both inside and out with inlaid flowers, ornaments and dancers. The doors open as if they are huge wings and the instrument takes on a whole new dimension.

With the doors open, the strings are revealed. The single bridge piece runs down the right-hand side of the instrument with the strings running obliquely upwards from left to right. The soundboard is located behind the strings and in its middle there is a rose of abstract design. This ornamentation was widely used by harpsichord and virginal manufacturers, and served purely as decoration or identification.

CHRISTIAN ERNST FRIEDERICI, Gera (Saxony), 1745, pyramid piano

CASEWORK:	*Possibly rosewood*
COMPASS:	*4¼ octaves; FF – d³*
ACTION:	*Stossmechanik*
MODIFIERS:	*2 hand stops; moderator, damper*
INSCRIPTION:	*Diese Pyramyte hat gefertiget und erfunden Christian Ernst Friederici Orgelbauer in Gera in Montas 7 tr Anno 1745 (inside case)*
DIMENSIONS (INS.):	*87 (Height incl. table stand) x 39 (W)*

This is the oldest extant pyramid piano, and possibly also the oldest vertical piano. Friederici's ideas were extremely advanced for the period. In this instrument he introduced diagonal stringing, facilitating strings of longer length. This concept was somewhat premature, and its advantages not to be realised for many years.

The instrument was designed to sit on a stand or on a table. The stand shown is probably not original. Friederici was believed to have nicknamed his pianos 'Bienforts', which has led to somewhat uncharitable speculation that he was referring to the need to play the instrument 'bien fort' for them to be heard at all.

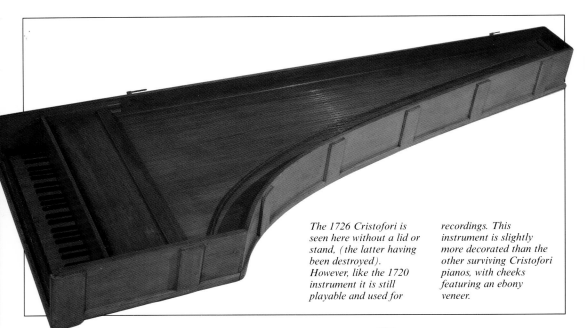

The 1726 Cristofori is seen here without a lid or stand, (the latter having been destroyed). However, like the 1720 instrument it is still playable and used for recordings. This instrument is slightly more decorated than the other surviving Cristofori pianos, with cheeks featuring an ebony veneer.

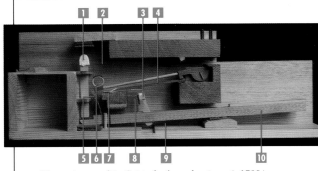

1 2 3 4

5 6 7 8 9 10

The action used in Cristofori's early piano (c1709), as described by Maffei, was remarkably sophisticated considering it was the first of its type. But Cristofori went on to improve the design considerably. This action comes from the 1726 piano.

BARTOLOMEO CRISTOFORI, Florence, 1726, grand piano ✳

CASEWORK:	*Cypress veneer with poplar or lime decoration*
COMPASS:	*4 octaves; C – c³*
ACTION:	*Cristofori jack with check and escapement*
STRINGS:	*Bichord*
MODIFIERS:	*1 hand stop; keyboard shift to 'una corda'*
INSCRIPTION:	*BARTHOLOMAEVS DE CHRISTOPHORIS PATAVINVS INVENTOR FACIEBAT FLORENTIAE MDCCXXVI*
DIMENSIONS (INS.):	*98½ (L) x 36 (W) x 8 (Depth of case)*

Cristofori built this grand piano (above) and a harpsichord in 1726. The cases of the two instruments are very similar, suggesting they were designed to be kept together. Both had the same four-octave compass, although the harpsichord was slightly larger. The bottom bass string is 77 in and the top string 5⅞ in, both greater than in the 1720 instrument. Assuming Cristofori used a single gauge of string, those in the upper octaves would be under slightly greater tension. The stand of this instrument was destroyed in World War II, but the piano survived and is now housed in the musical instrument museum at the University of Leipzig. The instrument's keyboard and action are shown after removal from the piano (right).

more animated and more dramatic. The change was led by string orchestras which were able to adapt with ease to developing tastes.

THE FIRST PIANO

Harpsichord manufacturers went to great lengths to try to produce a mechanism that would give them the desired dynamic response. But it was Bartolomeo Cristofali (Cristofori), of Padua, keeper of instruments in the court of Prince Ferdinand de' Medici of Florence, who actually solved the problem.

The date of Cristofori's first 'piano' is unclear. The 1700 inventory of the musical instruments belonging to the Florentine court includes an *'arpicembalo che fà il piano e il forte'* ('a harpsichord that can play quietly and loudly'). Later writings suggest this was built in about 1698. This was probably Cristofori's first pianoforte, although it has been suggested that he made a prototype as early as 1694.

Until recently, history had decreed that the piano was invented in 1709. Cristofori was visited then by Scipione Maffei, a journalist from Rome. In 1711 an article written by Maffei

appeared in the *Giornale dei letterati d'Italia*, giving a detailed description of Cristofori's new instrument, including drawings of the action. Here the instrument was described as a *'gravicembalo col piano e forte'* ('a harpsichord with soft and loud'). Maffei's account of his meetings with Cristofori also revealed that at that time he had sold three such instruments.

CHANGING MUSICAL TASTES

The invention of the pianoforte meant that there was now a keyboard instrument that could be used expressively. This led in due course to a new breed of keyboard performers who could put their own expressive stamp on musical works. But all this was to come: surprisingly, the pianoforte's invention did not generate much interest in Italy.

Cristofori's instruments were remarkably mature. The action worked well and was acceptable to most musicians. Nevertheless Cristofori continued to perfect his instruments, with greatest attention being paid to the action. In 1722 he developed the 'una corda' mechanism, which enabled the player, with the aid of a

hand stop, to direct the hammer at just one of the two strings used for each note. This provided greater control over dynamics and timbre. An example of his 1726 action is shown above and demonstrates considerable improvement over his original design.

The piano he made in 1726 was to be his last. He reverted to making harpsichords until he died, in 1731, at the age of 75. After Cristofori's death the Italians failed to capitalise on his work and develop a piano industry. This was left to other nations. Despite the popularity of the Viennese piano in southern Europe, including Italy, in the 1780s, it wasn't until 1840 that Italy established a commercial piano manufacturing base.

CONSTRUCTION

In total Cristofori made fewer than 20 pianos. Three of them still exist. The oldest, made in 1720, is at the Metropolitan Museum of Art, New York. A 1722 piano is to be found at the Musical Instrument Museum in Rome. The third, built in 1726, is in the instrument collection at Leipzig University in Germany. The construction of Cristofori's pianos is, as one would expect, very

The jack (3) is pivoted through the key (10), and acts on a lip on the intermediate lever (4), with its left end attached to a fixed rail by means of a vellum hinge (7). The lightweight hammer (6) is a parchment cylinder with a leather pad glued to the end of a cedar shank. The hammer assembly rotates about its pivot point (right).

As the key is pressed, the jack pushed up on the intermediate lever. This in turn acts on the hammer assembly, causing it to start its travel towards the string (2). At the same time the back end of the key pushes up on the damper assembly, which lifts the damper (1) off the string.

The hammer is launched at the string and the tip of the jack trips off the lip on the intermediate lever. The lever then falls back, disengaging itself from the pivot end of the hammer mechanism.

The hammer can now bounce back away from the string and is caught by the check (5), which prevents it from bouncing up and striking the string again. The key is still being held, and it can be seen that the tip of the jack has now yet been relocated under the intermediate lever.

As the key is released, its far end drops and the hammer is freed from the check.

When the key is fully released the spring (9) under the key causes the jack to relocate under the intermediate lever, precisely positioned by the adjustment (8), and the damper to fall back on to the string, thus damping any vibrations. The action is now ready to be played again.

BARTOLOMEO CRISTOFORI

Bartolomeo Cristofori was born in 1655 and served in the court of Prince Ferdinand de' Medici (1663-1713) in Florence from 1690. He was responsible for the court's instruments. For the first fifty or so years of his life, Cristofori's name was spelt in several different ways: Cristofali, Cristofani and Christofani. Prince Ferdinand was a great benefactor of the arts. He commissioned many operas and ballets as well as assembling an impressive collection of paintings. The artists and craftsmen he employed were organized in specialist 'workshops' devoted to specific skills. Cristofori's work initially involved the restoration, design and construction of musical instruments: mostly harpsichords, spinets and organs. After inventing the revolutionary pianoforte, Cristofori seems to have become disillusioned with it. He is thought to have had three students. They failed to build on his work, although one, Giovanni Ferrini, made a few harpsichord-pianos (harpsichords fitted with hammer mechanisms that can both pluck and strike the strings) before his death in 1758.

Cristofori is also known to have made other stringed instruments including horizontal and upright harpsichords, spinets,

double basses, and several violoncellos. Despite being undated, this cello was probably made between 1715 and 1720.

similar to that of the contemporary harpsichord. The main difference, apart from the action, is in the case. From his earlier experiments, Cristofori realized that the strings of the piano needed to be thicker and longer in order to achieve the volume and tone he required. Increasing the length of a string lowers its pitch. To get the right combination of volume, timbre and pitch, the tension of the string had to be increased. Cristofori therefore had to strengthen the case considerably.

One of the main areas of concern when increasing the tension on the strings is the pin block, the strip of wood into which the tuning pins are mounted. To prevent any twisting or warping under the strain, extra bracing to attach the pin block to the body of the piano was required. Cristofori's later pianos have an inverted pin block.

CRISTOFORI'S ACTION

A piano's sound comes from striking a string held under tension with some form of hammer. The string and soundboard assembly had been in existence for many years prior to Cristofori's work,

but Cristofori managed to develop an effective mechanism that took the downward pressure on a key and used it to 'project' a small hammer towards the strings. The 'action' of a piano is that mechanism.

Although it would initially appear relatively simple to build such a device, various complications arise. The speed at which the hammer strikes the string should be proportional to the force with which the key is played. If a key is played and held, the hammer must not be trapped against the string or the string won't vibrate.

Another problem concerns the vibrations of the string when the key is released: they need to be damped in some way. And if a key is played repeatedly, the hammer should respond accordingly, striking the string each time. All these design problems serve to complicate the mechanism.

Cristofori realized that to achieve his goal he had to produce an action that turned the single downward movement of the key into two distinct movements of the hammer: up, to hit the string, then instantly back down, leaving the string free to vibrate. To do this he developed an escapement mechanism.

Escapement means that the hammer and shank can 'escape' from the rest of the mechanism, hit the string and fall back, leaving the string free to vibrate. Cristofori arranged for the hammer to be thrown at the string, losing all contact with the rest of the action. It would then bounce off the string and fall away with the aid of gravity. Even though the key may continue to be held, the hammer still falls away from the string, because it no longer has any linkage to the key.

The Cristofori pianos have two strings for each note, tuned in unison. The later instruments feature an 'una corda' hand-stop which adjusts the striking position of the hammers so they only strike one of the strings.

In tonal character the Cristofori piano bears little relationship to the instruments of today. The sound is somewhat delicate, with none of the power associated with later instruments. The touch is light, as the hammers are very small in size. Overall, Cristofori's pianos are quieter than the harpsichord. They do, however, have the desired dynamic range and are considerably more powerful than the clavichord.

The first known piece of music specifically for the fortepiano was written by Lodovico Giustini of Pistoia and was published in Florence in 1732. It was a set of 12 sonatas entitled 'Sonate Da Cimbalo di piano e forte detto volgarmente di martelletti'. The piece, Giustini's first, was dedicated to Prince Antonio of Portugal. The resources of the new instrument are exploited in dynamic markings such as più forte and più piano. In general the music shows Giustini to have been a capable composer if not a great one. He died in 1743.

GOTTFRIED SILBERMANN, Freiberg (poss. Dresden), 1746, grand piano

CASEWORK:	Oak
COMPASS:	4½ octaves; FF – d³
ACTION:	Cristofori style
MODIFIERS:	1 hand stop; dampers
INSCRIPTION:	None
DIMENSIONS (INS.):	90½ (L) x 36½ (W) x 37 (Height incl. legs)

This piano is one of the 15 instruments purported to have been purchased by Frederick II ('the Great') of Prussia for his royal palaces. Only three of these instruments are known to survive. These were the 'improved' pianos that Silbermann produced after his earlier efforts. This was one of the first to have been delivered to Frederick's court and was probably one of the those which JS Bach played and this time found to his liking.

THE SECOND WAVE

The hundred years between c1750 and c1850 were crucial in the development of the piano. During this period, the instrument evolved from a 'workshop' experiment to what is essentially the piano, both upright and grand, that we know today. The evolution of the piano represents a search for more power, more volume, a greater dynamic range and a wider compass. The basis of the instrument, a mechanism that used hammers to strike strings, evolved first. After that the other desirable features of the modern instrument were slowly added.

The success of Hebenstreit's pantaleon in the early years of the 18th century spurred at least two other instrument manufacturers into action. In 1708, a Parisian, Cuisinié, produced an instrument known as a 'clavier', based on Hans Haiden's 'geigenwerck'. Like the geigenwerck, it was based on the hurdy-gurdy, with a treadle to rotate a rosined wheel that bowed the strings.

Another Frenchman, Jean Marius, saw the clavier and combined Cuisinié's ideas with those of Hebenstreit to develop the clavecin à maillets, which he showed to the Académie Royale Des Sciences in 1716. He developed four different designs, all using hammers to strike the strings. The first resembled the clavichord, in that the hammers struck the strings directly. The second used a down-striking action, possibly in imitation of the way a dulcimer or pantaleon is played. The third incorporated a primitive form of damper, and the fourth used both harpsichord jacks and pianoforte hammers.

Unfortunately it seems that, owing to various technical problems, the instruments were never more than a curiosity. These were, however, ground-breaking experiments and, had

further financial support been available, Marius would have established himself as one of the great pioneers in the development of the piano.

GERMANY

In Germany, Gottlieb Schröter (b. Saxony 1699), a teacher of clavichord playing, also heard Hebenstreit play his pantaleon, probably in 1717. He devised two actions, one up-striking, one down-striking, for playing the harpsichord with hammers.

The up-striking action looked most promising, but the cost of further developing the instruments was considerable. Unable to secure financial backing, he was forced to suspend all development work. For many years, Schröter was credited with being the inventor of the piano.

Gottfried Silbermann was a great maker of organs, clavichords, and pantaleons (until restrained by Hebenstreit's legal action). In 1726 he came across a German translation (in Johann Mattheson's *Critica musica*) of Scipione Maffei's account of Cristofori's pianoforte. Silbermann set about producing two

This engraving is of a 1781 painting by Johann Nepomuk de la Croce. It shows Wolfgang Mozart, aged 25, with his sister Nannerl playing a piano by Christian Ernst Friederici. This instrument was based on Silbermann's grand piano design. The piano is said to have featured a device known as a koretzug, that moved the point at which the hammers struck the strings. This would have had the effect of changing the harmonic content of the strings' vibration and hence the tone. Leopold Mozart, Wolfgang's father, can be seen holding a violin. The family is completed by the portrait of Leopold's wife, Anna Maria, who had died three years earlier.

JOHANN ANDREAS STEIN, Augsburg, 1781, double manual organ-grand (claviorganum)

CASEWORK:	*Walnut*
COMPASS:	*2 x 5 octaves; FF – f³*
ACTION:	*German with escapement (Prellzungenmechanik)*
STRINGS:	*Bichord (FF-g♯²); trichord (a²-f³)*
MODIFIERS:	*2 hand stops; moderator [piano]*
	2 hand stops, dampers; 8 ft diapason [organ]
DIMENSIONS (INS):	*72 (L) x 37½ (W) x 8½ (Height of piano section only)*

The lower keyboard of this instrument operates a set of organ pipes whilst the upper is used for the piano section, although there is no coupling between the keyboards. The term 'claviorganum' is used to describe both harpsichord/organ and piano/organ combinations. German piano makers liked to offer a choice between a straight piano and a piano with an organ, but the popularity of the combined instruments waned during the 18th century. This instrument is particularly important as it the first to incorporate Stein's Prellzungenmechanik action, which was to prove so influential in the development of the Viennese instrument.

KEY DATES

1708 Cuisinié exhibits his 'clavecin', based on Hans Haiden's earlier design, at L'Académie Royale des Sciences in Paris.

c1714 Gottlieb Schröter, a keyboard teacher, produces two piano actions (one up-striking, the other down-striking), for playing a traditional harpsichord with hammers.

1716 Jean Marius develops his *clavecin à maillets* (harpsichord with hammers) in Paris.

1725 The Maffei account of the Cristofori piano is translated and published by Mattheson in German, leading to a sudden burst of interest in the design and construction of the piano.

1726 Gottfried Silbermann, a clavichord maker, produces two further refinements on the 'harpsichord with hammers' theme but without commercial success.

1732 Publication of Giustini's 12 Sonatas "for soft and loud harpsichord", the first composition written specifically for piano.

1735 First upright grand piano made.

1736 Silbermann shows JS Bach his two pianos, but Bach is highly critical.

1739 Schröter (Dresden) develops tangent action which uses a sprung jack.

c1742 First square piano probably made.

1745 Christian Ernst Friederici builds first pyramid piano with innovative, if premature, oblique stringing.

1747 J.S. Bach plays a Silbermann piano in presence of King Frederick the Great and is more impressed.

c1752 First piano imported into England by Samuel Crisp, built in Rome by a Father Wood, an English monk, to Cristofori's designs.

1753 C.P.E. Bach publishes 'An Essay On The True Art Of Playing Keyboard Instruments' in Berlin. His first work to include reference to piano technique.

1753 Gottfried Silbermann dies.

instruments on the 'harpsichord with hammers' theme. He developed an action known generally as the *Prellmechanik*. The term derives from the word *Prelleiste*, which means 'rebound-rail', an essential element in the action.

In 1736 he showed his instruments to Johann Sebastian Bach, who was impressed but stated that the action was heavy and the upper register weak.

For ten years Silbermann refined his pianos, until in 1746 he took one to the court of King Frederick II of Prussia (Frederick the Great). The king was delighted with it and supposedly purchased 15 instruments. Thereafter, Silbermann failed to develop the piano further and died in 1753.

Silbermann had had access to both Cristofori's and Schröter's actions, and those who had worked with him had been exposed to both designs. As a result, his factory spawned two distinct lines of piano development. These eventually became known as the 'English' and 'German' styles of piano

One of Silbermann's students, Christian Ernst Friederici, continued his master's work and eventually made a small 'square'

piano, based on the design of the harpsichord, called the 'Bienfort'. It was the first commercially successful instrument. Friederici also produced upright pianos with vertical strings.

ENGLISH, GERMAN & VIENNESE ACTIONS

Initially there were two basic types of action, both up-striking: the English and the German. In their simplified forms they were known as the *Stossmechanik* and the *Prellmechanik*. The *Prellmechanik* has the hammer fixed by a pivot to the key with the hammer head towards the player. As the key is pressed, the rear end of the hammer shank catches on a fixed part of the casework, the *Prelleiste* (rebound rail), and flicks up so that the hammer strikes the string.

The *Stossmechanik*, sometimes known as the primitive Anglo-German action, usually has the hammer, with its head away from the player, hinged to a rail attached to the casework so that it is free to move up and down. Pressing the key causes a jack attached to the end of the key to act on the hammer shank, causing the hammer to flick up and strike the string.

Cristofori's later action was known as a *Stosszungenmechanik* (or *Englische Mechanik*). The *zunge* refers to the fact that the action features an escapement. Although not the same as the English grand action, this was to form the basis for Backers' important development of c1772.

It was Johann Andreas Stein who took his mentor Gottfried Andreas Silbermann's *Prellmechanik* and transformed it by adding an escapement. Stein's *Prellzungenmechanik* first appeared in 1781 and the 'claviorganum', shown on this page, is the earliest known piano with this type of action.

Stein's *Prellzungenmechanik*, or German action, was to be extremely popular with other German manufacturers. With the advent of a check mechanism at the turn of the century it started to be known as the Viennese action.

The invention of the pianoforte meant that there was now a keyboard instrument that could be used expressively. With instruments such as the harpsichord, the tempo could be varied, and so could the phrasing, but the lack of control over the volume of each note meant that it was hard for a musician to stand out.

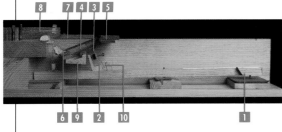

The English Double Action (*shown above at rest*) *was pioneered by Zumpe and patented by Geib in 1786. When the* **key** (*1*) *is pressed, the* **hopper** (*2*) *pushes up against the* **intermediate lever** (*3*)*, which in turn presses on the* **hammer shank** (*4*) *near the* **hinge** (*5*) *and launches the* **hammer** (*6*) *at the* **string** (*7*).

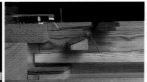

As the hammer moves, the hopper slips off the intermediate lever, which falls back. This forms the escapement, breaking the linkage between key and hammer. The far end of the key raises the **damper** (*8*) *off the string.*

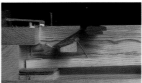

The key continues to be held, but the hammer, free of the hopper and intermediate lever, has bounced back from the string and dropped down to its **rest** (*9*)*. The damper remains off the string.*

As the key is released, the **spring** (*10*) *pushes the hopper to the left, repositioning it under the intermediate lever. The action is now ready to be played again. The damper is lowered back on to the string.*

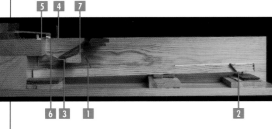

The English Single Action (*shown here at rest*)*. This early action was developed by Zumpe around 1760 from Cristofori's designs. Instead of an intermediate lever, a* **jack** (*1*) (*or 'pilot'*) *links the* **key** (*2*) *with the* **hammer** (*3*)*. When the key is pressed, the jack launches the hammer towards the* **string** (*4*)*. The key also pushes up the* **damper stick** (*5*)*, lifting the* **damper** (*6*).

Hitting the string, the hammer bounces back and, unless the key has been quickly released, collides with the jack again. There is no escapement, so the hammer can rebound and re-strike the string.

As the key is released the jack lowers and the hammer returns to its **rest** (*7*) *under the force of gravity, and the damper is simultaneously lowered.*

JOHANNES ZUMPE & GABRIEL BUNTEBART,
London, 1769, square piano

CASEWORK:	*Mahogany*
COMPASS:	*5 octaves; FF-f³*
ACTION:	*Zumpe's English single*
STRINGS:	*Bichord*
MODIFIERS:	*3 hand stops; bass and treble dampers, buff*
INSCRIPTION:	*Johannes Zumpe Londini Fecit 1769/et Buntebart Princes Street Hanover Square*
DIMENSIONS (INS.):	*50 (W) x 19 (D) x 6 (Height of case)*

This square piano from Johannes Zumpe (left) used his English single action with no escapement and no check, limiting its performance somewhat. This piano was typical of the basic, relatively low-cost instruments (around £15-£20) with which Zumpe made his fortune. Zumpe and Gabriel Buntebart, a fellow German, were partners from 1768 to 1778. J.C. Bach, who was a friend of Buntebart's, used a similar instrument for the first public piano recital, in 1768. With the lid open the modifiers and their levers can be seen to the left side of the instrument. The dampers sit above the strings and are raised or lowered by the relevant lever. The right hand 'compartment' houses the single bridge and the tuning pins.

Brass hand stops are used to raise and lower the treble and bass dampers (left and center respectively) while the right lever, known as a buff stop, is used to press a strip of buffalo leather up against the strings.

THE RISE OF THE SQUARE PIANO

The square piano was probably invented in southern Germany in the early 1740s. But it was not commercially produced until more than 20 years later, in England, where it met with great acclaim. Grand pianos had descended from the harpsichord and had their strings in line with the keys. The new instrument, with its strings at right angles to the keys, was more compact and economical. Manufactured and sold in quantity, it paved the way for the piano's later rise to dominance.

The origins of the square piano can be traced directly to the clavichord, with which it shares a rectangular (not square) shape and basic layout of strings and soundboard. The keyboard is positioned along one of the broad sides, and the strings run horizontally at right angles to the keys.

The square piano first appeared in the early 1740s in Germany, where it is known as the tafelklavier, or 'table piano', because of its shape. The oldest surviving example was made by Johannes Socher of Sonthofen, Bavaria, in 1742, according to a label inside it. The man who made the square piano a commercial success, however, was Johannes Zumpe, an associate of the Silbermann family.

The Seven Years War, which broke out in Germany in 1756, drove many German instrument makers to England. Twelve major figures in piano making were amongst these émigrés. They were later romantically labelled the 'Twelve Apostles', although little is known about some of them. Three of the most significant figures among them were: Americus Backers, a Dutchman; Johannes Pohlmann; and Zumpe. Others included Frederick Beck, who

arrived from Paris, Adam Beyer, initially an organ builder, and Gabriel Buntebart, a friend of Johann Christian Bach.

THE ENGLISH SQUARE

Backers, who worked in London from 1763 to 1778, and Zumpe both took Cristofori's action as the starting point for their innovations. Zumpe designed a square piano based on a much simplified form of the action, resembling that used by Socher. It was a low-cost, easily-built instrument, especially when compared to a harpsichord. The new square pianos became very fashionable in London and demand quickly outstripped supply.

"He could not make them fast enough to gratify the craving of the public" DR CHARLES BURNEY, on Zumpe's square pianos, Rees's *Cyclopaedia*

In June 1768 J.C. Bach (the 'English Bach') played one of Zumpe's square pianos in London, to much acclaim, and this led to even greater sales of the instruments: indeed, he is thought to

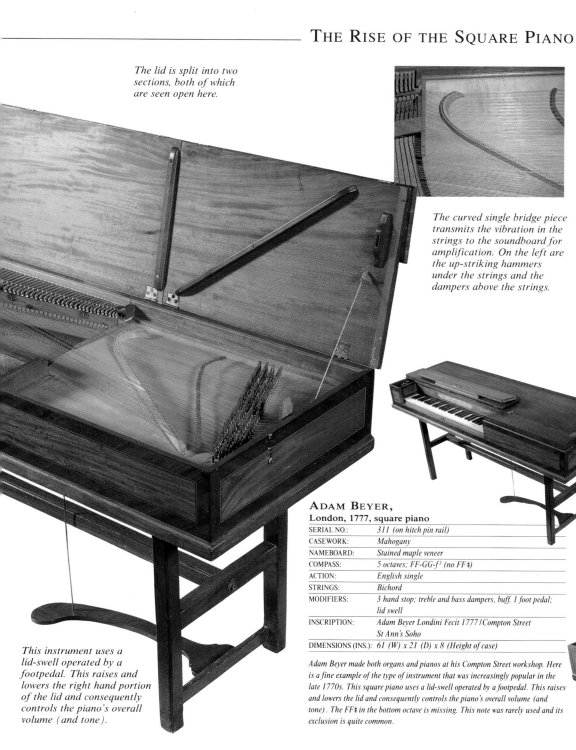

The lid is split into two sections, both of which are seen open here.

The curved single bridge piece transmits the vibration in the strings to the soundboard for amplification. On the left are the up-striking hammers under the strings and the dampers above the strings.

This instrument uses a lid-swell operated by a footpedal. This raises and lowers the right hand portion of the lid and consequently controls the piano's overall volume (and tone).

JOHANNES POHLMANN,
London, 1769, square piano

CASEWORK:	*Oak with mahogany veneer*
NAMEBOARD:	*Walnut burr veneer with box stringing*
COMPASS:	*5 octaves; FF-f³*
ACTION:	*English single*
STRINGS:	*Bichord*
MODIFIERS:	*2 hand stops*
INSCRIPTION:	*Johannes Pohlmann Londini Fecit 1769*
DIMENSIONS (INS.):	*51½ (W) x 18½ (D) x 10½ (Height of case)*

One of the earliest examples of the square piano, built much along the same lines as Zumpe's instruments. Zumpe sub-contracted a considerable volume of work out to Johannes Pohlmann, which no doubt led to considerable cross-fertilization of ideas. Pohlmann made pianos at Compton Street, Soho and Great Russell Street, Bloomsbury, London. He produced a piano similar to the one above for the composer Gluck. According to the 18th century musicologist Dr Burney, whereas Zumpe could not meet contemporary demand "Pohlmann, whose instruments were very inferior in tone, fabricated an almost infinite number for such [customers] as Zumpe was unable to supply." In 1823, a new company, Pohlmann & Sons, started trading in Halifax, Yorkshire, claiming direct links with the original workshop.

ADAM BEYER,
London, 1777, square piano

SERIAL NO.:	*311 (on hitch pin rail)*
CASEWORK:	*Mahogany*
NAMEBOARD:	*Stained maple veneer*
COMPASS:	*5 octaves; FF-GG-f³ (no FF♯)*
ACTION:	*English single*
STRINGS:	*Bichord*
MODIFIERS:	*3 hand stop; treble and bass dampers, buff. 1 foot pedal; lid swell*
INSCRIPTION:	*Adam Beyer Londini Fecit 1777 / Compton Street St Ann's Soho*
DIMENSIONS (INS.):	*61 (W) x 21 (D) x 8 (Height of case)*

Adam Beyer made both organs and pianos at his Compton Street workshop. Here is a fine example of the type of instrument that was increasingly popular in the late 1770s. This square piano uses a lid-swell operated by a footpedal. This raises and lowers the lid and consequently controls the piano's overall volume (and tone). The FF♯ in the bottom octave is missing. This note was rarely used and its exclusion is quite common.

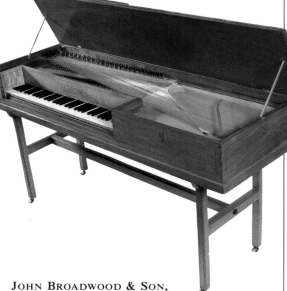

JOHN BROADWOOD & SON,
London, 1795, square piano ❋

SERIAL NO.:	*244 (written on the pin block, but probably incorrect; it could be 3244)*
CASEWORK:	*Mahogany with light and dark stringing*
COMPASS:	*5 octaves; FF-f³*
ACTION:	*English single*
STRINGS:	*Bichord*
MODIFIERS:	*None*
INSCRIPTION:	*John Broadwood and Son / Great Pulteney Street, Golden Square / Patent London 1795*
DIMENSIONS (INS.):	*45 (W) x 19 (D) x 5¼ (Height of case)*

Broadwood made his first square piano in 1771, so this was quite an established instrument. The action is single with Broadwood's patented (1783) brass underdampers: these were known as peacock dampers because of their graceful curved shape. This piano has the hitch pin rail located on the right, and the tuning pins positioned at the back of the instrument. This greatly improved the tone.

❋ *For information on recordings on this instrument, see Pianos on Record, p104.*

have bought one himself, a month earlier, for £50. Pohlmann also began turning out square pianos to meet the demand. Contemporary observers, such as the musicologist Dr Charles Burney, complained that Pohlmann's instruments were "very inferior in tone" to Zumpe's. But Pohlmann added a few ideas of his own, as well as hand-operated dampers and swell pedals.

The early Zumpe pianos were crude. The action had no escapement, making it impossible to play the same note repeatedly, nor was there any form of hammer check, meaning that the hammer could easily bounce back and re-hit the string. Zumpe rectified some of these problems in the early 1780s with his double action, though it still had no escapement.

John Broadwood (whose contributions to the piano industry are more fully discussed later in this book) started building square pianos around 1771. By 1783, however, he had produced a vastly enhanced version. He improved the tone of the instrument by repositioning the strings and moving the pin block and tuning pins to the back of the instrument. He also used underdampers (dampers mounted below the string) and introduced a sustain pedal.

Other manufacturers gradually improved the design of the square piano, making it a more sophisticated instrument. However, its commercial success is mostly credited to the design work and marketing of Zumpe.

PHYSICAL DESIGN

The square piano often suffers from diagonal distortion. The forces generated by the tensioning of the strings are considerable and the bodies of all square pianos are prone to twisting. To try to combat this distortion and to ensure integrity, the base board of the instrument was made at least 1½ in thick.

By 1770 most square pianos had a compass of five octaves, typically FF to f³. However, from around 1800 the musical works of the period demanded more notes and so the keyboard was expanded to 5½ octaves by extending the treble to c⁴.

Initially hand stops were used to raise and lower dampers, then knee levers, and finally foot pedals. Some southern European instruments featured up to six pedals for various musical and percussive effects such as bells, drums and cymbals.

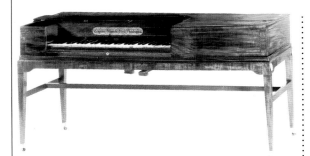

CHARLES ALBRECHT, Philadelphia, c1790-91, square piano

CASEWORK:	Mahogany, with satinwood, walnut and ebony inlay
COMPASS:	5 octaves; FF-f³
ACTION:	Single without escapement
STRINGS:	Bichord
MODIFIERS:	3 knee levers; dampers; shutter swell; lute
INSCRIPTION:	Charles Albrecht fecit Philadelphia
DIMENSIONS (INS.):	63½ (W) x 21½ (D) x 9 (Height of case)

Charles Albrecht was born in Germany, and emigrated to America in the 1780s. He moved to Philadelphia, an area known for its cabinet-making and furniture industries. In 1789 he built his first piano in America. Although Johann Behrent had made a square piano in America some 15 years earlier, Albrecht is considered to be the first important American manufacturer. Albrecht's designs, like this instrument, were closely based on English instruments although interestingly the octave span used by Albrecht is slightly less than that used by most European makers of the period.

KEY DATES

c1742 First square pianos made in southern Germany.

1760 German and Dutch piano makers (romantically known as the 'Twelve Apostles') including Johannes Zumpe, start to arrive in England, having fled the German Seven Years War.

1762 Production of oldest surviving Zumpe square piano.

1767 Piano first used for accompaniment in London at Covent Garden Theatre.

1768 First solo piano performances in England when J.C. Bach uses one of Zumpe's instruments at the Thatched Cottage in London.

1771 John Broadwood launches his first square pianoforte.

1771 Square pianos start to be made in Russia.

c1772 Americus Backers joins Broadwood and, with Robert Stodart (a Broadwood apprentice), perfects what was to develop into the English grand action.

1773 First piano concert in New York.

1775 Johann Behrent of Philadelphia, a German immigrant, builds the first piano in America – a square.

1781 Broadwood repositions pin block along the back of the case to increase volume and enhance tone.

1783 Broadwood produces a vastly improved square piano with efficient underdampers and a sustain pedal in place of the standard knee lever.

1786 Geib patents his double action, based on Zumpe's second action, introducing an intermediate lever to facilitate escapement.

1789 Charles Albrecht opens piano factory in Philadelphia.

1821 Broadwood builds first square piano with iron hitch pin plate.

1825 Babcock produces the first square piano with an iron frame, designed to support greater string tensions.

1837 Chickering improves frame.

1855 Steinway introduce overstrung square piano.

1874 Steinway perfects the sostenuto pedal for square pianos.

1880s Manufacture of square pianos ceases.

1903 Society of American Piano Manufacturers ceremonially burns a massive pile of square pianos at Atlantic City convention.

WILLIAM AND MATTHEW STODART, London, 1807, square piano

SERIAL NO.:	1026 (in ink on soundboard)
CASEWORK:	Satinwood veneer
KEYWELL:	Maple veneer
COMPASS:	5½ octaves; FF-c⁴
ACTION:	English double
STRINGS:	Bichord
MODIFIERS:	1; dampers
INSCRIPTION:	W&M Stodart / Makers to Their Majesties / And Royal Family / Golden Square / London
DIMENSIONS (INS.):	66 (W) x 24½ (D) x 9½ (Height of case)

A highly decorated piano from the London manufacturer. The company was established in 1775 by Robert Stodart, who worked with Broadwood and Backers on the grand piano action. This instrument was made after his sons William and Matthew had taken over the business. It uses the English double action, patented by Geib in 1786, for the main five octave compass of the keyboard, and a single action for the 'additional notes' (f♯³ to c⁴).

The painting on the casework depicts Cupid with a group of women.

THE FALL OF THE SQUARE PIANO

The square piano began as a small, quiet instrument for personal or domestic use. But over its life, which lasted about 100 years, increases in the tension and length of its strings raised its potential volume and improved its tone. And so the square piano grew and grew. The wooden casework wasn't strong enough to cope with the forces involved, meaning that many of the pianos that have survived have twisted and distorted cases. The arrival of the iron frame provided the strength the instrument needed, but led ironically to its downfall.

To aid tuning, which is more awkward with a downstriking action as wedges are difficult to use, two levers for damping the strings are located just to the left of the keyboard.

The piano has a second music rest to the right of the keyboard. This would be for use by a violinist, flautist or possibly a singer.

Schubert: **Impromptus D.899 and D.935,** *Peter Katin* Here a Clementi square piano of 1832 is recorded in a fairly dry acoustic environment. Square pianos were designed to be played in homes and this recording captures that atmosphere.

Johannes Zumpe wanted to build pianos for the wealthy middle-class rather than the aristocracy. Consequently, the casework of his early instruments was usually fairly basic, the only decoration being simple stringing (narrow strips of wood inlay). The visible parts, the front, sides and lid, were usually made of solid mahogany, with the back of oak or spruce. The internal parts were generally of spruce.

More elaborate later pianos used veneers and crossbanding. The keywell, or nameboard, was often highly decorated, with much use of contrasting veneers, fretwork and painting. However, by 1820 such ostentation had given way to better choice of woods.

As demand grew for instruments capable of producing greater volume, the strings had to be made longer and thicker and held under greater tension. Pianos had to become larger and stronger to prevent distortion. The problem was eased by the introduction of an iron hitch pin plate above the soundboard. Doubts exist about who did this first (Broadwood or Erard), but it is generally accepted that Broadwood & Sons had built a square piano featuring a metal hitch pin plate by 1821.

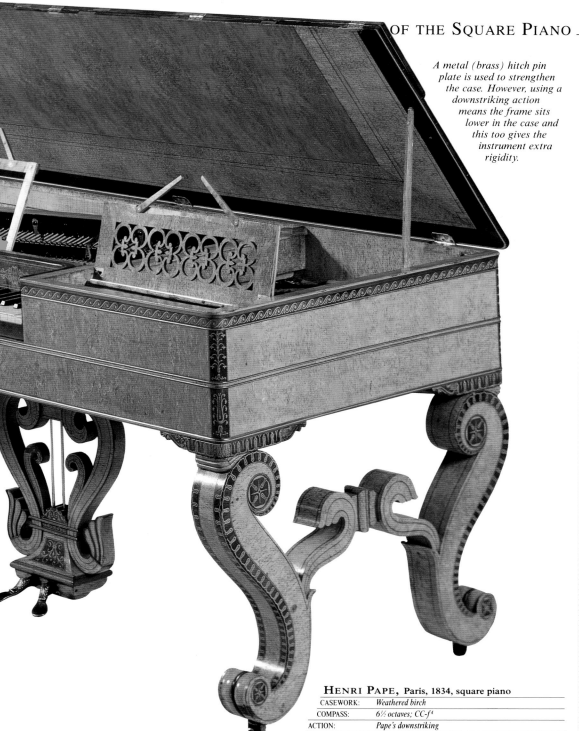

A metal (brass) hitch pin plate is used to strengthen the case. However, using a downstriking action means the frame sits lower in the case and this too gives the instrument extra rigidity.

JOHN BROADWOOD & SONS, London, c1860, square piano

SERIAL NO.:	63459
CASEWORK:	Rosewood
COMPASS:	6½ octaves; CC-a⁴
ACTION:	Improved English square
STRINGS:	Single CC to E; bichord F-a⁴
MODIFIERS:	1 footpedal; dampers
INSCRIPTION:	Patent / John Broadwood & Sons / Manufacturers to her Majesty / Great Pulteney Street / Golden Square London
DIMENSIONS (INS.):	72½ (W) x 33 (D) x 14 (Height of case)

An English square piano from a later period. The instrument has obviously grown in size and strength to support the greater tension of the strings. This

instrument was originally used by the servants of Buckingham Palace. This instrument is one of the very last English square pianos to be made. Broadwood actually made his very last square piano in 1866 (serial no. 64161), although full commercial production had ceased a few years earlier.

In 1825, an American, Alpheus Babcock, developed the first iron frame for the piano, which enabled far greater tension to be applied to the strings. Jonas Chickering took the design a stage further and most other manufacturers followed suit.

By the late 1840s, the square piano was as wide as a medium sized grand piano, and heavier. In the concert hall, the square piano had one advantage over the grand piano: the direct line of view from the audience to the pianist. But for domestic use people wanted something smaller. European manufacturers had been experimenting with upright designs for many years, but the Americans persisted with the square format. The last commercial square pianos were built in England in around 1860, but in America production continued. As late as 1868, 80 per cent of Steinway's output was still square pianos.

Production in America effectively ceased in the 1880s, and in 1903 the Society of American Piano Manufacturers asked its members to bring any square pianos they might have in stock to that year's Atlantic City convention. The pianos were stacked in a large pyramid shape and ceremonially burned.

HENRI PAPE, Paris, 1834, square piano

CASEWORK:	Weathered birch
COMPASS:	6½ octaves; CC-f⁴
ACTION:	Pape's downstriking
STRINGS:	Bichord
MODIFIERS:	2 footpedals
INSCRIPTION:	PAPE / A PARIS (on nameboard) 1ᵉʳ MEDAILLE D'OR DECERNÉE PAR LE JURY DE 1834 (on metal plaque)
DIMENSIONS (INS.):	72¼ (W) x 32½ (D) x 9¼ (Height of case)

This piano, which won Pape a gold medal in 1834, is very like one supplied to Queen Victoria. It is made from weathered birch, which comes from a tree that has died and subsequently suffered an ingress of rainwater. This causes the wood to be stained in a particularly distinctive and attractive way. (See p44-55 for more information on Henri Pape.)

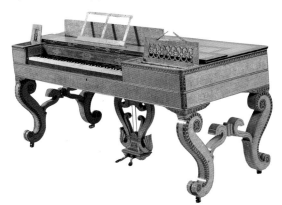

STEINWAY & SONS, New York, 1871, square piano

SERIAL NO.:	24380
CASEWORK:	Rosewood
COMPASS:	7 octaves; AAA-a⁴
ACTION:	Steinway square
STRINGS:	AAA-FF♯ single; GG-E bichord, F-a⁴ trichord
MODIFIERS:	2 footpedals; damper and moderator
INSCRIPTION:	Steinway & Sons / New York
DIMENSIONS (INS.):	79½ (W) x 40 (D) x 14 (Height of case)

The way in which the square piano grew in size can be clearly seen in this powerful instrument from Steinway & Sons. Even the lid weighs more than those of most grand pianos. This design, with a full iron frame, is probably the most powerful type of square piano ever built. When the lid is raised, the sound is reflected directly at the player, further enhancing the power of the instrument – though not to the benefit of an audience, as with the lid of a grand.

UNKNOWN, southern Germany, c1780, recumbent harp piano

CASEWORK:	Cherrywood
COMPASS:	4½ octaves; C - f³
OCTAVE SPAN (INS.):	6⅓
ACTION:	German, no check
STRINGS:	Single
MODIFIERS:	2 knee levers; dampers and moderator
INSCRIPTION:	None
DIMENSIONS (INS.):	45 (W) x 19 (D) x 5¼ (Height of case)

This piano is known as a 'lying harp' piano because of its shape when seen from above. However, it is still classified as a square piano, since its strings are perpendicular to its keys. Like the piano attributed to Schmahl, this was a light instrument designed to be portable. Unlike that piano, it certainly always had legs.

LUDOVICUS VEREL, London, 1783, portable square piano

SERIAL NO.:	62
CASEWORK:	Satinwood, with rosewood crossbanding
COMPASS:	4 octaves; F/G-f³, (no F♯)
OCTAVE SPAN (INS.):	6
ACTION:	English single
STRINGS:	Single (F and G); bichord (G♯-f³)
MODIFIERS:	None
INSCRIPTION:	No. 62 / Ludovicus Verel / Londini fecit / No 2 Great Maddax Street, Hanover Square / 1783
DIMENSIONS (INS.):	45 (W) x 19 (D) x 6 (Height of case)

Little is known of the life of Ludovicus Verel, and this elegant instrument, made in 1783, is one of the few surviving examples of his work. Other portable square pianos were made, but this is one of the more unusual. Interestingly the tuning pins are positioned at the rear of the case with the soundboard covering the whole area above the keyboard. This arrangement didn't find favor in England until the 1840s, though it was not uncommon elsewhere in Europe.

RICHARD HORSBURGH, Edinburgh, c.1786, portable upright

CASEWORK:	Satinwood veneer
NAMEBOARD:	Burr walnut veneer
COMPASS:	3½ octaves; G - c³
OCTAVE SPAN (INS.):	6½
ACTION:	Primitive sticker
STRINGS:	Bichord
MODIFIERS:	1 hand stop; buff
INSCRIPTION:	Richardus Horsburgh Edini fecit 1786
DIMENSIONS (INS.):	26 (W) x 37 (H) x 12¾ (D)

Richard Horsburgh was a piano maker based in Edinburgh. This is an unusual instrument which was supposedly invented by Domenico Corri, an Italian

entrepreneur living in the city at the time. It was often subsequently referred to as a 'conductor's piano', possibly because Sir George Smart (the 19th century conductor), took a small square piano of similar size around with him everywhere he went.

ANTON WALTER & SOHN, Vienna, c1803, portable square piano ❋

CASEWORK:	Walnut veneer
COMPASS:	4½ octaves; C - f³
OCTAVE SPAN (INS.):	6
ACTION:	Viennese
STRINGS:	Single
MODIFIERS:	1 knee lever; dampers
INSCRIPTION:	Anton / Walter und Sohn / IN WIEN
DIMENSIONS (INS.):	39 (L) x 15½ (D) x 6¼ (Height of case)

Anton Walter was born in southwest Germany, but moved to Vienna in about 1780. He was primarily an organ maker, and married the widow of Franz Schöffstoß, a renowned Viennese organ builder. He produced pianos from the 1780s, and at the turn of the century set up a partnership with his stepson Joseph Schöffstoß. Walter is one of the most important Viennese piano-makers of the era. This instrument is a portable square piano, typically Viennese in quality.

JOHANN SCHMAHL (ATTR.), Ulm, Germany, c1770, recumbent harp piano

CASEWORK:	Oak
COMPASS:	5 octaves; FF - f³
OCTAVE SPAN (INS.):	6⅓
ACTION:	Anglo-German single
STRINGS:	Single
MODIFIERS:	5 hand stops; dampers, moderators (silk/leather/wool fringe), drum
INSCRIPTION:	None
DIMENSIONS (INS.):	49½ (W) x 13 to 19½ (D) x 34¼ (Height incl. stand)

Johann Matthäus Schmahl worked in Ulm, southern Germany, in the late 18th century. He is known for this type of instrument, sometimes called a 'recumbent harp' or 'lying harp' piano, and this example is believed to have come from his workshop. Designed for journeys, it is considered to have developed from the 'ottavina' (a virginal tuned an octave above standard). The action has no escapement, which limits playing style. Schmahl often incorporated several hand stops but it is unusual to find five on an instrument of this period.

THE EARLY PORTABLE PIANO

The large horizontal pianos and early uprights were cumbersome, expensive and produced in tiny numbers. Only the highest levels of society could afford either to own them or house them. The square piano made the instrument more accessible but it was still bulky compared to the earlier virginals and spinets. Those who had made such instruments applied their skills to building small and portable pianos. These instruments proved popular with those with limited space in their homes, touring musicians and those who just wanted to take a piano on their travels.

Many 'recumbent harp' pianos such as this are attributed to Johann Schmahl. But none of the surviving instruments is signed by him.

This album features many of the instruments in this book (see Pianos on Record, p104). The small piano by Anton Walter, pictured opposite, is used to beautiful effect in one of Haydn's sonatas.

The natural keys are covered with ebony, while the accidentals are covered with bone. This coloring is typical of instruments from this region in this period.

Hand stops (above) include silk and leather moderators, 'lute' and 'celeste' effects, and a stop which presses a block of wood against the underside of the soundboard.

UNKNOWN, Southern Germany, c1805, sewing box piano

CASEWORK:	*Pine, with mahogany and sycamore veneer*
COMPASS:	*2½ octaves; f²-c⁵ (8' pitch); f¹-c⁴ (4' pitch)*
OCTAVE SPAN (INS.):	*4*
ACTION:	*German*
STRINGS:	*Single (f²-c³); bichord (c#³-c⁵)*
MODIFIERS:	*None*
INSCRIPTION:	*None*
DIMENSIONS (INS.):	*9½ (W) x 13½ (D) x 5½ (Height of case)*

Possibly made by one of Stein's pupils, this piano is a serious musical instrument and not a toy. Having no legs, it would probably have been placed on a table for playing. This would also serve as a supplementary soundboard to enhance the small spruce one which is integral to it. The keyboard and action slide back into the case when the piano is not in use or when it is being moved: there are no key check or damper mechanisms to get in the way. Under the keyboard is a drawer, and another would probably have been located under the lid. Here writing materials or possibly sewing equipment would have been stored (giving rise to the term 'sewing box' piano). The strings run parallel to the keys, so despite its shape it is not defined as a square piano.

Both 'miniature' and 'portable' pianos are small and light, and no clear dividing line can be drawn between them. One important guide, however, when evaluating these instruments is the actual physical size of the keyboard, as represented by the octave span.

The octave span is the distance between the center of a key and the center of a key of the same note an octave higher. On a modern keyboard instrument the accepted distance is 6½ in.

This dimension has remained essentially the same since the 16th century, with occasional minor variations, particularly in the 18th century. Cristofori's pianos had an octave span of just under 6½ in. In addition to being easily moved, a portable piano will generally have a keyboard with an octave span in the region of 6½ in.

A miniature piano, on the other hand, will usually have an octave span that is markedly smaller than that norm. Miniature pianos were sometimes made by manufacturers for promotional purposes. Rich prospective clients welcomed the chance to see how a piano might look rather than merely seeing drawings. These very small instruments should not be confused with 'toy pianos', which generally use metal plates instead of strings.

JOSEPH DOHNAL, Vienna, c1800, Orphica

CASEWORK:	*Mahogany and maple*
COMPASS:	*3 octaves; c-c³*
OCTAVE SPAN (INS.):	*5¼*
ACTION:	*Viennese*
STRINGS:	*Single*
MODIFIERS:	*None*
INSCRIPTION:	*None*
DIMENSIONS (INS.):	*43½ (W) x 13½ (D) x 3½ (Height)*

The orphica was invented by Carl Röllig and first appeared around 1795. Röllig was a virtuoso glass harmonica player and composer, and probably used Joseph Dohnal's workshops to construct his instruments. This one, however, is attributed to Dohnal. The orphica is designed to be portable and can be worn around the neck using a leather strap. It is sometimes known as a 'weekend' piano by virtue of its portability.

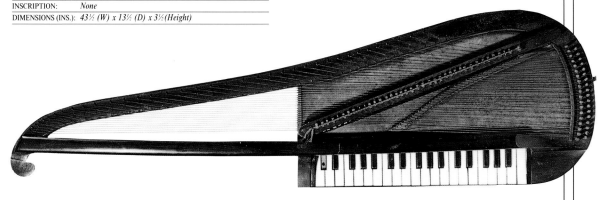

✻ For information on recordings on this instrument, see Pianos on Record, p104.

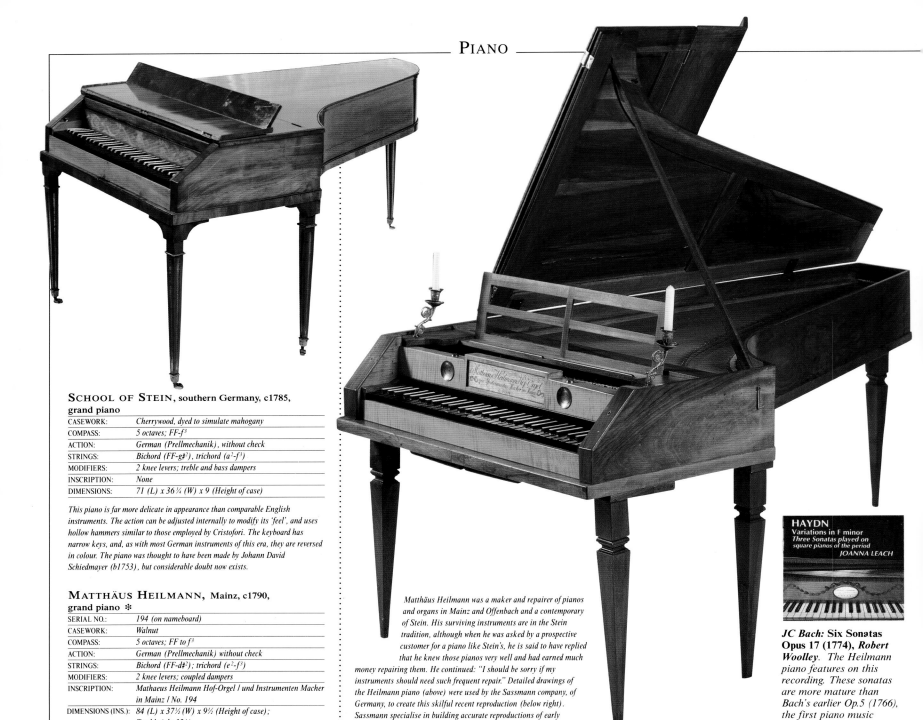

SCHOOL OF STEIN, southern Germany, c1785, grand piano

CASEWORK:	Cherrywood, dyed to simulate mahogany
COMPASS:	5 octaves; FF-f³
ACTION:	German (Prellmechanik), without check
STRINGS:	Bichord (FF-g♯²), trichord (a²-f³)
MODIFIERS:	2 knee levers; treble and bass dampers
INSCRIPTION:	None
DIMENSIONS:	71 (L) x 36¼ (W) x 9 (Height of case)

This piano is far more delicate in appearance than comparable English instruments. The action can be adjusted internally to modify its 'feel', and uses hollow hammers similar to those employed by Cristofori. The keyboard has narrow keys, and, as with most German instruments of this era, they are reversed in colour. The piano was thought to have been made by Johann David Schiedmayer (b1753), but considerable doubt now exists.

MATTHÄUS HEILMANN, Mainz, c1790, grand piano ✷

SERIAL NO.:	194 (on nameboard)
CASEWORK:	Walnut
COMPASS:	5 octaves; FF to f³
ACTION:	German (Prellmechanik) without check
STRINGS:	Bichord (FF-d♯²); trichord (e²-f³)
MODIFIERS:	2 knee levers; coupled dampers
INSCRIPTION:	Mathaeus Heilmann Hof-Orgel / und Instrumenten Macher in Mainz / No. 194
DIMENSIONS (INS.):	84 (L) x 37½ (W) x 9½ (Height of case); Total height 32½

Matthäus Heilmann was a maker and repairer of pianos and organs in Mainz and Offenbach and a contemporary of Stein. His surviving instruments are in the Stein tradition, although when he was asked by a prospective customer for a piano like Stein's, he is said to have replied that he knew those pianos very well and had earned much money repairing them. He continued: "I should be sorry if my instruments should need such frequent repair." Detailed drawings of the Heilmann piano (above) were used by the Sassmann company, of Germany, to create this skilful recent reproduction (below right). Sassmann specialise in building accurate reproductions of early keyboard instruments.

HAYDN Variations in F minor Three Sonatas played on square pianos of the period JOANNA LEACH

JC Bach: Six Sonatas Opus 17 (1774), Robert Woolley. *The Heilmann piano features on this recording. These sonatas are more mature than Bach's earlier Op.5 (1766), the first piano music published in England.*

THE EARLY VIENNESE PIANO

Vienna held a dominant position in the musical life of Europe from the 1770s until well into the 1830s. The Habsburg Empire encouraged music and theater and as a result craftsmen and artists were drawn to the city. Artistic activity encouraged associated industries, such as instrument-making. Like London, Vienna became a center of the piano industry, but the instruments produced in each city were quite different. Two distinct schools of construction emerged, based on different approaches to the piano's action: the 'English' and the 'Viennese' (sometimes known as the 'German' action).

Cristofori, Silbermann, and others had produced instruments of great technical merit and potential, but none had achieved real commercial success. Johann Andreas Stein's improvements to the action, incorporated in subsequent Viennese pianos, dramatically enhanced the appeal of the instrument.

The young Mozart had seen Stein's earlier instruments, and in 1777 wrote to his father praising them. But it was Stein's new action, the *Prellzungenmechanik*, that guaranteed him a place in history (see p17). This transformed the piano from a rather awkward device that needed to be played in a precise manner, to a more expressive, responsive instrument that was considerably easier to master.

By the end of the 18th century, the wealthy bourgeoisie and nobility of Vienna had made it a center of musical patronage and industry. Like London, the city attracted a number of German piano makers, many of whom used, or were to use, Stein's German action.

Johann Andreas Stein reputedly had 16 children. After his death in 1792, Nannette (the sixth) and Matthäus Andreas Stein

SEBASTIAN LENGERER, Kufstein, 1793, grand piano

CASEWORK:	*Tyrolean cherrywood with maple and walnut stringing*
COMPASS:	*5 octaves; FF-f³*
ACTION:	*German (Prellzungenmechanik), without check*
STRINGS:	*Bichord (FF-b) and trichord (c¹-f³)*
MODIFIERS:	*2 knee levers; damper and moderator*
INSCRIPTION:	*Lengerer In / strumentmacher zu Kuf- / stein in Tirol fecit / Anno / 1793*
DIMENSIONS (INS.):	*85½ (L) x 38½ (W) x 11 (Height of case)*

Lengerer originally worked in Kufstein, but moved to Vienna at the end of the 18th century. This instrument is attractively decorated and the inside of the lid is

covered by pre-printed patterned paper (though this probably isn't the original). Pianos like this, made by craftsmen in small towns away from metropolitan influences, were somewhat out of date. The cabinetry is in a style fashionable some two decades earlier. Early Viennese pianos had black naturals and white accidentals. Here the accidentals are probably made of beech, covered with bone, and the naturals made of ebony. The keys are also slightly narrower than those found on English pianos of the period, and the modern instrument. Viennese manufacturers were also inclined to produce attractively styled keyboards, as shown here.

FERDINAND HOFMANN, Vienna, c1800, grand piano

CASEWORK:	*Spruce (probably) with mahogany veneer*
COMPASS:	*5 octaves; FF – f³*
ACTION:	*Viennese with escapement*
STRINGS:	*Bichord (FF-b¹); trichord (c²-f³)*
MODIFIERS:	*1 hand stop; moderator*
	1 knee lever; damper
INSCRIPTION:	*Ferdinand Hofmann / Clavier Instrumentenmacher / in Wien*
DIMENSIONS (INS.):	*83 (L) x 38 (W) x 10 (Height of case)*

An attractive Viennese instrument. The delicate square-tapered legs feature brass cuffs, and have medallions depicting classical female figures set at their tops. The nameboard incorporates gilt bronze decorations of birds and leaves in relief. The moderator stop is located directly above the nameplate. Hofmann lived in Vienna his whole life and in 1812 became keyboard instrument maker to the Royal Court. The white naturals with mahogany veneer are typical of the more luxurious Viennese instruments built after about 1785. These features show the influence of the English style in Vienna.

The keyboard and action of the Rosenberger are easily removed by sliding the action assembly forward.

MICHAEL ROSENBERGER, Vienna, 1800-1805, grand piano ✻

CASEWORK:	*Cherry veneer*
COMPASS:	*5½ octaves (FF-c⁴)*
ACTION:	*Viennese*
STRINGS:	*Bichord (FF-a♯¹); trichord (b¹-c⁴)*
MODIFIERS:	*2 knee levers; damper, moderator*
INSCRIPTION:	*(On enamelled plaque) Michael Rosenberger / in Wien*
DIMENSIONS (INS.):	*86 (L) x 42 (W) x 10½ (Height of case)*

Similar in design to the instruments of Anton Walter, of whom Rosenberger was probably a pupil. This instrument, although exceedingly good in terms of performance, is typical of 'lower-priced' Viennese pianos of this era in its more primitive appearance. The use of cherry or walnut veneer with black naturals is also a sign of a less expensive instrument.

(the twelfth) took over the running of the business. Nannette married the pianist Johann Andreas Streicher in 1794 and that year the company moved to Vienna.

Stein's improved action, with the introduction of checks to prevent hammer bounce, became known as the Viennese action. It was adopted by more and more makers and continued to be used until the beginning of the 20th century.

In 1802 Matthäus Stein and Nannette Streicher ended their partnership and set up separate piano companies. Streicher, assisted by her husband, went on to become one of the world's leading piano makers. Matthäus continued to build pianos, inscribed with the French form of his name: André Stein.

Many great piano houses were based in Vienna at the beginning of the 19th century. They included: Matthias Müller, best known for his Ditanaklasis upright piano; Joseph Brodmann, whose student Ignaz Bösendorfer was to found of one of the world's best known piano houses; Conrad Graf; Anton Walter; Joseph Schöffstoß; Johann Schantz and others. More than 100 companies were then producing keyboard instruments in Vienna.

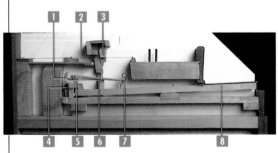

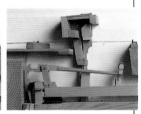

The action shown is from a Lengerer grand piano and is typical of the action of Viennese instruments at the end of the 18th century and during the 19th century. As the **key (8)** *is depressed, the* **kapsel (5)** *is raised and the rear end of the shank of the* **hammer (7)**, *known as the* **beak (6)**, *catches on the escapement* **(auslöser) (1)**. *This causes the hammer to flick up toward the* **string (2)**. *At the same time the key causes the* **damper (3)** *assembly to be lifted from the string.*

The escapement is hinged at its lower edge, and as the hammer approaches the string, the beak disengages from the escapement, which moves slighty to the left.

The key continues to be held and the hammer strikes the string and bounces and falls back to its rest. The escapement is still disengaged from the hammer. As the key is released the kapsel and beak are lowered. The escapement is pushed towards the beak by the **escapement spring (4)** *and eventually is re-engaged ready for the next note to be played.*

✻ *For information on recordings on this instrument, see Pianos on Record, p104.*

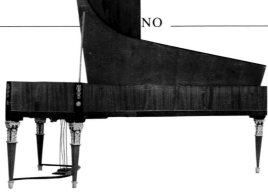

The straight side of the
piano is very plain,
indicating that it was
designed to be positioned
against a wall.

JANISSARY MUSIC

*From the 14th century to the early 19th, a janizary
or janissary was a Turkish soldier in the Sultan's
guard. This part of the Turkish army marched to the
sound of drums and percussion, including bells,*

*cymbals, triangles
and the 'cymbalstern',
a star on a pole with
bells and Turkish
crescents attached.
Such 'Turkish' music
became very popular
in Europe towards the
end of the 18th
century. Many
important composers
were influenced by it,
including Mozart, who indicated that his Rondo
(1778) should be played "alla Turca".
To capitalise on this vogue (and perhaps to outdo the
harpsichord) early 19th century Viennese pianos
often incorporated a 'janissary music' stop including
bass drum, bells and cymbals, and sometimes
triangles and tambourines. It would usually be
applied by means of footpedals or knee levers.
Richard Burnett's 'Keyboard Collection', shown
above, features the pianist playing several of the
instruments illustrated in this book. Of particular
interest is Mozart's 'Turkish' Rondo played on the*

*Fritz grand piano
shown, which provides
an excellent
demonstration of the
use of moderator,
janissary and bassoon
stops.
Some of the janissary
effects from Johann
Fritz's grand piano
(c1815) are shown
left. The three
concentric bells are
struck with a metal
beater linked to a
footpedal. Drum
sounds are provided
by a large beater
striking the underside
of the soundboard.
Associated with the janissaries is the 'bassoon' stop
located just beneath the bells, which lowers a roll of
parchment, or occasionally wood or silk, on to the
strings. The resulting buzzing is supposed to
resemble the sound of a bassoon. These effects
represented the first attempt to use the piano as a
replacement for an orchestra.*

The attractive convex
fascia board, finished in
lacquers, depicts Apollo
and the Muses, the nine
patron goddesses of the
arts and sciences.

JOHANN FRITZ, Vienna, 1814, grand piano ✳

CASEWORK:	Mahogany veneer, gilt-brass decorations; interior veneered in alder
COMPASS:	6 octaves; FF – f⁴
ACTION:	Viennese
STRINGS:	Bichord (FF-e¹); trichord (f¹-c⁴)
MODIFIERS:	1 knee lever; bassoon; 4 footpedals; keyboard shift (due corde), moderator, damper, janissary (drum, cymbal, bells).
INSCRIPTIONS:	Johann Fritz / in Wien (in ink on plaque set into nameboard). Johann Fritz / prov. Clavier-Instrumentenmacher / auf der Mariahülfer Haupstrasse / in grünen Kranz No.13 (on soundboard)
DIMENSIONS (INS.):	88½ (L) x 46 (W) x 12 (Height of case); Height incl. stand 35

*This grand piano from Johann Fritz incorporates the janissary or Turkish music
stop (see Janissary Music, left). In this case it includes a drum, cymbals and
bells. In addition this piano has a bassoon stop, activated by a knee lever, which
lowers a roll of parchment on to the strings, causing them to buzz when the string
is struck. This highly decorated instrument features four tapered mahogany legs*

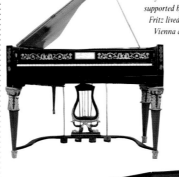

*with gilt carvings of the acanthus leaf
(a device commonly used to decorate
the capitals of Corinthian columns).
The lyre is also interesting in that it is
supported by carved dolphins. Johann
Fritz lived and worked in and around
Vienna and Graz, primarily making
grand pianos.*

The large number of
pedals, extraordinary by
modern standards, was
often prompted by the
need for one piano maker
to outdo the others.

THE EVOLUTION OF THE
VIENNESE PIANO

*Pianos using the Viennese action were
visually and acoustically more delicate than
those being made in England and France at
the time. The incessant demand for more
volume and power meant piano makers had
a constant struggle to strengthen and
redesign their instruments. This is
immediately apparent if you compare the
robust 1830 Graf piano (far right) with
the delicate 18th century instruments seen
on the previous pages. Ultimately, though,
the Viennese action, by virtue of its design,
could only adapt so far to the demands
made upon it and gave way to the more
sturdy English action.*

GEORG HASCHKA, Vienna, 1815-20, grand piano

CASEWORK:	*Stained cherrywood (simulating mahogany)*
COMPASS:	*6 octaves; FF – f⁴*
ACTION:	*Viennese*
STRINGS:	*Trichord*
MODIFIERS:	*7 pedals; drum, bells & cymbal (janissary), moderator, keyboard shift, damper, bassoon, and a duplicate moderator for the right foot.*
INSCRIPTION:	*none*
DIMENSIONS (INS.):	*89 (L) x 46½ (W) x 10½ (Height of case)*

This instrument is in empire style. Essentially similar to most other Viennese instruments of the period, its casework depicts a selection of Egyptian motifs, popular after the Battle of the Nile (1798), a crucial event in the Napoleonic Wars. Georg Haschka's instruments were often highly decorated.

CONRAD GRAF, Vienna, 1826, grand piano ✷

SERIAL NO.:	*Opus 988 (on soundboard)*
CASEWORK:	*Mahogany veneer*
COMPASS:	*6½ octaves; CC – f⁴*
ACTION:	*Viennese*
STRINGS:	*Bichord (CC-EE); trichord (FF-f⁴)*
MODIFIERS:	*4 pedals; keyboard shift (due corde), cembalo, moderator, dampers*
INSCRIPTION:	*Conrad Graf / k. k. Hof-Fortepiano-Macher / in Wien*
DIMENSIONS (INS.):	*95½ (L) x 47½ (W) x 12½ (Height of case)*

Conrad Graf made pianos in Vienna from 1811 to 1841, when he sold the business to Carl Stein, the grandson of Johann Andreas Stein. Graf never used iron framework on his instruments. Almost all his work (with the exception of an experiment with quadruple stringing) closely followed his initial designs.

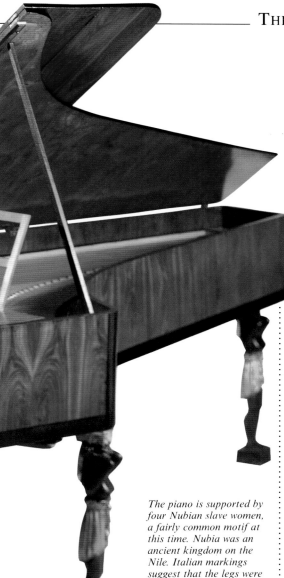

The piano is supported by four Nubian slave women, a fairly common motif at this time. Nubia was an ancient kingdom on the Nile. Italian markings suggest that the legs were probably made in Italy.

CONRAD GRAF, Vienna, c.1830, grand piano

CASEWORK:	*Cherrywood*
COMPASS:	*6½ octaves; CC – g⁴*
ACTION:	*Viennese*
STRINGS:	*Bichord (CC-EE); trichord (FF-g⁴); divided bridge*
MODIFIERS:	*4 pedals; keyboard shift, moderato, half moderato, dampers*
INSCRIPTION:	*Conrad Graf / kaiserl: kön: hof-fortepianomacher / nächst der carls-Kirche im Mondschein No. 102.*
DIMENSIONS (INS.):	*95½ (L) x 49 (W) x 13 (Height of case)*

Graf's pianos were regularly used by Beethoven, Chopin, Brahms, Schumann and others. The demand for louder instruments had resulted in the casework having to become stronger and more 'Germanic' in style. The instruments of new manufacturers such as Götting, Schneider, and Bösendorfer followed suit.

The sound made by a Viennese piano of this type is much lighter and more delicate than that of a modern instrument. The great Viennese composers, Mozart, Beethoven, Haydn and others, would have played the Viennese piano: to hear their compositions performed on such an instrument today alters our perspective quite radically. The whole balance of the music changes, with the melody much emphasised. Only when the music is played in this way can the composers' intentions be accurately realized.

By the 1780s, the English and Viennese pianos had become two distinct types of instrument. The Viennese instrument is comparatively light in construction and is typically double strung, whereas the English piano is usually triple strung and of much sturdier build. The Viennese action is lighter and simpler, using a hammer mounted on the far end of the key. The English action is more complex, using a hammer mounted on a separate hammer rail on the piano body.

The way in which the hammer strikes the string has important effects on the instrument's sound. The hammers of the English instruments strike the strings in a direct manner whereas the

hammers of the Viennese pianos tend to stroke the string as they hit it. This gives the Viennese piano a gentler sound than that of the more powerful English instrument. Curiously, this difference is reflected in the actual shape and appearance of the instruments.

There were several reasons for the decline and eventual disappearance of the Viennese instrument. The pianists of the time were unrelenting in their demand for more volume. But the way the construction and design of these pianos had evolved meant that it wasn't possible to get more volume without sacrificing touch response. Using larger hammers and increasing the weight of the action was difficult because the action could not be counter-balanced as it could be with the English approach. Attempting to increase the volume simply made the response of the instrument more sluggish and less desirable.

The pianists of the romantic movement, notably Franz Liszt, wished to draw music of great power and expressiveness from the piano. Instruments had to be extremely robust to withstand the pounding that this implied. The delicate Viennese instrument was not up to the demands of this kind of work. French and English

makers, however, used a completely different action and found that their instruments could deliver what was required.

The thinner, sweeter sound of the Viennese instrument became less fashionable, with an increasing number of players moving on to the fuller, richer timbres of the English-style piano. At the same time, the focus of the musical world's attention was also moving north, to Paris.

This, too, had an adverse effect on the piano makers of Vienna and southern Germany, who also suffered from the superiority of the French and English in manufacturing and marketing their instruments in quantity. In south Europe, mechanisation had made few inroads into the manufacturing process. But in London considerable use was being made of machinery in piano production as early as the 1850s.

By the second half of the 19th century, the Viennese action had effectively succumbed to the onslaught of the powerful northern European piano. In our own time, however, the search for 'authenticity' in musical performance has led to renewed interest in the Viennese piano.

✷ *For information on recordings on this instrument, see Pianos on Record, p104.*

CRANG HANCOCK, London, 1779,
transverse grand piano

CASEWORK:	Mahogany, shaped like a bentside spinet
COMPASS:	5 octaves; FF – f³, no FF♯
ACTION:	Anglo-German (Hancock's own hybrid action)
STRINGING:	Bichord
MODIFIERS:	Dampers
INSCRIPTION:	Crang Hancock Tavistock Street Londini / Inventor 1779 (in ink on holly plaque)
DIMENSIONS (INS.):	74 (L) x 27 (W) x 9 (Height of case)

John Crang Hancock was an instrument maker in London. He seemed to specialise in transverse grands and built them into bentside spinet cases. This type of instrument was to become very popular in Germany where it was known as a Querflügel. Hancock also patented a sprung key action to correct the heavy action of the English pianos.

*Broadwood regularly altered the design of his nameboards, not only to reflect changes in the name of the company (eg from "and Son" to "and Sons") and the year, but also for aesthetic reasons. In **1794** he changed from using the Latin "Johannes Broadwood" to the English form and introduced an oval etiquette inlaid on a satinwood fascia board. In about **1813** a rectangular printed nameboard became the norm. Fretwork was often used from **c1795**. From the 1820s, simpler, less decorated designs were introduced. The nameboard is not a true indication of the date of an instrument. When a piano was returned to the factory to be serviced or modified Broadwood would, upon request, give it a new nameboard.*

THE GRAND PIANO IN ENGLAND

In England the success of the square piano during the late 1760s had also triggered demand for a better instrument, especially for public performance. Musicians wanted a louder piano with better tone and greater dynamic response. The action that was to facilitate this, and to form the basis of the 'English' grand piano, was developed by Americus Backers in conjunction with John Broadwood and his apprentice Robert Stodart. It was based on the designs of Cristofori and Silbermann, but was distinctly different to the 'German' action developed by Stein.

BROADWOOD

John Broadwood was born in Cockburnspath, Scotland, in 1732. A joiner by trade, he moved to London in about 1752. He managed to get work with the harpsichord maker Burkat Shudi and proved himself a most trusted employee. In 1769 he married Shudi's daughter Barbara and thereafter Shudi's harpsichords bore the name 'Burkat Shudi et Johannes Broadwood'. In 1771 Shudi signed the business over to him, dying two years later. Broadwood had been keeping an eye on the development of the piano, especially as one of his fellow workers at Shudi's had been Johannes Zumpe, and in 1774 he made his first square piano. In 1783, he patented his first major improvements, and by 1784 demand was exceeding that for harpsichords: the company sold more than 130 pianos that year. Broadwood built his last harpsichord in 1793.

Broadwood was a great friend of Muzio Clementi, a prominent musician, piano maker and entrepreneur who had arrived in England from Rome at the age of 14 to study. Clementi warned Broadwood of the threat posed by the Erard company of Paris. But the French Revolution meant Sébastien Erard had to move to London and Broadwood's market was protected at the most sensitive time in the company's expansion. Broadwood's square pianos initially bore the name 'Johannes Broadwood'. Then, in 1795, his son James (below left) joined the company, which became

John Broadwood and Son. Another son, Thomas (above right), joined in 1808, prompting a further change to John Broadwood and Sons. John Broadwood died in 1812, and James took control, going on to make Broadwood the greatest English piano manufacturer.

At the heart of the English grand piano was a new action, designed by Americus Backers. The earliest surviving grand piano with the action was made in 1772. The design, which became known as the 'English grand action', was not patented until 1777, when Robert Stodart included an improved version of it in his application covering a harpsichord/piano combination.

John Broadwood did not build his first grand piano until c1781. Broadwood was probably the first manufacturer to introduce scientists to the art of piano making. Previous designs of instruments had been based on intuition and 'hit and miss' experimentation. Broadwood wanted more consistency. He tried to maintain an even tension over all the strings of the instrument and he wanted to ensure that all the hammers struck at the same point along the string.

In 1788, he sought help from Dr Edward Gray and Signor Tiberius Cavallo, two experts from the British Museum. Armed with their recommendations, Broadwood immediately changed the point of attack, the point at which the hammer hits the string, which is crucial to a piano's tone. The optimum position to

The long side of the piano is not finished or veneered, as the instrument would have been positioned against a wall.

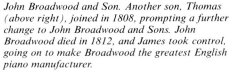

produce the tone Broadwood wanted proved to be one-ninth of the way along the string. He also divided the bridge into two sections. All these improvements enabled him to add half an octave at the top and bottom. By 1790 Broadwood was manufacturing 5½-octave instruments. His first six-octave pianos appeared in 1795.

At the end of the 18th century Broadwood was making approximately 400 pianos a year, significantly more than any other manufacturer. With the easing of political crises in Germany and France, many of London's émigré pianomakers had gone home, leaving the English market to Broadwood. Nevertheless, in 1800 there were still 30 to 40 companies producing pianos in London alone, and by 1850 some 400 firms had manufactured pianos in England.

English grand pianos at the turn of the 19th century still had casework reminiscent of the English harpsichord. But this was about to change, with the advent of the metal frame.

Janissary stops had never become popular in England but other stops were sometimes used to vary the tone of the piano.

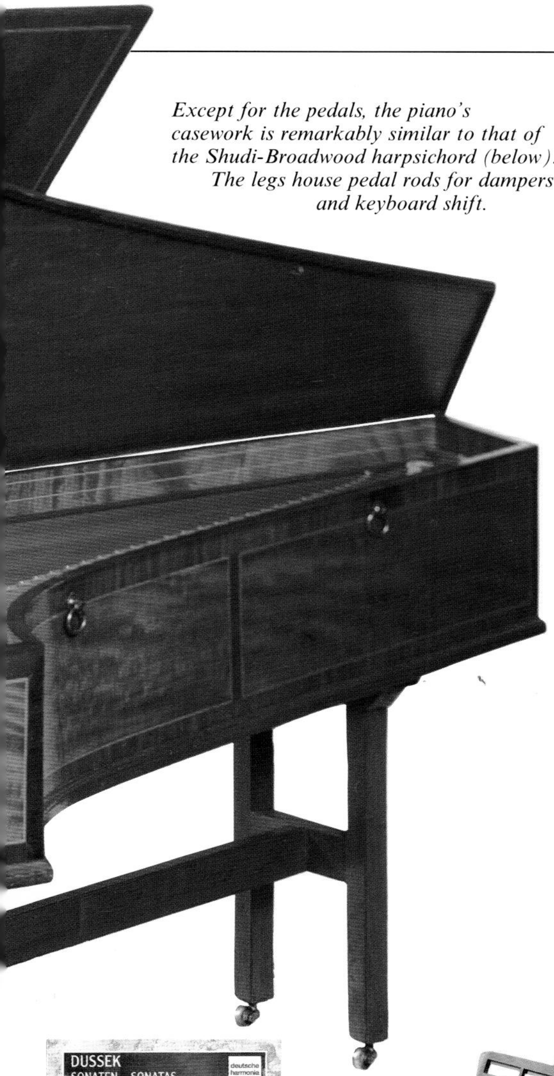

Except for the pedals, the piano's casework is remarkably similar to that of the Shudi-Broadwood harpsichord (below). The legs house pedal rods for dampers and keyboard shift.

JOHN BROADWOOD, London, 1787, grand piano

SERIAL NO.:	203
CASEWORK:	*Mahogany and oak with boxwood stringing*
COMPASS:	*5 octaves; FF-f³*
ACTION:	*English (improved)*
STRINGS:	*Trichord*
MODIFIERS:	*2 footpedals; una corda, dampers*
INSCRIPTION:	*Johannes Broadwood Londini fecit 1787 / Great Pulteney Street Golden Square*
DIMENSIONS (INS.):	*88 (L) x 37½ (W) x 11¾ (H); Height incl. stand 35½*

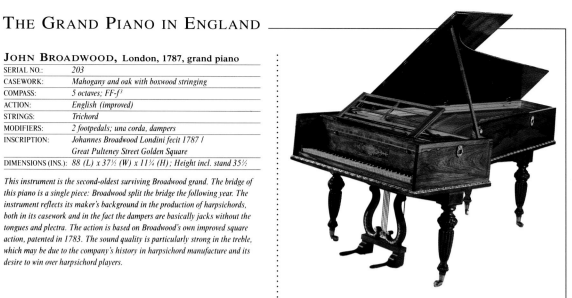

This instrument is the second-oldest surviving Broadwood grand. The bridge of this piano is a single piece: Broadwood split the bridge the following year. The instrument reflects its maker's background in the production of harpsichords, both in its casework and in the fact the dampers are basically jacks without the tongues and plectra. The action is based on Broadwood's own improved square action, patented in 1783. The sound quality is particularly strong in the treble, which may be due to the company's history in harpsichord manufacture and its desire to win over harpsichord players.

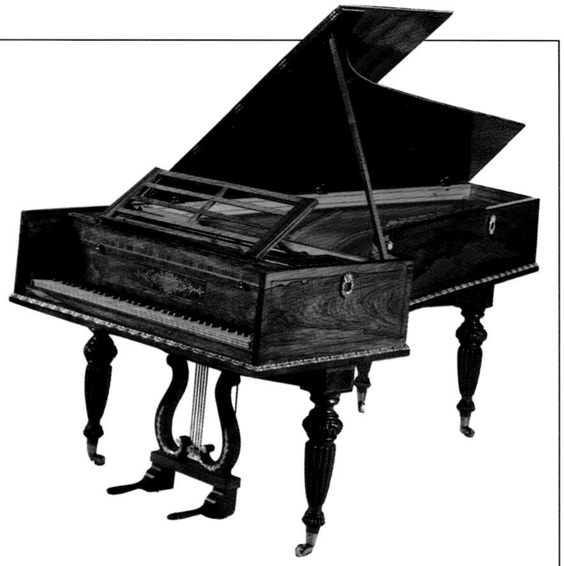

SHUDI-BROADWOOD, London, 1790, harpsichord

CASEWORK:	*Spanish mahogany with mahogany crossbanding*
COMPASS:	*2 x 5 octaves; FF-f³*
MODIFIERS:	*2; machine (a mechanism used in conjunction with the stops for selecting voicing), and Venetian swell*
DIMENSIONS (INS.):	*96½ (L) x 37½ (W) x 12¾ (Height of case)*

This instrument illustrates the harpsichord manufacturer's attempt to compete with the new piano. Shudi, one of the two main English-based harpsichord manufacturers, patented the Venetian swell in 1769 in an attempt to circumvent one of the older instrument's principal disadvantages. Previously, the only method of controlling the volume of the harpsichord had been to adjust the number of strings sounding per note, to select different types of plucking material, or to adjust the point at which the string was plucked. The Venetian swell simulated the effect of raising or lowering the lid, by means of a series of variable slats above the strings controlled by a footpedal. However this attempt to emulate the piano's features somewhat missed the point, in that it only allowed expression to be applied to the overall sound: a pianist can adjust the relative volume of each individual note. Nonetheless, other harpsichord manufacturers incorporated the Venetian swell into their instruments, and the device was also used in some pianos to control overall volume.

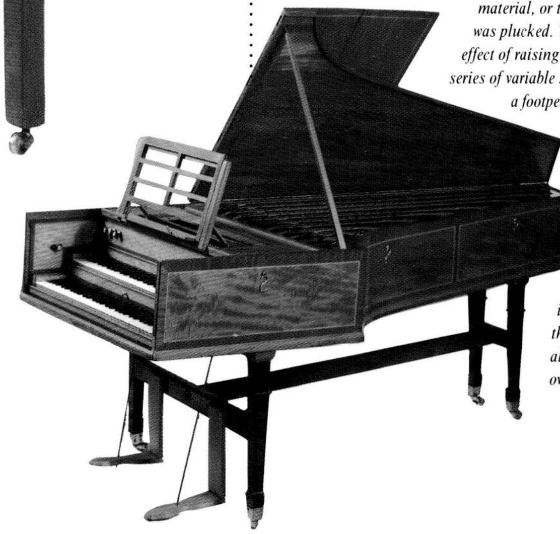

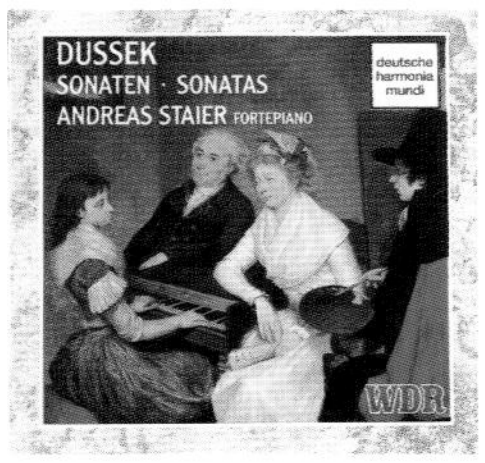

Andreas Staier here plays an 1805 Broadwood grand. Johann Dussek was a German friend of John Broadwood who came to London in 1790 and wrote for the English piano.

KIRKMAN, London, 1820, grand piano

CASEWORK:	*Figured rosewood, with brass stringing and gilt mouldings*
COMPASS:	*6 octaves; CC – c⁴*
ACTION:	*English grand*
STRINGS:	*Trichord; extra bridge for 4 ft and 8 ft strings*
MODIFIERS:	*2 footpedals; keyboard shift (8 ft, or 8 ft and 4 ft) and dampers*
INSCRIPTION:	*Kirkman / London / Patent*
DIMENSIONS (INS.):	*92½ (L) x 44½ (W) x 12½ (Height of case)*

An interesting and important instrument from the firm of Kirkman. Jacob Kirchmann came to England from Alsace in the 1730s and changed his name, first to Kirchman and then, when he made his first grand piano, to Kirkman.

This instrument would have been built when his great nephew Joseph was running the company. It is believed to have been owned by King George IV and kept at Brighton Pavilion. Like Shudi, Kirchmann had worked with Tabel, building harpsichords. This historical link manifests itself in the inclusion of Kirkman's patented 'octave stop'. Instead of having three unison strings (8 ft) per note, one of the strings is set an octave higher (4 ft). The keyboard shift can be used to move the hammer so that it strikes all three strings or just the two unison 8 ft strings. The effect of the 4 ft string is a sound that is harmonically rich and very bright.

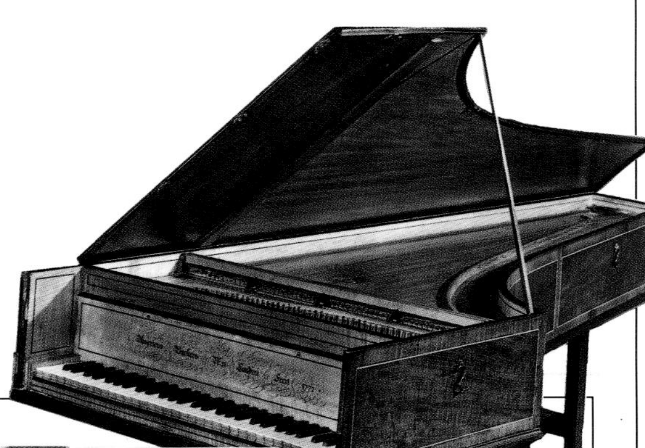

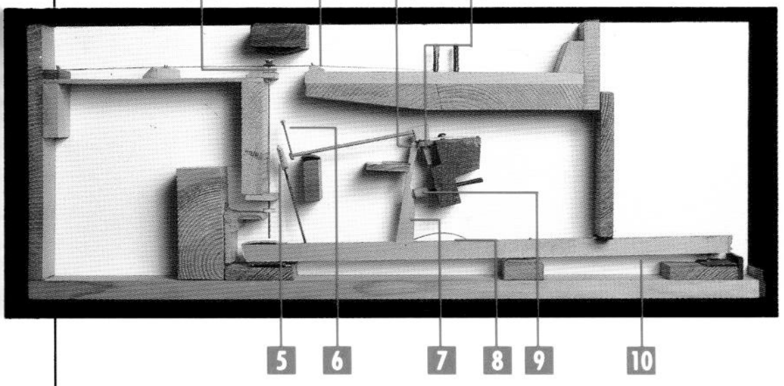

*This 'grand' action, developed by Americus Backers, has no intermediate lever, unlike Cristofori's later designs. As the **key (10)** is pressed, the **jack [7]**, the top end of which is located in the notch of the **hammer butt [2]**, pushes upwards causing the **hammer (6)**, which is free to rotate about the **pivot (1)**, to rise. At the same time the back end of the key causes the **damper (4)** to lift up off the **string (3)**.*

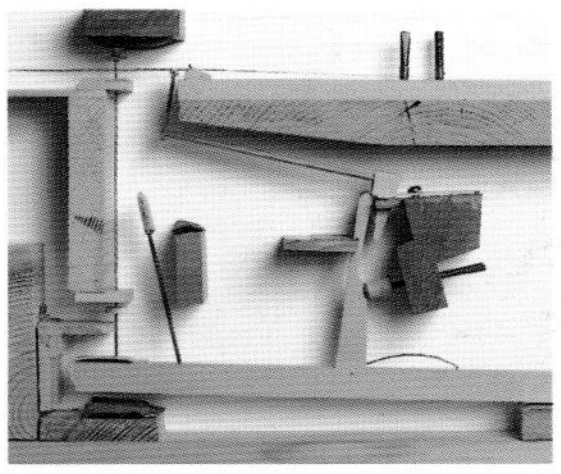

*As the key rises, the **set-off button (9)** causes the jack to disengage from the notch and escape from the hammer and shank, leaving the hammer still being propelled towards the string.*

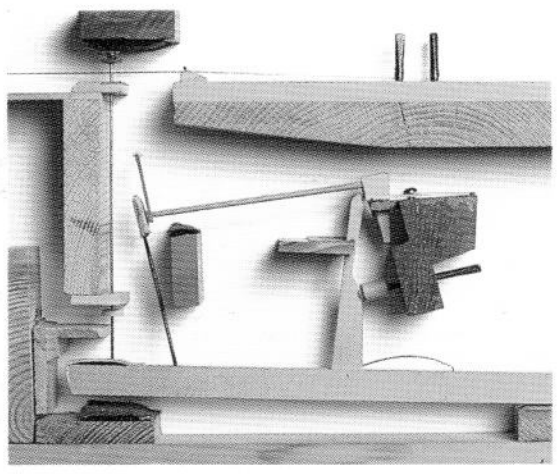

*Upon striking the string, the hammer bounces back and is 'caught' by the **check (5)**.*

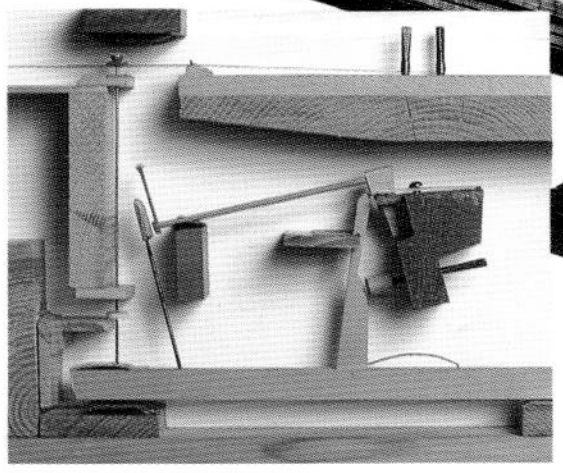

*As the key is released, the hammer is freed from the check and the **spring (8)** tries to re-establish the jack into the notch. By the time the key has returned to rest, the jack has repositioned itself and the damper lowered back on the string.*

Built in 1772, this is the first piano to feature the English grand piano action, developed by Americus Backers with Broadwood and Stodart. It is believed to have been the first to incorporate the modern pedal configuration.

SÉBASTIEN ERARD

Sébastien Erard, born in Strasbourg in 1752, was the most important of the French exiles in London. In Paris, Erard had started as an apprentice to a harpsichord maker but as Zumpe's square pianos appeared in quantity he decided there was more future in the new instrument. In 1777 he built his first piano, a square based on Zumpe's action, and many more followed, despite protests from the local harpsichord manufacturers, who saw the piano as a threat to their livelihoods. His own designs won favor not only with the French piano-buying public but with Louis XVI.

In 1792, in order to escape the Revolution, Erard moved to London with his brother, Jean-Baptiste. They built their first grand in 1796.

Erard was acutely aware that the action of the piano needed improvement. He first patented an escapement action in 1808, which was a great step forward. However it was the 'double escapement' (or 'repetition') mechanism, invented by Sébastien but patented by his nephew Pierre Erard in 1821, which was to become the basis of virtually all modern actions. It was an essential step in the development of the modern instrument which helped to put the Erards' company at the forefront.

Sébastien Erard died in 1831, leaving the business in the hands of Pierre, the son of Jean-Baptiste.

One of Erard's most important innovations was the 'agraffe' of 1808. The strings are threaded through this device, which prevents them moving when they are struck, improving tuning stability and dramatically enhancing tone. The agraffe shown is a simple staple from an 1818 Erard grand piano. Later it evolved into

a metal stud with one, two or three holes (for single, bichord or trichord notes) through which the strings passed. It is still used today.

THE EVOLUTION OF THE GRAND PIANO

The early 19th century was a time of great innovation in the piano industry. Patent lawyers were kept extremely busy with a flood of new inventions and enhancements to every element of the piano, from the action to the design of the music desk. Most of these ingenious ideas fell by the wayside, but the triumphant conclusion of the long struggle to improve the piano's action was the key to the instrument's total acceptance.

ERARD FRÈRES, Paris, 1808, grand piano

SERIAL NO.:	234 (on soundboard)
CASEWORK:	Mahogany with ormolu mounts
COMPASS:	5½ octaves; FF – c⁴
ACTION:	Erard's escapement action of 1796.
STRINGS:	Trichord
MODIFIERS:	4 footpedals; lute, dampers, moderator, keyboard shift (una corda)
	1 knee lever; bassoon (FF-f¹)
INSCRIPTION:	Erard Frères (on the nameboard); Erard Frères à Paris 1808 / No 234 (on the soundboard)
DIMENSIONS (INS.):	88 (L) x 43 (W)

This instrument was ordered from Erard's Paris office by Louis, King of the Netherlands, who was Napoleon Bonaparte's brother. Louis and his wife, Hortense de Beauharnais, were converting Amsterdam's town hall into their palace and the piano was intended as part of the decor. The piano is now owned by HM Queen Beatrice of the Netherlands. The nameboard is made of glass, with painting and gilding on the back (known as verre eglomisé), and signed by P. Rascalon.

TOMPKINSON, London, 1821, grand piano

CASEWORK:	Rosewood with brass inlays
COMPASS:	6 octaves; CC – c⁴
ACTION:	English grand
STRINGS:	Bichord (CC – FF); trichord (FF♯-c⁴)
MODIFIERS:	2 pedals; keyboard shift, dampers
INSCRIPTION:	For the King (on bottom key)
DIMENSIONS (INS.):	96½ (L) x 46½ (W) x 11½ (Height of case)

Another instrument that was made for King George IV and kept at Brighton Pavilion. It can clearly be seen in Thomas Nash's painting of the Pavilion's entrance hall. Thomas Tompkinson worked in London during the first half of the 19th century, when he was appointed piano maker to the Prince of Wales (later George IV), and in his life is said to have made more than 9,000 instruments. Tompkinson had a reputation for quality and he paid particular attention to the detail of casework. In this instance the inlay work is especially fine: note the winged lions at either end of the keyboard.

The casework of this piano features rosewood crossbanding and brass stringing. The side cheeks are still squared off: sloping cheeks, as found on Viennese instruments, were only just starting to appear on English and French pianos at this time.

The keyboard assembly of this type of piano is easily removed to reveal the action. The leather-covered hammers are small by comparison with those found in today's instruments

When the keyboard shift pedal is pressed, the keyboard and action slide so that the hammers strike either two strings (due corde) or one string (una corda) per note. A small peg (illustrated), to the right of the keyboard, determines how far the keyboard will move and thus whether one, two or three strings are to be struck by the hammer.

The Clementi's innovative harmonic swell mechanism can be seen here. When the pedal is pressed, a damping bar (the red 's-shaped' device) lifts off the strings to allow the extra length of string to vibrate. The player gains new control over the power of the instrument.

CLEMENTI, London, 1822, grand piano ✳

CASEWORK:	Oak with mahogany and rosewood veneer
COMPASS:	6 octaves; CC – c⁴
ACTION:	English grand
STRINGS:	Bichord (CC – FF); trichord (FF♯-c⁴)
MODIFIERS:	3 pedals; keyboard shift to due corde and una corda, (forte) dampers, harmonic swell
INSCRIPTION:	Imperial Patent / Clementi and Compᶦ London
DIMENSIONS (INS.):	97 (L) x 46 (W) x 13 (Height of case)

This Clementi grand piano is an exceptionally fine unaltered example of its type. Muzio Clementi (1752-1832), who was born in Rome but came to England as a child, was known in his lifetime as 'the father of the pianoforte', and is described as such on his gravestone in Westminster Abbey. He was primarily a composer and pianist but was closely involved in the design of the instruments that bore his name. This instrument features a device known as a 'harmonic swell', which was patented in 1821 by Frederick Collard, a partner in the company. The harmonic swell was an excellent feature of the piano which introduced a kind of reverberation effect to give the instrument a fuller, richer sound. The effect uses the sympathetic vibrations set up in the un-tuned non-speaking length of the strings. Here the soundboard is bigger than usual to accommodate a second bridge (the 'bridge of reverberation').

DIRECTIONS FOR THE USE OF THE PEDALS.

The harmonic swell feature was peculiar to Clementi instruments, so the player needed to be instructed on its use. Most manufacturers would include instructions for any special features on a label fixed to the body of the instrument.

COLLARD & COLLARD, London, c.1835, grand piano ✳

CASEWORK:	Maple veneer with marquetry decoration in various exotic woods
COMPASS:	6 octaves; FF – g⁴
ACTION:	English grand
STRINGS:	Bichord
MODIFIERS:	2 footpedals; keyboard shift (una corda), dampers
INSCRIPTION:	PATENT REPEATER / COLLARD & COLLARD / LATE / CLEMENTI, COLLARD & COLLARD / LONDON
DIMENSIONS (INS.):	80½ (L) x 46½ (W) x 13 (Height of case)

From 1822 to 1832, the company Muzio Clementi had set up was known as Clementi, Collard & Collard. However, upon Clementi's death the name was changed to Collard & Collard. Rococo instruments such as this are adorned with shell-like flourishes. The style was prominent in Europe during the 18th century and was revived in the middle of the 19th. This piano is from the revival.

✳ *For more on recordings using this piano see Pianos on Record, p104.*

Like the Seven Years War, which had convulsed Germany earlier in the century, the French Revolution led to several important piano manufacturers leaving their native country to set up factories in England. This was one of the main reasons why, by the end of the 18th century, London was the world's main center for piano production. But the city's success was due to more than just an influx of creative manufacturing talent. It also benefited from the increasing affluence of the local population, who were the industry's customers.

One of the most important of the French piano makers in London was Sébastien Erard. His contribution to the development of the instrument was enormous. Initially he studied the Zumpe design of square piano and made improvements to it, but he soon realized that the market was changing and that he should concentrate on the grand piano.

Erard's most important innovation was the 'double escapement' (or 'repetition') action mechanism. This action allows a note to be replayed without the key being fully released. Erard's double escapement action works by holding the hammer close to

the strings while the escapement mechanism re-engages itself ready for the next note. This means that the note can be quickly and easily re-played.

Early actions of this type were rather too complex, and consequently unreliable. Erard patented his first repetition action in 1808, and a slightly modified version was patented in France a year later. But the action for which he is justly celebrated was developed and patented in England in 1821. The German pianist and piano maker Henri Herz subsequently improved it. It was to ensure the success of the Erard company.

The English piano makers doubted the durability of this complex action, which works through an elaborate system of levers. They failed to realize its potential and ignored it, to their disadvantage, for many decades. Nevertheless, in the early 19th century the English market for grand pianos was still dominated by Broadwood, and to some extent Clementi (renamed Collard & Collard after 1830) and Tompkinson. But the Erard company, with its improved action and factories in both Paris and London, soon started to compete most effectively.

The soundboard is mounted high in the instrument. This appears to improve its tonal quality by helping to compensate for the relatively short string lengths.

Chopin, Piano Concerto No. 1; *Weber*, Konzertstück in F minor, *Christopher Kite*
This recording, by Christopher Kite, highlights the differences between the English piano (an 1848 Broadwood grand, mechanically similar to that shown) and the Viennese instruments of the same era.

This 1852 Robert Wornum piano uses a downstriking action, enabling him to position the strings and soundboard right at the bottom of the case. This makes the wooden frame far more rigid and able to withstand greater string tension. With the strings low in the instrument more energy is reflected from the case, increasing sustain and 'throw'.

ROBERT WORNUM, London, 1837, pocket grand piano

CASEWORK:	*Rosewood*
COMPASS:	*6 octaves; FF-f⁴*
ACTION:	*Wornum's tape-check grand*
STRINGS:	*Bichord*
MODIFIERS:	*2 footpedals; keyboard shift, dampers.*
INSCRIPTION:	*Royal Patent Equal Tension / Pocket Grand Piano-forte Imperial Manufactured by / Robert Wornum / Music Hall Store Street Bedford Square London*
DIMENSIONS (INS.):	*66 (L) x 45 (W) x 14 (Height of case)*

Wornum calls this instrument a 'Pocket Grand Piano-forte' and it was one of the first grands built with space-saving in mind. The action sits at the bottom of the case. The strings, soundboard and frame are mounted as a self-contained unit

above that and this whole section hinges upwards for access (see photograph). As the strings are mounted above the hammers, the action is in essence of the down-striking variety, but upside down. Wornum also employs a tape check, similar to that in his 'piccolo' upright pianos. The keyboard shift is unusual in that it only moves that part of the action that includes the hammers, and the sustain pedal actually lowers the dampers, which are located below the strings. Wornum tried to have all the strings at a similar tension, hence "Royal Patent Equal Tension".

FROM STRENGTH TO STRENGTH

By the middle of the 19th century the furious pace of innovation that had surrounded the piano almost since its invention had started to slacken. The main elements that make up the modern piano had been invented. A long period of development and refinement, rather than radical innovation, was in prospect. But the dramatic new music of the era brought new demands for piano makers.

The 19th century saw the rise of the romantic movement in music. The order and decorum of the classical era gave way to passion and drama in both composition and performance.

The age of musical showmanship had arrived, and audiences wanted to see musicians in artistic and emotional fervor. Sadly, the instruments of the early 19th century were not up to the job, and many a concert ended with a wrecked piano. Most virtuoso pianists required at least one spare piano to be on hand. It became vital for the piano to become more robust to withstand the aggressive playing of Beethoven, Liszt and others.

Surprisingly, the action, which was a complex mechanical device, generally faired better than the strings. These days it is hard to imagine a pianist breaking a string, but the grand piano strings of the day were under considerably less tension and needed to be much thinner to achieve the desired pitch. Strengthening the frame assembly would allow for greater tensioning of the strings, and thus thicker strings.

Broadwood had been using a metal hitch-pin plate and a metal brace for the pin block on his square pianos since around 1808.

This strengthened the fixings of the strings, preventing twist and distortion. But as you tension a string, forces are exerted on either end (the pin block and hitch-pin plate), tending to pull them together. Strengthening was required to keep these two elements apart from one another.

The use of iron spacers between the pin block and the belly rail, to which the hitch-pin plate is ultimately attached, was commonplace by the 1820s. But it only provided a modicum of extra resistance, because it didn't resist bowing. As a result iron braces were developed, running above the soundboard on the same plane as the strings and fixed to the hitch pin plate. Broadwood and Erard both lay claim to this development. The number of braces increased until the 1840s, when more efficient fixings allowed for greater forces to be applied to them. Consequently fewer such members were required.

With the increase in string tensioning came larger hammers and more robust actions. The remaining major advance was 'overstringing' — running the bass strings diagonally over the treble strings — which was patented in 1859 by Henry Steinway Jr.

KEY DATES

1772 Backers builds what is believed to the first piano to feature the English grand action.

1777 Stodart obtains the patent for the 'English Grand Action', subsequently used by American and English manufacturers. This is the first use of the word 'grand'.

1781 Stein (Augsburg) introduces his escapement action.

1781 Broadwood builds his first grand.

1788 Broadwood discovers, with help of Signor Cavallo and Dr Gray of the British Museum, that the string should be hit 1/9th of the way along its length to produce the tone he requires.

1792 Sébastien Erard flees the French Revolution and sets up his piano factory in London.

1794 Broadwood introduces pianos with a compass of six octaves.

1797 *Pianoforte*, the first magazine devoted exclusively to the piano, begins publishing in London.

1797 William Rolfe and Samuel Davis file patent for a janissary drum mechanism.

1808 Sébastien Erard develops the agraffe, which helps clamp piano strings into position, stabilizes tuning, and forms one terminal of the speaking length of the string.

1810 Sébastien Erard designs what was to become the modern pedal mechanism.

1820 Allen & Thom of London patent grand piano having a frame braced with iron tubes, their compensating frame. They sell the rights to Stodart.

1821 Sébastien Erard introduces double escapement (repetition) action, allowing extremely fast note repetition – patented by Pierre Erard.

1823 Erard patents grand piano with six resistance iron bars placed over the soundboard.

1823 Jonas Chickering starts in business with James Stewart.

c1825 Loud Brothers of Philadelphia build 7½ octave piano.

1826 Henri Pape uses tempered steel piano strings and felt-covered hammers.

1827 Broadwood patents a combination of a metal hitch-pin plate with resistance iron bars (virtually a full iron frame).

1827 James Stewart (partner of Jonas Chickering) develops the method, still in use today, of employing one length of wire to serve as two adjacent strings.

1828 Ignaz Bösendorfer takes over management of the Brodmann instrument workshop in Vienna.

1835 First example of automation in the piano manufacturing process with the introduction in Germany of a device for automatically covering hammers.

1838 Pierre Erard patents the pressure bar, which is designed to provide a force to prevent the hammers from lifting the strings away from the bridge.

c1840 Henri Herz produces the simplified Erard action, which is still used in today's instruments.

1842 The first workshop to specialize solely in the production of piano actions is opened by JCL Ishermann in Hamburg.

1843 Chickering patents a one-piece iron frame for the grand piano.

1844 Pape becomes the first known company to produce an eight-octave grand piano.

1859 H Steinway Jr. patents overstrung grand piano.

The instrument is straight-strung and the substantial bracing bars which keep the pin block and the hitch pin plate apart can be clearly seen.

Despite the success of Erard's double escapement action, Broadwood continued to use the English grand action on their pianos for many years.

▼ *This diagram traces the evolution of the piano frame, from the wooden structure used by harpsichord makers and employed by Cristofori and Silbermann, to the modern iron frameworks of today.*

◀ *The compensating frame (F) was developed by Thom Allen in 1820, and was designed to offset the effect of changes of temperature on the piano by using iron tubes that expanded with temperature to maintain string tension.*

◀ *These two types of frame (B&C) were found on German and Viennese pianos. Other than the small struts, these instruments didn't use much metalwork, relying more on increasingly heavy timbers.*

The size of a piano is dictated by the length of the strings and the tension under which they are held. The 18th century pianos of Cristofori and Silbermann had relatively simple wooden frames (A), like those in harpsichords of the period. As demand grew for more volume and power, pianos of the Viennese school were strengthened, initially by the addition of cross bracings, as seen on an early Stein piano (B), and later with an iron strut between the pin block and rim/bracings (C). In the 19th century heavier timbers facilitated greater string tensions. The English grand pianos of the late 18th century also used metal braces to tie the framework together (D), and during the early 19th century the amount of metalwork increased (E). The compensating frame (F) was an attempt to produce a frame that allowed for changes in temperature, but it never achieved lasting popularity. In 1827 Broadwood introduced iron hitch pin plates (G) with iron braces directly attached, which were anchored to the pin block, providing considerable strength. This was just one step away from the full iron frame (H) which was patented by Chickering in 1843, though not widely adopted for some years.

Today's grand pianos sometimes arrange the braces so the sound is directed to the collector, a focal point on the belly bar, for improved sound quality.

JC BACH'S ZUMPE SQUARE PIANO
Attrib. Johannes Zumpe, London, c1778

CASEWORK:	*Mahogany*
COMPASS:	*5 octaves; FF/GG – f³*
ACTION:	*English single*
STRINGS:	*Bichord*
MODIFIERS:	*3 hand stops; treble and bass dampers, buff*
INSCRIPTION:	*None*
DIMENSIONS (INS.):	*58 (W) x 20½ (D) x 8 (Height of case)*

This piano is believed to have been made by Johannes Zumpe and to have belonged to Johann Christian Bach, or at least to have been played by him. The evidence is a faint signature on the rear right part of the soundboard. JC Bach, the 'English' Bach, was a pioneer of the early piano. He was born in 1735 in Germany, the youngest son of Johann Sebastian Bach. Following the death of his father, in 1750, he joined his half-brother Carl Philipp Emanuel Bach in Berlin, where he was taught composition and keyboard playing. He probably spent most of his formative years playing the harpsichord, but he may also have tried Silbermann's piano. In 1754 JC Bach went to Italy, becoming organist of Milan Cathedral in 1760 and writing a considerable amount of church music. In 1762 he was invited to London to write two Italian operas. Bach's first piece composed with the piano in mind was his 'Sonatas For Piano Forte or Harpsichord Op. 5' of 1766. This is the earliest piano music known to have been published in England. It appeared just as Zumpe started to produce his square pianos. The music was simplistic, but this may have been deliberate. Zumpe's single action was difficult to play: by publishing a relatively simple work Bach helped to ensure that the piano became established. His Op.17 (c1774, reissued 1779) was far more mature. Bach is also known to have acted as a sales agent for Zumpe's pianos, not only in England but also in France where there were no established piano makers. Queen Charlotte, wife of George III, appointed Bach to the post of Master of the Queen's Music. He had already written the 'Six Concertos for Harpsichord Op.1' for her, in 1762. At a concert at the Thatched House in St James's in 1768, Bach gave the piano its first solo public performance in England, in effect giving royal approval to the instrument and ensuring its acceptance.

This piano is believed to be one of Zumpe's later instruments. Americus Backers started building grand pianos from around 1772, and Bach would probably have switched to his instruments for public performance. JC Bach died in 1782.

CHOPIN'S BROADWOOD GRAND PIANO
John Broadwood & Sons, London, 1848 ❋

SERIAL NO.:	*17047*
CASEWORK:	*Mahogany*
COMPASS:	*6½ octaves; CC – g⁴*
ACTION:	*English grand*
STRINGS:	*Bichord (CC – FF♯); trichord (GG – g⁴)*
MODIFIERS:	*2 footpedals; keyboard shift (due corde), dampers*
INSCRIPTION:	*Patent / Repetition Grand Piano / John Broadwood & Sons / Manufacturers to Her Majesty / 33 Great Pulteney Street Golden Square / London (on nameboard). THIS GRAND PIANO WAS USED BY FREDERIC CHOPIN AT HIS RECITALS IN LONDON IN 1848 (on plaque)*
DIMENSIONS (INS.):	*97½ (L) x 50 (W) x 13½ (Depth of case)*

In 1848 Polish composer Frédéric François Chopin came to England at the age of 38 to give a series of performances. He was always extremely careful in his choice of instrument. In Paris, where he lived, he chose to play Pleyel pianos, in preference to the more advanced Erard instruments. When he gave his first performance in Vienna he chose a Graf. Chopin was a great friend of Camille Pleyel, who in turn was a friend of the Broadwood family. Pleyel had introduced Chopin to the Broadwoods on an earlier visit to London. For the 1848 tour, Chopin came to London and chose three pianos: this one, which he used for his London recitals; no. 17093, which he chose for his rooms; and no. 17001, which he used for his Scottish recitals. His first London engagement was at Stafford House for Lady Gainsborough; the second was at Mrs Sartori's house, where he played his 'Nocturnes'; and the third was at Lord Falmouth's London house in St James's Square. He used the piano again in Manchester and finally at a charity performance in aid of Polish refugees. He returned to Paris and died the following year.

MAHLER'S GRAF GRAND PIANO
Conrad Graf, Vienna, c1830

SERIAL NO.:	*2257 (on pin block)*
CASEWORK:	*Laminated case: spruce and oak*
COMPASS:	*6½ octaves; CC – g⁴*
ACTION:	*Viennese with continuous back check*
STRINGS:	*Bichord (CC – EE); trichord (FF – g⁴)*
MODIFIERS:	*2 footpedals; keyboard shift, dampers*
INSCRIPTION:	*Conrad Graf / kaiserl: kön: hof-fortepianomacher/WIEN / nächst der carls-Kirche im Mondschein No. 102.*
DIMENSIONS (INS.):	*96 (L) x 49 (W) x 13 (Height of case)*

This was Gustav Mahler's first grand piano. Mahler was born in Austria in 1860 and was a composer and conductor rather than a pianist. This piano was made in 1830. Graf's pianos were widely used by the Viennese composers and performers of the 19th century. Schubert and Beethoven both possessed Grafs, and Brahms acquired one previously owned by Schumann. Conrad Graf was a very consistent manufacturer who rarely deviated from his original grand piano design. The quad-strung piano shown right is one exception. Mahler considered this to be "a delicate instrument". As much of his work followed the Viennese symphonic tradition of incorporating elements of folk music, this instrument's heritage made it preferable to a piano of his own time. The instrument's compass of just 6½ octaves is almost an octave less than that of a more modern instrument. Mahler had a close affinity with Vienna. In 1897 he became principal conductor at the Vienna State Opera House, a post he was to hold for ten years. This piano remained in Mahler's possession until about 1902. He died in 1911.

PIANOS AND PEOPLE

The musical qualities of the piano provided the platform upon which a whole wave of new composers and performers were to build international reputations. At the same time, the enthusiasm with which musicians embraced the instrument saved it from the obscurity into which other such innovations had fallen. Despite the apparent false starts suffered by Cristofori and Silbermann, the piano was the instrument that the musical world had been waiting for. Once people became aware of its existence, its success was inevitable.

The first great composer to know the piano was Johann Sebastian Bach (1685-1750). He saw Silbermann's early instruments in the 1730s but was not enthusiastic. He was, however, astute enough to appreciate what Silbermann was attempting to do. With his son, Carl Philipp Emanuel Bach (1714-88), he kept an eye on developments and is even said to have become an agent for Silbermann in Leipzig.

CPE Bach had risen to the position of chamber harpsichordist at Frederick the Great's court in Berlin, and had free access to the Silbermann pianos. JS Bach visited his son at court in 1747 and was asked by the king to improvise a fugue to mark his visit. This he did, on piano, now greatly improved, rather than on harpsichord. Sadly, JS Bach died just three years later, before he was able to exploit the potential of the new instrument.

His son, however, continued to work at court. In 1753 he stated that the clavichord was to be preferred to the piano, which was too difficult to play. At that time, this was probably accurate. But in his second *Essays on the True Art of Playing Keyboard Instruments*, published in 1763, CPE Bach acknowledged the importance of the piano. His sonatas of that period acquired new freedom, with extensive changes of tempo and dynamics.

His younger brother, Johann Christian Bach, had studied with him in Berlin. After working in Italy, JC Bach came to England where, in conjunction with Johannes Zumpe, he helped establish the piano industry during the 1760s and 1770s.

SONATAS AND PIANO TRIOS

The 'sonata' (from the Italian sonare, 'to sound') was to become the main type of composition associated with the piano. The sonata originally appeared in Italy in the 17th century, and was simply an instrumental composition, as opposed to a 'cantata', which was for voice. A vast number of the 'baroque sonatas' of the late 17th century took the form of the 'trio sonata', meaning they had written parts for three instruments (usually two violins and a viola da gamba or cello). They also had a 'continuo' harpsichord accompaniment, a basic harmonic backdrop improvised by the player from a bass line and chord symbols provided by the composer.

In the early 18th century more sonatas were written for a single

GRAF GRAND PIANO AS PLAYED BY BEETHOVEN
Conrad Graf, Vienna, c.1820, grand piano with quadruple stringing

SERIAL NO.:	365
CASEWORK:	Mahogany
COMPASS:	6½ octaves; CC – f⁴
ACTION:	Viennese
STRINGS:	Trichord (CC – C#); quadchord (D – f⁴); single bridge
MODIFIERS:	5 footpedals; keyboard shift (quad to due corde), bassoon, moderator 1, moderator 2, dampers
INSCRIPTION:	Conrad Grafl in Wien / Weiden No. 182
DIMENSIONS (INS.):	95 (L) x 48 (W) x 12½ (Depth of case)

This instrument is one of three such instruments known to have been made by Graf. One of them was made by Graf in c1824, especially for Beethoven. With his failing hearing, the composer needed as loud an instrument as possible. By adding an extra string Graf attempted to obtain a tone that was richer and more

powerful, though it didn't make the instrument any louder than his Broadwood. Beethoven didn't write again specifically for the piano from the date that the Graf instrument arrived to his death in 1827. The rival piano maker Matthäus

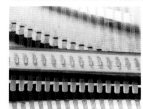

Andreas Stein was unimpressed with the quadruple stringing (left). "There's nothing worse than [instruments] with four strings," he said. "I now have excellent strings. If you have such strings you don't need quadruple strings." Stein was either worried by the possible threat this might cause his business or genuinely felt that the extra string

was nonsense. His son Carl Stein went on to acquire the Graf company in 1841, when Conrad Graf retired. The footpedals are also of interest. There are two moderators. In conjunction with the keyboard shift from four to two strings, these provide a much wider control over the character of the sound than is possible on Graf's usual instruments.

MARIE ANTOINETTE'S ERARD SQUARE PIANO
Sébastien Erard, Paris, 1787

CASEWORK:	Mahogany
COMPASS:	5 octaves; FF – f³
ACTION:	English single
STRINGS:	Bichord
MODIFIERS:	2 knee levers; dampers, buff
INSCRIPTION:	Sebastianus Erard Parisiis / 1787 / Rue du Mail No 37
DIMENSIONS (INS.):	58 (W) x 22 (D) x 7¼ (Height of case)

Marie Antoinette (1755-93) was born in Austria, the daughter of Holy Roman Emperor Francis I. She married the heir to the French throne in 1774, the year he became King Louis XVI. Sébastien Erard had begun making pianos in Paris, based on Zumpe's English designs. In 1777, however, he ran into problems with the local instrument makers and was imprisoned. Louis XVI had him released, and Erard subsequently produced this instrument for the queen. Very few instruments from the court of Louis XVI survive, owing to the destruction unleashed by the French Revolution. This instrument is one of the finest.

---

instrument and keyboard. George Frederick Handel's sonatas of this type still stuck with the continuo system, but his exact contemporary JS Bach started to write out the harpsichord part in his instrumental sonatas, giving it a melodic interest of its own. There were also important sonatas for solo keyboard, notably by Scarlatti.

These developments prefigured the acceptance of the piano. Unlike the harpsichord, the piano was designed for expression. Now it was given a prominent written part in the sonata rather than simply a supporting role. The familiar piano trio (piano, violin, cello) evolved, to be popularized by Haydn and Mozart in the 1790s.

Franz Joseph Haydn (1732-1809), one of the great masters of classical music, was largely responsible for promoting the use of the piano. He also transformed the sonata, by now given a more defined form by CPE Bach, into the classical string quartet and the symphony. Wolfgang Amadeus Mozart (1756-91) learned to play and compose at an extremely early age. His music drew on the formal innovations of Haydn, and both men were strongly influenced by the sonatas of CPE Bach. Mozart, unlike Haydn, was an accomplished performer.

The effect of the increasing power and enhanced tone achieved by piano manufacturers in this period can be observed in Mozart's piano trios. The cello had traditionally been used to support the bass of the piano (or the harpsichord). But with the increasing richness of tone produced by the Viennese piano there was less need for this support. The cello was thus allowed to range more freely, on an equal footing with the violin.

Playing techniques were also evolving. The piano was still considered merely an alternative to the harpsichord. Most piano players, including the great composers, had learnt their keyboard skills on the harpsichord or clavichord. Notes on these instruments have a strong initial attack followed by a fast decay: consequently they are less suited to playing in a 'legato' or flowing manner. Early players tended to play the piano as if it were a harpsichord, precisely but not smoothly. But as they became more familiar with the piano, legato playing became more widespread.

Ludwig van Beethoven (1770-1827), the third great master of the classical piano, still wrote much of his music to accommodate the early style. However, his work tends to present

more technical difficulties than that of the earlier composers, partly because improvements to the instrument had increased the possiblities. The action, compass and sound quality had all been improved. Beethoven could use a wider range than previous composers, and the finer, less cluttered timbre of contemporary pianos permitted the introduction of bass chords and more subtlety in the extreme treble.

THE ROMANTICS

Beethoven's last years saw the end of the classical era and the beginning of the romantic period. It was the time of virtuoso piano playing, from the fireworks of Liszt to the delicate articulation of Chopin. Pianos had become stronger and the action had improved, enabling the keyboard to respond faster. But it was probably the damper (or sustain) pedal that was the most important element of the romantic era. Composers such as Chopin, Schubert and Schumann (one of the first to specify the use of the pedal on the score) were keen to exploit its possibilities. It was to shape the sound of the romantic piano.

The point at which the bracing bars, which were forged as part of the hitch-pin plate, are attached to the pin block is shown here. This point endures considerable stress, and it took a long time for manufacturers to develop a stable fixing.

FRANZ LISZT

The composer and piano virtuoso Franz Liszt (1811-1886) was born in Reiding, a small village in Burgenland, which was at that time part of Hungary and is now the most eastern province of Austria. Liszt was a revolutionary figure in romantic music and was recognised as the greatest pianist of his day. His playing style both excited and delighted audiences. He became totally engrossed in his playing, and as a result his emotions took control. Coupled with his remarkably strong hands, this resulted in the destruction of many a piano, especially at the beginning of his career when the instruments were less robust. Liszt courted most of the major European piano houses at some point in his life and was personal friends with several of the proprietors. In the picture above, Liszt is shown playing a Bösendorfer piano, one of his oldest and longest loves, in the presence of the Emperor Franz Josef I. The lid has been removed.

JOHN BROADWOOD & SONS, London, 1848, grand piano ✷

SERIAL NO.:	*16368 (on pin block)*
CASEWORK:	*Amboyna veneer with gilt limewood foliate decoration*
COMPASS:	*6½ octaves; CC – g⁴*
ACTION:	*English grand*
STRINGS:	*Bichord (CC – FF♯); trichord (GG – g⁴),*
MODIFIERS:	*2 footpedals; keyboard shift (due corde), dampers*
INSCRIPTION:	*Patent / Repetition Grand Piano / John Broadwood & Sons / Manufacturers to Her Majesty / 33 Great Pulteney Street Golden Square / London*
DIMENSIONS (INS):	*98½ (L) x 53 (W) x 13½ (Height of case)*

Broadwood & Sons constructed their first grand piano with a full iron frame in 1846, but this instrument still utilizes the iron bracing bars which the company had introduced in the 1820s. The piano is extremely ornate, and it is said that it once resided in 'Agapemone', or 'The Abode of Love', at Spaxton in Somerset. This was the headquarters of the 'Family of Love', a bizarre and scandalous religious cult established in the 1850s. A similar if somewhat less decorated grand (serial no. 17,047) was sent to Manchester in 1848 for a Chopin concert. At the time an instrument of this type (without the decoration) would sell for around 155 guineas (£162.75). The Broadwood nameplate reflects the styling of the period and publicizes Broadwood's new idea.

✷ For information on recordings on this instrument, see Pianos on Record, p104.

Broadwood generally gave their grand pianos large footpedals – far larger than you would find on today's instruments.

Broadwood would probably have contracted outside craftsmen to decorate this extraordinary instrument.

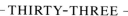

LEOPOLD SAUER, Prague, c1805, pyramid piano

CASEWORK:	Cherry veneer, mahogany fretted panel over the upper part of the casework
COMPASS:	5½ octaves; FF – a³
ACTION:	Hanging German
STRINGS:	Bichord (FF-b); trichord (c¹-a³)
MODIFIERS:	1 knee lever; dampers. 2 hand stops; bassoon and moderator
INSCRIPTION:	Leopold Sauer / Instrumentmacher / in Prag (on an oval plaque)
DIMENSIONS (INS.):	103 (H) x 43 (W) x 21½ (Depth of case)

Built in Prague by Leopold Sauer, this pyramid piano is fairly typical of the genre, although it is somewhat unusual to find a clock mounted in the upper casework. This instrument marks a revival in the pyramid shape, which originated with Christian Ernst Friederici (see p17) and his fellow piano makers in the first half of the 18th century, and which died out around 1760. The piano uses a 'hanging German' action, which makes it comparatively light to the touch, although this instrument is no longer in a playable condition. Sauer primarily made only pyramid and upright grand pianos and this is one of the very few of his instruments to have survived.

JONES, ROUND AND COMPANY, London, c1810, cabinet upright grand piano

SERIAL NO.:	707 (on yoke – a strengthening bar glued to pin block)
CASEWORK:	Mahogany veneer with satinwood banding
COMPASS:	6 octaves; CC – c⁴
ACTION:	English upright grand
STRINGS:	Bichord
MODIFIERS:	2 pedals; keyboard shift (due corde and una corda), damper
INSCRIPTION:	Jones Round and Co. / UPRIGHT GRAND & SQUARE PIANOFORTE / Makers / To His Royal Highness The Prince of Wales / No 11 Golden Square / London
DIMENSIONS (INS.):	104½ (H) x 45 (W) x 22 (Depth of case)

One of the tallest pianos ever made. The same company also made a similar instrument but in gothic style for King George IV, which is believed to have been some four inches taller. Opening the doors reveals a set of shelves.

MUZIO CLEMENTI & CO., London, c1816, upright grand piano

CASEWORK:	Mahogany with satinwood keywell
COMPASS:	5½ octaves; FF – c⁴
ACTION:	English upright grand (no stickers)
STRINGS:	Trichord (unverified)
MODIFIERS:	2 footpedals; keyboard shift (una corda), dampers
INSCRIPTION:	Muzio Clementi & Co / Cheapside, London
DIMENSIONS (INS.):	103 (L) x 42½ (W) x 23 (Depth of case)

Clementi made many upright grand pianos in his lifetime and quite a number still survive. This instrument has a timbral quality virtually identical to the English grand pianos of the time. The attractive floral design is found on other Clementi instruments of this period. An identical design is also found on the pianos of William Rolfe, also of Cheapside, London, indicating that manufacturers would often bring in outsiders to decorate their instruments.

UPRIGHT GRANDS AND UPRIGHT SQUARES

The early upright grand pianos were essentially horizontal grands with the frame/string/soundboard assembly rotated up to the vertical. They were able to use strings of similar length and consequently their tone could be as good as that of a horizontal grand. They did, however, have several disadvantages. They were large cumbersome pieces of furniture, too big for many homes. And when used for recitals, as the front of the instrument needed to face outwards, the player had to sit with his back to the audience. This was unacceptable, especially if the pianist was also a singer.

The upright grand piano has strings that run vertically. In effect it is a grand piano with the strings, soundboard and frame assembly raised up to the vertical and the action adapted accordingly. Early upright grand pianos had the strings rising straight up from the keyboard. From the end of the 18th century, however, manufacturers started to bring the whole broad end of the grand almost down to the ground. In some instances, as in the case of certain giraffe and lyre pianos, the strings ran obliquely rather than vertically.

The upright grands made from c1735 to c1850 had the pin block at the bottom and as such are very different to the upright pianos of today, which have this broad end of the frame running along the top.

There are four main types of upright grand piano. One of the earliest was the 'pyramid' piano (Pyramidenflügel). Christian Ernst Friederici pioneered it, building his first in 1745, with a triangular case that tapered to a flat top. The bass strings rose obliquely to the right, permitting a symmetrical appearance with the apex of the case in the middle. There was little interest in this

Although one of a new generation of Broadwood pianos, this piano was in essence a fairly standard model. It was, however, hand picked for its quality. The casework is made of Spanish mahogany, inlaid with marquetry and ormolu, and the handles are of brass shaped to resemble a laurel wreath.

Broadwood's pianos had become much stronger in the preceding decade. The string tension of this instrument would be at least half as much again as in a piano of 1805.

This piano had a six-octave keyboard, which Beethoven used to the absolute limit. Towards the end of his life, it was suggested he get a newer piano with a larger compass but Beethoven remained faithful to the Broadwood.

The right hand pedal is split into two halves, with the left half raising the bass dampers and the right half the treble dampers.

ELGAR'S BROADWOOD SQUARE PIANO
John Broadwood & Sons, London, 1844 ✳

SERIAL NO.:	56785
CASEWORK:	Mahogany
COMPASS:	6 octaves; FF – f⁴
ACTION:	English single
STRINGS:	Single (FF – D♯), bichord (E – f⁴)
MODIFIERS:	Footpedal; dampers
INSCRIPTION:	John Broadwood & Sons / Makers to her Majesty / Great Pulteney Street Golden Square / London
DIMENSIONS (INS.):	67 (W) x 27 (D) x 11 (Height of case)

This Broadwood square piano was made in 1844 and classified as their 'school model'. It was purchased by a Mrs Skelton of Worcester in that same year. Composer Edward Elgar's father, William Henry Elgar, ran a piano dealership

and repair workshop in Worcester. In 1867 this piano was repaired by the firm, Elgar Brothers, a fact that is recorded on an inscription on the B flat key immediately below middle C. Whether the piano remained in the possession of Elgar brothers for the next 30 years is not known, but in 1898 Edward Elgar rented a country retreat, Birchwood Cottage, just outside of Worcester, and acquired the piano to use there. On the soundboard of the piano Elgar wrote down the titles of some of the pieces that he composed on it. These include two of his best known works: 'Caractacus'

and 'The Dream of Gerontius'. He undoubtedly used the Broadwood when writing his famous 'Enigma Variations', but this is not mentioned on the soundboard. Curiously, the words "Mr Rabbit" are, however. This may refer to a pet belonging to his daughter Carrice. With Elgar's increasing fame, he ended his tenancy of Birchwood and the piano was dispatched to his sister's house in Stoke. As Birchwood was such a small house, the square piano suited Elgar's needs. It was not, however, the easiest of instruments to play as it had no back check.

'Elgar: His Music Performed On His Piano' *by Anthony Goldstone*
The 1844 Broadwood square piano is used exclusively here to recreate some of Edward Elgar's most famous pieces. Elgar would have used this instrument in composing many of these pieces. The works include 'Variations of an Original Theme (Enigma)', Op.36; and 'Dream Children', Op.43.

✳ *For information on recordings on this instrument see Pianos on Record, p104.*

ERARD GRAND PIANO AS PLAYED BY MENDELSSOHN AND LISZT
Pierre Erard, London, 1837

SERIAL NO.:	15484
CASEWORK:	Mahogany
COMPASS:	6½ octaves; CC – g⁴
ACTION:	Erard patent double escapement
STRINGS:	Bichord (CC – EE); trichord (FF – g⁴)
MODIFIERS:	2 footpedals; keyboard shift, dampers
Inscription:	Erard / Patent Harp and Piano Fort Maker / To the Queen / No 18 Great Marlborough Street / London
DIMENSIONS (INS.):	94½ (L) x 50 (W) x 12½ (Depth of case)

Erard was the only major manufacturer that had factories in both London and Paris, then the two main cultural centers of the world. This fine instrument is typical of the grand pianos that Pierre Erard, nephew to Sébastien, was producing at the time. The Erard piano was technically superior to any other instrument on the market, thanks mostly to its double escapement action. Erard's pianos were

used by many of the major pianists and composers of the era, including Mendelssohn, Liszt, Thalberg and Dussek. Erard's main competitor in Paris was Pleyel, whose instruments were favored by pianists such as Chopin, Cramer, Field and Friedrich Kalkbrenner. Erard's instruments were the most technically advanced pianos available, but there were pianists who preferred a more traditional instrument. The endorsement of products by the great players was very important to the manufacturers of high quality pianos.

The photograph (below) comes from the film 'Immortal Beloved', a free dramatization of the life of Beethoven. The scene captures the atmosphere of an aristocratic Viennese garden party in the grounds of a country house. Beethoven is performing as part of a piano trio (with violin and cello), a musical grouping for which he composed enthusiastically and prolifically.

BEETHOVEN'S BROADWOOD GRAND PIANO
John Broadwood & Sons, London, 1817 ✳

SERIAL NO.:	7362
CASEWORK:	Spanish mahogany
COMPASS:	6 octaves; CC – c⁴
ACTION:	English grand
STRINGS:	Trichord
MODIFIERS:	2 footpedals; keyboard shift to una corda, split pedal for treble and bass dampers
INSCRIPTION:	John Broadwood & Sons / Makers to his Majesty and the Princesses / Great Pulteney Street Golden Square / London (on nameboard) Hoc instrumentum est Thomas Broadwood londini donum propter ingenium illustrissimi Beethoven (on plaque directly above nameboard)
DIMENSIONS (INS.):	97¼ (L) x 45¼ (W) x 11½ (Depth of case); Height incl. stand 36

This is one of the most famous early grand pianos. It is known as the 'Beethoven Broadwood'. In 1817 Thomas Broadwood, fourth son of John Broadwood, was running the company jointly with his brother James. He set off on an extended tour of Switzerland, Austria and Germany. In Vienna he met Beethoven, who was by now quite unwell and also becoming deaf. Broadwood decided to present the composer with his latest grand piano. He asked five of the most accomplished pianists in London – Kalkbrenner, Ferdinand Ries (who was also Beethoven's London agent), Cramer, Ferrari and Knyvett – to choose an instrument from his factory. As well as bearing a special inscription, the piano was also signed by the five. The piano was sent from London on 27th December, 1817, and arrived at Trieste in early spring, from where it was taken by cart to Vienna. Upon hearing of this gift Beethoven wrote to thank Broadwood: "I have never felt a greater pleasure than your honor's intimation of the arrival of this piano, with which you are honoring me as a present. I shall look upon it as an altar upon which I shall place the most beautiful offerings of my spirit to the divine Apollo. As soon as I receive your excellent instrument, I shall immediately send you the fruits of the first moments of inspiration I spend at it, as a souvenir for you from me my very dear B.; and I hope that they will be worthy of your instrument." Frustrated by deafness, Beethoven inflicted severe damage on the piano. It was reported to Broadwood in 1824 that "the broken strings were mixed up like a thorn bush in a gale". After Beethoven's death the piano was bought by C Anton Spina, who presented it to Franz Liszt in 1845. Liszt put it in his library in Weimar. He later donated it to the Hungarian National Museum.

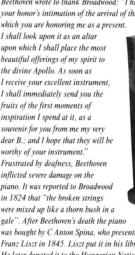

'The Beethoven Broadwood Fortepiano', played by Melvyn Tan
In 1992 the Beethoven Broadwood piano was carefully restored by David Winston, and taken on a special tour of European cities. The piano was played by Melvyn Tan, who also made this celebratory studio recording of Beethoven's music.

Beethoven had kept the Broadwood piano in his flat in Schwarzspanierhaus in Vienna. The picture above shows a recreation of the flat, based on an engraving by L Hoechle.

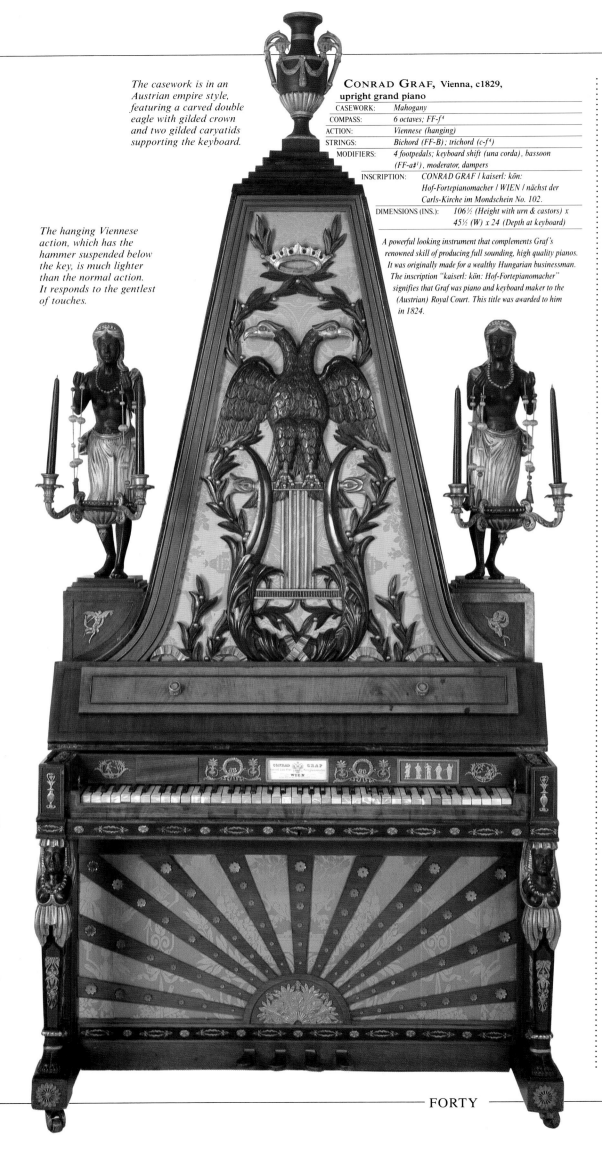

The casework is in an Austrian empire style, featuring a carved double eagle with gilded crown and two gilded caryatids supporting the keyboard.

The hanging Viennese action, which has the hammer suspended below the key, is much lighter than the normal action. It responds to the gentlest of touches.

CONRAD GRAF, Vienna, c1829, upright grand piano

CASEWORK:	*Mahogany*
COMPASS:	*6 octaves; FF-f⁴*
ACTION:	*Viennese (hanging)*
STRINGS:	*Bichord (FF-B); trichord (c-f⁴)*
MODIFIERS:	*4 footpedals; keyboard shift (una corda), bassoon (FF-a♯¹), moderator, dampers*
INSCRIPTION:	*CONRAD GRAF / kaiserl: kön: Hof-Fortepianomacher / WIEN / nächst der Carls-Kirche im Mondschein No. 102.*
DIMENSIONS (INS.):	*106½ (Height with urn & castors) x 45½ (W) x 24 (Depth at keyboard)*

A powerful looking instrument that complements Graf's renowned skill of producing full sounding, high quality pianos. It was originally made for a wealthy Hungarian businessman. The inscription "kaiserl: kön: Hof-Fortepianomacher" signifies that Graf was piano and keyboard maker to the (Austrian) Royal Court. This title was awarded to him in 1824.

UNKNOWN, probably Vienna, c1835, giraffe piano

CASEWORK:	*Mahogany*
COMPASS:	*7 octaves; CC-c⁵*
ACTION:	*Hanging Viennese*
STRINGS:	*Bichord (CC-EE); trichord (FF-c⁵)*
MODIFIERS:	*2 footpedals*
INSCRIPTION:	*None remaining*
DIMENSIONS (INS.):	*92 (H) x 54 (W) x 21½ (Depth of case)*

The giraffe piano was invented in Vienna and first appeared around 1798. This instrument could have been made by Schlimbach, Seuffert, Ehrlich or possibly Wachtl, all keen exponents of the giraffe piano. The hanging Viennese (or hanging German) action is developed from the basic Viennese action, but with the hammers suspended below the level of the keys, enabling it to respond to a very light touch. This instrument once belonged to Dr Helmholtz, the eminent physicist and physiologist.

type of instrument until it was revived in the early 19th century by Joseph Wachtl and his then partner Franz Seuffert.

Another approach was represented by the 'bookcase' (or 'cabinet') piano. These are extremely tall, rectangular instruments. The strings run vertically up from the keyboard, and the empty space on the treble side would often be filled with shelves. The top section would frequently also have doors fitted in the casework.

The 'giraffe' piano (Giraffenflügel) has its strings perpendicular to the keyboard. Its case slopes down elegantly from an extremely tall left side to the short treble side. At the top there is normally a scroll motif. A 'lying giraffe' has the strings running obliquely from the bass side up to the treble side, with the latter being vertical. This makes the instrument less tall, and gives a recumbent effect.

A third type of giraffe piano, the 'double giraffe', exists, but it is more an affectation of casework than a specific type of piano. The giraffe piano first appeared in about 1800, and was popular in Europe for more than 50 years. In America giraffe pianos were

UNKNOWN, probably Berlin, c1825, lyre piano

CASEWORK:	Mahogany veneer
COMPASS:	6½ octaves; DD – f#⁴
ACTION:	English upright grand
STRINGS:	Bichord
MODIFIERS:	2 footpedals; keyboard shift to due corde, and dampers
INSCRIPTION:	None
DIMENSIONS (INS.):	81½ (H) x 47½ (W) x 23½ (Depth of case)

This lyre piano is thought to have been made by Johann Schleip. It is much more simply decorated than the c1830 Schleip on this page, but there are marked similarities between the two. Interestingly, this piano uses bass strings that have a core overspun with two extra layers to enhance the string's mass while still retaining a degree of flexibility. This design is relatively unusual.

WILLIAM SOUTHWELL, London (& Dublin), 1800, upright square

CASEWORK:	Mahogany and satinwood veneer,
COMPASS:	6 octaves; FF – f⁴
ACTION:	English single, with stickers
STRINGS:	Bichord
MODIFIERS:	2 footpedals; both connected to the damper mechanism
INSCRIPTION:	None
DIMENSIONS (INS.):	58 (H) x 62 (W) x 18½ (Depth of case)

Southwell pioneered the upright square type of piano. He patented the design in 1798. With the front cover removed, it can be seen that this is in effect a square piano, rotated up and resting on its long side. 'Stickers' are used to raise the hammer part of the action so that the strings are struck at the desired point.

JOHANN SCHLEIP, Berlin, c1830, lyre piano

CASEWORK:	Mahogany (empire style)
COMPASS:	6½ octaves; DD – g⁴
ACTION:	English upright grand
STRINGS:	Single (DD-FF#); bichord (GG-g⁴)
MODIFIERS:	3 knee levers; bassoon, keyboard shift, damper
INSCRIPTION:	J. C. Schleip / in / Berlin
DIMENSIONS (INS.):	82 (H) x 47 (W) x 24 (Depth of case)

This fine instrument was once housed at Caernarfon Castle in Wales. As can be seen from the internal shot the strings run obliquely in order to maximize their length within the casework. Interestingly, the soundboard is free standing.

---

still being made as late as the 20th century despite their evident impracticality as a domestic instrument.

The fourth type of upright grand piano is the 'lyre' piano (Lyraflügel). This evolved from the pyramid, and was built almost exclusively by Berlin piano makers in the second quarter of the 19th century. Sylig, a piano maker in Berlin, is thought to have invented this type of instrument. But the best-known manufacturer of lyre pianos was Johann Schleip, who worked with Sylig and in 1822 took over his workshops.

The upright square piano, developed by the Irish piano maker William Southwell in 1798, was a different instrument altogether. It takes the string/soundboard assembly of the square piano and rotates it forward to the perpendicular. Its simple 'sticker' action moved the hammers to the top of the instrument, linking them by wooden rods to intermediate lever above the keys. This type of piano never achieved great popularity. Southwell also developed the sloping upright square, which was similar in concept except that the string/soundboard assembly wasn't raised up fully to the vertical, instead sloping away from the player.

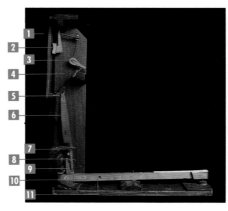

*The basic sticker action, with no check, was pioneered by John Landreth in the 1780s and William Southwell at the beginning of the 19th century. It is an adaptation of Geib's double action. The **hammer (3)** is connected to the sticker by a flexible vellum **hinge (5)**. When the key is pressed the **jack** or **hopper (9)** pushes up on the **intermediate lever (7)**, causing the **sticker (6)** to push up onto the butt of the hammer and thus propel the hammer head towards the **string (1)**. The sticker simultaneously raises the **damper wire (4)** which lifts the **damper (2)** from the string.*

*With momentum transferred to the hammer, the jack escapes from the intermediate lever, which falls back to rest on the **ledge (8)** which forms part of the jack. The hammer strikes the string and bounces away.*

*As the **key (11)** is released, the **jack spring (10)** pushes the jack back under the intermediate lever. The note is then ready to be played again. One advantage of this action was that it could be used for both large and small pianos.*

JOHN ISAAC HAWKINS, Philadelphia, 1801, portable upright piano

CASEWORK:	*Light wood veneer*
COMPASS:	*5 octaves; FF-f³*
ACTION:	*Sticker; no check or escapement*
STRINGS:	*Trichord*
MODIFIERS:	*2 footpedals; swell and moderator*
INSCRIPTION:	*J Hawkins / Invenit et Fecit / Patent / No 61801 / Philadelphia*
DIMENSIONS (INS.):	*35½ (W) x 43¼ (H) x 15¼ (Depth of case)*

This piano and the Ditanaklasis of Matthias Müller were the first uprights to extend the strings down to the floor. The instrument was designed to be transportable. The keyboard folds into the cabinet and carrying handles are provided on both sides. Hawkins, who was born in England and had emigrated to Philadelphia, incorporated both new and old ideas in this revolutionary and important instrument. There is no pedal to raise the dampers: instead a Venetian swell mechanism (see Shudi's harpsichord p8-10) governs the amplitude of the instrument by opening and closing the slats under the keyboard. The soundboard is supported by a metal frame, and the strings are tensioned by means of mechanically operated tuning pins sitting in a metal pin block. Hawkins' pianos were not a great success either as musical instruments or as commercial products. Thomas Jefferson is alleged to have bought one and found the tuning so unstable that he sought redress.

SÉBASTIEN MERCIER, Paris, 1831, upright piano

SERIAL NO.:	*62*
CASEWORK:	*Mahogany*
COMPASS:	*6 octaves; FF-f⁴*
ACTION:	*English upright*
STRINGS:	*Bichord FF-f²; trichord f♯²-f⁴*
MODIFIERS:	*2 footpedals; sustain, moderator*
INSCRIPTION:	*S. Mercier / Facteur de Pianos droits perfectionnés à / Auteil / Paris*
DIMENSIONS (INS.):	*60¼ (W) x 40 (H) x 21¼ (Depth of case)*

In France this kind of instrument is known as a 'piano droit'. French makers, in particular Blanchet et Roller (Paris) pioneered this compact upright design in the late 1820s. The French didn't like the taller upright instruments, because they obscured the player from the audiences, so the manufacturers set about making a more compact design. At the 1827 Louvre Exhibition, Blanchet and Roller unveiled a piano of this type that was less than 40 in high. This particular instrument was made by Sébastien Mercier in 1831 and is an early example of an obliquely strung upright. The French pianos of this era are particularly well engineered with great attention to detail. For example this instrument hinges open effortlessly to expose the action and strings. Mercier even included a place in the frame for a tuning hammer.

In order to access the strings and action, the piano hinges open from one side. The action is housed in the front assembly along with the keyboard, and the strings, frame and soundboard are left in the rear body.

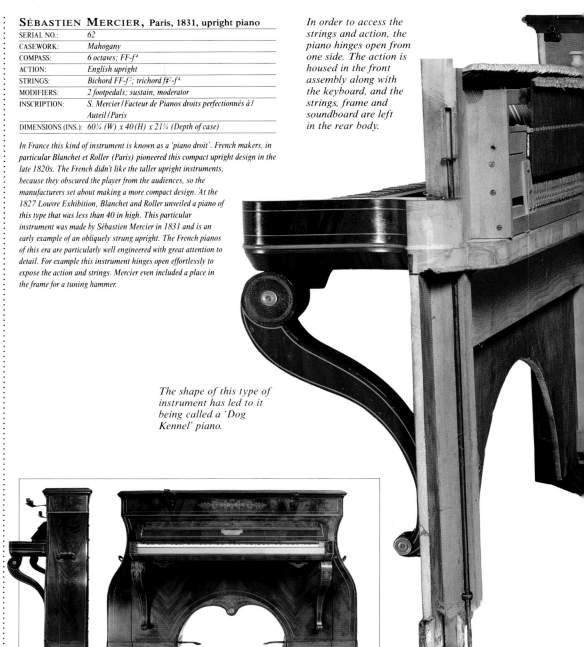

The shape of this type of instrument has led to it being called a 'Dog Kennel' piano.

THE EARLY UPRIGHT PIANO

The upright was developed to be a smaller, more economical and perhaps more portable instrument. At the same time manufacturers and inventors wanted to produce a sound that was as close as possible in power and quality to that of the grand piano. These objectives are, however, often incompatible. Over the years there have been smaller instruments, louder instruments, cheaper instruments and better sounding instruments, but an improvement made to one characteristic was generally detrimental to the others. Consequently, the story of the upright piano is one of compromise.

The upright piano that we know today first took shape in 1800, following earlier experiments with vertical grand pianos. Credit for the invention of the upright has to be shared between two piano makers on either side of the Atlantic. Attempts have been made to link the two or to try and put one before the other, but without sufficient authority. Working independently, Matthias Müller in Vienna and John Isaac Hawkins in Philadelphia both realized that the stand, or leg assembly, of the upright grand was a redundant feature and that the bass strings should be lowered to the floor.

The two instruments — Müller's 'Ditanaklasis' and Hawkins' 'Portable Grand Piano' — were fairly similar in concept. Müller, who was born in Wernborn, Germany in 1770, used a version of the grand action of the day. However, he elected to have the hammers strike the strings nearer to their mid-point than usual and this led to a sound that had fewer harmonics, and was thus less piano-like.

Hawkins was an engineer by profession and his instrument was exceptionally ingenious, with an iron frame and a fold-up keyboard. It was purported to have been designed for use on board ship. Unfortunately, it is believed to have had a horrible tone and gone out of tune easily. Perhaps for these reasons, neither instrument achieved the recognition its invention deserved.

"Pleyel is making too many pianos. He no longer has the time to take care over them."
GIOACCHINO ROSSINI, quoted by Franz Liszt in a letter of 1839

In 1802, Thomas Loud of London suggested that the strings of the upright should be run diagonally thus enabling the instrument to accommodate longer strings (and hence produce a better sound) or to be housed in a smaller case. This was not a new idea, but Loud was the first to incorporate it into an upright design. He secured a patent but is not thought to have produced any practical examples. Loud emigrated to New York in about 1813, where he subsequently produced small vertically-strung pianos. In Europe such pianos of between 50 and 70 inches in height would have been known as 'pianinos'. But from 1840 the term was used for any small, obliquely-strung upright piano.

By running the strings diagonally and at a fairly obtuse angle, the height of the instrument could be significantly reduced. The longest string is 58 in, considerably more than the height of the piano. However, the instrument does need to be to made somewhat wider than normal, as can be seen from the front elevation.

The oblique stringing leaves a semi circular void under the instrument. This is effectively used for placing one's feet and thus locating the footpedals.

IGNACE PLEYEL & CIE

One of the most important French piano houses was that founded by Ignace Pleyel in 1807. A child prodigy, Pleyel was trained as a composer by Haydn, and then became chapel-master at Strasbourg. Unfortunately, in 1789, he fell foul of the French Revolution and was repeatedly condemned to death. He escaped only by writing the score for a republican drama: its subsequent popular acclaim was taken as evidence of his loyalty. At some point he moved to England, where he became acquainted with London's burgeoning piano industry. On returning to Paris, he set up a piano factory of his own, in 1807, copying the early pianos of Robert Wornum. Henri Pape, then foreman to the Pleyel factory, further developed the upright, and it became so popular in France that there was little demand for the square piano. Pleyel also developed a range of grand pianos based on the Broadwood grand action. Ignace and his son Camille, who took over the factory in 1824, were friends of Frédéric Chopin, who was a devoted user of Pleyel pianos. Camille died in 1855, after which his partner Auguste Wolff took control, changing the name to Pleyel, Wolff & Cie. Eventually, in 1887, it became Pleyel, Lyon & Co.

In 1798 William Southwell of London had introduced the 'sticker' action, which allowed for the hammer to be positioned at the optimum point on the string. He subsequently improved this action and added an escapement and, in 1821, a check.

However, Robert Wornum was the man who transformed the upright piano into the instrument we know today. One of his early upright pianos, of 1811, was only just over a meter tall. This piano used diagonal stringing and an adaptation of the English double action. Later, in the 1830s, he maintained his innovative reputation by developing a new action that combined precision with durability. It used a length of tape to provide the check that prevents the hammer from striking the string more than once. He developed it originally for the grand piano and then applied it to the upright. With some modifications, this action has been the basis of the upright piano ever since.

Wornum's pianos are sometimes called 'cottage pianos' or 'piccolo pianos'. Both have a small proportion of their casework above the keyboard, giving them a total height of between 40 and 50 in. The 'cottage' pianos are around 48 in high, while

'piccolo' pianos are only around 43 in. The term 'cabinet piano' refers to uprights with a high upper casework, reaching 70-100 inches in total height. A 'console piano', on the other hand, is an upright with no upper section. When the lid is closed it is virtually flat-topped and looks almost like a desk.

Wornum's action was subsequently developed in Paris by Pleyel and Pape, with the result that it became known, erroneously, as the 'French' action. Pleyel and other French manufacturers became so commercially successful with upright designs that the square piano never really established itself there. During the 19th century, there was a feeling that the piano makers had lost sight of their artistic ideals and were merely interested in mass production. Franz Liszt, in a letter to his friend Pierre Érard the French piano maker, in 1839, complained about a Pleyel piano he had just been using in Bologna. "This piano is one of the least successful examples of the make — the keyboard was prodigiously uneven and the middle, high and low ranges so veiled as to be frightening. To sum up, the effect of the piano was detestable."

IGNACE PLEYEL, Paris, c.1840, pianino

SERIAL NO.:	3748 (on pin block)
CASEWORK:	Mahogany veneer
COMPASS:	6 octaves; FF – f⁴
ACTION:	Tape check (Wornum)
STRINGS:	Single FF-f; bichord f♯-f⁴
MODIFIERS:	2 footpedals; hammer shift (una corda), dampers
INSCRIPTION:	Medailles d'OR, 1827 & 1834 / Ignace Pleyel & Compie / Facteurs du Roi / PARIS
DIMENSIONS (INS.):	45 (W) x 42¼ (H) x 23¼ (Depth of case)

This small upright piano was based on Wornum's vertically strung uprights, and used the 'tape check' action that was Wornum's greatest innovation. Pleyel called this type of instrument a "pianino". The name came to be widely used on the  *continent for this style of small vertically-strung instrument, as opposed to the obliquely-strung 'piano droit'. Note that the foot-pedal modifier introduces a hammer shift to achieve una corda (the softer sound of a single string rather than double strings). The whole set of hammers is moved so that only one string is struck, a system also commonly used in grand pianos.*

HENRI PAPE, Paris, 1841, console piano

SERIAL NO.:	*4688 (on pin block)*
CASEWORK:	*Rosewood veneer*
COMPASS:	*6½ octaves; CC – f⁴*
ACTION:	*Pape's 1839 patent action*
STRINGS:	*Single (CC-FF); bichord (FF♯-D♯); trichord (E-f⁴)*
MODIFIERS:	*2 footpedals; keyboard shift (due corde), dampers*
INSCRIPTION:	*PAPE / PARIS & LONDRES (on nameboard)*
DIMENSIONS (INS.):	*54 (W) x 39½ (H) x 20½ (Depth of case)*

This is more typical of the type of console pianos made by Henri Pape than the 1840 example shown below. The legs here are of a 'barley-sugar' style. Again, with the lid closed, the fretwork along the back top is set just in front of the tuning pins. Pape, amongst other things, was responsible for much of the development associated with using felt as a hammer covering. Both these instruments originally used hair felt normally used to make beaver hats.

JEAN-HENRI PAPE

Jean-Henri Pape was probably the most inventive of the 19th century piano makers. He constantly developed new concepts and ideas in manufacture and design. Some of his instruments were bizarre in shape, and in 1850 he took out a patent for a piano with six strings per note. But among the vast number of patents he filed (more than 120) were some ideas of great importance.

Pape was born in Sarstedt, Germany, in 1789. He moved to Paris in 1809, but almost immediately left to spend a couple of years in London studying piano manufacture. On his return he became foreman at the Pleyel factory, where he put into effect much he'd learned in London. In 1817 he set up his own workshop and this gave him the freedom to experiment. He is best known for his elegant design, as can be seen in the square and console instruments shown in this book. His main technological contributions, however, include what became known as the French down-

striking action (inspired by Wornum's and Streicher's designs), the use of felt to cover hammers, his console pianos, and his use of tempered steel wire for strings. The table piano shown above was typical of Pape's designs. Many of his instruments, including the console piano (left), doubled as pieces of furniture. Pape, at one point, ran the largest piano factory in Paris, employing more than 300 men. He also sponsored training for students from all over the world: Carl Bechstein was a Pape student. Yet, despite his apparent success, he died poor in 1842.

The pedals are of brass and are attractively finished. The left shifts the keyboard and action to una corda and the right lifts the dampers.

HENRI PAPE, Paris, 1840, upright console

CASEWORK:	*Burr Elm*
COMPASS:	*6½ octaves; CC – f⁴*
ACTION:	*Pape's 1839 patent action*
STRINGS:	*Single (CC-FF♯); bichord (GG-ᶜ); trichord (f-f⁴)*
MODIFIERS:	*2 footpedals; keyboard shift and dampers*
INSCRIPTION:	*PAPE / PARIS & LONDRES (on nameboard); PAPE facteur de Pianos du ROI / PIANO CONSOLE BREVET D'INVENTION (on music rest, centre); EXPOSITION DE / 1859 / 1er RAPPEL DE LA MEDAILLE / D'OR (on music rest, right)*
DIMENSIONS (INS.):	*39½ (H) x 52 (W) x 20 (Depth of case)*

Henri Pape invented the console piano in 1828. However, a refined action wasn't to be patented until 1839. With the lid closed the instrument appears to be a chiffonier or sideboard, especially with these bracket-type legs. The term console refers to the fact that there is no upper body to the instrument. Pape's console pianos incorporated an iron frame, with the soundboard located behind the frame forming the actual back of the instrument. In some instances this would be painted to simulate the wood used for the main casework. The fretwork that runs around the back of the instrument, and can be seen fully when the lid is closed, actually covers the tuning pins, which are just 6 inches above the keyboard.

The upright pianos of this era used leather covered hammers. This instrument still bears the original set.

New ideas led to pianos suffering at the hands of technicians who weren't briefed with the correct servicing instructions. So manufacturers used labels explaining their intricacies. This example explains how to replace a broken string and how to set up the action.

ROBERT WORNUM, London, c1835, piccolo piano

CASEWORK:	Mahogany veneer
COMPASS:	6 octaves; $FF - f^4$
ACTION:	Wornum tape-check
STRINGS:	Single (FF-G♯); bichord (A-f^4)
MODIFIERS:	2 footpedals
INSCRIPTION:	Royal Patent Equal Tension / Piccolo Piano Forte Invented and Manufactured by / Robert Wornum / Music Hall Store Street Bedford Square London
DIMENSIONS (INS.):	40¼ (H) x 44 (W) x 21 (Depth of case)

This is one of Wornum's first 'piccolo' upright pianos and uses his advanced tape-check action. Wornum is often credited with having invented the tape-check mechanism but the idea was actually formulated by Herman Lichtenthal of Brussels. The purpose of the tape is to aid the relocation of the hammer and to prevent it bouncing back and re-hitting the string when a note is held. Wornum's designs were some of the most important in the development of the piano, and this instrument has a lot of similarities to the modern upright. The reference on the nameboard to "Royal Patent Equal Tension" refers to Wornum's patent of 1820, which describes how the strings are held at approximately the same tension but wound with wire to bring them to the correct pitch.

ROBERT WORNUM

Robert Wornum Jr., born in England in 1780, was the son of a music publisher. He set up in partnership with George Wilkinson in 1811, and worked with him for two years before taking over the family business. Wornum contributed more to the development of the upright piano than any other maker. His design of 1811, later to be known as a 'cottage piano' with diagonal stringing, was an important advance. He produced several important actions. These included his 1826 upright design, the blueprint for the action of the modern upright, and the tape-check action which is used, with minor modifications, to the present day. Nevertheless, his upright pianos were generally rather delicate and lacking in power and volume. It was left to other manufacturers, most notably the French houses, to fulfill their potential. This lack of power is strange, but it can probably be explained by their lack of metal strengthening. Wornum died in 1852.

THE EVOLUTION OF THE UPRIGHT PIANO

Demand for pianos became quite phenomenal during the 19th century, leading to a consumer boom of a type that had never been seen before. There were few other luxury goods to purchase and the piano was a status symbol to which a large proportion of the population could aspire.

Many homes acquired a piano for show, with little intention that anyone in the family would actually learn to play it. For that reason, some manufacturers tended to produce instruments that looked far better than they sounded. Tone and playability took second place to appearance.

The upright piano was the answer to the piano manufacturers' prayers. It was a consumer product that could be sold to the middle classes but one that came with immense prestige value because it had evolved from the grand pianos of the social elite. The ownership of a piano was something of which aspiring 19th-century families could be proud.

Size was of extreme importance in the case of the upright instrument. Manufacturers had tried to strengthen grand and square pianos, making them bigger and more unwieldy in order to produce more volume and improve the tone, but it was clear that this was not the way to approach the upright market. The typical middle class home in the industrialized mid-19th century was not big: rooms were kept fairly small to make them easier to heat. In any case, a grand piano dominates all but the largest rooms. Piano designers realized that the domestic market needed smaller, more compact instruments which wouldn't unduly dominate or stand out in a room.

As can be seen from the instruments on this page, the upright piano was often disguised as something else or given another use when not required as a piano. Unlike the grand, the upright gave piano makers scope to be inventive. Pianos would appear not only as tables and writing desks, but as bookcases, chests of drawers, and secrétaires. There were even triangular designs which enabled the piano to fit into the corner of a room.

The English and French makers were the most inventive in making the piano appeal to the domestic consumer. The designs of Pape, in particular, although rather expensive, served as a catalyst to other innovators.

"The upright will never be the piano for the artist, because of its incapacity to give any satisfaction to artistic temperament."
ALFRED DOLGE, *Pianos And Their Makers*, 1911

It should be appreciated, however, that even in the 1850s only around 50,000 pianos a year were being made. The big boom in piano sales was yet to come. This would be led, not by the piano makers, but by the marketing men with their new weapon, the Three Year Plan (see p49).

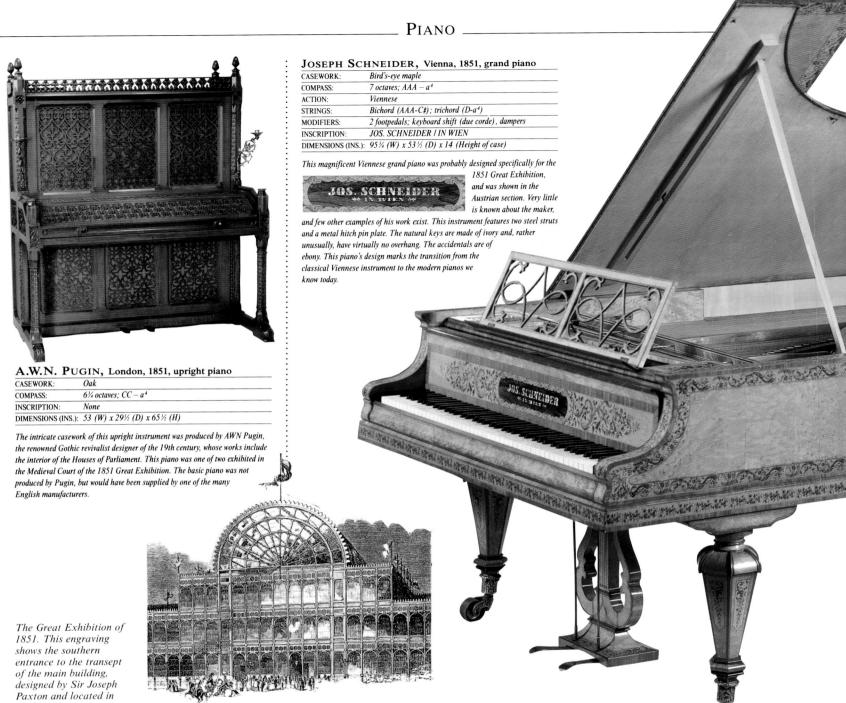

JOSEPH SCHNEIDER, Vienna, 1851, grand piano

CASEWORK:	*Bird's-eye maple*
COMPASS:	*7 octaves; AAA – a⁴*
ACTION:	*Viennese*
STRINGS:	*Bichord (AAA-C♯); trichord (D-a⁴)*
MODIFIERS:	*2 footpedals; keyboard shift (due corde), dampers*
INSCRIPTION:	*JOS. SCHNEIDER / IN WIEN*
DIMENSIONS (INS.):	*95¼ (W) x 53½ (D) x 14 (Height of case)*

This magnificent Viennese grand piano was probably designed specifically for the 1851 Great Exhibition, and was shown in the Austrian section. Very little is known about the maker, and few other examples of his work exist. This instrument features two steel struts and a metal hitch pin plate. The natural keys are made of ivory and, rather unusually, have virtually no overhang. The accidentals are of ebony. This piano's design marks the transition from the classical Viennese instrument to the modern pianos we know today.

A.W.N. PUGIN, London, 1851, upright piano

CASEWORK:	*Oak*
COMPASS:	*6¾ octaves; CC – a⁴*
INSCRIPTION:	*None*
DIMENSIONS (INS.):	*53 (W) x 29½ (D) x 65½ (H)*

The intricate casework of this upright instrument was produced by AWN Pugin, the renowned Gothic revivalist designer of the 19th century, whose works include the interior of the Houses of Parliament. This piano was one of two exhibited in the Medieval Court of the 1851 Great Exhibition. The basic piano was not produced by Pugin, but would have been supplied by one of the many English manufacturers.

The Great Exhibition of 1851. This engraving shows the southern entrance to the transept of the main building, designed by Sir Joseph Paxton and located in Hyde Park.

THE GREAT EXHIBITIONS

The great exhibitions and expositions of the second half of the 19th century were the shop-windows for the major piano houses. In the same way that today we find 'concept cars' at the motor shows, manufacturers would use the exhibitions to display some of their more spectacular instruments. They also demonstrated their latest technical developments and competed fiercely for prizes that recognized the advances they had made.

The concept of the 'World's Fair' began in the middle of the 19th century and grew to immense proportions. Such fairs and expositions still occur every three to five years but their importance as shop-windows for the technology of the present and future has declined somewhat, owing to the powerful influence of other more immediate technologies.

The World's Fairs featured exhibits from around the globe in the fields of arts and crafts, scientific discoveries, and industry and agriculture. The fairs also served as a meeting point for those involved in each industry, where developments and inventions could be discussed and new ideas aired. In addition awards were given for the best products and developments in pre-defined classes. These awards were hotly pursued, because success was excellent publicity for a product and an invaluable marketing tool. Despite the fact that piano makers would build special instruments for the fairs, they would be keen to advertize the fact that they had won an award across their entire range of instruments. The choice of winners of these awards nearly always led to bitter arguments, particularly amongst piano manufacturers.

The Great Exhibition of 1851, held in London, was the first of the true World's Fairs, sponsored as it was by a national government. It was planned by Prince Albert and was intended to show the technical supremacy of Britain. It included about 13,000 exhibits and attracted some six million visitors. There were 178 pianos by 102 different manufacturers on display. This gives some idea of the piano's importance as a commercial product. It should be remembered that this was a time of strong economic growth, and many people had a lot of disposable income and few consumer goods on which to spend it.

The success of the London exhibition fuelled other events. In 1853 both Dublin and New York hosted fairs, the latter of similar proportions to the 1851 London exhibition. Two years later Paris held its own Exposition, which was more elaborate, but a financial flop. Other fairs followed in London (1862), Paris (1867), Vienna (1873), Philadelphia (1876), Paris (1878), London (1886), Paris again (1889) and Chicago (1893). In 1900 the highly successful Paris World Exposition attracted more than 39 million visitors.

The piano's hammers have a layer of leather that is subsequently covered with felt. This helps to produce the melodious tone typical of the latter Viennese instruments.

The piano is beautifully decorated in bird's-eye maple with a fine wood mosaic inlay.

Three hexagonally tapered legs support the body of the piano, which is typical of the classical Viennese instruments of the period. This piano illustrates the change of style from its solid Germanic predecessors to the more flamboyant design of the second half of the 19th century.

The piano features intricate fretwork, dominated by a rather austere carved head (above). Carvings of full figures are used as the columns appearing to support the keyboard.

BÖSENDORFER, Vienna, 1858, grand piano

Ludwig Bösendorfer made this piano for Emperor Franz Josef I, and it was also shown to the public at the World Exhibition in Paris. Bösendorfer was not only an important figure in the piano world, but also a leading figure in the Viennese social scene. He was a personal friend of the Kaiser, who in turn had a keen interest in music, and he also regularly attended the World's Fairs across Europe. The instrument was designed by Theophil von Hansen and is particularly stylishly decorated, without being too ornate. Gold statuettes are positioned at the edge of each panel and the intricate fretwork of the music rest is upheld by two mythological creatures. The piano appears somewhat deeper than was the norm for instruments of this period. This is probably to accommodate the artistic elements of the casework, as the strings and frame assembly can be seen to be sitting fairly low in the body of the case. This instrument still uses the Viennese action. The keyboard has a 7-octave compass (AAA – a⁴), typical of the period. Compare this instrument with the piano Bösendorfer made for the Kaiser's wife, Empress Elizabeth, which she gave as a present to Empress Eugenie of France, wife of Napoleon III (p 63-64-65).

LAMBERT, London, 1851, upright piano

COMPASS:	6¾ octaves; CC – a⁴
MODIFIERS:	2 footpedals; keyboard shift, dampers
INSCRIPTION:	Lambert / from Collard / Inventor of the Patent Action Check
DIMENSIONS (INS.):	51 (W) x 31 (D) x 59 (Height of case)

This instrument was made specifically for the 1851 Exhibition. Unfortunately some of the original decoration has been painted over. However, it can be seen

untouched on the lower panel beneath the keyboard, and on the insides of the two side panels. The piano's keyboard is exquisitely styled, featuring tortoiseshell accidentals and ivory naturals with an inlaid motif. The footpedals are also covered with tortoiseshell. This piano has a wooden frame. The actual instrument was made by the Collard brothers and then decorated and styled by Lambert of London. Little is known of this company, but they were probably furniture makers or interior designers. This was probably a 'one-off' for the Great Exhibition. Lambert are not known to have produced any further pianos.

LW MÜLLER, Hamburg, 1863, Upright Piano

COMPASS:	7 octaves; AAA – a⁴
MODIFIERS:	2 footpedals; keyboard shift, dampers
INSCRIPTION:	L.W. Müller / Hamburg
DIMENSIONS (INS.):	56 (W) x 28 (D) x 68 (H)

This rather monstrous upright piano is believed to have been shown at the 1863 Exhibition in London. Its most notable feature is the painting of St Cecilia, the patron saint of music. This is set in an oval cut out of the front panel (top door).

The piano's appearance tends to suggest that it would have been used in a church or other religious meeting place. There is also some rather unusual inlay work of brass and coloured enamels, used to embellish the inscription and somewhat out of keeping with the instrument's overall design.

STEINWAY & SON, New York, 1857, grand piano

This piano, serial no. 1225, was the first art-case piano to be made by Steinway & Sons in New York, barely a year after they made their first grand (no. 791). Steinway's first brochure and price list (right) was produced in 1888, and shows two styles of grand piano, ranging in size from 6 ft 10½ in to 8 ft 10 in ($1100 to $1800), six upright pianos and a 7½ octave square piano.

STEINWAY & SONS

Heinrich Engelhard Steinweg Snr was a cabinet maker by trade, but showed great interest in musical instruments: he made his first piano in 1836 at the age of 39. The Steinway family subsequently ran a small shop in Seesen, Germany, where they made many types of instrument, including up to ten pianos a year. With the 1848 revolution in Germany, Heinrich decided to emigrate to America, taking his entire family, with the exception of his eldest son, CF Theodor Steinweg. On arriving, the family decided to Americanize their names, and found work with American piano-making companies.

By 1853 the Steinway family decided to set up their own manufacturing company. Their first instrument was a conventional square piano. In ten years they were running the world's largest piano factory. Meanwhile, in Germany, Theodor continued to manufacture pianos under the Steinweg name, joining the rest of the family in the US some years later. The first major Steinway innovation was the introduction of cross-stringing to their square piano (1855), enabling the use of much longer strings.

They also simultaneously introduced a cast-iron frame (plate). In 1860 they produced the overstrung grand, the forerunner to the modern concert grand. It received universal acclaim. The company soon achieved world-wide fame and opened a factory in Hamburg, Germany, in order to challenge the European dominance of companies such as Bechstein, Blüthner and Ibach.

The Great Depression of the 1930s saw Steinway's annual output fall from 280,000 pianos (1927) to 50,000 (1931). But the company survived this setback, as well as two world wars, and continues to build some of the best pianos in the world at its Hamburg and New York factories.

ERARD, London, 1866, grand piano ✳

DIMENSIONS (INS.): *100 (L) x 57 (W) x 14 (Depth of case)*

This beautiful grand piano, serial no. 9772, was constructed in London. The casework uses an amboyna veneer with an stained fruitwood inlay. The letters that make up the inscription on the nameboard, "Patent Erard London", are actually individually inlaid. The piano uses a metal hitch pin plate with additional iron bars to provide the strength required for sufficient tensioning of the strings. By this time most grand pianos had a compass of seven octaves. This instrument spans from AAA to a⁴.

The instrument is straight strung, with the four strengthening braces clearly visible. These were fabricated as part of the metal hitch pin plate.

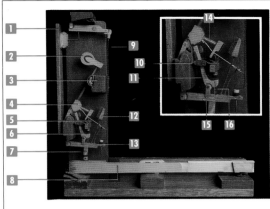

This 19th century overdamped action is based on Robert Wornum's 1842 patent. As the **key (8)** is pressed, the **capstan screw (7)** lifts the **wippen (13)**. This causes the tip of the **jack (6)** to press up on the **notch (10)** in the **hammer butt (4)**, propelling the **hammer (2)** towards the **string (1)**. At the same time the **damper wire (9)** lifts the damper, and the **hammer check (12)** rises, ready to catch the hammer.

As the hammer travels towards the string, the **toe (15)** meets the **set-off button (11)**, causing the tip of the jack to flick out from the notch. The hammer strikes the string, and with the aid of the **tape (5)** falls back so the **balance hammer (14)** is caught by the check.

Releasing the key lowers the wippen and frees the hammer, which falls back to the **hammer rest (3)**. The damper swings back on to the string and the jack, helped by the **repetition spring (16)**, relocates itself ready for the note to be played again.

KUHN & RIDGEWAY, Baltimore, 1857, harp piano

This instrument uses a metal frame, the top part of which is exposed and decorated to become the feature that provides its name. The keyboard has a seven octave span (CC to c⁵), and the piano is straight strung. The bottom door has been removed, as has the fall, hollow and top, revealing the action. The soundboard can be seen not to extend past the strike line, giving the piano a somewhat insubstantial sound. The harp piano did not succeed commercially.

FRANZ LISZT
SONATA IN B MINOR - PRELUDE AND FUGUE
CSÁRDÁS MACABRE - NORMA FANTASY

ALEXEI ORLOWETSKY

***Franz Liszt:* Sonata in B Minor, Prelude & Fugue, Csárdás Macabre, Norman Fantasy,** *played by Alexei Orlowetsky Franz Liszt used pianos by several major different manufacturers in his career - and broke a good many of them. This recording is made on an Erard concert grand piano made in 1889, a little later than the one shown. It lends itself well to recapturing the magic of a Liszt performance.*

ROBERT WORNUM,
London, c1860, upright piano
DIMENSIONS: 53 (W) x 39 (H) x 25 (Depth of case)

This attractive seven-octave 'piccolo piano' is just 39 in tall. It uses Wornum's improved tape-check action, patented in 1842. Except for its use of overdampers rather than underdampers, it varies little from the upright pianos of today. The fretwork on the top door was damaged during World War II.

The English piano makers, Brinsmead, pioneered the 'top tuner' in 1884. Instead of using wrest pins, the strings are attached to a screw threaded bolt that is mounted directly on to the iron frame, parallel to the strings. A nut was incorporated on the thread such that when it was tightened, tension was applied to the strings. Tuning then became a far simpler matter involving the adjustment of these nuts.

A PERIOD OF CONSOLIDATION

The second half of the 19th century saw few dramatic changes to the mechanics of the piano. The grand piano had almost completed its evolution from the delicate instrument of the late 18th century to the robust, powerful one we know today. The upright piano had also come of age, and most refinements were in the manufacturing process rather than in design. In Europe in the 1850s, the piano industry was still small and inefficient. Even Broadwood, the largest piano maker in the world, employed fewer than 350 men. But in the following 60 years, world production grew from under 50,000 pianos a year to more than 500,000.

Despite the pioneering work of Babcock, Albrecht and Hawkins, the Americans were still lagging behind the European manufacturers as the 19th century began. Only after the War of 1812, between Britain and the United States, did the American piano industry develop. A look at the history of virtually any American piano house of the period will reveal that the company was owned by, and employed, skilled European craftsmen who had emigrated to the US.

American piano makers, led by Steinway and Chickering, swept into the European market in the second half of the 19th century. They shocked the established piano houses by winning many awards at the major exhibitions and with their advanced production techniques and new ideas, both in design and marketing, they became serious challengers on the world market.

The most important contributory factor in the success of the piano was the 'three year plan', yet it is often overlooked. It was a 'hire purchase' scheme, introduced in the late 1850s, that boosted sales dramatically. As demand for pianos increased, however, quality declined. People bought inferior instruments

just to have pianos in their homes. Nevertheless, by the 1890s, the economies of scale, a more educated public and stabilized demand brought the quality back to an acceptable level.

"So baneful and so reprehensible – yet unfortunately not illegal – a system of trading" The three year plan, described by FJ Crowest in *Phases of Musical England*, 1881.

With the exception of overstringing, few major advances in piano design came after 1850, but the manufacturing process was transformed by increasing mechanization. Newcomers to the market, especially the Americans, introduced the latest machinery, forcing established piano houses to change.

The century ended with the world piano industry efficient, profitable and successful — and dominated by the Americans. In 1850 America produced approximately 10,000 pianos each year to Europe's 33,000. By 1910 the figures were 370,000 (US) and 215,000 (Europe). This was a stunning achievement.

✳ *For information on recordings on this instrument, see Pianos on Record, p104.*

JOHN MERLIN, London, 1784, claviorganum

John Joseph Merlin was a prolific inventor. In addition to his work with musical instruments, he also invented the wheelchair and roller-skates. He produced a

piano/harpsichord combination in 1780, a downstriking grand in 1786 (long before anyone else), and employed quad-stringing 40 years before Graf built his famous instrument for Beethoven. This piano-organ combines a square five-octave piano (FF/GG-f³ – no FF♯) with a set of 8 ft wooden pipes. The piano section, although it looks conventional, incorporates some interesting features. The instrument is bichord throughout,

and the single English action can be slid fractionally forward so that the hammer strikes just one of the strings for each note to provide a softer sound (una corda). The music rest, which isn't clearly visible, is longer than that of the square pianos of the time, so as to be able to accommodate organ music which was published in the wider landscape format. The octave span of the instrument, approaching seven inches, is greater than normal for this period, probably to accommodate the organ pipes.

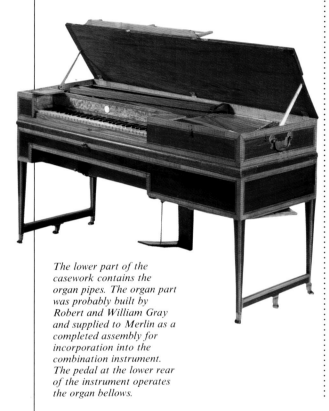

The lower part of the casework contains the organ pipes. The organ part was probably built by Robert and William Gray and supplied to Merlin as a completed assembly for incorporation into the combination instrument. The pedal at the lower rear of the instrument operates the organ bellows.

ROBERT WORNUM, London, c1844, Albion square piano

It is not thought that Robert Wornum actually made any square pianos of the traditional type. This instrument, although squarer than any other square piano,

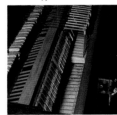

cannot accurately bear that label because its strings run perpendicular to the keyboard, as in a grand piano. The piano is single strung and, unusually, features a down-striking action with tape-check, a modification of Wornum's important 1842 action. The Albion square pianos were essentially table shaped and were sometimes built as pairs. This design was not particularly popular, however.

The Tribune Piano
A common problem for players of the tall early upright pianos was that the musician had to sit with his or her back to the audience. Auguste Herce's 'tribune piano' inverted the instrument so that the keyboard was at the top and the strings ran down to the ground. In order for the player to reach the keyboard a raised platform was required. Obviously this instrument had little application in the home.

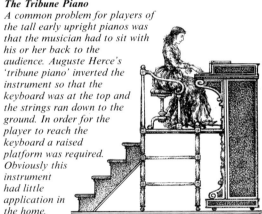

HENRY PERCIVAL, London, 1878, perpendicular piano

This instrument was developed by Henry Percival of Bayswater, London, who filed a patent (no. 2597) for it in 1878. It has two keyboards mounted vertically, each encompassing just over four octaves. There is an overlap of notes in the middle

register so some can be played from either keyboard. Together both keyboards encompass a seven octave (AAA to a⁴) range. The bass notes are found at the bottom of the left hand keyboard, and the treble notes at the bottom of the right hand keyboard. This perpendicular piano was relatively small (just 33 inches high excluding the stand) and light, and could be played facing an audience, which made it suitable for touring performers, especially those who sang. Despite these apparent benefits, the instrument enjoyed no popular success.

VARIATIONS ON A THEME

Over the years, pianos have appeared in many different forms and mutations. Innovations in design produced publicity for the manufacturers, which was particularly necessary in the 19th century when there were so many of them. In some cases the innovation was a feature of the instrument – a new tuning system, or method of frame construction – but in others it represented a totally new concept of how to throw a hammer at a string. The patents of the period contain much of interest, if not of great scientific value.

Consumers are often reluctant to embrace new technology. Two centuries and more ago, instrument makers were faced with the problem of popularizing the piano. They decided that the best approach would be to bring it in on the back of another instrument, in some cases quite literally, by combining it with something people already knew and felt comfortable with.

COMBINATION INSTRUMENTS

This was one of the reasons behind the arrival of piano-organ combinations, piano-spinets, piano-harpsichords, and later piano-harmoniums, right across Europe. Johann Andreas Stein, one of the most important piano makers in southern Germany, produced a piano and organ combination (see p17) and piano-harpsichord combinations. Many of the piano makers had previously built other types of instrument, so these combinations were an obvious step.

The 19th century was a particularly rich period for piano exotica. With the piano becoming increasingly popular in the home, manufacturers attempted to adapt it to the domestic

environment. Pianos were disguised as pieces of furniture, such as bookcases and tables, but instruments were also built that incorporated beds, drinks cabinets and even commodes.

THE WALL PIANO

Pianos took up a lot of space in the home and one solution was to have a piano that was mounted on a substantial hinge mechanism. When the piano was not in use it was turned on its end, rather like a fold-up bed.

This idea was taken a stage further by Daniel Hewitt, a professor of music in London and a fairly prolific inventor, who developed the 'wall piano' in 1854. He decided that instead of having to use an expensive braced wooden case to support the strings of a piano, he would design an upright instrument that used a wall as the supporting structure. He filed a patent showing the pin block and hitch pins mounted directly to the wall, with the soundboard positioned between it and the strings. It is not known whether Hewitt continued to live with a roof over his head, but the idea, like so many at the time, failed to catch on.

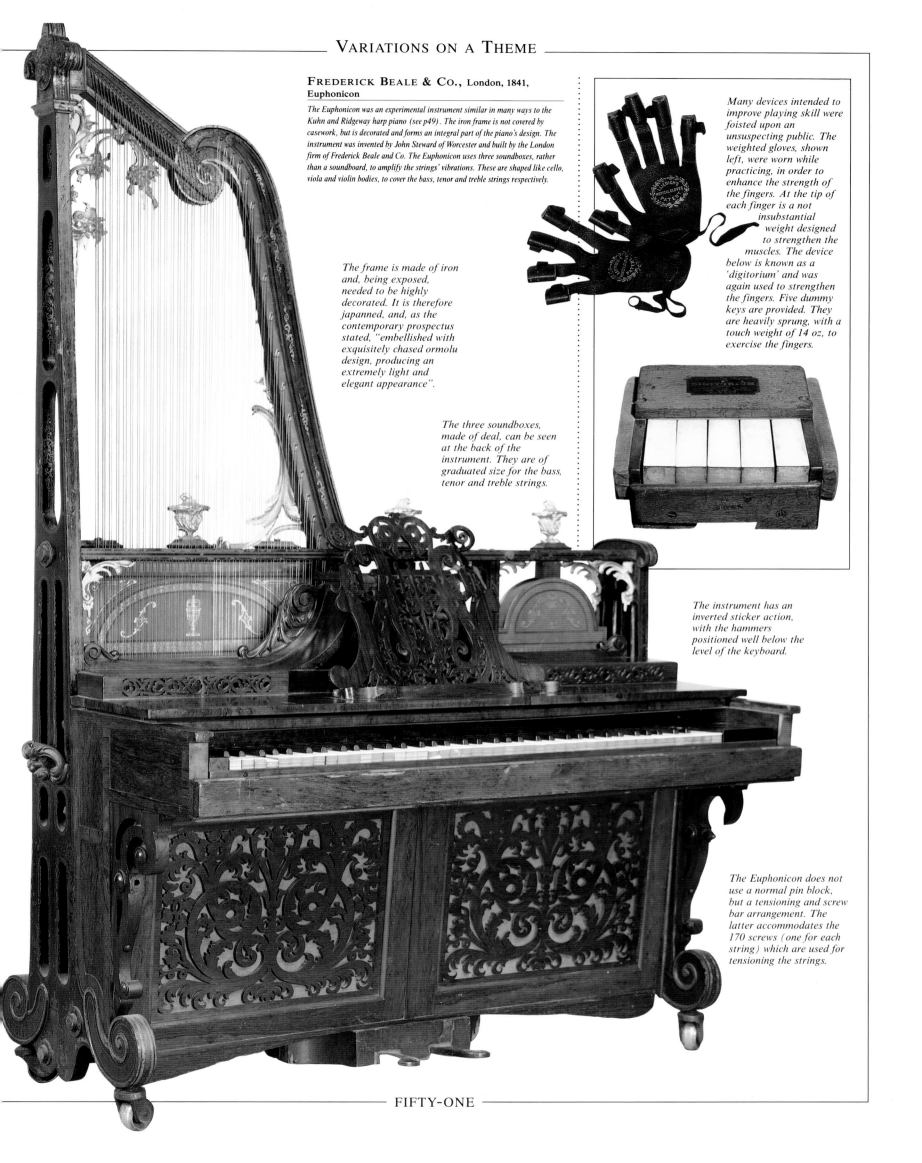

FREDERICK BEALE & CO., London, 1841, Euphonicon

The Euphonicon was an experimental instrument similar in many ways to the Kuhn and Ridgeway harp piano (see p49). The iron frame is not covered by casework, but is decorated and forms an integral part of the piano's design. The instrument was invented by John Steward of Worcester and built by the London firm of Frederick Beale and Co. The Euphonicon uses three soundboxes, rather than a soundboard, to amplify the strings' vibrations. These are shaped like cello, viola and violin bodies, to cover the bass, tenor and treble strings respectively.

The frame is made of iron and, being exposed, needed to be highly decorated. It is therefore japanned, and, as the contemporary prospectus stated, "embellished with exquisitely chased ormolu design, producing an extremely light and elegant appearance".

The three soundboxes, made of deal, can be seen at the back of the instrument. They are of graduated size for the bass, tenor and treble strings.

Many devices intended to improve playing skill were foisted upon an unsuspecting public. The weighted gloves, shown left, were worn while practicing, in order to enhance the strength of the fingers. At the tip of each finger is a not insubstantial weight designed to strengthen the muscles. The device below is known as a 'digitorium' and was again used to strengthen the fingers. Five dummy keys are provided. They are heavily sprung, with a touch weight of 14 oz, to exercise the fingers.

The instrument has an inverted sticker action, with the hammers positioned well below the level of the keyboard.

The Euphonicon does not use a normal pin block, but a tensioning and screw bar arrangement. The latter accommodates the 170 screws (one for each string) which are used for tensioning the strings.

HENDERSON, London, 1826, cabinet grand piano with barrel mechanism

This instrument is thought to have been made by John Broadwood & Sons, with the barrel mechanism supplied by Henderson. This mechanism is clockwork, 'powered' by a series of lead weights. It drives a second set of hammers, which strike the damped strings. Expression can be added to the music 'played' by the barrel by altering the speed at which the drum rotates. The loudness and softness of the notes can also be varied by means of a sliding ball at the side of the instrument, and of course the dampers can be raised and lowered to change the sound quality. The drum fitted to this instrument is a replica of the original and incorporates ten different pieces. The piano uses an English sticker action, is 79 inches high, and features a six-octave FF – f⁴ keyboard.

PASQUALE & CO., London, c1905, barrel piano

Pasquale and Company were an Italian company that made and rented out instruments from 1900 to 1914. This piano would probably have been used in a public house with an electric motor and coin box fitted. The mechanism is essentially the same as that used on the Tomasso street piano (right) and features ten different tunes. This instrument has just 48 notes altogether, and unlike the street pianos, it has felted hammers.

MONTANINI, Italy, c1900, barrel piano

From 1890 to 1920 the barrel piano was at the peak of its popularity. Montanini was one of the main Italian constructors, each of whom had his own barrel 'pinners'. A tune played on one instrument would have a different arrangement to one played on another. This attractively decorated piano, shown with its top door removed, incorporates drums and a cymbal.

Music of the Streets, *Roy Mickleburgh*
A selection of popular Victorian tunes is featured on this recording, which is played on a variety of street instruments, including a Tomasso street piano and a Hicks cylinder piano of 1846.

THE BARREL PIANO

Mechanized music dates back to about 1300, when clockwork devices were used to drive musical boxes. These had a simple barrel mechanism using carefully positioned pins on a metal or wooden drum. Ways were sought to bring music into homes where no one could play an instrument. The solution was to mechanise the instruments themselves. Virginals and spinets fitted with a barrel mechanism are known to have existed as early as the 17th century.

The barrel mechanism was almost certainly the first method of automating the production of music. Nails were inserted in a rotating cylinder, with each nail representing a musical event. As the cylinder turned, the nail would activate a lever, causing a note to sound. In the earliest mechanised instruments, the lever itself was the vibrating medium: the nail actually plucked the note.

Using a circular medium to store the information also solved the problem of what happened when the music finished — it automatically began again.

The barrel mechanism was fitted to all manner of instruments, including the organ. The oldest surviving cylinder organ is in Salzburg. It uses 350 pipes, was completed in 1502, and is affectionately known as the 'Bull of Salzburg'. An original cylinder, supposedly 'pinned' under the direction of Leopold Mozart, still exists.

The construction of a working mechanism for stringed keyboard instruments was more challenging. In c1650, Samuel Bidermann of Breslau (now Wroclaw in Poland) built three virginals incorporating barrel mechanisms.

Interestingly, the great masters, such as C.P.E. Bach, Haydn, Handel and Mozart, did not frown upon automatic instruments. It is believed that Mozart wrote three compositions for the musical clock (a small mechanical pipe-organ operated by a pegged cylinder and housed within a clock). His *Andante* K616 (1791) can be seen to have been written directly for a barrel mechanism and not specially adapted.

Father Marie-Dominique Joseph Engramelle improved the way in which cylinders were 'nailed'. In his 1775 book *Tonotechnie*, he described a system that enabled cylinders to be nailed with an extremely high degree of accuracy. This went a long way to ensuring the acceptance of the barrel mechanism.

In the early 19th century, the piano became a popular and fashionable musical instrument. Inevitably manufacturers began to fit barrel mechanisms to their pianos, but with the exception of the street piano, they had little commercial success.

Two types of street instrument used the barrel mechanism. The portable instrument, carried by the player on a shoulder strap, was often known as the Hicks piano after the Bristol family firm

A TOMASSO & SONS, London, c1885, street piano

During the late 19th century a large number of Italian émigrés moved to England. Many of the families established businesses making, renting, selling and operating barrel pianos. They also manufactured and 'pinned' barrels with the latest popular tunes - an extremely skilled job. These street pianos, which evolved from the earlier cylinder pianos, would have been transported on a low slung cart as shown, and were common on the streets until the mid 1920s. This piano had 44 notes (CC to c³) but no B flats (they didn't feature in the instrument's tunes).

The hammers are made of a hard wood without felt. This produces a bright sound which carries well.

Each barrel includes ten tunes, each lasting approximately 45 seconds. The lever on the right of the instrument moves the barrel slightly to the left or right to select a new tune.

A solution to the problems of the barrel mechanism was already in existence in 1801 when French inventor Joseph Marie Jacquard developed an automatic loom that used a length of punched card to guide its movements when weaving figured silk fabrics. This mechanism was seen by Seytre, a French inventor from Lyon, as the ideal replacement for the rather inefficient barrel mechanism.

SIMONI, Bologna, c1900, barrel piano

Gaetano Simoni from Bologna was another important Italian manufacturer at the turn of the 20th century. This piano features an 'amusement', a street scene with a barrel piano being played and two mechanised couples dancing to the music. Such visual elements were fairly commonplace. Simoni's instruments are renowned for their excellent tone and mechanical construction but are let down by less impressive musical arrangements.

The piano is operated simply by turning the handle on the front. This turns the barrel, which replaces the keyboard, bringing the pins in contact with the action mechanism.

that made many of them. The more substantial street piano had to be carried around on a wheelbarrow-like cart.

The sound production elements of these instruments were similar to those of the traditional piano. However, the hammers were often left uncovered, producing a brittle sound capable of cutting through the noise of busy urban streets.

Street music had a very poor reputation. In London laws controlled the performers.

The barrel mechanism was limited. The barrels were bulky and sometimes difficult to replace. Consequently the instrument could often only play one set of tunes (usually up to ten on a barrel). In the 1840s Alexander Debain developed a system to 'open out' the barrels into a series of wooden blocks, still with pins, which were 'fed' sequentially into the machine.

Using pinned barrels or blocks of wood was still limiting. They were expensive and time-consuming to produce. A more efficient way of storing the musical information was required. With the arrival of the age of industrialization and mechanisation, manufactures found a solution already existed — in the textile industry.

DEBAIN, Paris, 1851, 'planchette' piano

Alexandre-François Debain pioneered the 'planchette' mechanical piano. He replaced the barrel with an oblong piece of wood (the 'planchette') carrying pins. Along one edge of the planchette is a toothed rack, which mates with a pinion along the top of the instrument. By turning a crank, the planchette is drawn, pins downwards, over a series of jacks linked to the relevant keys. Several planchettes (typically four) were required for each piece of music. The idea was originally developed as an attachment for church organs, then incorporated into small upright pianos. The instrument shown has two separate actions, although it is not possible to play the piano's keyboard at the same time as using the planchettes. This instrument also features four castanets.

The mechanism is operated by a crank, and the music is drawn over a set of sprung levers. When a hole is encountered the respective lever is activated and the hammer triggered.

The Piano Melodico uses folded cardboard as the storage medium. The piano was popular across Europe and Racca released new music 'books' every year.

HUPFELD, Leipzig, c1904, Vorsetzer piano player

The Vorsetzer was a piano player developed by Hupfeld, one of the most important European manufacturers. The cabinet was wheeled up to the keys of a piano and the levers aligned with the keyboard. This player uses Welte-Red piano rolls, which were the first of the reproducing systems.

ORCHESTRELLE COMPANY, New York & London, c1900, Pianola piano player

The Pianola was invented by Edwin Votey and was the foundation on which the Aeolian company, which owned Orchestrelle, was based. The player can be seen here 'pushed up' to a grand piano: it was often called a 'push-up'. Pedals are used to drive the pneumatic system, and levers are used to set the speed of the performance, the strength with which the keys are played, and the balance between low and high notes. Non-musical customers were told that they would have all the benefits of playing because the means of adding expression were at hand and "expression is the soul of music". This device cost £65 ($250) at the turn of the century.

The sound produced by the Piano Melodico was delicate, yet it had depth. It has been compared to that of a mandolin in terms of tonal clarity.

The device has 65 'fingers' and therefore doesn't entirely span the piano's compass. The Orchestrelle company made great play of the fact that their Pianolas didn't affect the workings of the piano stating that their player "doesn't mar or injure the piano in any way".

HARPER ELECTRIC PIANO CO.,
London, 1905, player piano

This instrument from The Harper Electric Piano Company Ltd, was built in their workshops in Holloway, London. The instrument has a 7-octave (AAA to a⁵) compass. Its appearance, and the fact that it is fitted with a coin box, tends to

suggest that it was originally installed in a public house. The instrument is powered by an electric motor and uses special Harper piano rolls as the storage material. This type of piano uses what is known as an expression mechanism, which means that the rolls contain additional information relating to the way in which the music should be played. For example, the roll might specify that the treble notes should be played louder than the bass notes. The degree of expression is limited compared to that of the reproducing systems that were to come.

AEOLIAN

William B Tremaine entered the musical instrument business in 1868, at the age of 28, becoming a piano maker in the family firm of Tremaine Brothers. Nevertheless, in 1878 he formed the Mechanical Orguinette Company to market an automatic 'orguinette', and in 1883 the Aeolian organ appeared. Following the purchase of the Automatic Music Paper Company of Boston, Tremaine overhauled his companies and in 1888 set-up the Aeolian Organ & Music Company. His son Harry B. Tremaine saw that the future for automatic instruments lay with the piano. Over the next 40 years Aeolian was to dominate the American automatic piano market. The foundation for this was the Pianola, a pneumatic piano player developed by Edwin Votey in 1897. The name has since become a generic term for all types of player pianos. The success of the Pianola was in many ways attributable to Aeolian's incredibly aggressive marketing campaign. The Pianola evolved considerably over the years, with models actually being incorporated into pianos. Steinway were one such company to incorporate the Pianola in their instruments. One important advance made by Aeolian was the introduction of the Duo-Art Reproducing Piano, a sophisticated mechanism fitted to high quality pianos (see p56).

This instrument was not only popular, it was easy to use and maintain and relatively inexpensive to buy. It would be commonly found in bars, taverns and dance halls as well as in affluent homes.

G. RACCA, Bologna, c1900, Piano Melodico

The Piano Melodico, or melody piano, was patented in 1886 by Giovanni Racca and utilizes cardboard music books as the storage medium. This was an improvement over the earlier barrel pianos, as tunes of greater duration could be played, and a wider selection of tunes assembled. The mechanism would, however, be made obsolete by the piano roll. This is the 'grande' version of the piano melodico. For situations where space was at a premium, Racca also developed upright and table top versions of the instrument.

QRS Music Rolls Inc. was established in 1900, by Melville Clark, one of the pioneers of the pneumatic player mechanism, and founder of Story & Clark. At its peak in 1926 the company was producing a staggering 11 million rolls a year. The company still produces rolls to this day. However the meaning of the letters QRS has been lost to the passing of time.

THE PIANO PLAYER AND PLAYER PIANO

The pinned barrel had many limitations. For an automatic instrument to gain wide appeal a more sophisticated way of storing music was required. This came about through an adaptation of the method invented by Vaucanson of Paris to operate his celebrated automata in the middle of the 18th century. He used a cylinder with punched holes rather than raised nails. Adapted first by Joseph Marie Jacquard to the loom, the idea was subsequently applied to musical instruments with great success.

Between 1840 and 1850, Seytre and Pape in France and Bain in Scotland produced workable automatic instruments using a punched hole system, but neither achieved commercial success. Giovanni Racca was the first to produce a successful automatic piano based on this principle.

In 1863 a Frenchman, Fourneaux, developed the Pianista. This was the first pneumatic 'piano player'. It was a large box, about the size of an upright piano, that was wheeled up to the instrument so that its mechanical 'fingers' actually played the keys. The power came from a crank-operated bellow-driven pneumatic system.

A distinction should be made between the 'piano player' and the 'player piano'. The former, of which the Pianista is an example, is a free-standing device that plays an ordinary piano with mechanical 'fingers'. The latter is a piano with a player mechanism built into it.

The appearance of the piano roll (initially in the 1870s), a long roll of paper with holes punched into it, was to change things dramatically. This compact, efficient way of storing information

made the automatic piano a viable proposition. John McTammany developed a system, but Edwin Welte got it into production.

"Gentleman – I desire to order another Pianola for use in my residence. Will you kindly select an instrument in rosewood and have it packed with its rolls of music and shipped by steamer?" I.J. PADEREWSKI
(from an advertisement of 1900)

The piano player became very popular in the 1890s. As a free standing device it didn't interfere with the internal workings of the piano. By the end of the century, however, the player piano had gained popularity because it allowed access to the keyboard and took up less room.

Most of the music rolls for the early piano players and the player pianos included no expression or dynamic information. It was, however, possible for the operator to add expression by controlling tempo, volume and pedalling.

STECK, New York, 1919, reproducing piano

The Steck company was founded in New York in 1857 by George Steck. In the 1870s Steck also opened a factory in Gotha, Germany. Aeolian took over the firm in 1904, using Steck's pianos as a good quality upright to house the Duo-Art reproducing mechanism. They also fitted their mechanisms into Steck grands. The Duo-Art system employs separate expression controls for theme and accompaniment. Notes are designated as either melody or accompaniment, and it is possible to set the volume independently for each group. The design of the Duo-Art system remained fairly constant so all Duo-Art rolls are compatible with any Duo-Art piano made before the merger with Ampico in 1932.

The Steck piano shown has had its doors removed to reveal the player mechanism. The action and individual note mechanisms are behind the black panel above the keyboard.

The Duo-Art mechanism is capable of reading standard 88-note rolls (which require expression to be provided by the operator), Thermodist rolls and Duo-Art rolls. A selector switch is provided on the left side of the spool box.

The pair of bellows (below) ensures the roll remains correctly aligned on the tracker bar.

The original piano rolls shown here were all published by the Aeolian Company. They feature Glinka's 'The Lark' (far left), a fox-trot by M.V. Bucci (left) and MacDowell's 'To A Water Lily' (below). Most piano rolls have an introductory section with information and pictures relating to the composer, composition and performance. In the case of the Audiograph roll (below) the illustrations, lyrics and words of the story can be seen as the roll plays. The red line on the Metrostyle roll (left) dictates the tempo.

The expression system is located in the bottom left-hand corner. This controls the dynamics of the notes and other elements of the performance, including pedalling.

THE REPRODUCING PIANO AND OTHER AUTOMATIC INSTRUMENTS

The mechanical piano players and player pianos of the early 20th century were not capable of exactly recreating the playing of the great pianists. The perforations in the music rolls identified only when a particular note should be played and for how long the key should be held. There was no scope for controlling the dynamics of a note, nor any way of recreating the original pedalling action. The race was on to develop a genuinely faithful system for reproducing piano performances.

A reproducing piano is a mechanised instrument designed to recreate a pre-recorded performance of a work as closely as possible. Unlike the player piano, the reproducing piano can record and reproduce information not only about notes and their durations, but also about dynamics, tempo changes and, in many cases, pedalling.

Many great pianists recorded rolls for use with reproducing pianos, and these instruments can still recreate their original performances with a fairly high degree of accuracy.

In 1904, Edwin Welte of Freiberg, Germany, invented a system for encoding virtually every nuance of a pianist's playing on to a paper roll. He also replaced the pedalled bellows used to drive the instrument with an electric motor. The reproducing piano didn't appear in America for another ten years, but then it soon replaced the more basic player pianos.

THE MECHANISM

The player piano, the piano player and the reproducing piano all depend upon the piano roll. The operation of an automatic instrument is relatively simple, despite appearances to the contrary. The instrument works on a pneumatic system using a vacuum created either by foot-operated bellows or by an electric motor. The paper roll runs over a tracker bar, a metal strip with a row of holes in it, one for each note. In more advanced systems there are also holes for dynamics and pedalling. Each hole is connected to the pneumatic action by a pipe known as the pneumatic tube. At the end of the tube there is a flexible pouch, above which is a valve. This area is normally held in a vacuum.

When a hole in the piano roll passes over the corresponding hole in the tracker bar, the vacuum is broken and air rushes down the pneumatic tube, causing the flexible pouch to expand and push open the valve. This in turn causes air to rush from a hinged bellows associated with that note down into the instrument's vacuum chamber. The bellows collapses, and as it does so it operates the piano action and plays a note. Because the bellows are collapsing rather than inflating, the action responds immediately.

The piano players and player pianos initially operated over 65 notes, and used rolls that were 11¼ inches wide with six holes

Finish: *This instrument has five layers of black lacquer, hand rubbed between each coat.*

Strings: *The strings are made from hardened drawn polished steel, the bass strings being wound with pure copper. Single stringing is used for AAA-EE, double stringing for FF-AA, and the remaining notes are all triple strung. The average string tension is 180 lb per string, though the figure varies with pitch. The Model D uses 2¼ miles of wire in its construction and the longest string has a length of 79¼ in.*

Solids: *All solid elements are made from ebonized birch.*

Braces: *Five solid spruce members are attached at points around the inner rim using maple dowels. Their other ends join at a metal 'shoe'. This provides a strong supportive structure for the sound-producing elements of the piano.*

Ribs: *Made from sugar pine, the ribs support the soundboard, which has to endure considerable down-bearing forces from the strings.*

Legs: *Made from ebonized birch.*

"It's wonderful, but the thing about the Hamburg Steinway is that you can't play the blues on it."
KEITH JARRETT

Artur Rubenstein (above), one of the world's greatest classical pianists, playing an 1853 Steinway (serial no. 483). This was the first Steinway piano to be made in New York.

Steinway artist Keith Jarrett (left), released **The Köln Concert** *in 1975. It has subsequently become the most important jazz album of recent times. Jarrett possesses both an American and a German Steinway grand piano.*

Pin block: *This is constructed from six layers of laminated quarter-sawn hard rock maple, laminations being aligned at 45° and 90° to each other. This angling of the laminations is designed to make the gripping force on the tuning pins stronger and more constant. Most pin blocks consist of many more laminations, requiring more layers of glue. Glue provides no grip to the wrest pin: it follows that the greater the amount of wood in contact with the tuning pin the better. This design of pin block was patented in 1963 by Steinway employee Frank Walsh.*

STEINWAY, New York, c1877, grand piano

This is one of the finest examples of the art-case piano. It is based on the 7¼ octave Model D, and is made of burred walnut and satinwood. Known as a 'Centennial Grand', it was built in 1876, 100 years after the American Declaration of Independence. It is an overstrung grand with a full cast-iron frame, mounted in a heavily braced laminated case and supported by three substantial carved baluster legs. The casework was designed and produced by the firm of Pottier & Stymus, which decorated a number of Steinway pianos. This is believed to be the only surviving instrument on which the name appears. The company was at the forefront of American design. In 1994 this instrument, serial number 36922, became the second most expensive piano ever sold, after the 1883 Steinway (p65).

The three pedals are housed in a traditional pedal lyre, rather than the more common pillared lyre. Like the legs, it has been given extra weight in order not to be swamped by the elaborate gilding.

ERARD, Paris, 1855, grand piano

This elegant seven-octave grand piano was built in an ebonized case to provide a particularly strong black base. Against that is set the ormolu, a gold-colored alloy, which runs around the piano's bottom edge and outlines the shape of the lid. The bright satinwood interior highlights the frame and strings assembly and again contrasts strongly with the rich black casework. The piano stands on three elaborately carved legs that are also decorated with ormolu mounts. This instrument was built in the year that Pierre Erard died. He had been responsible for introducing the double escapement action. From this date the company went into a gradual decline. This piano, which was awarded a Seal of Honour at the Paris Exposition of 1867, can be said to have been built at the height of the Erard company's fortunes.

BROADWOOD, London, 1879, grand piano

In 1879 the painter Edward Burne-Jones was asked by a friend, William Graham, to design a piano which he could give as a wedding present to his daughter Frances. Burne-Jones commissioned Broadwood to build a grand piano with a traditional harpsichord-like shape, supported by a trestle stand, that would be in keeping with the aims of the Arts and Crafts movement he was establishing with

the craftsman and poet William Morris (see p66). Burne-Jones himself painted the lid, which shows Mother Earth. The side of the case depicts the Greek myth of Orpheus, who descends to the underworld to search for his dead wife Eurydice, finds her, but breaks his promise not to look back and loses her forever. This sad story was believed to have been chosen by Burne-Jones to reflect his unhappiness at the marriage: he is said to have been in love with Frances Graham.

The lid is decorated on both sides. These large expanses of wood, with their sweeping curves, make interesting and spacious 'canvasses' on which the artist can work.

The sides and lid of the piano were painted by the Parisian landscape artist Lucien Simonnet. The detail is taken from the top of the lid and shows a rural scene in which a youth has taken a bird's nest from a tree and is showing it to a group of young women, one of whom can be seen shearing a sheep. In the background, two cherubs can be seen. Cherubs also appear around the side of the case of this Steinway grand piano.

STEINWAY, Hamburg, 1897, grand piano

This instrument was built at Steinway's German factory in Hamburg. The piano is a Model C, measuring 7 ft 5 in long. The Model C was first built in 1861, as a seven-octave 7 ft 1 in piano, but was increased to the full 88 notes in 1886. The Model C is referred to as a 'parlor grand'. Many consider that its scaling (the relationship between string length and pitch) and balance make it the best instrument in the Steinway line. After manufacture in Hamburg, the piano was dispatched to France where G Brunenhausen was commissioned to design and build the decorative casework. This was common practice in Europe. There was no art department in Hamburg and Paris was still considered to be the design capital of Europe. Brunenhausen and Cuel & Co. was the most commonly used designer. Art-case pianos made in Europe were nearly always built on commission.

THE ART-CASE PIANO

The piano has always been a musical instrument first and foremost, but at the same time the need to win acceptance has meant its appearance has had to take account of its surroundings. So pianos have always reflected the furniture styles of their day. Once the internal layout of the piano, whether square, upright or grand, had become firmly established, the casework could be used to make an aesthetic statement. The true art-case piano is an art form in its own right.

When a piano was to be decorated out of house, Steinway would normally send the instrument in an unfinished state, without legs, pedal lyre or music desk and rest, which would be supplied by the company doing the decoration. In this instance, though, the music rest is simply a gilded version of that found on standard grands.

BROADWOOD, London, 1895, grand piano

Broadwood called this instrument a 'short grand' and at just over 6 ft (73 in), with a seven-octave (AAA – a⁴) keyboard, this is certainly one of the smaller art-case grands. The case is of Spanish mahogany decorated with ormolu. Three of the panels feature the ubiquitous cherubs (see below). Broadwood refers to this instrument as being in Adam style (although it has elements of the earlier Sheraton style). It still features a single escapement action and has a straight-strung scale mounted on a composite iron and steel frame. Made in 1895, the piano (serial number 44070) was built when Broadwood was starting to experience a considerable degree of financial difficulty. This forced the company to advertise, and in the same year it released the Album of Artistic Pianofortes, designed to promote the company's more expensive instruments.

Musical instruments have often been highly decorated. The Flemish and Italian harpsichord and virginal makers, in particular, had produced extremely ornate instruments. The Ruckers family, for instance, employed great painters to decorate their instruments. This approach was inevitably applied to the piano. Many of the great piano houses, for instance Broadwood, Steinway and Blüthner, were founded by skilled woodworkers and furniture designers who wanted their pianos to be attractive pieces of furniture.

Pianos reflected the styles of their eras. The mid-17th century to the 1720s was the period of the baroque, an exuberant style based on curving forms derived from classical antiquity. In France, the fashion began to change in the latter years of the reign of Louis XIV (1643-1715) and the early years of Louis XV (1715-1774). The new rococo style was a reaction against the pomp of the baroque. It made light-hearted use of elaborate motifs such as shells, scrolls, and flowers that taxed even the most accomplished of craftsmen. English designers, meanwhile, were more reserved, tending to use the beauty of the wood rather than to decorate it.

The neo-classical style prevalent during the reign of Louis XVI

Action: *All wooden parts of the Steinway Accelerated Action are of quarter-sawn white maple bushed with wool action cloth to reduce friction.*

Panels: *The panels (lid, etc) have a core made from 5-ply yellow poplar and have the inner and outer faces veneered.*

Hammers: *The cores of the hammers are made by hand from hard birch and covered using 18 lb premium wool felt from merino sheep. The hammer shanks are of maple.*

Action Rail: *Clover-leaf shaped (for stability), with a core of maple running down its length inside the metal. This wooden core securely holds the screws that secure the action.*

STEINWAY MODEL D

It takes just over 9 months to produce a Model D from seasoned wood to the instrument shown above. This illustration shows the piano as it would appear on the concert platform, with the full prop stick supporting the lid. The piano is 107¾ in long, 61¼ in wide and 39 in high. The exploded view (right) has had the fall assembly removed. The keyboard and action have then been freed from the casework and partially pulled out to show the keys and key bed. The action has been lifted from the key assembly. The capstan screws, which can be seen on the keys, would sit directly under the action. The Model D is overstrung, featuring combination agraffe, capo d'astro bar, and front and rear duplex.

Keys: *Made from Bavarian spruce, individually weighted off. Ivory was used for key coverings until 1989, but now a mock-ivory polymer known as "Ivo-Plast" is preferred. The touch weight of the keys is 52 g for AAA (bottom A) graduating to 47 g for c⁵ (top C). The octave span is 6½ in.*

GERMAN AND AMERICAN MODEL DS

Approximately 150 Model D pianos are made each year in Hamburg, Germany, and New York, USA. There are minor differences between the American and German instruments, mostly associated with the materials used. Most of the components used to make the American Model D come from North or South America, while the materials for the German-made pianos can come from anywhere in the world.

Each factory has its own production team. The shapes of the pianos' cases differ slightly, and the American Steinway has a slightly different 'feel' to the German piano, although this would only be apparent to the most sensitive of players. The German Model D has a knob for a lid lock on the bent side.

Some pianists are predisposed to either the German or American instrument. As a result Steinway can tailor the Model D to suit its purchaser. For example the pianist may want a German action fitted into an American instrument. In addition, every Model D is adjusted to the pianist's liking, and is voiced to give a tone and response that suits a player's style and taste.

Keybed: *Made from heavy quarter-sawn planks of spruce (1¾ in thick). The keybed has large maple dowel ends which provide a solid mount for the adjustable brass touch-regulation screws.*

Hardware: *Locks, castors, etc, are solid brass, polished and lacquered.*

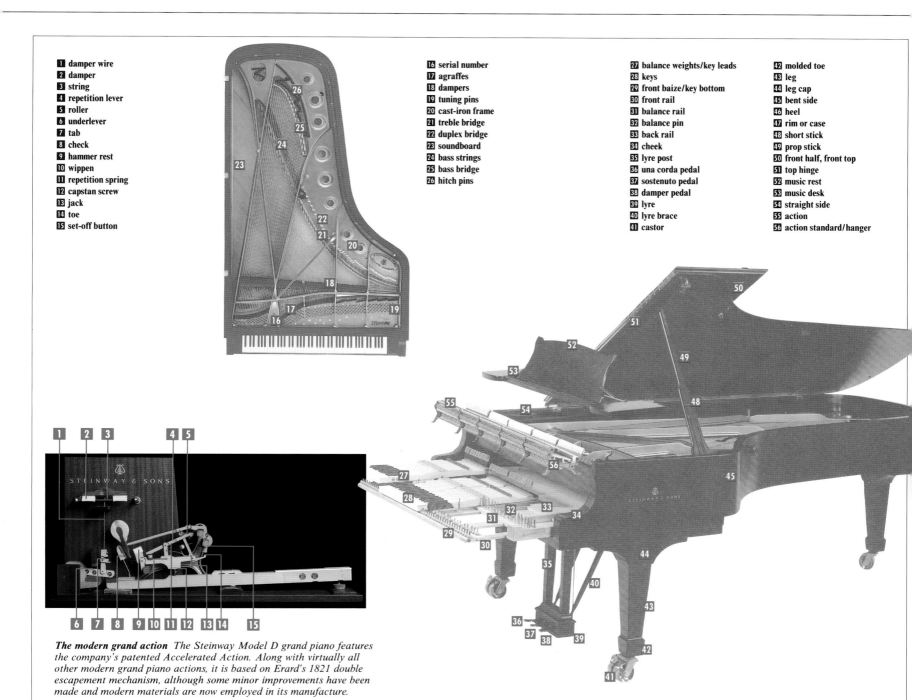

1 damper wire
2 damper
3 string
4 repetition lever
5 roller
6 underlever
7 tab
8 check
9 hammer rest
10 wippen
11 repetition spring
12 capstan screw
13 jack
14 toe
15 set-off button

16 serial number
17 agraffes
18 dampers
19 tuning pins
20 cast-iron frame
21 treble bridge
22 duplex bridge
23 soundboard
24 bass strings
25 bass bridge
26 hitch pins

27 balance weights/key leads
28 keys
29 front baize/key bottom
30 front rail
31 balance rail
32 balance pin
33 back rail
34 cheek
35 lyre post
36 una corda pedal
37 sostenuto pedal
38 damper pedal
39 lyre
40 lyre brace
41 castor

42 molded toe
43 leg
44 leg cap
45 bent side
46 heel
47 rim or case
48 short stick
49 prop stick
50 front half, front top
51 top hinge
52 music rest
53 music desk
54 straight side
55 action
56 action standard/hanger

The modern grand action The Steinway Model D grand piano features the company's patented Accelerated Action. Along with virtually all other modern grand piano actions, it is based on Erard's 1821 double escapement mechanism, although some minor improvements have been made and modern materials are now employed in its manufacture.

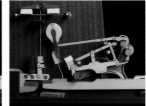
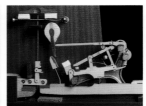

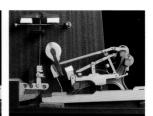

At rest As the key is pressed, the **capstan screw (12)** pushes up on the **wippen (10)** causing the **jack (13)** to push up on the **roller (5)** (which is attached to the hammer) through a slot in the **repetition lever (4)**.

Hammer strikes string The jack continues to move upwards until its **toe (14)** encounters the **set-off button (15)**, causing the jack to flick off the roller, leaving the hammer moving in free flight towards the **string (3)**. Meanwhile the **damper (2)** has been lifted off the string by the **damper wire (1)**.

Hammer in check With the key still held, the hammer bounces back off the string and is 'grabbed' by the **check (8)**. The downward movement of the hammer has caused the repetition lever to compress the **repetition spring (11)**.

Hammer freed As the key is partly released, the hammer is freed from the check and rises slightly under the force of the repetition spring. This allows the jack back under the roller. If the key is played again, the hammer will hit at the string, albeit less forcefully than it would from its initial rest position.

Back to rest When the key is fully released the hammer falls back so that it is just clear of the **hammer rest (9)**. The toe of the jack leaves the set-off button and the jack is fully repositioned under the roller. The damper is lowered simultaneously on to the string.

At rest, dampers raised When the damper pedal is pressed, a series of levers raises the **underlever (6)**, which lifts the dampers via the damper wire. The **tab (7)** is part of the sostenuto assembly. Once a string has been played and the pedal pressed, a tab prevents the damper wire of any note being held from falling back.

Three pairs of bellows are used to drive the roll mechanism. The gearing chain can be seen to their left.

To the far right is the main on/off switch. The switch is controlled remotely by a knob located to the right of the spoolbox: a metal rod links it to the actual switch.

The large circular knob below the keyboard can be used to control tempo and expression. Turning it adjusts the volume of the melody; sliding it adjusts the tempo. The knob is linked to the pointer in the spoolbox. Certain rolls indicate the tempo with a line, so that it can be adjusted manually. The far right lever puts the piano into play mode and rewinds the roll.

The bottom right chamber houses the electric pump. This is used instead of the bellows when the piano is used in reproducing mode.

The foot-bellows are used for expression – the harder the pedals are pumped the louder the notes. As the bellows hide the soft and damper pedals, hand operated levers are provided just below the keyboard. If the electric motor is used, the pedals are folded away.

KEY DATES

c1800 Jacquard develops a loom controlled by punched cards.

1846 Patent granted for the use of perforated cardboard to produce mechanized music.

1863 Fourneaux develops the Pianista, the first pneumatic piano player mechanism.

1880 William Tremaine sets up the Mechanical Orguinette Co. (later the Aeolian Co.) to manufacture automated reed organs.

1880 First automatic piano unveiled by Needham and Sons, New York. It was built by R.W. Paine and was an adaptation of the orguinette mechanism.

1887 Edwin Welte (Germany) introduces the use of the perforated paper roll.

1890s Domestic electricity first becomes available.

1897 Edwin Votey develops 'push up' player for the Aeolian company.

1900 Votey mechanism refined and called the Pianola.

1904 Welte Red reproducing system introduced.

1905 Hupfeld DEA reproducing system introduced.

1912 Aeolian Duo-Art reproducing system introduced.

1923 Reproducing mechanisms incorporated in 10 per cent of total piano sales.

1925 US piano production: 137,000 conventional instruments, 169,000 player pianos.

1929 Ampico introduce Model B reproducing system.

1938 Manufacture effectively ceases.

MILLS NOVELTY COMPANY, Chicago, c.1920, Violano-Virtuoso

The Violano-Virtuoso, seen here with its front off, was invented by Henry Conrad Sandell in c1905. The special piano rolls play five tunes, with the melody played on the violin, which has four strings bowed by discs of cellulose acetate driven by a variable speed motor. The accompaniment is played by the 44-note piano section. The machine is coin-operated and would originally have cost about $1,000.

Conlon Nancarrow: Studies For Player Piano *'played'* by Conlon Nancarrow
Conlon Nancarrow is unique among composers. Nancarrow decided in the 1940s to write for one instrument: the player piano. Since then he has produced a breathtaking array of pieces focusing both on complex rhythms and polyphonic texturing. He cuts his own rolls directly and this offers him possibilities unavailable to composers working with a normal piano. Some of his studies have been transcribed for standard instruments.

per inch. However, standardisation between manufacturers took place towards the end of the 19th century and rolls were produced with nine holes per inch, allowing all 88 notes to be played.

The four main companies producing reproducing systems were: the German Welte organisation, with their original Welte Red (1904), and later Green systems; Hupfeld, also German, with their DEA system of 1905, and their subsequent Solo-Phonola, Duo-Phonola and Tri-Phonola; Aeolian, which pioneered the hugely successful Duo-Art; and the Ampico system, made by the American Piano Corporation (which became the Ampico Corporation in 1915). But there were many other systems. In 1928 there were more than 35 competing player mechanisms in the US alone.

Cutting piano rolls was a difficult and time-consuming job. The music was played first and the dynamics added later. All the great performers of the day created piano rolls, including Paderewski (Duo-Art and Welte); Rachmaninoff and Rubinstein (Ampico); Gershwin (Duo-Art); Debussy, Mahler and Richard Strauss (Welte); and Fats Waller (Hupfeld). Their rolls provide the only historical record of how they actually played their works.

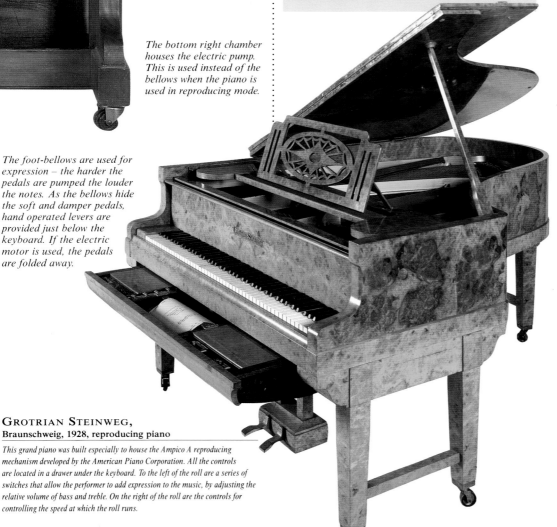

GROTRIAN STEINWEG,
Braunschweig, 1928, reproducing piano

This grand piano was built especially to house the Ampico A reproducing mechanism developed by the American Piano Corporation. All the controls are located in a drawer under the keyboard. To the left of the roll are a series of switches that allow the performer to add expression to the music, by adjusting the relative volume of bass and treble. On the right of the roll are the controls for controlling the speed at which the roll runs.

CLASSIFICATION OF GRAND PIANOS

There are various terms used to describe the size of a grand piano. The simplest approximate designations are:

CONCERT GRAND	7 ft 6 in or more
MEDIUM GRAND	5 ft 6 in-7 ft 6 in
BABY GRAND	4 ft 6 in-5 ft 6 in

However, various manufacturers use other names for their instruments: the following examples give an approximate idea of the relative sizes.

IMPERIAL CONCERT GRAND	9 ft 6 in Bösendorfer
SEMI-CONCERT GRAND	7 ft 5 in Kawai
HALF CONCERT GRAND	7 ft 4 in Bösendorfer
PARLOR GRAND	6 ft 7 in Bösendorfer
BOUDOIR GRAND	6 ft 2 in Steinway
MINIATURE GRAND	5 ft 10 in Steinway
MIGNON GRAND	5 ft 8 in Bösendorfer

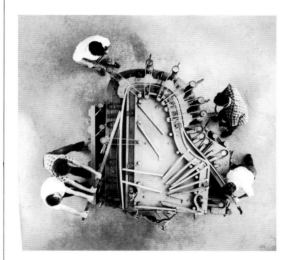

Soundboard: The wood used for the soundboard must have a very straight, close and even grain. Quarter-sawn Alaskan Sitka spruce (in America) or European pine (Germany) is favored. The timber generally comes from around 3,000 ft. Wood grown at that height has equal amounts of light and dark grain because growth in the spring and summer (which produces light grain) matches that in the rest of the year. Typically it has between 10 and 15 growth rings per inch. Sound travels along the grain of the soundboard, so the soundboard is arranged with the grain following the lie of the long bridge. The soundboard is tapered from 9 mm at its center to 6 mm at the outer edge, allowing freer movement and producing a tone richer in harmonics.

The rim-bending clamp shown here was designed by CF Theodore Steinway in 1880. The 18 layers of maple that form the inner and outer rims are glued and clamped in this press and left overnight for the glue to set. The assembly is then released from the clamp and left for 4-6 weeks to ensure correct moisture content. This process achieves the desired inner and outer rim shape without the need to introduce heat or humidity, which results in a stable and appropriately resonant structure.

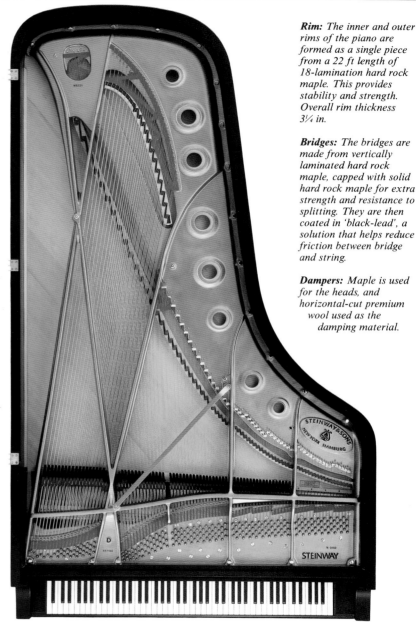

Rim: The inner and outer rims of the piano are formed as a single piece from a 22 ft length of 18-lamination hard rock maple. This provides stability and strength. Overall rim thickness 3¼ in.

Bridges: The bridges are made from vertically laminated hard rock maple, capped with solid hard rock maple for extra strength and resistance to splitting. They are then coated in 'black-lead', a solution that helps reduce friction between bridge and string.

Dampers: Maple is used for the heads, and horizontal-cut premium wool used as the damping material.

Frame: The frame is made from cast iron, which is filed, sanded, coated with red oxide paint followed by several coats of bronze spray and finished with a coat of lacquer. It weighs approximately 340 lb – more than a third of the total weight of the piano. The frame has to withstand a stress of around 20 tons.

Tuning Pins: Made of blued steel and finished with rust-resistant nickel.

THE MODERN GRAND PIANO

The instrument shown here is said to be the most complicated piece of machinery ever built by hand. The Steinway Model D Concert Grand Piano has 12,000 parts and takes the best part of a year to produce. It is probably the finest Steinway ever made, and the choice of the majority of the world's concert pianists today.

STEINWAY AND SONS: MODEL D

The Steinway Model D is the piano that the majority of contemporary concert pianists use in performance. The first D-style grand piano (serial no. 791) was made in about 1857, but it took a further ten years for Steinway to develop its unique rim-bending process. This allowed the rim to be made from a single piece of laminated maple and is one of the features that helps to give the Steinway its particular sound and character. The first instruments were 7-octave, parallel-strung pianos: the first overstrung Model D appeared in 1859 (serial no. 2552).

In 1884, the piano's compass was extended to that which we know today: 7⅓ octaves. At the same time the length of the instrument was increased to 8 ft 10 in. In 1914 the case was stretched to 8 ft 11¼ in (serial no. 178,700). It remained virtually the same until 1967 when it grew by an extra half inch to its present dimensions.

The Model D is the largest 'production' piano that Steinway has ever made. The piano is a quarter of an inch less than nine feet in length: Steinway has never called it a nine-foot grand.

The length of a grand piano is generally measured from the front, by the keyboard, to the overhang of the lid at the very back. Some manufacturers have been known to use a diagonal measurement which inflates the size of their grand pianos.

"Steinway is the only piano on which the pianist can do everything he wants and everything he dreams. Steinway gives the pianist every opportunity." VLADIMIR ASHKENAZY

The Steinway Model D is made up of about 12,000 parts, most of which are in the action, which derives ultimately from that invented by Erard in 1821. The piano has 243 strings, or rather 'speaking lengths', since many of the strings are looped around the hitch pin to form in effect two strings.

Steinway maintains that the Model D concert grand piano is "built to a standard not to a price". The fact that so many of the world's leading pianists choose this instrument more than justifies this claim.

MILLS NOVELTY COMPANY, Chicago, 1920s, Horse Race Piano

The Mills Novelty Company specialized in instruments with an 'optical amusement'. This piano features a mechanical horse race, and would probably have been located in a bar or arcade. When a coin is inserted, the 'Mills magnetic expression piano' begins to play its roll and the race begins. With the back of the instrument opened up, the frame and the electrical actuators (solenoids) controlling the action are revealed. Like the Violano-Virtuoso, the piano has no keyboard, so the strings can be arranged in any order. To keep stress to a minimum, and to maintain tuning, the frame is symmetrical, with the longer bass strings located in the middle. The date on the frame, June 4th, 1912, is the date of Henry C Sandell's patent.

The popularity of the reproducing piano peaked in the mid-1920s, after which the Depression, and the arrival of radio and gramophone, took their toll. By 1936 it was virtually dead.

OTHER INSTRUMENTS

As the automatic instrument technology evolved, inventors sought to apply it to other instruments. Companies in Germany and America set about devizing elaborate mechanisms to automate the violin. The sound of the violin on its own, however, wasn't marketable, so violin/piano combinations were devized from about 1910. The Mills Novelty Company in America and Hupfeld in Leipzig were the leaders in this field.

The automated piano was the juke box of the day, and many different types appeared at the beginning of the 20th century. The arrival of the gramophone, and subsequently the juke box, was to lead to their rapid decline.

The reproducing piano enjoyed a limited revival in the 1950s and 1960s. Later, electromechanical and computerized systems gave the concept a new lease on life.

AMERICAN PHOTO PLAYER COMPANY, USA, 1920-25, Fotoplayer Model 20

Instruments such as this were used in cinemas and theatres in the 1910s and 1920s. Originally, silent movies were accompanied by live piano, but the instrument's limitations and the difficulty of finding suitable pianists led to the development of mechanical substitutes. The Fotoplayer Model 20 is a player piano with additional organ pipes, percussion instruments and sound effects devices. It has two spoolboxes, so that one roll can be re-wound while the other is playing. The strap-handles along the top door of the instrument, the switches below the keyboard and the four footpedals are for triggering the effects, including gunshot, thunder, cymbals, wind/siren, whistle and chimes.

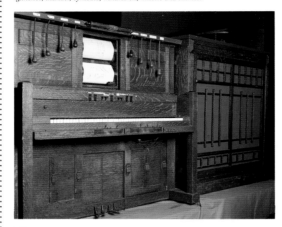

HUPFELD, Leipzig, c1910, Phonoliszt-Violina

This massive device incorporates an 88-note piano keyboard and three violins, all driven by special rolls. The violins are single stringed, tuned to D, A and E (there is no G) and played by a circular hoop with horsehair inside. The violin moves to the revolving 'bow' and mechanical fingers pitch the note as required. Dynamics are introduced by increasing the pressure of the bow or changing its speed.

HUPFELD

Ludwig Hupfeld (b1864) was a pioneer of the automatic instrument, and his company, Ludwig Hupfeld AG, of Leipzig, became the world's largest manufacturer of the devices. Hupfeld's firm was probably the first to use an electric motor to drive a piano player. In 1902 the company produced the Phonola, which had a 73-note compass (later extended to 88 notes) and offered considerable control over dynamics, with separate bellows for the treble and bass.

In 1904, Welte, Hupfeld's main rival, introduced their Welte-Mignon (or Welte-Red) reproducing system and Hupfeld had to act quickly to retain market share. The company released its DEA reproducing system in 1905. By 1911 Hupfeld employed 1300 workers to produce many automatic instruments, including the Phonoliszt-Violina and various Orchestrions.

Hupfeld was best known for its Solo-Phonola and its Duo- and Tri-Phonola reproducing piano systems. A special piano was used for recording a roll, with every note connected to an electric switch. The switches operated a row of pencils corresponding to the notes of the piano. Dynamics were measured by a pneumatic device. The pencil lines indicated where holes were to be cut in the rolls, and additional expression perforations were added in the margins. When demand for automatic instruments declined, Hupfeld concentrated on grand pianos. The company survived, but the heyday of the automatic instrument was gone.

The advertising of player pianos and reproducing pianos was directed primarily at people who had no musical ability. Anyone could 'play' and thus benefit from having an automatic piano, and the manufacturers and distributors were only too keen to promote this fact. This advertisement for Hupfeld player pianos ran in The Times c1926.

Ignaz Bösendorfer was born in 1794 in Vienna. At the age of 33 he was granted a license to start building pianos. Franz Liszt, then 17, was recommended to try them. Liszt found the instrument strong and its tone and color very much to his liking. He endorsed it and immediately the reputation of the pianos started spreading throughout Europe.

In 1859 Ignaz (left) died and his son Ludwig (below) took control. He built a new factory, in 1860. Ten years later, the company moved again. Construction was moved to its present site in Vienna's Fourth District. Ludwig Bösendorfer (seen below in 1892 demonstrating to Emperor Franz Josef I the company's new Imperial Grand Piano) had no direct descendants to take over the business, so in 1909, upon retirement, he sold the company to his friend Carl Hutterstrasser. Ludwig died in 1919. World War II saw much of the company's reserves of wood destroyed. In 1945, the Bösendorfer premises were devastated in heavy fighting and the remaining pianos used for firewood. The company slowly revived. A handful of workers managed to build eleven pianos during 1946/7, rising to some 100 pianos a year from 1950 to 1966. Arnold H Habig, head of the Jasper Corporation and subsequently the President of Kimball, bought Bösendorfer in 1966. His aim was to use their expertise to help improve the Kimball range of pianos. The purchase worked well for both companies. By 1978 production had reached more than 500 instruments a year.

(1774-1793) represented a rejection of the rococo. It featured restrained Greco-Roman patterns, while furniture became lighter and simpler, using straight tapering legs later adapted to the English square piano. Robert Adam and Thomas Sheraton were the leading designers in England in this period and they had some influence on piano design.

At the start of the 19th century the neo-classical spawned the empire style, which developed during Napoleon's imperial period (1804-14). In England the empire movement found a reflection in the Regency style. Both had classical elements with strong Greek and Egyptian influences.

At the same time, however, waves of revivalism were sweeping Europe. First came the rococo revival of the 1820s (see the Collard & Collard piano, p31). Then Gothic revivalism built upon the style of the Middle Ages (see AWN Pugin's upright piano p46), becoming extremely fashionable in the mid-19th century. Finally there was the Renaissance revival, which returned to neo-classical motifs and elegant decoration, before mass production began to confuse the picture.

BÖSENDORFER, Vienna, 1867, grand piano

This instrument is one of the world's most famous pianos, and is known as the 'Empress Eugénie' Bösendorfer. It was designed by Viennese craftsman Hans Makart. Some doubt exists about whom the piano was originally made for. Some

sources state that it was built for the Empress Elizabeth, wife of Austrian Emperor Franz Joseph I, who presented it as a gift to Empress Eugénie of France, wife of Louis Philippe Napoleon III. Other sources say that it was commissioned directly from Bösendorfer by Napoleon, as a birthday gift for the Empress Eugénie. It certainly appeared at the 1867 Exposition in Paris and was the prized possession of the Empress. When Emperor and Empress were exiled in England in 1871, following a bloodless coup the previous year, they took the piano with them. The Empress kept it in her house in Torquay, and after her death in 1920 it was left to friends in the town.

The casework is mahogany, inlaid with kingwood, and the legs and the cherubs on the end-cheeks are hollow cast bronze.

STEINWAY, New York, 1883, grand piano

In 1989 this Model D piano was sold at auction for $360,000, the highest price ever paid for a piano. It was made by Steinway in New York and shipped to London in 1884, where the case was designed and exquisitely decorated by Sir Lawrence Alma-Tadema, the Dutch-born British designer. The painting above the keyboard, 'The Wandering Minstrels', was by Sir Edward Poynter, president of the Royal Academy. The piano was subsequently returned to its owner Henry G Marquand, then president of the Metropolitan Museum of Art in New York.

BECHSTEIN, Berlin, 1898, grand piano

Bechstein was probably the most prolific European maker of art-case pianos at the turn of the century. However, many of these instruments were destroyed during the two world wars. Bechstein was best known for its line of 'Empire' grands, which are still to be encountered around the world. This instrument, made just before the death of Carl Bechstein, has a simplified rococo flavor.

RUHLMANN/GAVEAU, Paris, c1924, grand piano

Emile-Jacques Ruhlmann was one of the most important French furniture designers of the 20th century. In 1925, the Exposition Internationale des Arts Décoratifs et Industriels Modernes took place in Paris, giving rise to the art deco style. Ruhlmann, with the assistance of architect Pierre Patout, designed a pavilion, entitled L'Hôtel du Collectionneur, housing his designs. The show was an enormous success and Ruhlmann was propelled to the front of the modern design movement. This piano was the focal point of the Grand Salon, the room that was the talk of the entire exhibition. It is believed that Ruhlmann built six instruments to this design. The workings of the instrument are by Gaveau, but casework styling and design is by Ruhlmann.

STEINWAY, New York, 1903, grand piano

This piano, the 'first' White House Steinway, was presented to President Theodore Roosevelt, representing the American people, in 1903 to mark Steinway's 50th anniversary. It was designed by RD and JH Hunt under the auspices of interior designer Joseph Burr Tiffany, head of Steinway's Art Department, and was carved by Jean Ayuso. It cost $20,000 to produce. The painting on the lid is by Thomas Dewing, and shows the nine Muses. The sides of the casework feature the seals of the original 13 states. This piano was given the serial number 100,000, although Steinway had been producing instruments with six-figure serial numbers from 1901.

The shape of the piano is unusual, in that it is roughly square but with a bowed bent side and four tapered legs.

Ruhlmann signed both the piano and the chair, the latter being specially designed with upholstered scrolling back and flared square legs to complement the instrument.

BECHSTEIN

Carl Bechstein was born in 1826 and served his apprenticeship as a piano maker in Berlin. In 1849 Bechstein went to Paris to study the methods of both Pape and Kriegelstein. In 1853, back in Berlin, he designed and built his own piano. By 1856 he had attracted the attention of the pianist Hans von Bülow. Bechstein went to a concert by Liszt and, like Bösendorfer some three decades earlier, was amazed by the ferocity of his playing. Bechstein decided his instruments would have to be able to take this kind of punishment. He eventually persuaded Liszt and Bülow to perform together on his pianos and Liszt became a great supporter.

Bechstein saw art-case instruments as a way of creating an image of quality. A classic Bechstein art piano is shown below, its pure white casework supported, empire style, by two Greek sphinxes. The Bechstein factory was virtually destroyed in World War II but the company survived. Initially it restored and repaired instruments, but by 1950 the company was making about 100 instruments a year. In 1963

Baldwin purchased the Bechstein company. Karl Schulze, a retailer and master technician, and two partners bought the company back into German hands in 1986.

The unusual shaped case is made of mahogany, veneered with matched Macassar ebony. The nameboard, labeled Gaveau, Paris, is of burl amboyna, and the tapered legs are inlaid with ivory. The pedals are suspended by a fluted bow and finished in silvered bronze.

STROHMENGER, London, c1900, upright piano

This type of upright piano, with hinged doors, was originally designed by MH Baillie Scott in 1896. Baillie Scott came from the Isle of Man and this type of instrument became known as a Manxman. This particular piano was built some years later by the London firm of Strohmenger & Sons, which was bought by Chappells in 1938.

ERARD, Paris, 1905, grand piano

This 7 ft 5 in piano from the House of Erard is modeled on one of the most famous pieces of furniture ever made, the Bureau du Roi Louis XV by Jean Francois Oeben and Jean-Henri Riesiner, which can be seen at Versailles. The instrument was made in 1902 by Erard, and sent to the Jansen workshop, where it was completed in 1905. The casework is extensively veneered in several woods. The piano features highly decorative ormolu mountings, which are particularly effective around the cheeks at each end of the keyboard, on the legs and on the pedal lyre. Ormolu is a gilded bronze, or gold colored alloy of copper, zinc and tin, used to decorate furniture. These ormolu mountings, as well as the mahogany parquetry, are believed to have been produced by François Linke, one of the most renowned French cabinet makers at the turn of the century. The quality of the craftsmanship can be seen from the detail on the lid, of which the top heel end is shown (right). The instrument is straight strung, with a seven-octave (AAA — a⁴) compass, and naturally uses Erard's double escapement action. It is believed that this is one of only two such instruments.

BROADWOOD, London, 1898, 'square' grand piano.

CR Ashbee, a leading London architect, designed this unusual instrument as a wedding present for his wife. The piano is square in plan, with an overstrung iron frame, made up, unusually, of several castings. A long hinge runs across the width of the instrument, so that the two halves of the lid can fold upwards. The piano is painted in an art nouveau style and features pastoral scenes in which young women are playing instruments.

ERARD, Paris, 1921, grand piano

This instrument, like the piano above, is designed to reflect the French regal style of the 18th century. The casework, however, can be seen to be somewhat different, with the extra cabriole legs at the middle and rear. Ormolu mountings are still used, but the effect is less extreme. By the 1920s, demand for this kind of instrument was decreasing. Interior designers were looking towards the modernism of the Bauhaus and art deco schools.

THE ART-CASE PIANO: INTO THE MODERN ERA

The true art-case piano, like a great painting, is an individual object, an artistic entity in its own right. It is also made with scant regard for cost. Consequently such instruments are extremely rare. More recently, though, the term has come to be used for a group of instruments, still highly decorated or designed for an aesthetic purpose, but made in slightly larger numbers. The distinction between the two was blurred by the arrival of mass production.

By the late 19th century, the furniture-making process had largely been mechanized. This provoked a strong reaction in the shape of the Arts and Crafts movement. Its designs, intended to sustain traditional craftsmanship, were to prove influential.

The architects and interior designers who built grand houses for the industrialists of the late 19th and early 20th centuries insisted that everything in them should adhere to the dominant style. This had implications for the creators of art-case pianos.

In the 20th century, the decorative styles favored by the rich were seized upon and manufactured in quantity for the mass market. Art nouveau, pervasive in the 1890s and early 1900s, used undulating, organic forms. After World War I, the Bauhaus in Germany preached a simple functionalism. Art deco, appearing in France in the 1920s and 1930s, explored geometrical lines and man-made materials.

Since then, design has benefited from Scandinavian influences, but revivalism has become dominant. Although designers such as Wendell Castle in America (see p83 and p86) continue to make art-case pianos, the commissioning of such instruments is now rare.

GRANFELDT, Stockholm, 1827, square piano

This piano was made in Sweden by Olof Granfeldt in 1827. The curved keyboard is intended to facilitate playing at each end of the piano's compass. Granfeldt built several such instruments. Experiments with curved keyboards date back to the late 18th century, but the first patent was only taken out in 1910, by F Cludsam (sometimes referred to as Clutsam), a German piano maker. Cludsam's keyboard was considerably more curved than this.

GEORGE ROGERS AND SONS, London, c1920, organist's piano

Like most pedal pianos, this instrument was designed for organ practice. The music rack is long, to fit organ music, which is generally in a wide format. The piano has two seven-octave (AAA – a⁴) keyboards. The mechanism is not as complex as that on the Moór double manual pianos. Here both sets of keys are linked to a single action. Playing middle C on the upper keyboard prevents the use of the same note on the bottom keyboard. The piano is raised to accommodate a 2½-octave (AAA-G) pedalboard. The player sits on a wooden bench that straddles the pedals.

This is a Milner pedal piano (right) with a single keyboard. The bottom door has been removed and the pedalboard assembly pulled out slightly to reveal the mechanism. The piano has been raised to allow the pedal assembly to slide in underneath the footpedals. The pedals are linked by a series of levers to vertical 'stickers' and thence to the action.

JANKÓ

Paul von Jankó was born in western Hungary in 1856. He was trained as a mathematician and became a musician and engineer, studying under physiologist and physicist Hermann von Helmholtz. In 1882, he patented a new form of keyboard layout, designed to allow the player to cover a wider span of notes with each hand and to make all keys equally easy to play. Jankó's keyboard drew upon earlier designs by Conrad Henfling (1708), Johann Rohleder (1791) and William Lunn (1843). He used short narrow keys akin to buttons, and stacked them up to form six tiers. The notes were arranged in whole-tone intervals. The first tier, the third and the fifth play a whole-tone scale beginning from C. The second, fourth and sixth tiers play a whole-tone scale beginning from C♯. The shape and fingering of a given scale or chord is the same in any key and the octave span is reduced to 5in as opposed to 6½in on a normal piano. In 1886, RW Kurka incorporated a Jankó keyboard into a piano, and Paul von Jankó himself demonstrated it in Vienna, playing works by Liszt, Schubert and Chopin.

C♯	D♯		F		G		A		B	C♯	D♯		F		G		A		B
C		D		E	F♯		G♯		A♯		C		D		E	F♯		G♯		A♯		C
C♯	D♯		F		G		A		B	C♯	D♯		F		G		A		B
C		D		E	F♯		G♯		A♯		C		D		E	F♯		G♯		A♯		C
C♯	D♯		F		G		A		B	C♯	D♯		F		G		A		B
C		D		E	F♯		G♯		A♯		C		D		E	F♯		G♯		A♯		C

It was not taken up by the Viennese piano makers, but in Germany Blüthner, Kaps and Ibach all built pianos using the keyboard. In England, Hopkinson was the first to fit a Jankó keyboard, in 1888, and Broadwood soon followed. The pictures show an 1890s Broadwood grand with a 7⅓-octave Jankó keyboard (above), and a Decker Brothers upright of c1892 (left). Many acclaimed the keyboard as the most important development of the age. Few players, however, were prepared to learn the new fingering, simple though it was. By the turn of the century it had become clear that the new keyboard was not going to replace the traditional design. Jankó died in Constantinople in 1919. No more than a handful of his keyboards remain.

KEYBOARD VARIATIONS

The design of the keyboard has remained virtually the same for more than four hundred years, despite the fact that it does not represent an ergonomic or musical ideal. Over the centuries various attempts have been made to improve its ease of use and its suitability for musical experimentation. But, as so often happens, these designs have ultimately come to nothing. It seems that after spending years mastering one keyboard, however flawed, few pianists are prepared to leave it behind to embrace a new design with no guaranteed future.

The piano has a seven-octave span. However, the keyboard can slide up a fifth or down a fourth, and so requires an extra

octave of keys and space for the keyboard to slide. As a result the piano is, at 68 in, considerably wider than a standard upright.

Two brass plates cover the parts of the keyboard that fall outside the range of the strings (AAA – a⁴). When the keyboard is slid, these plates mask off the keys that fall outside this range.

BROADWOOD, London, 1904, upright transposing piano

This transposing piano (left) allows the player to learn a piece, then to use the piano's mechanism to change it to a different key. The first patent for a transposing piano was granted to Edward Ryley in 1801, after the acceptance of equal temperament tuning had made such devices possible. Three systems of mechanical transposition have appeared over the years. The first transposing pianos used a sliding keyboard that moves up or down half an octave so that the action strikes higher or lower strings. An alternative was to move the frame and strings in some way. In 1812 Erard produced a piano with a circular soundboard that rotated, while others utilized footpedals to move a traditional frame and strings to the desired position. The third method was to mount an additional keyboard over the keys of the piano at the point which would provide the appropriate transposition.

Here the keyboard can be seen transposed down four semitones, so that playing the key C actually causes the hammer to strike the lower A flat strings. The left lever under the keyboard 'unlocks' it from its current location, while the right is used to move it to a new position. An alignment scale is provided just above the keyboard.

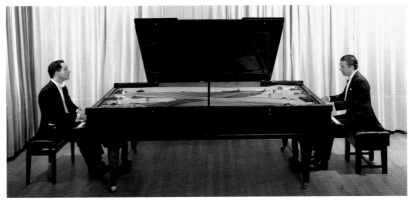

As early as 1753, CPE Bach praised equal temperament tuning in his *Essays On The True Art of Playing Keyboard Instruments*. In the 19th century this tuning, designed to allow composers to move easily between all 12 keys, became widely accepted across Europe.

Equal temperament makes transposition of a theme from one key to another musically straightforward; not so the change of fingering. The layout of the keyboard means that the musical scale associated with each key has its own individual fingering.

Many inventors have sought to make one scale fingering work for all keys, either by changing the layout of the keyboard or by making the hammers strike different strings for different keys.

New keyboards have sometimes attracted their devotees, but they have never succeeded in overcoming the weight of tradition and vested interests. Repositioning the action or keyboard (or both) to produce the 'transposing piano' has been more successful. The songwriter Irving Berlin liked to play and compose in F♯ and had three transposing pianos made for him by the Sohmer company.

These weren't the only attempts to change the way the piano was actually played. Manufacturers added additional keyboards

and pedalboards. In the 1920s Emanuel Moór, a Hungarian composer and pianist, added a second keyboard tuned an octave higher which could be coupled to the first. Passages in octaves could thus be played in single notes on one keyboard. Pianos were also built to be played by two players at once. These 'duoclaves' used two keyboards which shared the same casework and might also share the same strings, frame and soundboard.

In the late 19th and early 20th centuries, interest developed in 'quarter-tone' and 'micro-tonal' music, which divides the octave into more notes than the 12 semitones used in conventional tuning. This required new keyboard instruments. A typical 'quarter-tone' piano consisted of two grand or upright pianos, tuned a quarter of a tone apart, and a special keyboard with mechanical linkages permitting it to play both pianos. The quarter-tone keyboard had red and brown keys between the normal black and white keys. When a black or white key was played a note emerged from the piano tuned to concert pitch: when a red or brown key was played it came from the piano tuned a quarter-tone higher.

PLEYEL, Paris, 1928, Duoclave

The 'Duoclave' or 'Double Grand Piano' (Vis à vis in French) was patented by J Pirsson of New York in 1850 and shown at the Great Exhibition of 1851. There had been several example of pianos with more than one keyboard before this. In 1800 Matthias Müller of Vienna suggested adding a second keyboard to his 'Ditanaklasis' upright piano, and in 1812 Erard took out a patent showing a second keyboard added to one of their upright pianos.

The Duoclave illustrated is one of a handful of such instruments made by Pleyel of Paris. It consists of two overstrung pianos, sharing just the soundboard, lid and rectangular case. Originally this instrument was in the Théâtre du Châtelet. It is of standard width (60 in), and 9 ft 5 in long. Pleyel had made a smaller 8 ft model in the 1890s. The piano is seen here being played by David Nettle and Richard Markham, who currently tour with the instrument.

EAVESTAFF, London, c1937, 'De Luxe' Minipiano

The Minipiano design was brought to England from Sweden by Percy Brasted. He put it into production in 1934, using the Eavestaff name. The piano is bichord throughout, and the pin block and tuning pins are reached by folding down a panel beneath the keyboard. In the first year Brasted sold more than 7000 of these instruments. The success of the Minipiano was due to its styling and its low price: just over £30. Soon all the mass market manufacturers were producing similar types of piano.

MORLEY, London, c1950, orchestral upright grand piano

Morley was a pioneer of symmetrical pianos. This model, seen here with the top door, fall and hollow removed, is known as the orchestral grand. Its heritage lies in the early pyramid and lyre pianos of the 18th and 19th century, but it has a full iron frame. The hammers strike the strings away from the soundboard and toward the player, just as they do in the horizontal grand piano. This instrument was designed for use in a small orchestra where floor space is limited.

MORLEY, London, c1934, symmetrical grand piano

Morley referred to this instrument as its perpendicular symmetrical grand. It catered to the public taste for novelty. The piano has the same basic frame/soundboard assembly as the orchestral grand above. However, here it has been rotated through 180 degrees and positioned on the floor. Again, the hammers strike the string away from the soundboard. The whole front assembly is detachable from the soundboard and frame to make the piano easier to move. In 1934 this instrument sold for 55 guineas (£57.75).

BRAM MARTIN AND HIS ORCHESTRA, WITH A MINX MINIATURE PIANO, BROADCASTING FROM THE HOLBORN RESTAURANT

In 1934, Challen, along with Bösendorfer and Steinway, signed a deal to supply the BBC with pianos, an essential part of daily broadcasting in the days before recorded programming. Challen seized upon this opportunity to bring the sound of their instruments into homes across the country. Advertisements such as this made the most of the situation, neglecting to mention the presence of pianos made by Bösendorfer and Steinway in the BBC's London studios.

The Minx Miniature piano was an incredible success before and after the Second World War. This instrument, produced by Kemble Pianos, was aimed primarily at the domestic market. It also had, however, advantages in a small orchestra, as seen here. It took up little floor space, and didn't obscure the performer. Nevertheless when Kemble introduced the Minx Miniature in 1935 it was taking a risk. Many doubted that the instrument would sell. But the growing success of Eavestaff's Minipiano spurred Kemble on. Incredibly, the Minx continued to be made for another 31 years.

An open invitation to meet

CHALLEN

THE LARGEST GRAND PIANO IN THE WORLD

AT

THE BRITISH INDUSTRIES FAIR
MAY 5th—16th, 1952

CHAS. H. CHALLEN & SON, LTD.
Omega Works, Hermitage Road, Finsbury Park, London, N.4.

The 'Challen Giant' is the largest functioning horizontal grand piano ever known to have been built. It was made in London in 1935 by Chas. H Challen & Son Ltd and weighed slightly less than 1¼ tons. The piano was *11 ft 8 in long, and the longest bass string measured 9 ft 11 in. The total tensile force of the strings was estimated at 30 tons. Unfortunately the present whereabouts of this remarkable instrument are not known.*

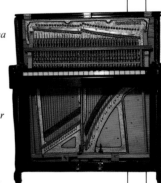

This 3⅓ octave (A – c³) instrument, made by Schoenberg of South Korea in 1989, is a mere 28 in wide and 33 in high. The keyboard is just 22 in above the floor as opposed to about 27½ in on a full size instrument. It was probably built either for promotional purposes or for use by a child. It is, however, a fully working piano and is shown here with the top and bottom doors removed. It is single strung (vertically) throughout, and has a metal frame and a laminated beech pin block.

KEMBLE, London and Bletchley, c1938, Minx Miniature piano

The Minx Miniature is just under 3 ft tall. One style in the range is shown here, with the top and bottom door, the keyboard and the action removed to reveal the acute angle of the overstringing. Kemble used a drop action (see p94) on the Minx, and they also offered to incorporate a device they called the modulator as an extra. This was a buff stop that damped the strings as they were hit to reduce the overall volume of the instrument and make the piano more acceptable to people who didn't want the noise of their practising to carry to adjacent rooms.

ALL SHAPES AND SIZES

Paradoxically, the global economic depression of the 1930s led to a resurgence of innovative piano design. Manufacturers responded to the lack of money in people's pockets by producing cheaper pianos and appealing new designs. In the end, though, the salvation of many companies proved to be the new miniature 'drop-action' pianos.

Design was the key to selling pianos in the middle part of the 20th century. From the depression of the early 1930s through to the early 1950s ways were sought to rekindle the excitement of owning a piano in the age of the wireless and the gramophone. But piano makers were also conscious of the economic conditions of the time. The miniature piano was one answer.

The British piano maker Percy Brasted acquired the basic design for the miniature piano from Sweden but had to work hard at making it a success. He changed its name from miniature piano to 'Minipiano', becoming the first person to register the prefix 'mini-' anywhere in the world. At the 1935 Radio Show, singer Paula Green sang from atop what appeared to be a pyramid of Minipianos. The following year Brasted presented a concert featuring 50 young female pianists, each playing a Minipiano.

By producing a range of minipianos, Brasted was able to maximize the market impact of the instruments. There were initially three versions of the six-octave piano: the Ritz, a simple design similar to the original; the Modern, using wood and chrome; and the De Luxe, with electric lights. They came in

various finishes, including different woods, enameled coatings (crackle, satin and high gloss) and even colored keyboards. Traditionalists were appalled.

"Pianos are like perambulators. They will not go unless they are pushed." PERCY BRASTED, in *Musical Opinion and Musical Trades Review,* July 1935

Nevertheless, the Minipiano was an incredible success in both Britain and America, where Brasted had sold the manufacturing rights to the Hardman Peck company. Other companies copied and improved the design to produce, among others, the 'Minx Miniature' (see above) and the 'Ministrelle'. In France, Pleyel produced the 'Elite' and Gaveau 'le Menuet'. In Germany, Feurich was producing similar instruments.

At the other end of the scale, however, demand was not good, and manufacturers had to go to extreme lengths to maintain sales. Challen, for instance, built the massive 'Challen Giant' to celebrate George V's silver jubilee of 1935.

THOMAS MACHELL & SONS, Glasgow, c1920, Dulcitone

The 'Dulcitone' was invented by Thomas Machell in 1860, although not perfected until 1880. It is usually described as a 'tuning-fork' instrument. This five-octave example uses a down-striking version of the English grand action. The inverted action assembly can be seen on top of the casework in the picture below. The jack (or hopper) is beneath the front of the key. Each hammer strikes a U-shaped metal bar, mounted in rubber. The sound bears little relationship to that of a piano but the instrument feels similar to play. The lack of a real frame makes the Dulcitone relatively light and portable. It was the most popular of the early 'tuning-fork' instruments. Other examples included the 'Typophone', the 'Adiaphon' and the 'Euphonium'. The most famous, however, was the electric piano designed by Harold Rhodes in the late 1950s.

The Hindenburg airship was designed to replace the Graf Zeppelin on the transatlantic crossing between Frankfurt and New Jersey. The Graf Zeppelin had already made more than 140 crossings, and had carried more than 13,000 passengers. The new Hindenburg carried 50 passengers, in private cabins, at an impressive 78 miles per hour. Even so, the journey took 48 hours, so the operators felt it essential to provide entertainment for their wealthy passengers. Thus the Hindenburg included a music salon, complete with a grand piano. The piano was made by the Blüthner company to be as light as possible. As the instrument was played only to an intimate audience, the strings could be thinner and held under reduced tension. That meant the frame, usually the heaviest part of a piano, could be made from aluminum. The piano perished with the 33 passengers and crew of the Hindenburg when it crashed at Lakehurst, New Jersey, in 1937. The subsequent abandonment of airship travel meant no further pianos of that type were ever made.

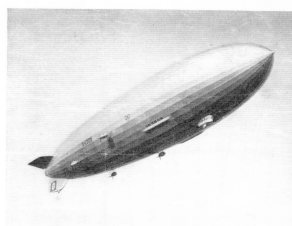

The New German Airship "Hindenburg"

with a Blüthner Grand Pianofor on boa

The Blüthner Grand Pianoforte specially made in leather and l

The eminent engineers who have been associated with the building of the new German Airship have selected the Blüthner Piano for use on their wonderful craft, as they regard the Blüthner as being the highest achievement in Pianoforte construction.

JULIUS BLÜTHNER LEIPZIG

Sole Concessionaires for Gt. Britain and the British Empire:
BLÜTHNER & CO. LTD., 17/23, WIGMORE ST. LONDON W 1

The Music Salon on the Airship showing the Blüthner Grand

ON THE MOVE

The standard piano is a bulky instrument. Moving it is not a task to be undertaken lightly, especially as this puts additional stress on the frame, necessitating the services of a piano tuner. Nevertheless, there are circumstances in which pianos have to be moved from place to place, and that has meant piano makers developing special instruments capable of withstanding such treatment. In particular, the need to provide wealthy travelers with a versatile medium for entertainment has provided the impetus for the creation of some extraordinary pianos.

Before the establishment of air travel as the principal means of mass transport, long journeys were slow affairs. Entertainment was essential to keep travelers happy during these periods of enforced leisure. By the early 20th century the piano had become ubiquitous as an accompaniment to musical and theatrical entertainments of all kinds: it was equally at home in solo performance, as an alternative to light orchestras and small instrumental groups, or for use with singers.

The steamship or ocean liner was the most widespread form of intercontinental travel in the west. Passenger ships invariably carried at least one piano. Piano makers recognized the glamour associated with sea travel and seized upon the association for promotional purposes.

With the arrival of long distance air travel, the liners turned to cruise work. However, they still needed pianos, so the makers continued to equip the on-board bars, music rooms and entertainment halls with specially designed instruments.

The great liners were not the only form of luxury long-distance transport that required entertainment. Pianos were developed that

could be accommodated on private yachts (right), trains and even airships (above). The strict weight constraints of fixed-wing aircraft design, however, ruled out the on-board use of the acoustic piano.

Piano designers soon found other solutions to the problem of making the piano more mobile. The bulkiest elements of the traditional piano are the frame and the soundboard, so it seemed obvious to try to reduce these in size or remove them altogether.

To remove the frame it was necessary to employ a different vibrating element. Various different ideas were tried, including the use of the prongs of specially designed tuning forks ('tines') and tuned metal strips ('reeds'). Although it was possible to build a keyboard instrument with an adequate dynamic response, the character of its sound was always somewhat removed from that of the acoustic piano.

Removing the soundboard meant finding some new means of amplification. This became possible with the development of the electronic amplifier, which followed the invention of the thermionic valve in the early part of the century.

WELMAR PIANOS

take music round · · the world . . .

aboard the M.V. "AUREOL"

WELMAR BABY GRAND in sycamore and burr maple installed on M.V. "AUREOL." (To the order of Messrs. Waring & Gillow.)

WELMAR PIANOS
specially designed for use on board ship, have been supplied to the following:—

★ S.S. "Nova Scotia" ★ M.V. "Derbyshire"
★ S.S. "Newfoundland" ★ M.V. "Warwickshire"
★ S.S. "El Nawk Food" ★ M.V. "Guidonia"
★ S.S. "Gothic" ★ S.S. "Princess Marguerite"
★ S.S. "Queen of Bermuda" ★ M.V. "Princess Patricia"
★ S.S. "Presidenta Peron" ★ M.V. "Angola"
★ S.S. "Empress of Scotland" ★ S.S. "Ocean Monarch"

(★ To the order of Messrs. Hampton & Sons, Ltd.)
(● To the order of Messrs. Waring & Gillow)

WHELPDALE, MAXWELL & CODD, LTD.

47 CONDUIT STREET, LONDON, W.1

SHOWROOM: GRO 7361 FACTORY: MAC 4702

WHELPDALE, MAXWELL & CODD, LTD.

47 CONDUIT STREET, LONDON, W.1

SHOWROOM: GRO 7361 FACTORY: MAC 4702

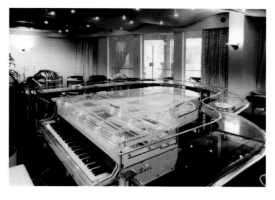

SCHIMMEL, Braunschweig, Germany, c1980, transparent grand piano

This piano is located in the lower rear bar (the 'Yacht' bar) of the liner Queen Elizabeth II. Cunard, owners of the QEII, commissioned Schimmel to produce a transparent piano to form the centerpiece of a matching bar. The frame, action and keyboard are similar to those on other Schimmel grand pianos, but the acrylic casework allows onlookers to see what is going on inside. Acrylic sheets do not have the same acoustic properties as wood, so the piano has a slightly different tone. The material is also very dense: the lid of this piano is approximately twice the weight of a traditional piano's lid. The QEII boasts at least five pianos on board at any time. The instrument shown to the left is a Chappell piano with a strengthened leg assembly to withstand ocean travel. It came from the Queen Mary, one of the QEII's predecessors.

Welmar (whose trade advertisement from 1952 is shown above) was one of the leading makers of ship pianos, equipping the British royal yacht Britannia, among others. The leg assembly of a ship piano has to withstand more stress than that of a conventional instrument: castors are replaced by bolts. Materials have to be suitable for a wide range of climates.

The folding keyboard required considerable modifications to the piano's action, making it somewhat heavy and sluggish.

The castors were removed when the piano was aboard ship to prevent any chance of accident.

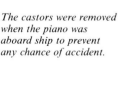

Despite its modest size, the instrument incorporated a seven-octave ($AAA - a^4$) keyboard.

When not in use, the keyboard was disconnected from the action and tilted upwards to fold neatly into the main body of the instrument.

CHAPPELL & CO, London, c1910, upright yacht piano

This small upright piano was made by the Chappell company, for use where space is at a premium. Its most notable feature is the keyboard, which can be folded up into the body of the instrument when it is not in use. This instrument was originally installed in the warship HMS Edinburgh, based in Scotland. Although known as a 'yacht piano', this type of instrument is often found in other locations, including the home. Despite its apparent advantages, however, the piano was not a great success and few were made.

THE PIANO SENSATION OF THE WORLD
at the "show place of the nation"

NEW ELECTRONIC 'MINIPIANO'

This advertisement was used to help launch the Hardman, Peck and Co Minipiano in the US in 1940. It shows three Minipianos on stage at the Radio City Music Hall in New York, and explains that each instrument, with its electronic amplification, can produce the sound of several concert grand pianos. It also suggests that the instrument is ideal for practice, since in that mode it is only audible within a radius of a few feet.

WURLITZER, Corinth, Mississippi, 1955, EP-100 electric piano

Wurlitzer's first electric piano was based on Miessner's 'stringless' piano, which used metal reeds (strips of metal anchored at one end) rather than strings. These are struck by hammers and their oscillations translated into electrical signals by a pickup. Wurlitzer enjoyed great success with different versions of this instrument. The most popular and enduring was the EP-200.

MIESSNER

Benjamin Franklin Miessner, born in 1890, worked initially in early radio. He was, however, always interested in the use of electricity in musical instruments. In 1921 he developed an electrostatic pickup for pianos and subsequently a pickup for guitars. But he also wanted to produce a small low-cost electric piano for music students. Realizing that the soundboard could be dispensed with, he developed what is known as his Electronic Piano, using an electrostatic pickup. He licensed it to at least half a dozen different piano makers across America. The pianos were relatively successful, but, with no soundboard, the decay of the bass notes produced a muddy, cluttered sound. Miessner decided to use reeds as the vibrating element, because their shape produced the desired decay characteristic. This concept, known as Miessner's 'stringless' piano, was taken up by Wurlitzer and marketed as the EP 100 (left). This was the first low cost, truly portable electric piano, made for 20 years. Although Miessner went on to produce further innovations, he will always be best-known for his contribution to the electric piano. He died in 1980.

HARDMAN PECK, New York, c1940, Minipiano (electric)

Hardman, Peck and Co licensed BF Miessner's 'electronic' piano design and fitted it into the Minipiano, which they had also licensed, this time from Brasted in England (see p71). This piano has the action and stringing of the Minipiano, but instead of a soundboard it uses a separate electrostatic pickup for each of the 88 pairs of strings. The signal is filtered, amplified and fed to built-in loudspeakers. Like many of the electric pianos of the day, the instrument also featured a radio and a gramophone, the latter built into the stool that came with it.

WURLITZER, Illinois, 1938, upright piano with electronics

This instrument was jointly developed with a German, Bruno Helberger, who had in 1928 designed the Hellertion, essentially a metal strip controlling a valve oscillator. The pitch of the note produced was dependent on where the player placed his finger. This piano incorporated a Hellertion, which makes it possible to produce glissando effects.

CLOSE TO YOU
CARPENTERS

The Carpenters: Close To You *The Carpenters used the Wurlitzer piano extensively on their 1970 album Close To You, and the single 'We've Only Just Begun'. Richard Carpenter praised the Wurlitzer's brightness and the warmth and beauty of its sound. The 1970s band Supertramp also used the Wurlitzer EP-200 for its distinctive sound.*

THE EARLY ELECTRIC PIANO

Piano makers have consistently sought to make the piano louder, to give it more sustaining power and to give it a wider range of sounds. Their starting point is an extraordinary piece of mechanical engineering. In the soundboard, the piano has its own powerful system of acoustic amplification. Many companies and individuals have tried to build on that to change the piano's character. At times mechanical additions, for instance the janissary stops of the early 19th century, have been used, or the piano has been 'prepared' in various ways. But it was the introduction of electricity that really offered possibilities for experimentation.

Towards the end of the 19th century, one focus of the piano makers' ingenuity was the way the sound of the strings decayed. Inventors went to great lengths to try to make the piano's strings continue sounding for as long as the key was held. One early method was to blow compressed air over the strings to try and sustain vibration.

Electricity proved a more effective solution. An alternating electric current was passed through electromagnets to set strings in vibration or keep them vibrating. These instruments, known as sostenente pianos, were still effectively acoustic but used electrical energy only to enhance their sound production.

The true electric piano evolved when the signal produced by a vibrating medium (a string, reed or metal rod) was turned into an electrical current for subsequent amplification. This had many advantages. The soundboard was no longer required, which meant the piano could be smaller. The absence of the soundboard also meant less damping effect on the vibrating medium, providing a sound with a slower decay. And with amplification the piano could be made much louder, although at first the quality was poor.

The electric piano owes its existence to the wireless industry, on two counts. In 1904 Sir John Fleming invented the diode valve, leading to Lee De Forest's 1906 invention of the triode. Both were essential components of radio. De Forest subsequently produced the first valve amplifier, in 1907. The development of the amplifier triggered research into methods of producing a piano-like signal that could be amplified.

"When a musical instrument is in its infancy, its musical validity is invariably subject to question. Is this so surprising?"
TOM RHEA, *Contemporary Keyboard*, January 1977.

But the radio was also of great consequence because of its effect on the home entertainment market in the early part of the century. Before radio, families had relied on the piano and automated piano for entertainment. Radio and the gramophone rapidly halved the sales of pianos. New sounds were one way for the piano industry to fight back.

The single bass strings pass under the electromagnetic pick-up at the rear in groups of five. Beneath the strings in a black box is a 3W audio amplifier.

BECHSTEIN, Berlin/Hradec Králové, 1931/2, electric grand piano

This instrument, commonly referred to as the Neo-Bechstein grand piano, was developed at Berlin University by Dr Walther Nernst and built by Bechstein and the electrical company Siemens, in Hradec Králové in what is now the Czech Republic. It has no soundboard but a series of electromagnetic pickups. The hammers are far lighter and smaller than those of a conventional instrument, and the strings are thinner and held under less tension. The sound is subtle and delicate, more akin to that of an early piano than a modern grand. The large black box in the void of the bent side is a radio. The separate amplifier unit incorporated a record player. Although the Neo-Bechstein achieved little lasting success, it marks the first major step from acoustic to electric piano.

KEY DATES

1886   **ELEKTROPHONISCHES KLAVIER**, *Richard Eisenmann* (Berlin) Early attempts to use electricity in conjunction with the acoustic piano consisted of using a current to activate the strings. Eisenmann positioned electromagnets close to the strings of the piano and these could produce an infinite sustain when a note was played. The system was fully perfected by 1913.

1891   **SOSTENENTE PIANO**, *Eugene Singer* (Paris) Singer worked along similar lines to Eisenmann, but introduced an alternating current with a frequency akin to the string it was to activate, thus achieving a more controlled effect. These are known as electromagnetic sostenente pianos.

1915   **AUDION PIANO**, *Lee De Forest* (New York) De Forest, inventor of the amplifier, developed this instrument and patented it in 1915. It was the first electronic (as opposed to electric) instrument, but doubt exists as to whether it was ever finished. It certainly was never put into commercial production.

1926   **PIANORAD**, *Hugo Gernsback* (New York) An early electronic instrument utilizing audio frequency oscillators. It had a two octave keyboard, each note of which controlled its own oscillator.

1928   **PIANO ÉLECTRIQUE**, *Joseph Béthenod* (Paris) An electric piano that used tone wheels as the sound source. These spinning serrated wheels (one per note) induce a signal in an electromagnetic pickup which is subsequently amplified.

1928-30   **NEO BECHSTEIN**, *Bechstein-Nernst-Siemens* (Berlin) A hybrid grand piano utilizing electromagnet pickups. It is probably the best known of the early electric instruments although its success was not long lasting. See main picture (left).

1930   **CREA-TONE**, *Simon Cooper* (New York) This was the most effective of the electromagnetic sostenente pianos using electrical feedback circuits to regenerate the vibration of the piano's strings. Although the Crea-Tone received a good press at the time, it failed to retain much interest.

1930   **ELECTRONIC PIANO**, *BF Miessner* (Milburn, New Jersey) An 88-note piano without a soundboard, with individual electrostatic pickups for each string. Strictly speaking an electric rather than an electronic piano. See 'BF Miessner' (left).

1931   **RADIOPIANO**, *Hiller* (Hamburg) An electric piano using struck strings amplified by electromagnetic pickups.

1931-34   **ELEKTROCHORD**, *Oskar Vierling / August Förster* (Berlin) The Elektrochord used two strings for each of all but the bottom eight notes of this grand piano-based instrument. Only one of these strings is actually hit by the hammer. The other, which is shorter and under less tension, vibrates in sympathy. This vibration is transduced using electrostatic pickups. These pickups are placed on different parts of the string to give different tonal qualities and are also set both vertically and horizontally, which leads to a wide range of timbres and attack characteristics.

1932   **SUPERPIANO**, *Emerick Spielmann* (Austria) An electronic instrument using a photoelectric effect to generate the tones. A series of spinning disks with holes is spun in front of a light source. The broken light fell on a photoelectric cell and thus generated an oscillating current. Not strictly a piano at all. However the Superpiano did offer a crude touch-responsive keyboard. The volume of each note could be determined by the depth to which the key was depressed. Again, not a successful product.

1933   **CLAVIER**, *Lloyd Loar* (Kalamazoo) An electric piano using struck reeds, marketed by Acousti-Lectric as part of its Vivi-Tone line of instruments.

c1933   **PIANOTRON (US)**, *Everett Piano Co.* (Michigan) An early combination piano, consisting of a traditional acoustic with electrostatic pickups on the strings which could be connected to an amplifier if desired.

c1935   **LAUTSPRECHERKLAVIER**, *Beier & von Dräger* An electromagnetic piano employing struck strings.

1937   **VARIACHORD**, *Dr Pollak-Rudin* (Vienna) A sostenente piano where the strings are both activated and amplified electromechanically.

1938   **ELECTONE**, *Krakauer Brothers* (New York) Designed by Maurice K Bretzfelder, and based on BF Miessner's patent. Incorporates three sets of electrostatic pickups to facilitate different timbres.

1938   **BERNHARDT ELECTRONIC PIANO**, *Bernhardt* (Canada) A licensee of the Miessner patent.

1938   **DYNATONE**, *Ansley Radio Corp.* (New York) 88-note upright electric piano designed by Arthur C Ansley, based on the Miessner patent.

1938   **PIANOTRON (UK)**, *The Selmer Co. Ltd* (London) Similar to the Hohner Pianet, using reeds that are plucked rather than hit. An electromagnetic pickup converts the reeds' vibrations into an electric current that can be amplified. Made until 1974.

1939   **MINIPIANO.** *Hardman Peck & Co.* (New York) Seven-octave upright electric based on Miessner's 1930 patent.

1939   **STORYTONE**, *Story & Clark Piano Co* (New York) A seven-octave electrostatic piano, again based on Miessner's patent. Incorporated a gramophone and a radio receiver.

1954   **PIANOPHON**, *Beleton* (Berlin) Designed for home use, the Pianophon utilized struck steel reeds as the vibrating medium. Their oscillations were transduced by electromagnetic pickups.

1955   **STRINGLESS PIANO**, *B.F. Miessner* (New Jersey) This piano employed struck reeds as opposed to strings and was used as the basic design for the Wurlitzer electric piano. See 'B.F. Miessner' (left).

1963   **RHODES PIANO**, *Harold Rhodes* (California) The classic electric piano using tines (metal rods) as the vibrating medium (see p77).

For details relating to the types of pickups detailed above please refer to pp.76-77.

KAWAI, Hamamatsu, Japan, c1983, electric grand piano

The EP-308s electric grand piano uses a traditional action to strike a set of strings and has a full 88-note compass. Instead of a soundboard the piano has three separate pickups for each string. Their output is combined to produce the desired sound. The keyboard on the top is a string synthesizer integrated into the design. The entire unit is housed in a transparent acrylic case.

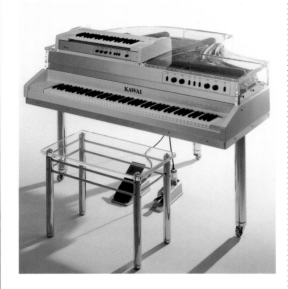

The controls on the front panel set the overall volume and tone, and add electronic tremolo if desired.

The top section of the piano, containing the strings and frame, is hinged along the back of the lower section so that it can tilt back for removal .

The Hohner Clavinet is essentially an electrified clavichord with the sound-board replaced by an electromagnetic pickup. The simple action has the tangent mounted under the key. The instrument shown is the Clavinet I of 1964. The most widely used model was the D6, which has a bright, percussive sound.

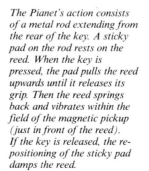

HOHNER, Trossingen, Germany, 1962, electric reed piano

The Pianet L (right) was designed by Ernst Zacharias, who was also responsible for the Hohner Clavinet and Cembalet. All were important electric keyboards. The Pianet uses metal reeds as the vibrating medium. These are not struck, however, but plucked (see below). Strictly speaking that makes the instrument an electric reed harpsichord, but history and its sound have branded it a type of electric piano. The Pianet L was the first of Hohner's Pianet range. The most popular was the Pianet T (from the mid 1970s), perhaps because it was the cheapest worthwhile electric keyboard on the market.

The CP-80, in common with most electric pianos, has a single pedal, which is used for raising the dampers.

FROM ELECTRIC TO ELECTRONIC

The history of the piano is filled with confusions over terminology, and the era of the electric and electronic instruments is no exception. The term 'electric piano' is often used to describe any keyboard instrument that uses electricity and produces piano-like sounds. But a distinction should be made between simple 'electric' pianos, whose sound derives from a physically vibrating element, and 'electronic' pianos, where the sound is generated by circuitry without the use of moving parts.

The Pianet's action consists of a metal rod extending from the rear of the key. A sticky pad on the rod rests on the reed. When the key is pressed, the pad pulls the reed upwards until it releases its grip. Then the reed springs back and vibrates within the field of the magnetic pickup (just in front of the reed). If the key is released, the re-positioning of the sticky pad damps the reed.

YAMAHA, Hamamatsu, Japan, 1978/9, electric grand piano

This is an 88-note CP-80 electric grand piano, based on the 73-note CP-70 produced by Yamaha in 1976-77. The later model operates on low voltages for reasons of safety: a mains transformer is supplied. The strings, which are considerably shorter than they are in a conventional acoustic instrument, are located, along with the frame, in the top half of the piano. This can easily be separated from the lower section, containing the action and the keyboard, for ease of transportation. As the strings are shorter than usual, they are made thicker, and this gives rise to the characteristically 'twangy' bass notes of this piano. The CP-70 and CP-80 were extremely popular instruments, especially for touring members of bands.

HAROLD RHODES

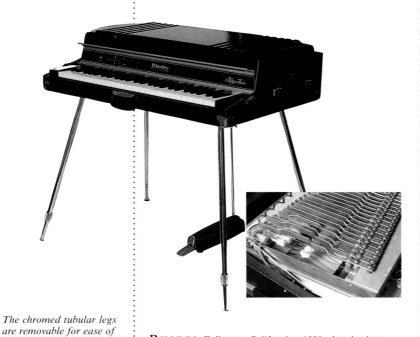

Harold Rhodes was born in 1910. In 1942, he devised the 'Air Corps Piano' for wounded airmen to play in hospital. In 1947, he launched the 'Pre-Piano', using tines (metal rods forming one half of a tuning fork) as the vibrating medium. It failed through poor manufacture. Later Rhodes showed guitar maker Leo Fender a 72-note piano built into a case, before joining the Fender company in 1955. But only the 32-note Piano Bass made it into production. When CBS took over Fender in 1965, Rhodes was finally given the opportunity to manufacture his 73-note and 88-note electric pianos, both using the tine system. Production ended in 1981.

Rocky Mount Instruments produced in 1967 the Rock-Si-Chord, an electronic keyboard. It was followed by the popular RMI Electra Piano, an all-electronic piano used by Steve Winwood, Ray Manzarek and others. The instrument shown is the later 668X.

SELMER, London, c1950, Clavioline

The Clavioline was designed to fit under a piano keyboard to provide the pianist with an alternative sound. A three-octave mini-keyboard (with a smaller octave span than a normal keyboard) controls a monophonic electronic oscillator. A bank of 18 rocker switches selects different timbres and there are stops for introducing vibrato. A knee lever can also control pitch changes. The Clavioline was invented in France in 1947 by Constant Martin and licensed to, among others, Selmer and Gibson. It was redesigned by Harald Bode in 1953 and marketed as the Combichord. The loudspeaker and amplifier are separate.

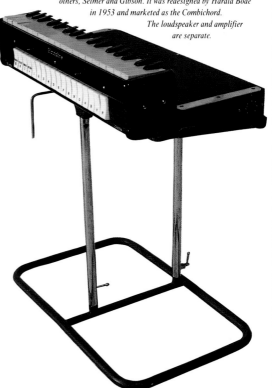

The chromed tubular legs are removable for ease of transportation.

RHODES, Fullerton, California, c1980, electric piano

The Stage 54 is a 54-note flat-topped variant of the familiar Stage 73 and Stage 88 pianos. It was the last of the Rhodes electro-mechanical pianos to be made, and was to have been produced in bass, middle and treble versions. The inset picture shows the tine mechanism. The rod hits the hammer and its vibrations are turned into electrical signals by the pickup at the end of the tine. Altering the position of the tine relative to the pickup can completely change the piano's tone. The tine is fine-tuned by moving a small spring down its length.

The electric piano (also known as the 'electroacoustic' or 'electromechanical' piano) uses a hammer to strike a mechanical medium such as a string or a reed, causing it to vibrate. A pickup turns these vibrations into electrical signals which are amplified.

"The all-electric [electronic] type of instrument has greater future possibilities, than the other [electric], which, after all, only presents a compromise."
Amateur Wireless, 7th October 1933

Various means have been used to induce these signals. In the 'electromagnetic' pickup, the vibrating medium disturbs a magnetic field. In the 'electrostatic' pickup, the vibrating medium varies the capacitance in a circuit. A 'photoelectric' pickup uses the vibrating medium to alter the amount of light falling on a photoelectric cell. The 'piezoelectric' pickup uses a crystalline or ceramic material that responds electrically to mechanical movements. The 'electro-acoustic' pickup is effectively a microphone.

With all these pickups, the frequency of the electrical signal mirrors the frequency of the vibrating medium. With appropriate positioning of the pickup and electronic filtering and amplification, a piano-like tone can be produced.

ELECTRONIC PIANOS

An electronic instrument uses circuitry, rather than a mechanical element, to generate an oscillating signal. The sound of a piano, however, is more complex. Each note changes amplitude and timbre from the moment it is struck. Producing an electronic facsimile of this proved difficult. However, World War II led to an upsurge in research in electronics, culminating in the 1947 invention of the transistor. By the early 1960s, the electronic piano was commercially viable. Early examples used the keys purely as switches to 'activate' the note.

The electronic piano has more stable tuning than the electric instrument. It is smaller, lighter and virtually silent when used for practice with headphones. However, many musicians continue to prefer the sound of the electric instrument.

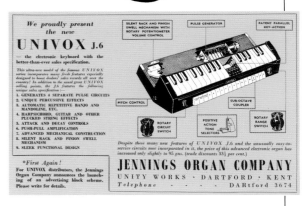

The Univox was similar in concept to the Clavioline, but featured a more advanced type of keyboard which could respond to the way in which the keys were played, opening up new avenues of expression. Other manufacturers introduced similar monophonic piano attachments in order to extend the range of the piano. Most notable were the Solovox, produced by the Hammond Organ Company, and the Clavioline (above).

KORG, Japan, 1994, digital home piano

The C303 is a typical digital piano from the Japanese manufacturer Korg. It uses digital samples of real acoustic pianos to create an authentic piano sound, delivered by the built-in loudspeakers. Adding more sounds is simply a case of loading more samples into the instrument's computer memory. In this case they include harpsichord, vibes, strings, and pipe organ. An additional advantage of this digital piano over its acoustic counterparts is that it can be instantly re-tuned: either into a different key or in terms of actual temperament.

Concert for Anarchy (1990) Since the early days of the piano, the instrument has been a canvas for artists. Great furniture makers have designed pianos in their own styles. And pianos have appeared in many significant paintings, usually as props in historical portraits. But the piano can also become a piece of art in its own right, no longer a musical instrument but a work intended to provoke thought, create debate and serve as a medium for expression. In this instance, the American artist Rebecca Horn has taken a grand piano, turned it upside down and suspended it high in the air. As observers pass beneath the instrument, the piano appears to explode above them, with the keys and workings of the instrument expelled from within the piano's frame. The piano then re-assembles itself and the cycle repeats. First shown in 1990, this work is entitled Concert for Anarchy.

ROLAND, Japan, 1993, digital stage piano

The 88-note RD-500 digital piano has neither speakers nor console. It is designed for use on stage, in a studio or as part of a MIDI-based music production facility. The keyboard is weighted to approximate the feel of a conventional action. Facilities are provided to manipulate the wide range of sounds available and to determine the response of the instrument's keyboard.

The Showmaster uses small but advanced pickups mounted on the soundboard, and these faithfully reproduce the timbral nuances of the piano.

RECENT TIMES

Popular music and the instruments employed to produce it invariably reflect the technology of the day. In recent times, the musical instrument industry has been quick to incorporate new ideas and technological advances. Computer technology and digital electronics are among the most rapidly changing fields of science, and their innovations are of increasing importance in the world of musical instrument design. The modern electronic piano works entirely in the digital domain, a world in which sound is processed as just another kind of numerical data.

Sound can be recorded and stored as a series of electrical pulses representing binary numbers. A digital piano has built into it recorded 'samples' of the sound of an acoustic grand piano. There may be more than 16 different samples (covering the range of *ppp* to *fff*) for each note.

When a key of the digital piano is played, the instrument's microprocessor selects the relevant sample. This is subsequently converted from numerical form back into sound and amplified.

As increasingly powerful processors became available, the concept of 'physical modeling' has evolved. The player selects the type of piano he wants. The piano has been 'taught' the characteristics of that type of piano and applies that type of shaping or 'modeling' to the notes being played. The result is intended to be a faithful recreation of the instrument being modeled. This requires considerable computing power but such instruments are becoming increasingly feasible.

The Musical Instrument Digital Interface (MIDI) is a somewhat simpler use of computer technology. Developed in the early 1980s, primarily by the Roland Corporation of Japan and

Sequential Circuits of the USA, it allows electronic musical instruments to communicate with one another.

In its simplest mode MIDI allows one instrument to control one or more others. An electronic piano could be linked to a string synthesizer, for instance, so that when the piano's keyboard is played both instruments sound. MIDI also allows communication with a computer. The musician can play music 'into' the computer, edit and correct it using a program akin to a word processor, and then listen to it being played back.

PRACTICE PIANOS

One interesting recent development is the 'silent' or 'practice' piano. Sensors are connected to each key of an acoustic instrument which record how the key is played. This information is turned into a MIDI signal and used to drive an electronic piano sound module. A rail is then positioned to prevent the piano's hammers from striking the strings. The player listens to the output of the sound module on headphones while the acoustic piano remains silent.

The piano has a normal soundboard, and can be played acoustically like a traditional piano. However it also has MIDI and audio signal outputs which vastly extend its potential.

TRIMPIN, Seattle, USA, 1990, MIDI-controlled prepared piano

Inventor and composer Trimpin built the Contraption IPP 71512 to extend the timbral range of the piano, in a similar way to those who modify or 'prepare'

pianos. Instead of simply striking the strings with hammers, Trimpin's Contraption mechanically bows, plucks and strikes the strings with all manner of different devices, producing sounds never heard before from a piano. The IPP (Instant Prepared Piano) 71512 is controlled by computer via a MIDI link. The music is composed within the computer, which subsequently sends commands to four rotating tracks which can be positioned at specified locations to lower various mechanisms to 'activate' the strings. The photograph below shows part of these tracks, with various mechanisms for exciting the strings mounted on them. The instrument can still be played from the keyboard, by hand, or by a special piano adapter which directs the mechanism on to the strings without the use of the computer.

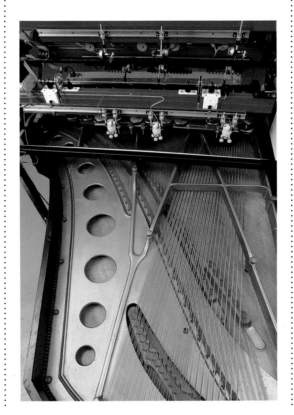

KLAVINS, Bonn, Germany, 1988, upright piano ✳

Believed to be the largest stringed instrument in the world, the Klavins Model 370 was initially built as an experimental instrument designed to obviate the compromises of the modern piano. The instrument stands 12 ft 1½ in tall, enabling it to be straight strung and houses a bottom bass string of about 10 ft in length. This reduces inharmonicity and gives a more natural sound. The soundboard has a surface area of more than four square yards, and is mounted vertically, thus projecting the sound towards the audience rather than the ceiling. The strings exert a total force of more than 27 tons. This instrument bears certain similarities to the Tribune piano (p50).

__Michael Ponti__ plays the Klavins Model 370 on this extremely interesting recording of works by Liszt, Chopin, and Mussorgsky. The depth and clarity of the Klavins' bass strings are particularly well demonstrated in Ponti's rendition of __Pictures At An Exhibition__.

SEILER, Kitzingen, Germany, 1992, electric upright piano

The Showmaster Junior 114 is a stylized 88-note upright piano designed primarily for stage and television use. It features a MIDI contact bar which measures the movement of the keys and produces a MIDI control signal. The piano's keyboard can therefore be used to play remote electronic sound modules. A control panel above the keyboard configures the MIDI set-up. The piano also has pick-ups mounted on the soundboard which provide an accurate signal that can be amplified or recorded.

ASTIN-WEIGHT, Salt Lake City, USA, c1980, upright piano

The picture (left) shows the unique Astin-Weight frame assembly. Traditionally the soundboard of an upright piano butts up along the edge of the pin block. However Astin-Weight has designed its uprights so that the soundboard sits behind the pin block, permitting a soundboard that is 15 per cent larger than normal. This produces a 'bigger' sound. To achieve this the bridge has to be deeper, giving the piano its own unique sound. Astin-Weight pianos use a full perimeter cast-iron frame, with no supporting back posts. Innovations such as these show that the development of the piano carries on.

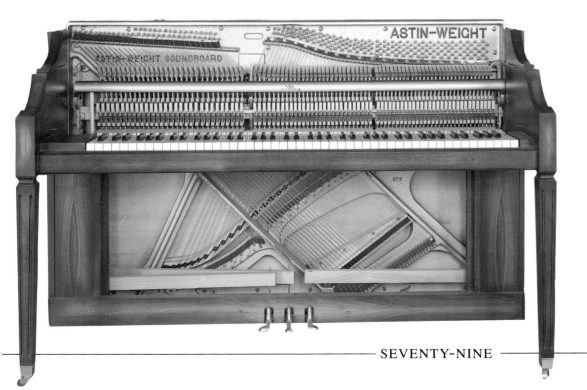

The model on the left shows a piano action largely made of plastic. Plastic actions first appeared in the 1940s, but before 1960 the material was unreliable. On more modern instruments the use of plastic improves uniformity across the compass of the keyboard, but despite the advantages many feel it destroys the character of the piano.

✳ *For information on recordings on this instrument, see Pianos on Record, p104.*

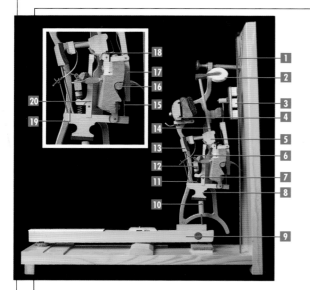

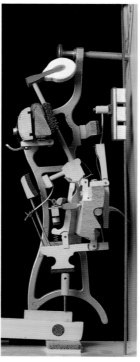

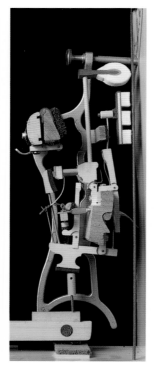

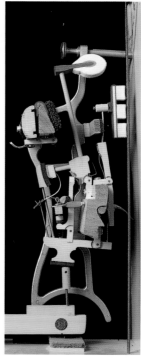

The modern upright action *The Bösendorfer Model 130 uses an action that is typical of most upright pianos. It is surprisingly close in design to Robert Wornum's tape-check action of 1842. It is made for the Bösendorfer company by Louis Renner GmbH.*

1 string	**11** repetition spring
2 hammer	**12** set-off button
3 damper head	**13** check
4 hammer rest rail	**14** hammer shank
5 hammer butt	**15** damper spoon
6 bridle strap	**16** damper rod
7 toe	**17** damper body
8 wippen	**18** knotch
9 key	**19** bridle wire
10 pilot (capstan screw)	**20** jack

*At rest The **hammer (2)** and **hammer shank (14)** are supported by the **hammer rest rail (4)**. The top of the **jack (20)** is located in the **notch (18)** of the **hammer butt (5)**. As the **key (9)** is depressed, the **pilot** or **capstan screw (10)** pushes up on the **wippen (8)**. This causes the jack to push up on the notch and propels the hammer towards the **string (1)**. At the same time the end of the wippen nearest the string falls slightly causing the **damper spoon (15)** to push the **damper body (17)**, lifting the **damper head (3)** away from the string.*

*Hammer strikes string Just before the hammer reaches the string, the **toe (7)** of the jack encounters the **set-off button (12)** which flicks the jack out of the notch, leaving the hammer moving towards the string under its own momentum. The hammer strikes the string and bounces back, aided by the **bridle strap (6)**, which is anchored to the wippen by the **bridle wire (19)** and is instantaneously tautened.*

*Hammer in check The hammer is then caught by the **check (13)**, which prevents the hammer from bouncing back and re-striking the strings. The key at this point is still held, and the therefore the damper remains off the string.*

*Key released As the key is partially released, the wippen lowers and this free the jack from the check. Further lowering of the key allows the jack, with the ai of the **repetition spring (11** to relocate in the notch. Th note can now be played again, albeit with less powe Only when the key is fully released will the action retu to its initial position with t damper on the string.*

THE MODERN UPRIGHT PIANO

The Model 130 Studio is a high quality, hand-built upright, made to the highest standards by Bösendorfer in Vienna. This instrument is considered to be one of the very best upright pianos in production.

In construction it is similar to many modern upright instruments. However, the quality of its manufacture, design and scaling make it among the most sought-after of pianos for studio, live performance and domestic purposes.

The Model 130 Studio has been made by Bösendorfer since 1978. It was restyled in March 1995, when longer keys were fitted to improve the response of the keyboard, and was subsequently renamed the Model 130 Classic.

The piano takes its name from its height: 130 cm or 51 in. It is 60 in wide and 25 in deep. Until 1995, Bösendorfer made a standard Model 130 as well as this Model 130 Studio. The difference was in the casework: the Model 130 had a more rounded console shape and was without columns 'supporting' the keyboard.

Bösendorfer produces only about 30 of this model each year. Some 80 per cent of the instrument is made by hand and each piano takes approximately a year to manufacture.

The main advantage of the upright piano over the grand piano is simply that of size. This upright piano occupies just over 10 sq ft of floor-space, whereas the Steinway Model D grand piano (on page 61) takes up approximately 45 sq ft. The disadvantage is the shorter string lengths, which produce less sound output and generally an inferior tone. The longest bass string (AAA) of the

Model 130 upright measures just under 50¾ in, compared to the Steinway's 79¼ in.

The other inherent difference between the upright and the grand is in the action. The grand piano can take a much longer key than the upright. Consequently its action has a much more controlled response.

OTHER MODERN UPRIGHTS

The Bösendorfer Model 130 at 51 inches in height is typical of the larger modern upright piano. The terms 'spinet' and 'console' are often used in connection with the upright piano, especially in America. A modern spinet piano will be between 36 in and 38 in high, while a console will measure between 38 in and 43 in. Above that height come standard uprights. To confuse matters further, however, in America upright pianos of between 43 in and 47 in are sometimes referred so as 'studio pianos'.

All except the smaller spinet piano use the standard upright action, though in the case of the console it is somewhat compressed. The spinet piano uses a drop action.

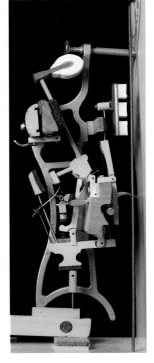

Frame: The single piece cast-iron frame is rubbed down, filled, sprayed with several coats of bronze spray and then lacquered.

Action: Few companies actually produce their own actions. Bösendorfer contract Louis Renner GmbH, one of the world's largest manufacturers of piano parts, to build its actions to its designs.

...blow This illustrates ...happens when, without ...ey being played, the ...low (soft) pedal is ...ssed. This causes the ...low rail to tilt forward, ...ing the hammer closer ... string. Thus when a ... is played, the hammer ...ble to attain the same ...ity at impact with the ... and the note sounds ... quietly.

Damper Again the action is at rest, but this time the damper pedal has been pressed and held. This causes the **damper rod (16)** to move down and out against the damper body, lifting the damper from the strings. When the pedal is released, the damper is lowered back onto the strings.

Keyboard: The keyboard spans the standard 7⅓ octaves, $AAA - a^5$. The keys are made of spruce and covered with a polymer called 'ivorine', a modern substitute for ivory.

Finish: The instrument has a 1 mm coat of black polyester finish applied to it. This is subsequently cut back to approximately 0.5 mm for a deep gloss appearance.

Soundboard: The soundboard is spruce, with the grain running parallel to the long bridge. To support the soundboard and to help spread the sound energy evenly over its surface, 12 spruce ribs (or belly bars) are set on its back at 90 degrees to the grain.

Hardware: All the hardware - the castors, locks and pedals - is made of solid brass.

Pedals: This Model 130 Studio has the standard two pedals. The left is the 'half blow' (soft) pedal, the right lifts the dampers.

BÖSENDORFER, Vienna, 1978-95, upright piano

Bösendorfer only makes two sizes of upright piano, the smaller Model 120 and this one, the Model 130. Few modern uprights are made with such care and attention to detail as the Bösendorfer. Exceptional care is taken with wood, for instance. Most makers speed up the seasoning process by drying their wood in kilns. Bösendorfer stores its raw timber outside for several years and then places it in a slow drying room for at least another 12 months before using it in manufacture. Such care is reflected in the piano's price. But this instrument shows that a modern piano can be comparable to any handmade piano in history.

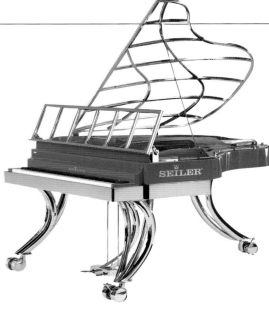

SEILER, Kitzingen, Germany, c1987, grand piano

This unusually styled grand piano, known as the Showmaster SM 180, is the parent of the Showmaster Junior 114 upright shown on page 79. The piano functions as a normal piano, with a traditional soundboard and action. However, it is designed to be easily modified to accept contact pickups, mounted on the soundboard. In addition a MIDI contact bar and control panel (not shown on this instrument) can be fitted for controlling other electronic sound modules if desired.

BALDWIN, Cincinnati, 1984, grand piano

Liberace, with his outrageously flamboyant style, became arguably the best known popular pianist of the 20th century. He idolized and in many ways imitated the great pianist, Paderewski. Wladziu Valentino Liberace was loved and loathed. The Musical Courier *said of him in 1954, "When a first-rate artist or musical ensemble has difficulty in filling a modest sized auditorium, and a third-rate pianist with a 'corny' line and a few bad dance steps captivates the nation, then it is high time for a national cultural appraisal …" Originally Liberace had a Baldwin SF-10 grand piano which he'd had covered with Austrian rhinestones. He called this his "Super Piano" and used it for his Radio City Music Hall appearances. The stage set would be black and the piano would be bathed in white light while he played it on a revolving dais. The effect was stunning. However, Liberace found the SF-10 hard to play for long periods of time, because of its*

action, and subsequently replaced it with a 9 ft Baldwin SD-10 (pictured right). This piano came from Baldwin's "Artist Service" collection of select instruments, and had been used in the past by many Baldwin Artists including George Shearing, Michael Tilson Thomas and Leonard Bernstein. Liberace called it his new "Super Piano". The instrument was again covered with Austrian rhinestones, this time weighing almost 200 lbs. Such was the extra weight on the lid that a second 'glass' lid prop was added. Authentic rhinestones are a rock crystallite found in or near the River Rhine. However the term has come to be more widely used to describe any artificial gem, of paste or glass, which sparkles like a diamond. Liberace used rhinestones not only on his piano but also his stage clothes and, of course, in his jewelry. Such was his impact on the rhinestone industry that the Austrian rhinestone suppliers awarded him with an enormous rhinestone, supposedly the world's largest, in recognition of his services to the industry. Liberace nearly always used Baldwin pianos for his shows, because Baldwin was the first company to provide him with a piano, even though at the time he was virtually unknown. Liberace used to say that Mr Steinway had come to one of his concerts and had subsequently joked with the press that Liberace had sold more of the company's pianos than anyone else.

KAWAI, Hamamatsu, Japan, from c1980, grand piano

'See-through' pianos have been made since the beginning of the 20th century. In 1929 the French modernist designer Pierre Legrain built a famous instrument using large panels of glass. Kawai, and Schimmel in Germany, are the two major manufacturers of this type of piano. Kawai originally built this, the CR-40N 'see-through' grand, for use at trade fairs, to show in detail the internal workings of their grand pianos. However, such was the response that the company started to make available the instruments by special order. The transparent elements, like those of the Schimmel piano on board the Queen Elizabeth II (see p72), are made of an acrylic material capable of supporting the considerable weight and stress imposed by the workings of the grand piano.

YAMAHA, Hamamatsu, Japan, 1987, grand piano

The Yamaha 'Centenary' piano shown above was built to celebrate the company's 100th Anniversary. Torakusu Yamaha built his first organ in 1887. One hundred years later Yamaha had become the world's largest manufacturer of musical instruments. Strictly speaking, however, the first Yamaha company wasn't founded until 1889.

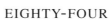

STEINWAY & SONS, New York, 1990, grand piano

The distinguishing feature of this instrument, which is based on a Model L, is the exquisite marquetry on the casework. Marqueteur Silas Kopf and cabinetmaker Tim Faner were commissioned by Steinway to produce the instrument, which is known as 'Vines of Morning Glories'. It features a frieze, showing a band of morning glories with vines and leaves, made from holly, walnut, mahogany and cherry veneers on a walnut burl veneer background. This prototype for a limited edition was given the serial number 500,001.

STEINWAY & SONS, New York, 1987, grand piano

In 1987, New York designer Wendell Castle was commissioned to produce the piano that was to bear the serial number 500,000 and celebrate Steinway's 135th birthday. The unusually shaped grand is embellished with the signatures of all the 'Steinway Artists' then living. These are engraved on exotic wood veneers and arranged in a diagonal pattern on the casework of the instrument. The piano was unveiled at a gala concert at Carnegie Hall, at which many of the artists performed.

THE SECOND WHITE HOUSE PIANO

In 1938, Steinway & Sons built the piano below and gave it the serial number 300,000. It was given to the American people and placed in the White House, where it replaced the 1903 Steinway, serial number 100,000 (see p66). It was presented to President Franklin Delano Roosevelt by Theodore Steinway on December 11th 1938. The piano case is made of Honduran mahogany and was designed by the New York architect Eric Gugler, who chose a square form rather than the more traditional 'S'-shaped or double curved bent side. The workings of the instrument are the same as a Model D but its casework makes it some seven inches longer than normal. Along the side of the instrument are vignettes, in gold leaf, representing traditional American musical forms. These were created by Dunbar Beck and show 'The New England Barn Dance'; 'The Song of the Cowboy'; 'The Virginia Reel'; 'The Song of the Black Slave'; and 'The Chant of the American Indian'. This impressive instrument stands on three gilded mahogany legs in

the shape of golden eagles, carved by Albert Stewart. President Roosevelt commented that he found them more ornithologically accurate than the eagles on the 1903 White House piano. The piano is normally used in the East Room of the White House. In 1979 it was found to be suffering somewhat in its high profile location and it was returned to Steinway & Sons for reconditioning.

20TH CENTURY INSTRUMENTS OF SIGNIFICANCE

Since the middle of the 20th century, the impact of technology on the traditional 'acoustic' piano has shown itself most clearly in the casework. The extraordinary art-case pianos of the turn of the century were unique individual creations. Now, however, improvements in materials and manufacturing technology have made it possible for visually stunning designs to be produced in greater numbers and on commercial production lines.

There will always be a demand for 'one-off' instruments, such as the remarkable Steinway pianos, designed by Wendell Castle, that are shown on these pages. The White House Steinway (the second to bear the name) is another example of an instrument created for a special purpose, in this case for presentation as a gift to the American people.

In the past it was neither economical nor practical to use these esoteric pianos as the basis for production instruments. Nowadays, however, new materials and computer-controlled machining techniques have made it possible to produce unusual designs in small numbers without costs reaching astronomical levels, as the Seiler and Hollein pianos here demonstrate.

One thing that virtually all the highly-decorated pianos on these pages share is the fact that they are based on standard components. The White House piano is a Model D; the 'Vines of Morning Glories' piano is a Model L; Liberace's Baldwin is an SD-10; Yamaha's 'The Moon and the Piano' instrument is a CF-11S and so on. By taking established piano assemblies and building them into special housings, costs can be controlled.

The future of the acoustic piano lies in producing instruments that customers both enjoy playing and find aesthetically pleasing. In the home, the standard wooden box may be becoming an anachronism, so manufacturers are looking for new ways of dealing with the instrument as a piece of furniture. The elegant simplicity of David Linley's design (far right) is one approach: using more color to produce a sense of fun is another.

"I think [the piano] has a future as furniture, or as durable goods for investment." FREDERIC RZEWSKI (pianist/composer), in *Keyboard*, December 1985

There will always be demand for the traditional, high quality, classical style of piano, but that is only part of the market. As sales of pianos shrink, manufacturers are bound to experiment with bolder designs. Many will dismiss these as gimmicks, but if they stimulate interest and sales they are helping to secure the instrument's future.

Bösendorfer Imperial
Bösendorfer's most famous instrument is the Imperial grand piano, built in Vienna since 1892. Its compass (CCC – c⁵) is nine notes wider than the 88 notes of the standard grand. The extra keys were originally added at the request of the Italian composer Ferruccio Busoni, who was transcribing Bach's Passacaglia in C minor *and found that he needed the bottom C. The extra nine notes, both naturals and accidentals, are black. This means that only the normal compass is immediately visible.*

Panels: *All body panels are made of 12 mm (½ in) laminated maple.*

Strings: *The strings are made of steel, and the bass strings are wound with pure copper. Single stringing is used for AAA – GG♯, double stringing for AA – B, and the remaining strings are triple strung.*

Bridges: *In the bass and tenor sections the bridges are made of a single piece of solid maple. However in the treble, the bridges are capped, also with maple.*

1 key block	**14** short (bass) bridge	**27** back half
2 lock rail	**15** hitch pins	**28** tuning pins
3 toe(s)	**16** columns	**29** half top
4 lock	**17** balance pin	**30** half-blow rail
5 side stick	**18** cheek	**31** hammer checks
6 soundboard (part)	**19** key weights	**32** bridle wire
7 long bridge	**20** pilot wire	**33** hammer rest rail
8 pedal rocker	**21** pilot (capstan screw)	**34** frame
9 half-blow (soft) pedal	**22** action standard	**35** hammers
10 damper pedal	**23** treble end	**36** bass end
11 key	**24** treble strings	**37** half-blow crank
12 bat (front) pin	**25** action rail	
13 bass strings	**26** agraffes	

HOW A PIANO WORKS: 1

Despite the many different types of acoustic piano, all create their basic sound from a set of strings which vibrate when hit by hammers. In fact there are three main sections that work together to produce the sound of a piano: the 'sound generators'; the 'amplifiers'; and the 'mechanism'.

The piano's 'sound generators' are the strings, the oscillations of which determine the pitch, harmonic content and relative amplitude (volume) of the final sound. The 'amplifiers' are the soundboard and other parts of the body of the instrument which together take the energy of the vibrating strings and amplify them to produce the sound we perceive as that of a piano. And the 'mechanism' is the part that turns an action by the player such as the pressing of keys into the desired vibrations of the strings, a job jointly undertaken by the keyboard (see p92) and the piano action.

WHAT IS SOUND?

Before we can understand how a piano produces its unique sound, it will be useful to know a little about how sound works.

Sound is the sensation we experience when our ears detect vibrations or changes in air pressure. The air around us is made up of billions of microscopic particles that form the atmosphere of our planet, and it is these particles that transmit sound from a source to our ear.

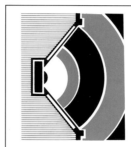

Loudspeaker *(left)*
The diagram represents waves of rarefied and compressed air radiating sound from a loudspeaker cone.

The simplest way to illustrate how sound is transmitted is to consider a loudspeaker (see diagram above). If you were to remove the cover of the speaker and then play some music through it you would see that the cone of the speaker oscillates back and forth. (This is easier to see when playing very low-frequency sustained bass notes, for example from the recording of a church organ.)

As the cone moves forward, the air particles in front of the speaker are compressed. The cone then moves back into the speaker causing 'rarefaction', where the air particles become less densely packed. Meanwhile the original compression has caused adjacent air particles to become compressed. These are then rarefied, and the process of compression and rarefaction continues as the sound radiates from the speaker.

Note that the air particles themselves do not move from source to listener, but move back and forth over a small space causing compressions and rarefactions; it is these 'waves' of compressions and rarefactions that move. A common analogy is the effect of dropping a stone into a pond. As a stone enters the pond an immediate displacement of liquid causes nearby water to rise above the normal level, then to fall, and so on. The water does not actually move out away from the point of the stone's impact. The undulating waves produced are simply peaks and troughs on the surface, analogous to compressions and rarefactions of air particles.

At the receiving end of the sound process, each of your ears acts like a loudspeaker in reverse. The changes in air pressure cause a membrane within the ear to move back and forth, and this movement is subsequently translated into minute electrical pulses which are transmitted via the auditory nerve to the brain, where they are interpreted as sound.

Sound can only be transmitted through a medium with a molecular structure – which is why sound will not travel through the vacuum of outer space. Sound does travel through gases, such as air or hydrogen, liquids, such as water, and solids, such as metal or wood. Thus the sound of a piano is produced by the transmission of sound not only through air but also through solid material, most significantly the wood of the piano's bridge and soundboard.

STRINGS

A piano manufacturer designing a new instrument strives for a harmonious combination of a large number of disparate qualities, such as: a good tone; as much volume as possible; as much sustain as possible; an instrument of sensible dimensions.

All of these elements are especially affected by the manufacturer's choice of strings, which are crucial to the sound and tone of the instrument. Many different types of piano strings have been developed over the years, principally because of

the large number of different design elements that can be adopted. The string maker can modify the string's material structure (wound or unwound), thickness, length and applied tension.

The top string of a seven-octave grand piano has a 'speaking length' (the portion of string that is struck by the hammer and is free to vibrate) of around two-and-a-half inches. If all the strings were under the same tension and made of the same material as that top string, the piano would need to be approximately 24ft long to accommodate the lowest-pitched string. Obviously this is not practical, and alternative solutions have to be found.

Manufacturers must combine strings of different lengths and thicknesses in order to build pianos of a manageable size, and there are a number of techniques that can be used to lower the pitch of a vibrating string. It is possible to do this by: decreasing the tension applied to it; making it thicker; making it longer; or making it of a material with a greater density.

STRING TENSION

The greater the tension of the string, the better the sound quality and the louder the instrument. These two qualities are high on the list of those sought by manufacturers and players alike. When the iron plate arrived in the early 19th century and made higher string tension a practical proposition there was a notable improvement in the performance of the piano.

In order to maintain stability and to maximize the overall tension that the piano's framework can handle it has always been necessary for piano makers to design instruments with as uniform a tension as possible across the piano's compass, or span. Each string of a square piano with a wooden frame is under approximately 80lbs of tension, while each string of a modern grand piano is under a force closer to 200lbs. By comparison, each string of an acoustic guitar is under only 10 to 15lbs of tension.

In fact, the frame of a modern grand piano has to withstand a total pulling force of up to 30 tons, while the strings of an upright piano can apply a pull of around 18 tons. It follows that the strength of the frame and backposts of a modern piano will determine the amount of tension that can be applied to a string, and pianos are designed with the string tension essentially fixed. (Relatively small changes in the tension are of course made when tuning the strings.)

STRING THICKNESS AND DENSITY

A thicker string will vibrate at a lower rate than a thin string, and as a consequence will have a lower pitch. Manufacturers therefore use progressively thicker strings as the required pitch becomes lower.

The massive lid is made of clear acrylic material some ¾ in thick.

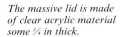

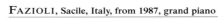

RAMEAU, Paris, 1993, upright piano

This modern piano, from the French manufacturer Rameau, is based on a design by Christian Adam, and is called 'Aurore'. The split top reflects the design of the 'butterfly' grand pianos of the mid 20th century. These were symmetrical in shape, with the lid hinged along the middle. This instrument uses a spruce soundboard with the casework finished in a vibrant red polyester. It also features a third pedal, which is a mute.

LINLEY, London, 1987, upright piano

David Linley's prestigious furniture manufacturing company produced this upright piano in 1987. The mechanics of the piano are based on a contemporary Broadwood design, thought to have been assembled by Kemble Pianos. David Linley Furniture subsequently produced this extremely elegant and stylish design using sycamore with inlays of ebony. A special type of sycamore, known as ripple-sycamore, was chosen for the casework. The wood is specially selected with a ripple feature in the grain, and is carefully matched in a herringbone pattern. Such top-quality sycamore has to be cut at a specific time of year in order to prevent the tree's pink sap from marring the pure white coloration of the wood. The casework is finally lacquered to preserve the wood's qualities.

FAZIOLI, Sacile, Italy, from 1987, grand piano

This instrument has the distinction of being the largest grand piano made commercially in the world today. It is also considered to be one of the very best. The Model F308 is made by Fazioli in Italy and measures, as the name implies, 308 cm (10 ft 2in) in length. It also weighs a massive 1518 lb, which is two-thirds of a ton. One unusual feature of this Fazioli are the four pedals: damper; sostenuto; a soft pedal, which brings the hammers closer to the strings; and una corda. Fazioli, despite having only been established since 1978, has earned such a reputation for quality that it is classed among the top three piano makers.

STEINWAY & SONS, New York, 1989, upright piano

This is another design from the leading New York artist and craftsman Wendell Castle. He has designed the best art-case pianos of recent years, including the Steinway (serial no. 500,000) shown on the far left. Castle has taken a standard Steinway upright piano and transformed it into this remarkable creation which he calls 'Ivory Spirit'. The piano has a highly 'streamlined' form, which attempts to get away from the traditional boxy shape of the upright. The chair forms part of the overall design, mirroring on a smaller scale the shape of the piano: its seat protrudes in a way that reflects the emergence of the keyboard from the piano's wedge-shaped body. Castle's name for the piano is apt, and is intended as an homage to the elephants killed as a result of the demand for ivory to cover piano keys. The instrument resembles the shape of an elephant's tusk, and also, by using sycamore in a similar way to the Linley piano (above), it has a creamy ivory-like color.

YAMAHA, Hamamatsu, Japan, 1991, grand piano

This startling instrument was designed by Yamaha for Tetsuya Komoro of the Japanese band TMN. It expresses a theme: 'The Moon and the Piano'. The idea is that the instrument should "capture the elements of both the past and the present, whilst embodying a spirit of timeless nature and humanity". The piano is based on a Yamaha CFIII-S concert grand, but also incorporates advanced electronics. These include a MIDI interface, for connection to other instruments and computers, and an on-board Disklavier system.

BÖSENDORFER, Vienna, 1990, grand piano

Designed for Bösendorfer by the world-renowned Austrian architect Hans Hollein, this piano employs a modern style based on strong color and extensive use of brass. The design is not a 'one-off' for a particular location, but was produced as a limited edition over several years. Hollein has headed a master-class in architecture at the Academy of Applied Arts in Vienna since 1979, and has designed many important buildings in Austria and Germany. Architects are quite often hired to design special casework. They are thought to combine a detailed knowledge of materials with artistic flair.

The piano is equipped with Yamaha's Disklavier system which digitally records the way the keyboard is played and enables the piano accurately to recreate pre-recorded performances.

The side of the instrument is 5⅛ in thick, and built up from 65 separate layers to create an instrument of exceptional strength and resonance

This piano is 7 ft 9¾ in long and weighs 1232 lb, 25 per cent more than a Steinway Model D, which is more than a foot longer.

Tuning *(left)* *Piano-tuning is a skilled job that involves far more than the accurate pitching of each string. An experienced piano-tuner will subtly adjust the tuning across the whole range of the instrument to achieve the most pleasing musical relationship between the notes rather than adopt a sequence that is based strictly on physics.*

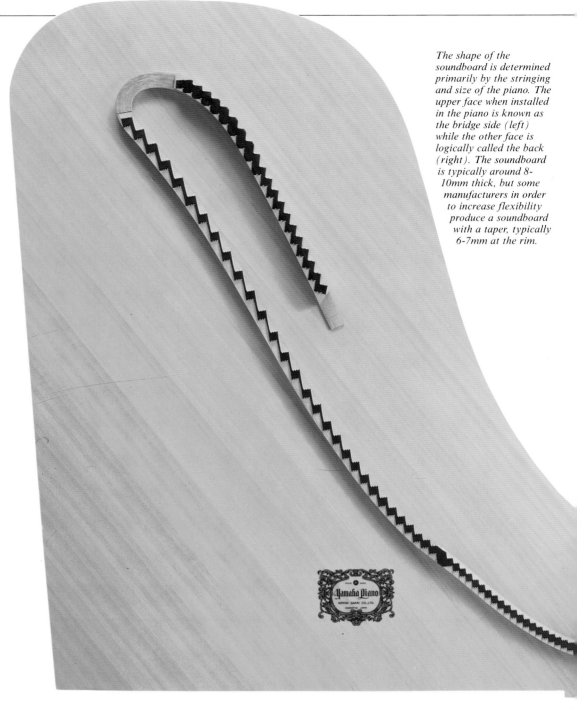

The shape of the soundboard is determined primarily by the stringing and size of the piano. The upper face when installed in the piano is known as the bridge side (left) while the other face is logically called the back (right). The soundboard is typically around 8-10mm thick, but some manufacturers in order to increase flexibility produce a soundboard with a taper, typically 6-7mm at the rim.

As the string gets thicker it also becomes stiffer, and its tone quality deteriorates. To overcome this deficiency some string makers wrap copper wire around the string, increasing its mass and effectively lowering its pitch without degrading tonal character. But it remains an inescapable fact that a longer string will have a better tone than a short one, and as a result smaller pianos will always suffer some inadequacies in sound quality.

STRING LENGTH

The length of the string determines its pitch – the longer the string, the lower the note. But in order to maintain both loudness and tone quality the string for a given note should be as long as possible. As a result, the piano designer must balance very carefully the relative size of an instrument against the quality of its performance.

STRING MATERIALS

The strings of a piano are generally made of very pure carbon steel. This material is chosen because it can stand considerable longitudinal pull as well as repeated striking by the hammer without distorting. In order to achieve a good tone the string must have a perfectly circular cross section. Without this the string will tend to vibrate in an elliptical motion rather than in a single plane, wasting energy and causing the string to perform less efficiently. The finish given to the string is also important, with a smooth clean surface essential to correct vibration.

Wound strings generally have a copper wire wrapped around the steel core, while some bass strings are copper plated. Copper is used because it provides a good tone and does not rust. Some older instruments had iron-wound bass strings, but these tended to lose their elasticity and tone quality with age. Virtually every manufacturer now uses copper-wound strings.

THE SOUNDBOARD

A piano string stretched tightly between two fixed points and plucked would sound relatively quiet – and nothing like a sustained note played on a piano. This is because the string vibrating on its own cannot activate enough air particles to produce a loud sound: it has a very small surface area, and the number of air particles that it can set into compression and rarefaction is relatively small.

Nevertheless, the isolated string when plucked would continue to vibrate for much longer than the sustained piano note. This is another consequence of such a string moving few air particles: it is not damped so readily by the action of the air and so continues to oscillate for a longer period (a property exploited by electric grand pianos, see p77).

In order to increase the amplitude of the sound produced by the vibrating string it is necessary to increase the number of air

particles with which the string comes into contact, and to do this the energy of the struck string is transmitted via the bridge to the soundboard.

The soundboard is the 'voice' of the piano, and the way in which it translates the strings' vibrations into the movement of air particles dictates the character and quality of the sound of a particular piano. The soundboard is responsible for ensuring that the instrument produces an acceptable sound with the highest fidelity, and it is not too surprising to learn that manufacturers put a great deal of time, money and effort into the design of the soundboard.

If the piano were a hi-fi system, the soundboard would be equivalent to the loudspeakers – and poor quality speakers will invariably provide inferior sound quality no matter how good is the source material.

The typical soundboard is not a flat piece of wood: the center of the bridge side of the soundboard is raised. This raised portion, known as the crown, serves two purposes. First, it pushes the soundboard-mounted bridge hard up against the strings to give a more efficient transfer of vibrations, and second, it encourages sound waves to move more freely over the soundboard.

In order to maintain the integrity and shape of the soundboard, ribs (sometimes known as belly bars) are attached to the back. These help to maintain the crown and the overall shape of the soundboard, and as they are mounted at right

angles to the grain of the soundboard they also contribute to the distribution of vibrations across the grain and thus over the whole area of the soundboard. The inner rim of the instrument, to which the soundboard of a grand piano is glued, also plays an important part in transmitting vibrations, and in this manner it will help to determine the character of a particular instrument's sound.

The soundboard of an upright piano is typically oblong in shape, but otherwise is much the same as that of a grand. Some modern soundboards are laminated, usually consisting of three thin layers of wood, often spruce but sometimes a composite of different woods. Laminated soundboards, found on less expensive instruments, are reputed to sound less good than solid versions. But they are more durable, and will retain their crown and not crack so readily.

THE BRIDGE

The bridge is a very important part of the instrument, conducting the energy of the vibrating strings to the soundboard. The strings are attached to both ends of the piano's frame: at one end to the hitch pin, and at the other indirectly via the tuning pin and pin block.

The bridge is positioned near to the crown of the soundboard so that the string exerts a strong downward pressure on to the bridge and, subsequently, to the soundboard. The precise placement of the bridge determines a string's 'speaking length',

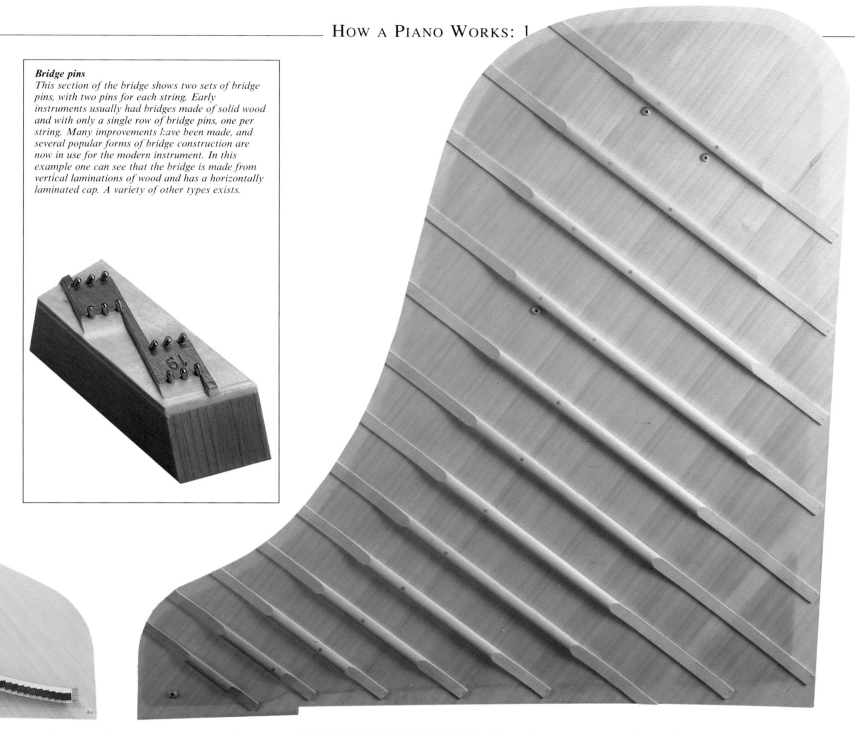

Bridge pins
This section of the bridge shows two sets of bridge pins, with two pins for each string. Early instruments usually had bridges made of solid wood and with only a single row of bridge pins, one per string. Many improvements have been made, and several popular forms of bridge construction are now in use for the modern instrument. In this example one can see that the bridge is made from vertical laminations of wood and has a horizontally laminated cap. A variety of other types exists.

the portion of string that is struck by the hammer and is free to vibrate. It is essential that the speaking length of the string comes into contact with the bridge pin and the bridge at exactly the same point, otherwise the sound can become muddled.

A grand piano usually has two bridges, one for the treble strings and a second bridge for the longer bass strings. In the large illustration (above) the two bridges are joined at the top. This arrangement is known as an overhanging bridge and is designed to enhance sound quality. Other instruments may have two separate bridges.

Bridges are usually similar in shape whatever the type of piano, but construction of the bridge can vary and is critical in ensuring that the strings' vibrations are transmitted efficiently to the soundboard. It is essential that the bridge is bonded securely to the soundboard. Usually the bridge is carefully glued in place; on better quality instruments there is also a dowel joint, a wooden pin that strengthens the joint. This is accomplished by passing the dowel through the bridge, soundboard and, in some cases, the ribs.

The total downward pressure of the piano's strings on the bridges and thus on the soundboard is approximately 1,000lbs. Sometimes this tremendous force can lead to a 'collapsed' or 'fallen' soundboard. This is the result of the strings pushing the bridge and soundboard away. It leads to the contact pressure between the string and bridge becoming dramatically reduced, as is the energy transferred to the soundboard.

A good soundboard is made from a solid sheet of wood, normally composed of glued strips of selected Alaskan spruce. This wood is chosen for its straight grain, light weight and relative flexibility, qualities that make for an efficient conversion of the energy of the vibrating strings into sound.

Ideally the spruce used for a piano soundboard should have a grain which has around ten growth rings per year. Piano makers know that sound travels much faster down the grain than it does across the grain of wood, and the spruce strips of the soundboard are arranged with the grain following the line of the treble bridge as closely as possible. This allows the vibrations to spread more easily over the full area of the soundboard.

HOW A PIANO WORKS: 2

*Enormous strains are imposed within a piano
in order to maintain the instrument's strings
in constant and stable tension. These forces
have posed some of the greatest problems
facing piano manufacturers during the past
300 years, and instruments must be
constructed very strongly in order to
withstand the colossal forces involved.
The strings of a grand piano can have a total
pull of over 30,000lbs, the like of which is
found in no other type of musical instrument.*

THE FRAME

At the heart of the piano's strength is the metal frame, sometimes known as the plate. It is a complex yet vital component, made from cast iron to an extremely high tolerance, large in surface area yet thin in cross-section, and bearing virtually the entire stress of the strings. Despite considerable advances in materials technology, cast iron is still found to be the best material to use for the frame. Many alloys have been tried as alternatives, but most were found to be costly and to suffer from compression when the strings were held under tension.

The frame contributes more than one-third of the total weight of a grand piano. Although it does not bear all the instrument's stresses the frame still needs a considerable amount of support, primarily from the backposts (or backframe) and the inner rim assembly. The backposts and inner rim form a solid structure on to which the soundboard is glued and the frame bolted. The construction of the inner rim and backposts

is not only important for the solidity of the structure, but it can also add to or detract from the overall sound quality of a particular instrument.

The backpost assembly for the upright instrument is generally of a relatively simple type, consisting most often of a rectangular structure which usually forms part of the outer casing of the piano. It has between two and five posts running vertically to add support.

PIN BLOCK AND TUNING PINS

The pin block is mounted under the frame of the grand piano and it is essential that it marries perfectly with the frame. Any gap between the two will cause problems when tension is applied to the strings.

On first appearance the pin block is of straightforward design. It is a piece of wood into which a tuning pin is bedded and around which one end of a string is coiled. The tension in

1 wrest plank
2 frame
3 wrest pin
4 up bearing
5 capo d'astro or agraffe
6 string
7 soundboard
8 bridge
9 damped section of string
10 hitch pin
11 hammer strike point

Grand frame assembly
(above) The speaking length of each string is determined at one end by the point at which it presses hard against the top edge of the capo d'astro, and at the other by the point where it meets the bridge and bridge pin. The string is struck by the hammer from beneath, at a point between one-seventh and one-ninth of the distance along the speaking length of the string. This upward action momentarily increases the force on the capo d'astro. Usually only the speaking length

of the string is left free to vibrate; all other lengths are damped off using strips of listing cloth.

Grand piano frame
(right) The bottom part of the frame of a grand piano sits just behind the keyboard. The small holes are for the tuning pins. A second set of single holes for the agraffes (brass string anchors) can be seen along the top left edges of the bottom section. The larger holes in the upper part of the plate influence the tone of the plate and help reduce its overall weight.

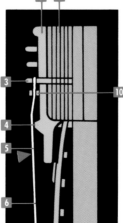

1 wrest plank
2 frame
3 wrest pin
4 up bearing
5 hammer strike point
6 string
7 soundboard
8 bridge
9 hitch pin
10 pressure bar

Upright frame assembly
(left) On an upright piano, the hammer strikes the string 'into' the frame. This means that the string runs from the tuning pin to pass under the pressure bar and over the upbearing edge of the frame, which marks one end of the string's speaking length. The string then runs to the bridge, the other end of its speaking length, and on to the hitch pin.

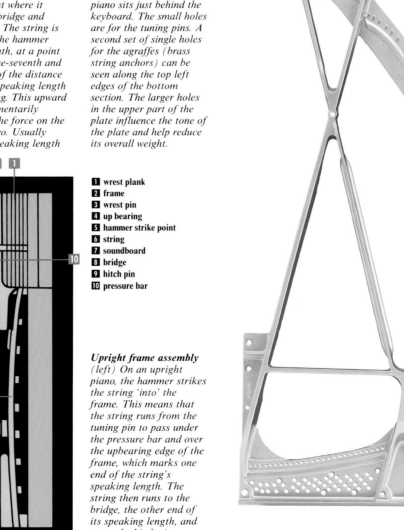

the string is varied simply by rotating the tuning pin, which provides an anchor for one end of each string. Twisting the pin clockwise applies additional tension to the string and its pitch rises; turning the pin counter-clockwise slackens the string and lowers its pitch. The pin block and tuning pins are usually considered to be among the most critical parts of the instrument: indeed, if the pin block does not work properly then the piano will not work properly.

The tuning pins are bedded into the pin block, usually to a depth of between an inch and an inch-and-a-half. Some makers use tuning pin bushes, providing the advantage of extra wood into which the pin can bed. The 'buried' length of the pin increases the frictional force between the metal pin and wooden pin block. The exposed length of the pin has a small hole drilled in it, and the top end of the pin is squared off to accept the tuning hammer. The string is secured through the hole and wrapped around the pin two or three times.

This shows the tuning pins around which the strings are coiled. By turning the tuning pins the strings are brought precisely into tune. They are arranged here as trichords – three strings per note. The tuning pins pass through the iron frame and fit tightly in the pin block. The strings can be seen here passing through the agraffes which serve to exert a downward force on the string and to ensure that the strings are correctly spaced.

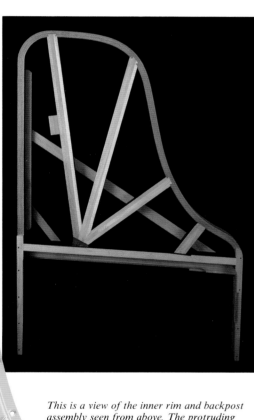

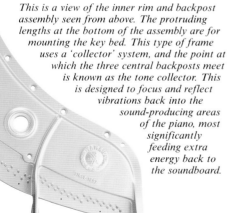

This is a view of the inner rim and backpost assembly seen from above. The protruding lengths at the bottom of the assembly are for mounting the key bed. This type of frame uses a 'collector' system, and the point at which the three central backposts meet is known as the tone collector. This is designed to focus and reflect vibrations back into the sound-producing areas of the piano, most significantly feeding extra energy back to the soundboard.

STRINGING

In order to give the piano a full, rich tone and to provide plenty of volume, all but the very lowest bass notes are produced by combinations of more than one string. Each of the treble notes, from an octave or so below middle C right up to the highest note, is generally produced by three strings tuned in unison, known as a trichord. For upper bass notes the stringing is bichord (two strings per note) while only the bottom few notes are single-strung. If the piano had three notes per string throughout its entire range the bass notes would sound too loud and swamp the tenor and treble strings, and the arrangement would impose an extra and unnecessary force on the frame of the piano.

Strings in a trichord or bichord are tuned in unison with one another (and together are in fact termed 'a unison'). Despite each string delivering exactly the same pitch, there will be minute discrepancies between the tunings and harmonic structure of their sounded notes, and these differences will cause additional harmonic 'movement' in the sound.

Although it is accurate to say that a piano has over 200 strings, in practice many of the strings actually provide two speaking lengths. This is achieved by running the string from one tuning pin down over the bridge and around the hitch pin, then back over the adjacent bridge and back to the corresponding tuning pin. The technique is known as loop stringing and is used for most of the treble strings. A good number of the strings in the bass section are wound, which means that looping is not practical for these. With a looped string, such is the tension and stiffness around the hitch pin that it will not slip. A change in tension made by adjusting the first

tuning pin will not affect the tension in the other half of the string (although in some cases the hitch pin is used only for one length of string).

STRING, SOUNDBOARD AND FRAME

The hammer in an upright piano hits the string 'into' the frame, while in a grand piano the hammer strikes upwards, sending the string up and away from the frame. This distinction requires the strings to be anchored in a different way in these two types of piano, and results in the reversal of the respective positions of the upbearing element of the frame and the downbearing pressure bar or agraffe.

The capo d'astro acts as a downbearing force on the strings and helps to anchor them securely. It was invented by Antonie Bord in Paris in 1843, and was modified and patented by C.F. Theodore Steinway 32 years later. The term comes from the Italian 'capo tasto' which referred to the nut of a lute.

Agraffes are used as an alternative to the capo d'astro, although they are generally found only in more expensive instruments. Their purpose is twofold: to exert a downward force on the string, and thus to mark one end of the speaking length of the string; and to ensure that the spacing between the strings for each note is exact and does not move. They are small pieces of brass, one per note, which screw into the iron frame. Each agraffe is drilled with one, two or three holes, for single, bichord or trichord use. Sometimes known as studs, agraffes were invented by Sébastien Erard at the beginning of the 19th century.

DUPLEX AND ALIQUOT SCALING

Duplex scaling is a means of using the non-speaking ends of a string, undamped, to enrich the sound of a note. It was developed by C.F. Theodore Steinway with the aid of acoustic engineer Herman von Helmholtz in 1872 (patented 1878), and it is used today by Steinway and other manufacturers for upright and grand pianos.

The length of non-speaking string nearest the tuning pin is known as the front duplex, the length nearest the hitch pin the back duplex; some instruments may use both duplexes, while others use either the front duplex or the back duplex. Sometimes this feature of the piano is called aliquot duplex scaling, which can be confusing. While strictly speaking this is a correct use of the term 'aliquot', it should not be mistaken for aliquot scaling, where an extra string per note is added to the existing string(s). The extra string is not struck by the hammer, nor is it damped, and it is designed to provide sympathetic vibration to add harmonics and overtones to the sound of that note.

Aliquot scaling *(left) Julius Blüthner invented this scheme in the 1870s, where an extra string adds overtones and harmonics, based on the fourth-string system of harpsichord maker Hans Rucker.*

HOW A PIANO WORKS: 3

The keyboard is the means by which the player controls the piano's mechanism, and other than the pedals it is the only part of the entire piano with which the player makes contact. Today's instruments generally have a keyboard compass, or span, of either 7 octaves (85 notes) or 7⅓ octaves (88 notes). This larger compass dates from around 1850 when the iron frame came into wide used and enabled the piano to support the considerable additional stress of the extra notes.

THE KEY

A piano key is, quite simply, a lever, although a great deal of care must go into its construction and design to ensure that it operates perfectly.

The key sits on the key frame and is located by two pins. The pin furthest from the front of the key is the balance pin, while the pin at the front is the bat pin (so-called because its shape resembles the bat used in the British game, cricket). The balance pin anchors the key in the correct position on the balance rail; the bat pin ensures that the key cannot move from side to side. The key rests on the back rail, and when pressed it rocks on the balance rail so that the rear part of the key rises. The capstan screw then transmits this movement to the action.

Keys for upright pianos and for grand pianos are designed differently: the relative locations of the balance pin vary, the upright's key is substantially shorter, and the hammer check of the upright instrument is not mounted on the key but is part of the action mechanism.

KEY SPECIFICATIONS

The key of a grand piano can be anything up to 24 inches long, while on an upright the key's total length is limited by the depth of the instrument and is generally around 13 inches, although some smaller instruments may have keys less than 11 inches long.

There is a problem of touch variation associated with shorter keys. To depress a key on a reasonably good piano, with the dampers raised, a force on its front edge of around two ounces is necessary. However, pianists do not play the keys at exactly the front edge, and each of our fingers is of a different length. The nearer to the balance pin that one presses a key, the greater the force required. If the length of the key is reduced – and consequently the distance between the key's front and the balance pin – the variation in the touch weight over the length of the key is much greater. In other words, shorter keys can be harder to play. A grand piano with its much longer keys reduces this problem.

The positioning of the balance pin and rail is also crucial in determining the performance of the keyboard. Typically on a grand piano the ratio of distances between bat pin to balance pin and balance pin to capstan is 2:1, while on an upright it is 3:2. This results in the grand offering a much better touch response.

It is interesting to note that the key of a grand piano is balanced so that when the action is removed it sits with the front end lower, while an upright key is balanced so that it sits with the back end lower. The playing lengths of the keys also vary between grand and upright, with those of an upright up to 15 per cent shorter than those on a grand piano.

KEY DIP

The vertical distance through which the front edge of the key can travel is called the key dip. Various factors influence the key dip such as the distance between the front of the key and the balance pin, and the height of the front rail. Typically a piano will have a key dip of around 10mm.

KEY WEIGHT

The keys of grand pianos and some upright pianos have added key weights, small disks of lead that slot into holes drilled in the key. These are used to ensure that the key has the correct touch weight, and that this is uniform across the compass of the keyboard. In some of the more expensive instruments the weighting is scaled across the compass so that the bass notes have a slightly heavier touch weight.

On better quality instruments keys are individually weighted after they have been installed on to the key frame. On cheaper models weights will be fitted before assembly, if at all.

KEY CONSTRUCTION

The individual keys for a keyboard are cut at once from a wide sheet of wood that has been carefully constructed from glued strips. This method ensures uniformity of key weight across the keyboard, and a grain alignment that should run down the length of the key.

Piano keys are generally made from hardwoods such as fir, spruce or sugar pine, woods that must be properly seasoned before they can be used in any fabrication process.

White keys were once covered in ivory and black keys were made from ebony. Ivory can no longer be used in any manufacturing process, and synthetic materials such as polymers and acrylic or phenolic resins are now used for both black and white key coverings. Ivory was an ideal key-covering material because it absorbed the sweat from a player's fingers.

The synthetic alternatives are good, but are considered by many to offer an inferior feel and lower sweat absorption properties when compared to the natural material.

HAMMERS

The hammer is the prime element of the piano that distinguishes it both in operation and sound from earlier keyboard instruments that preceded the piano such as the harpsichord, spinet, clavichord and virginal.

The introduction of the iron frame to the piano in the mid 18th century enabled manufacturers to increase the tension of the strings, which in turn required the use of larger hammers. Before this time piano hammers were considerably smaller. Today, hammers vary in size over the compass of the piano. Bass notes will inevitably require heavier hammers than those that strike the treble notes.

The demands made on a piano hammer are considerable. The hammer will have to strike the strings of the piano hundreds of thousands of times during its life. It therefore has to be strong and reliable. It also must have specific properties in order to be able to cope with the extremes of loud and soft playing. The striking surface needs to be soft, with a degree of elasticity to accommodate the gentler notes, while it should become progressively firmer towards its center to handle the playing of louder, more forceful notes.

DAMPERS

To prevent strings from vibrating when not required to do so, a system of felt dampers is used. In a grand piano the dampers sit on the strings. Usually they are held in place by their own mass, but sometimes weights are inserted on the damper's underlever (see picture of grand action, right) to ensure that the dampers sit more securely on the strings. In an upright piano the dampers are held against the string by individual damper return springs (see upright action, p94).

There are three occasions when the damper is lifted from the string:

- when a key is played, the damper lifts individually
- when the damper pedal is pressed, all the dampers lift together
- when the sostenuto pedal is pressed (where fitted), the dampers lift selectively.

The damper is lowered when the key or pedals are released. One damper is used to control all the strings for each note, so different shaped dampers are usually used for single-strung, bichord and trichord notes. The best felt for dampers is generally considered to be that made from the wool of Australian Merino sheep.

It is most important that the damper should work silently. When the damper lifts from the string it must do so cleanly; if it should catch a string in any way it will cause that string to sound, quietly but audibly.

UNDERDAMPED AND OVERDAMPED

Upright pianos are sometimes described as being underdamped or overdamped. An overdamped piano has its dampers located above the strike line of the hammers; on an underdamped piano the dampers are below the hammers. The former was used originally for vertically-strung instruments.

If a damper is positioned close to the center of a string it will operate more efficiently. Consequently, overdamped pianos with dampers close to the top of the instrument were not very effective. Today all pianos are underdamped, and the term overdamped is only used to describe older upright instruments.

ACTION

The action is the essential mechanism that translates the energy of the key pressed by the player into vibrations in the string. The only element of the action over which the player has control, other than the damper setting, is the speed at which the hammer strikes the string, which is directly related to the speed at which the key is depressed.

THE MODERN GRAND ACTION

The ancestry of the modern grand action can be traced back to Cristofori's original designs. Sébastien Erard and Henri Herz took these designs and improved them considerably, making piano playing easier and more expressive. The modern double escapement action, or repetition action as it is sometimes known, has in fact changed little since the early 19th century.

1. repetition lever
2. hammer shank
3. repetition lever regulating screw
4. hammer rest felt
5. damper felts
6. damper head
7. damper rail
8. string
9. damper wire
10. hammer top felt
11. hammer under felt
12. check leather
13. hammer molding
14. check felt
15. check
16. underlever frame
17. underlever frame flange
18. balancing weight
19. underlever
20. underlever top flange
21. underlever top flange screw
22. underlever key cushion
23. check wire
24. tail
25. key frame cloth
26. wippen flange
27. wippen
28. wippen top flange
29. repetition spring
30. undercarriage
31. capstan screw
32. spoon
33. key
34. key button bushing
35. balance washer
36. balance rail
37. key button
38. balance pin
39. action hanger
40. undercarriage base felt and cushion
41. jack regulating button
42. set-off button
43. jack
44. jack regulating screw
45. regulating rail
46. set-off screw
47. repetition lever covering
48. hammer roller
49. repetition felt block
50. drop screw
51. key covering
52. bat pin
53. key front
54. bat pin washer
55. key frame

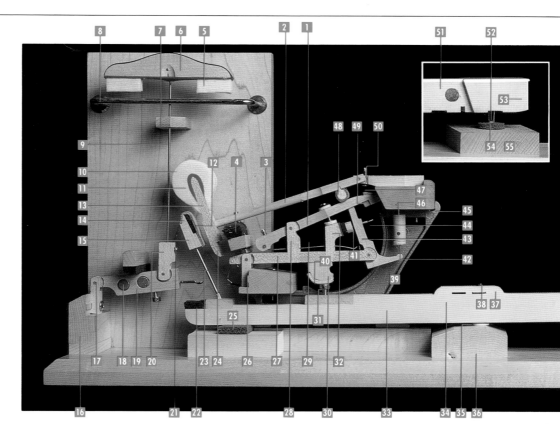

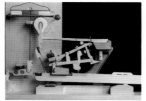

Action shots *The main annotated photograph (above right) is of a typical modern grand piano action made by the long-established firm of Herrburger Brooks, showing the action at rest with the damper pedal pressed. By means of a series of levers this causes the* **underlever (19)** *to be pushed upwards, lifting the* **damper felts (5)** *from the* **string (8)**.

At rest *As the* **key (33)** *is pressed, the* **capstan screw (31)** *pushes up on the* **undercarriage (30)**. *This in turn rotates the* **wippen (27)** *which is mounted in the* **wippen flange (26)**. *The* **jack (43)** *is pivoted to the wippen and is free to rock back and forth. As the wippen rises so does the jack, the top end of which passes though a slot in the* **repetition lever (1)** *which pushes up on the* **hammer roller (48)** *causing the* **hammer (13)** *to be projected towards the string.*

Hammer strikes string *The jack continues to move upwards until the toe of the jack encounters the* **set-off button (42)**, *causing the jack to flick up off the roller leaving the hammer being propelled upwards towards the string, free from the jack and other parts of the action. The damper mechanism rests on the top rear end of the key, a part known as the* **underlever key cushion (22)**. *As the key is pressed, the top rear end of the key rises causing an upward movement of the underlever. This causes the* **damper wire (9)** *to rise, and this in turn lifts the damper felt from the string.*

Hammer in check *With the key still held, the hammer bounces back off the string and its* **tail (24)** *is caught by the* **check (15)**, *a wooden pad covered in felt and leather that is attached to the rear of the key by the* **check wire (23)**. *The downward movement of the hammer has caused the repetition lever to be pushed downwards, slightly compressing the* **repetition spring (29)** *which is designed to pull the jack to the left. But because the tip of the jack is located to the right of the roller by the action of the set-off button on its toe, the jack cannot move and a kind of scissor tension exists between the jack and the repetition lever.*

Hammer freed from check *Upon partially releasing the key, the hammer is freed from the check and, under the upward force of the repetition spring and lever on the roller, the hammer rises slightly. The toe of the jack is also lowered slightly and this allows the repetition spring to pull the jack back under the roller. If the key is played again the hammer will be projected at the string but with less potential velocity than it would have at the initial rest position.*

Back to rest *When the key is fully released the hammer falls back so that it is just clear of the* **hammer rest felt (4)**, *and the toe of the jack leaves the set-off button allowing the jack to be fully repositioned under the roller. The damper is simultaneously lowered on to the string.*

The Upright Action *The example shown is a modern underdamped action, so-called because the dampers lie below the hammers. The modern upright action comes almost directly from Robert Wornum's action of 1842 which featured a tape-check mechanism, but with an overdamper. Like the grand action, little has changed in its design since the 19th century, other than general improvements in construction and manufacture and in the choice of materials.*

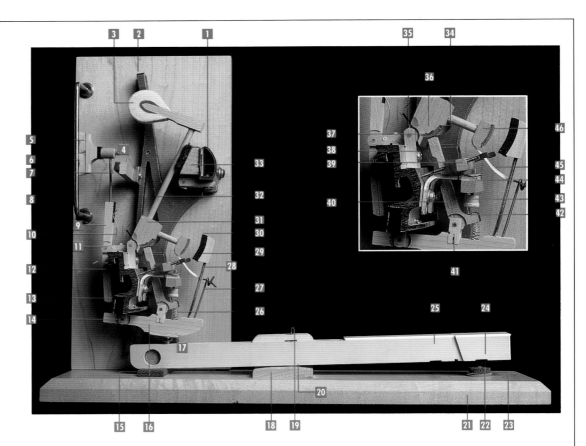

1 hammer rest rail	**24** bat pin
2 action standard	**25** key
3 hammer	**26** jack spring
4 damper screw	**27** bridle wire
5 damper head	**28** check wire
6 damper felt	**29** check
7 damper check rail	**30** check leather
8 string	**31** hammer butt
9 damper stem	**32** hammer shank
10 damper return spring	**33** half blow rest rail
11 damper stem flange	**34** hammer butt cushion
12 hammer rail beam	**35** hammer butt leather
13 damper spoon	**36** hammer butt notch pad
14 lever flange	**37** notch
15 back rail [location]	**38** butt flange
16 wippen	**39** jack check rail
17 capstan screw	**40** jack
18 balance rail	**41** jack flange
19 balance pin	**42** toe
20 balance washer	**43** set-off button
21 key frame	**44** set-off rail
22 bat pin washer	**45** tape (bridle strap)
23 front rail [location]	**46** balance hammer

   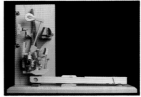 

At rest *The* **wippen** *(16), which is mounted on the* **lever flange** *(14), is free to move up and down. As the* **key** *(25) is pressed the* **capstan screw** *(17) pushes up on the wippen and this movement is transferred to the* **jack** *(40) through the* **jack flange** *(41). The* **hammer shank** *(32) is mounted on the* **hammer butt** *(31), into which a* **notch** *(37) is formed. The hammer butt is mounted on the butt flange so that it is free to rotate, causing the hammer to move towards the* **string** *(8). As the jack pushes*

against the notch quite quickly, the hammer assembly acquires a fair degree of momentum. Meanwhile the ball of the **damper spoon** *(13), located on the far end of the wippen, moves to the left as the wippen rises, causing the* **damper stem** *(9) to rotate, lifting the* **damper felt** *(6) off the string.*

Hammer strikes string *The jack continues to move upwards, pushing on the hammer butt until its* **toe** *(42) encounters the* **set-off button** *(43), which causes the jack to flick out of the notch. The hammer and hammer butt assembly have now escaped from the rest of the action, carrying the hammer towards the string, which it hits and then bounces back.*

Hammer in check *Having struck the string, the hammer falls back and the* **balance hammer** *(46), is 'caught' by the* **check** *(29), thus preventing the hammer from re-hitting. The* **tape** *(45), or bridle strap locates the balance hammer in the check. With the key held and the hammer assembly firmly in check, the* **jack spring** *(26) is kept compressed.*

Hammer freed from check *As the key is released the balance hammer is freed from the check, and the* **hammer shank** *(32) falls on to the* **half blow rest rail** *(33). Releasing the key a little more frees the toe of the jack from the set-off button, and the jack partly relocates in the notch, making it possible to replay the note, albeit with less potency.*

Key released *As the key is completely released the jack properly relocates in the notch and the damper is lowered back down on to the key under the influence of the damper return spring.*

PEDALS

The character of the notes being played on the piano is modified by its pedals. All acoustic pianos are fitted with a damper pedal, which lifts the dampers from the strings, and a soft pedal, which in the grand piano directs the hammer at just one (una corda) or two (due corde) of the three strings for each note, and in the upright piano reduces the distance between the hammer and the string (a 'half blow').

A sostenuto pedal is sometimes found on higher quality pianos. It lifts only those dampers of notes being held. Other pedals sometimes present include the bass sustain pedal, which lifts the dampers of only the bass notes, and the practice or muffler pedal, which softens the overall sound by introducing a strip of felt between the hammers and the strings.

Spinet piano action *This is a special form of the upright action used in very small upright pianos most commonly found in the United States and known as spinet pianos (not to be confused with the spinet itself). The action is positioned below the key to minimize the piano's height. The spinet action is broadly similar to that of the upright piano, but because it has an additional mechanical linkage between the keys and an inverted 'sticker' on the wippen, the spinet piano action is generally considered to be inferior to that of the conventional upright.*

VIBRATING STRINGS

When a key is played, the hammer is launched at the string, the hammer strikes the string, and it then bounces back. Consider this action in slow motion: the string is pushed away from its normal position by the force of the hammer, but the tension in the string pulls it back. In this way the string is set into vibration. The point at which the hammer strikes the string establishes how the string will vibrate, and is therefore crucial in determining the tone produced by that string.

As the piano string vibrates, it experiences a period of regularly repeating cycles, or oscillations. The number of times that the string completes these cycles each second will be the string's frequency. The pitch of a sound depends upon the frequency of vibration: the higher the frequency – measured in cycles per second or Hertz (Hz) – the higher the resulting musical pitch. In order for a piano string to oscillate faster, and hence produce a higher pitch, it can be given an increased tension, made shorter, or made thinner.

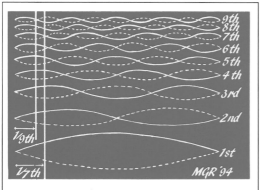

Vibrating strings (above) The diagram represents the way in which a vibrating string not only vibrates as a whole but also in two halves, three thirds and so on. This series of pitches, known as the 'harmonic series', is present in varying amounts depending on how and where the string is struck, and shapes the tonal quality of the resulting sound.

FREQUENCY, TONE AND HARMONICS

When a string vibrates, or oscillates, it responds in a complex manner, as represented in the diagram above. Not only does the string vibrate as a whole, between the two points that anchor it at each end, to produce a fundamental pitch, but also as two halves, three thirds and so on, producing a series of related musical pitches, or harmonics, known collectively as the harmonic series. These harmonics are all produced from one string, and are present in varying amounts depending on how and where the string is struck. The presence of harmonics in varying degrees helps to determine the tonal quality and 'color' of the resulting sound.

The bottom shape in the diagram illustrates the first harmonic, or fundamental. The points of maximum deflection of the string are known as anti-nodes, and the points of no deflection are called nodes (in the case of the fundamental, the nodes are at the two ends of the string). The string's shape changes during vibration, and the solid line in the diagram represents its shape at its maximum oscillation, while the dotted line represents the string's maximum position during the second part of its cycle. The rate at which it completes the cycles is its frequency, measured in cycles per second, or Hertz (Hz). The piano is tuned so that the A above middle C oscillates 440 times a second (which would be expressed as 440Hz, or 440 cycles per second).

The second harmonic, marked 2nd on the diagram, shows a node in the string effectively halving the string's vibrating length. This means that the string will oscillate twice as fast as the fundamental, and as a consequence its frequency and therefore its perceived pitch will be double that of the fundamental. The third harmonic oscillates at three times the

rate of the fundamental, and so on. For example, if the fundamental of a note oscillates at 100Hz, the second harmonic would have a frequency of 200Hz, the third 300Hz, the fourth 400Hz, and so on. If the frequency is doubled, the pitch is raised by an octave. So the second, fourth, eighth and sixteenth harmonics are (respectively) one, two, three and four octaves above the fundamental pitch. The third harmonic (3f) is an octave plus a musical fifth above the fundamental, and the fourth harmonic (4f) an octave plus a musical fifth plus a musical fourth above, and so on.

THE STRIKING POINT

The point at which the hammer actually strikes the string determines how the string will vibrate and, therefore, the harmonics that will be produced by the string.

It is possible to hear this for yourself by plucking the string of a piano (with dampers lifted). Plucking the string in the middle will produce mostly fundamental, giving a relatively rich, mellow tone; plucking the same string close to one end will produce a thinner, more 'nasal' sound that is rich in higher harmonics but lacks a strong fundamental and lower harmonics. As a guide, if you pluck a string near to the node of a harmonic, that harmonic will sound less strongly. (The node is the point at which the string has zero deflection from its resting position – see diagram left.)

Virtually all piano manufacturers position their instrument's hammers to strike at a point between one-ninth and one-seventh of the distance along the speaking length of the string. This area is chosen because it produces a sound rich in the more desirable harmonics, but reduces as much as possible the so-called 'dissonant harmonics', the seventh and ninth, that tend to blend less favorably with the rest.

The diagram on the left showing the harmonic series has two vertical lines marking the boundaries of this ideal striking area. Notice that the nodes for the seventh, eighth and ninth harmonics are within the area, meaning that they will barely be heard, whereas the anti-node of the fourth harmonic is very close to the area, meaning that this desirably pleasant harmonic will be heard more strongly.

Manufacturers go to great lengths to ensure that the hammers in their pianos consistently strike at exactly the desired point along the string. The slightest deviation can dramatically change the harmonic content of a note and give the instrument a considerably different tone.

TRANSIENTS

When a piano's hammer strikes a string, it remains in contact for approximately the time that it takes the string to 'bend' to its maximum displacement and to return for the first time to its initial central position. This time is equivalent to that taken to complete one-half of a cycle at the fundamental frequency of that note (although this may be modified by how hard the string is struck, the exact point at which it is struck, and, most importantly, what the hammer is made of). The harder the hammer, the more likely it is to bounce instantly off the string, resulting in less fundamental tone and more higher harmonics – especially the fourth. Essentially, however, the hammer is in contact with the string for one-half of a cycle.

Consider the strings of the note A-440 (the fundamental of which vibrates 440 times a second). One cycle takes 1/440th of a second to complete, so the hammer would remain in contact with the string for half that time – a mere 1/880th of a second. For lower notes the time is of course longer, while for higher notes it is shorter.

During this briefest of moments, the hammer coming into contact with the string produces an instantaneous burst of sound, in addition to the sound produced by the displacement of the string. This brief burst of sound is known as the transient, and is responsible for giving the note its 'edge', or 'bite'.

It is most important that the hammer leaves the string cleanly once it has struck. Even by remaining in contact for a period of one-half of a cycle, the hammer will have muted some of the higher harmonics. If it remains in contact longer than that it will necessarily dampen (in other words it will reduce the volume of) the fundamental.

INHARMONICITY

So far it has been assumed that the harmonics produced by a vibrating piano string are exact multiples of the fundamental. This would be the case if the tension of the string were the only force acting on the string, but one must also consider the stiffness of the string.

When the string is hit and displaced, both the tension applied to the string and its natural stiffness act as a restoring force. The more 'curved' the string, the greater the effect of the stiffness. Higher harmonics introduce a tighter curvature to the string – see the diagram – and so they are most affected.

The consequence of this phenomenon is that the frequencies of the higher harmonics become progressively sharper (higher in pitch). This is known as inharmonicity, a problem most often encountered in smaller pianos where the manufacturer has had to use unusually thick strings to achieve the deeper bass notes.

HARMONIC ENVELOPES

The tone of a note produced by a struck piano string is continually changing, and alters according to various factors. These include the part of the string struck by the hammer, the characteristics of the material used to make the string and the hammer, and the damping effect on the individual harmonics of the air and of the piano's bridge, soundboard and frame.

When a single note is played, the hammer strikes the string, and the amplitude (volume) of the note goes from zero to a maximum value. The note then dies away, rapidly at first and then more slowly. This sequence is more properly described as the 'envelope' of the note.

The sound is brighter to start with; as the note starts to die away the sound becomes not only quieter but more mellow. This is because the upper harmonics tend to fade more quickly than the lower harmonics, and as a consequence the tone becomes less bright. However, the relative amplitudes of the harmonics are constantly changing, and it is this 'animation' that breathes life into the sound of the piano. Each harmonic has its own amplitude envelope, and some harmonics may only appear late in the overall duration of the note.

With three strings per note sounding in unison and producing harmonics of varying amplitude envelopes, and in some cases the added benefit of duplex and aliquot scaling, it is hardly surprising that a well designed and correctly set up piano can produce some of the most breathtakingly rich and beautiful sounds of any musical instrument.

TONING

We have seen that a hammer's felt covering must be of optimum quality and of correct hardness and density to give it the desired amount of 'bounce'. Even if the head remains in contact with the string for one-half of the fundamental cycle, it will already have started to dampen, or reduce, the higher harmonics. Conversely, if the hammer is too hard it will bounce too quickly from the string and the resulting sound will be 'thin' because of the exaggerated amount of higher harmonics.

Once a new piano has been assembled, skilled technicians set about toning, or voicing, the instrument. This is different to tuning, which is concerned with the accurate pitch of the notes; toning ensures that the tone of each note is correct.

A toning needle is used for this job. It consists of up to three closely-spaced needles protruding about one-half of an inch from a holder. The needles are used to puncture the head of the hammer to make it softer – and thus to dampen the higher harmonics. If the head is too soft, all the harmonics are affected and the overall sound of the instrument deteriorates. A hammer that is too soft either needs to be replaced, or has to be hardened chemically.

PITCH AND TUNING

All pianos today are tuned to a standard reference pitch where A above middle C (a¹) is set to exactly 440Hz (440 cycles per second). This is known as International Standard Pitch and was agreed upon in 1939 at the Second International Tuning Pitch Conference in London. Before this standard was adopted there were no rules and every orchestra defined its own pitch – and up until very recent years the Moscow Philharmonic Orchestra, for example, tuned to a¹=445Hz. Those extra five cycles may not seem like much, but their effect on a piano's tuning is to increase the tension on the strings such that almost half a ton of extra stress is added to the frame.

A sound is generally audible to a young, healthy person if its frequency lies between 20 and 20,000 cycles per second (or 20Hz-20kHz, with a kHz equal to one thousand Hz), although the ability to hear the higher frequencies deteriorates as one becomes older. The compass of the modern piano is generally AAA to c⁵, which when tuned at A-440 translates to a frequency range of 27.5Hz to 4.2kHz. This means that, with the exception of the pipe organ, the piano produces the largest range of frequencies of any acoustic musical instrument.

PIANO HOUSES

The following compendium of piano manufacturers, or 'houses', is arranged in alphabetical order. A chronological chart showing which names appeared when can be seen below, and more information about the work of individual makers may be found throughout the book by consulting the index (see pages 108-111).

PIANO CHRONOLOGY

piano house	start year	piano house	start year
Broadwood	1728	Bechstein	1853
Erard	1777	Blüthner	1853
Ibach	1794	Schiedmayer	1853
Streicher	1802	Steinway & Sons	1853
Challen	1804	Gabler	1854
Pleyel	1807	Mason & Hamlin	1854
Babcock	1810	Stodart & Morris	1856
Chappell	1811	Wurlitzer	1856
Wornum	1811	Kimball	1857
Pape	1817	Steck	1857
Irmler	1818	Kaps	1858
Sauter	1819	August Förster	1859
William Hall & Co.	1820	Neumeyer	1861
Chickering	1823	Baldwin	1862
Nunns & Clark	1823	Decker Brothers	1862
Meyer	1824	Pfeiffer	1862
Dunham	1827	Kranich & Bach	1864
Bösendorfer	1828	Petrof	1864
Pirsson	1829	F. G. Smith	1866
Timothy Gilbert	1829	Marshall & Mittauer	1867
Firth Hall & Pond	1833	Estey Piano	
Schmidt-Flohr	1833	Corporation	1869
Thürmer	1834	Krakauer Bros	1869
Brinsmead	1835	Perzina	1871
Grotrian-Steinweg	1835	Uebel & Lechleitner	1871
Strohmenger	1835	Sohmer	1872
Lindemann	1836	Whelpdale Maxwell	
Worcester	1836	& Codd	1876
Boardman & Gray	1837	Barratt & Robinson	1877
Bradbury	1839	Aeolian	1878
Knabe	1839	Hupfeld	1880
Lemuel Gilbert	1839	Everett Piano Company	1883
J.C. Fischer	1840	Schiller	1884
Hopkinson	1840	Zimmermann	1884
Hulskamp	1840	Schimmel	1885
Hardman	1842	Mannborg	1889
Hallet & Davis	1843	Roth & Junius	1889
Luther	1843	Yamaha	1889
Woodward & Brown	1843	Kohler and Campbell	1896
Grovesteen	1844	Niendorf	1896
Story & Clark	1844	QRS	1900
Rönisch	1845	American Piano	
Gaveau	1847	Company	1908
Lighte & Newton	1848	Kemble	1911
Hallet & Cumston	1849	Kawai	1927
Hazelton Brothers	1849	Knight	1935
Seiler	1849	Young Chang	1956
Bacon & Raven	1850	Samick	1958
Feurich	1851	Astin Weight	1959
Haines Brothers	1851	Fazioli	1978
Steingraeber & Söhne	1852	Falcone	1984
Weber	1852	Boston	1991

At one time there were over 10,000 companies producing pianos; today there are but a few hundred. Consequently pianos may still be in production bearing the names of companies that we note as having ceased trading or having gone out of business. Many of these names survive on pianos that have no connection with the original company, but this does not necessarily mean that the instrument is made along the traditional lines of the old company. It is more likely that the piano will be a mass-produced instrument using the old name to add value or to provide a 'historic' identity. In other cases it is often more cost-effective for a company to contract another manufacturer to build instruments to which the company's name is added, than it is to fund the company's own manufacturing plant.

It may be that a name has been sold when a company goes out of business or is sold as an asset by one company to another. It should be noted in these cases that we are not suggesting that a piano bearing a particular name has been made by a company that has ceased trading, nor that a company producing pianos bearing a particular name is in any form of financial difficulty.

Some instruments may be described in the trade as 'stencil pianos'. These are pianos that are bought from a manufacturer and 'badged' by a particular dealer or distributor with its own name (in a similar way to a supermarket offering own-brand products). It is not a new phenomenon: instruments with a name other than that of the original manufacturer have been around since the end of the 18th century. A manufacturer may produce several thousand instruments of a particular design and subsequently sell them to several different dealers each of whom applies his own brand or trade name. Dealer A can thus appear to offer his own 'special' piano to a customer, who cannot compare prices of that instrument in another store because Brand A pianos are only on sale at Dealer A's store. Stenciling can also hide a poor-quality instrument behind a new identity.

On some occasions a manufacturer or dealer may even try to pass off a piano as that of a much more prestigious manufacturer by giving it a roughly similar-sounding brandname. Bechstein, for example, has over the years noted pianos on the market with such brandnames as Beckstein, Bachstein, Eckstein and Brechstein.

AEOLIAN

William B Tremaine, a piano maker in the family firm of Tremaine Brothers, entered the US musical instrument business in 1868 at the age of 28. Ten years later he formed the Mechanical Orguinette Company to market an automatic organ, and in 1883 the Aeolian organ appeared. (The term Aeolian is used for musical instruments which have sound-producing elements activated by the wind, and here refers to this company's original involvement in the manufacture of organs.) Following the purchase of the Automatic Music Paper Company (Boston), Tremaine overhauled his companies and set up the Aeolian Organ & Music Company in 1888. His son Harry B Tremaine guessed that the future for automatic instruments would be combined with the piano, and over the following 40 years Aeolian came to dominate the American automatic piano market.

The key to this domination was initially the pianola which was developed by Edwin Votey in 1897. The pianola was a pneumatic player made by Aeolian, and in 1903 the Aeolian Weber Piano & Pianola Company was formed, with Aeolian the principal partner. The pianola evolved considerably over the years, with some models being incorporated into pianos by makers such as Steinway.

The other great advance made by Aeolian was the introduction of the Duo-Art reproducing piano, a sophisticated mechanism fitted to the more expensive models. Such was the elegance of the Duo-Art system that the paper rolls could record virtually every nuance of dynamics, tempo and phrasing.

The Aeolian empire grew, and an Aeolian Hall was built in New York, similar in concept to the great concert halls built by Steinway and Bösendorfer. In 1932 the company merged with the American Piano Corporation to form the Aeolian American Corporation, the name of which was changed in 1959 to the Aeolian Corporation. In 1983 Aeolian, which was then producing poor quality instruments and suffering from the recession, was sold by the Heller family who had controlled the company since the time of the Tremaines.

The new owner was Peter Perez, former president of Steinway and Sons. He was unable to revitalize the failing company and in 1985 Aeolian closed. Most of the assets, primarily the brandnames, were sold to Wurlitzer, Young Chang and Sohmer & Co. In 1989 Sohmer sold the Mason & Hamlin, Knabe, and George Steck names to a Seattle-based businessman, Bernard Greer, owner of Falcone.

Companies bought or controlled at various times by Aeolian include: Acoustigrand; Ampico; Chickering; Duo-Art; Hardman Peck; Haines Bros.; Knabe; Ivers & Pond; Mason & Hamlin; Melodigrand; Pianola; Weber Piano Company; George Steck & Company; Vose.

AMERICAN PIANO COMPANY

The company was originally a marketing operation set up in 1908 and under which many American piano houses consolidated their business. These included Knabe, Chickering, Steck, Haines Bros., Weber, J.C. Fischer and, in 1922, Mason and Hamlin. In 1909 the company established a player piano department and produced the Ampico reproducing system, while in 1932 the company merged with Aeolian to become the Aeolian American Corporation.

ASTIN WEIGHT

Ray Astin and Don Weight together formed this small piano manufacturing company in Salt Lake City, Utah, in 1959. Its pianos are revolutionary in design: the uprights dispense with backposts, relying on a full-perimeter frame, and mount the soundboard behind the pin block instead of beside it so that the soundboard can be made much larger, taking up the entire back of the piano. The grands are equally innovative, with the straight side on the right allowing the lid hinge to run along the treble side.

BABCOCK

The US company was founded around 1810 in Boston, Massachusetts, by Alpheus Babcock and his brother Lewis, who both trained with Benjamin Crehore, supposedly the first native American piano maker. Crehore was primarily involved in making square pianos at his workshop just outside Boston but he did make several piano-organs in conjunction with William Goodrich in 1804. In 1807 Crehore and the Babcocks produced one of the first American transposing pianos. Crehore is said to have trained other great American piano makers including the Bent Brothers.

The Babcocks originally teamed up with Thomas Appleton, an organ builder from Boston, but with the death of Lewis in 1814 at the age of 35, Alpheus brought in the Hayt Brothers as partners, and pianos of that era bore the name Hayt, Babcock and Appleton. Subsequently Alpheus continued on his own, until in 1821 he struck up a working relationship with Jonas Chickering. Babcock is best known for pioneering the single cast metal frame which included the hitch pin plate, which he patented in December 1825. He worked for many companies over the following 20 years, including a spell with Klemm & Brothers in 1829. Babcock also ran William Swift's Piano Manufactory, but by 1837 had returned to Boston to work for Jonas Chickering.

BACON & RAVEN

This company was founded in New York in 1850 by George Bacon and Richard and Thomas Raven.

BALDWIN

The foundations for the Baldwin company were laid in 1857 when Dwight Hamilton Baldwin settled in Cincinnati, Ohio, and began to teach piano and organ. He subsequently set up an instrument dealership, primarily selling Decker Brothers pianos, and in 1866 he employed Lucien Wulsin as an office clerk. Wulsin became an important part of the organization and in 1873 became a partner in D.H. Baldwin & Company, and thanks in part to Wulsin's input Baldwin became the largest dealer in keyboard instruments in the American Midwest.

It was inevitable that the company would become a manufacturer, and from 1889 several production companies were formed, including the Hamilton Organ Company, which built reed organs, and the Baldwin Piano Company, which made higher-priced pianos.

Dwight Hamilton Baldwin died in 1899 and left his estate to fund missionary causes. Wulsin purchased the Baldwin estate and took control in 1903, after which the company grew rapidly. In the 1920s Baldwin was one of the first companies to experiment with electronics. The technology was used in the Baldwin electronic organ of 1946, an instrument so successful that the company mushroomed into the Baldwin Piano & Organ Co.

From 1963 to 1986 Baldwin controlled the Bechstein operation. The Corporation today makes pianos and organs under the Baldwin, Chickering and Wurlitzer names. One of the best known players of Baldwin pianos was Liberace, and most of his spectacular instruments were made especially for him by the company.

BARRATT & ROBINSON

This British company was established in 1877 in London. Its Minstrelle model was one of the more successful of the minipianos of the 1930s.

BECHSTEIN

Carl Bechstein was born in Germany in 1826 and while still young was taught by his stepfather to play piano, violin and cello. One of his sisters married a piano-maker, Johann Gleitz, and as Bechstein reached maturity it was decided that he was to become a piano-maker and would serve an apprenticeship with Gleitz.

Following his apprenticeship, Bechstein traveled. He visited the piano-maker Pleyel in Dresden, and then moved to Berlin where his talents soon got him a position of responsibility running the small factory of the famous German piano-maker G. Perau. But Bechstein wanted to learn more about the French school of piano-making, then considered the best in the world, and in 1849 he left Berlin for Paris where he was fortunate enough to be able to study the methods of both Pape and Kriegelstein. He learned much from the excellent French craftsmen and designers, in particular how to obtain greater sound levels from both upright and grand pianos, and also acquired valuable knowledge of the commercial side of the piano industry.

Bechstein returned to Berlin in 1852 to take charge of the Perau factory, and after another spell as superintendent at Kriegelstein in Paris he finally settled back in Berlin. He set about designing his own piano. By 1856 he had attracted the attention of the famous pianist Hans von Bülow, who subsequently praised the Bechstein instruments.

A few months later Bechstein went to a concert given by Franz Liszt and, like Ignaz Bösendorfer some three decades earlier, was amazed by the ferocity of Liszt's playing. Bechstein witnessed the snapping of the strings of Liszt's Erard piano, and decided his instruments had to be able to take this kind of punishment. He enlisted Bülow to test his designs and eventually persuaded Liszt and Bülow to perform together using Bechstein pianos. Liszt became a great supporter and a personal friend of Bechstein. In keeping with the other great piano manufacturers, Carl Bechstein established in 1892 the Bechstein Hall near Potsdamer Platz, Berlin.

In the first seven years of its existence, the Bechstein company produced 176 instruments. By 1900 (the year Carl Bechstein died) production had increased to nearly 3,700 instruments. Although Carl Bechstein had not been a great innovator, his forte had been to utilize the best ideas from other manufacturers and to put them together to make a truly great instrument. On his death Carl Bechstein left his sons Edwin, Carl and Johann in charge of the business.

Business continued to thrive after Carl's death, and in 1912 the 100,000th Bechstein was produced. The popularity of Bechstein instruments continued for many years, although output never increased above 5,000 pianos a year. The Bechstein company was always keen to innovate. In 1926 it introduced the Lilliput grand (a 7¼-octave instrument that was just 5ft 4in long) and was also active in producing player pianos using Welte & Söhne mechanisms. Bechstein embodied the Moór system for two keyboards (see p68) and also produced the Neo Bechstein, the company's first and only foray into the world of the electric piano (see p74).

The years of the Great Depression saw production slump (they built just over 600 instruments in 1933) and with the death of the brothers the company was owned primarily by Helene Bechstein. During the late 1930s production began to increase, and it was alleged primarily by other German manufacturers that Karl Bechstein was a personal friend of Adolph Hitler and that the Bechstein company made the official piano of the Third Reich, consequently obtaining great commercial gain at the time.

The Bechstein factory was badly damaged by bombing towards the end of World War II, although the Bechstein company managed to return to business soon after the cessation of hostilities. Initially it restored and repaired instruments, but by 1950 was making close to 100 instruments a year.

In 1963 Baldwin purchased the Bechstein company and continued to run it on traditional lines. In 1986 retailer and master technician Karl Schulze and two partners bought the company back into German hands from Baldwin. They completely restructured the Bechstein operation, closing down three of the company's factories, and setting up a new high-tech facility in Berlin in 1989.

BLÜTHNER

Julius Blüthner was born in Falkenhain, Germany, in 1824 and like so many piano makers started his career as a cabinet maker. In 1853, having worked for the German piano makers Hölling and Spangenburg in Zeitz, he set up on his own with very little capital to build grand pianos.

The key to the marketing achievements of the company followed the success of Blüthner's pianos at the Industrial Exhibition of 1854 in Munich. Julius Blüthner subsequently had his pianos accepted into the Leipzig Conservatory of Music, which attracted international students. Such was the quality of Blüthner's instruments that the Conservatory's students spread the word about these great new pianos, and demand for Blüthners soon followed from around the world.

The growth of the Blüthner company was remarkable. By the end of its fourth year the company employed 14 men and by 1864 there were 137 workers on the payroll. Until 1900 Blüthner was the second biggest manufacturer of pianos in Europe, making some 3,000 instruments a year. It is said that Julius Blüthner still managed to check every instrument that left the factory.

Blüthner was not highly educated but he did have a remarkable 'ear' and through constant experimentation developed several techniques to improve grand pianos and upright pianos. His greatest contribution was the aliquot system, in which he added a fourth string to notes in the upper octaves. This string was left free to vibrate sympathetically and was tuned in unison with the other three strings in the extreme treble (and an octave above in the tenor section). Blüthner developed this system over a period of several years following his theoretical work with H. Gretschel, and patented it in 1873. The extra strings add a pleasing 'singing' quality to the tone of the upper octaves, and the system is still used on Blüthner instruments of today.

Julius Blüthner died in 1910 in Leipzig, and the company was taken over by his sons Max, Robert and Bruno. However, the growth of the earlier years was not sustained. During World War II the German factory was completely destroyed by bombing, but after the war the company was encouraged by the East German government to resume production, and to facilitate production Blüthner shared many of its facilities with the Bechstein company.

BOARDMAN & GRAY

The company was established in 1837 by William G. Boardman, who was subsequently joined by James A. Gray. The company was based in Albany, New York.

BÖSENDORFER

The name Bösendorfer is firmly linked to the city of Vienna, the great cultural center of the 19th century and home to so many important musicians and composers. Ignaz Bösendorfer, born in 1794, began his apprenticeship with Joseph Brodmann, a respected organ and piano manufacturer. Brodmann is believed to be the first manufacturer to place supportive ribs above the soundboard rather than below it, and he also patented a very successful triple-laminated soundboard. Bösendorfer worked for Brodmann from the age of 19 until he was 33, when he was granted a license to commence the manufacture of his own pianos. In a short time the Bösendorfer piano would become world famous.

It was during the 1820s that the teenage Franz Liszt was receiving much acclaim for his dazzling and dynamic piano concerts. Unfortunately, such was the power of Liszt's technique and so great was his enthusiasm when performing that no piano in Vienna was able to withstand his musical demands. He regularly shattered the instruments he was playing. Friends of Liszt recommended that he consider the new pianos being made by Bösendorfer, and so he tried one of Bösendorfer's original instruments. Liszt not only found the piano strong enough to withstand his forceful playing style, but he also found its tone and color very pleasing. He immediately took up the instrument and overnight the House of Bösendorfer became famous for its high caliber concert grand piano. As with most virtuosi, Liszt 'endorsed' pianos by many other manufacturers during his career, devaluing specific recommendations. But there is little doubt that Liszt's recognition served to elevate the Bösendorfer piano on to the world stage.

Ignaz Bösendorfer continued to receive many accolades, including in 1830 the title of Austrian Court and Chamber Piano Maker, and the reputation of his pianos rapidly spread throughout Europe. Demand required a larger factory, but Ignaz died in 1859 at the age of 64, before the completion of his new factory, and his son Ludwig took over the business. Fortunately Ludwig had studied at the commercial and technical department of the Royal Imperial Polytechnic, as well as working in his father's workshop, and came to the business well versed in piano design and manufacture.

Ludwig Bösendorfer took care of the move to the new factory in Neu-Wein, Vienna, in 1860. It took only ten years for the company to outgrow those premises, and the factory was relocated to its present site in Vienna's Fourth District, while offices and showroom moved to Liechtenstein Palace in the city center.

Ludwig's love of horses led him to the Palace riding school, where he observed that the main riding area had unique acoustic properties and subsequently convinced the prince that it would make an outstanding concert hall. Ludwig's intuition paid off and in 1872 Bösendorfer Hall opened to great critical acclaim and much excitement. Like Steinway Hall in New York, Bösendorfer Hall was to become the city's cultural focal point.

Ludwig Bösendorfer was a true impresario and possessed a larger-than-life character, and mixed with high society and royalty. With no direct descendants who could take over the business, Ludwig decided upon reaching retirement age in 1909 that he would sell the company to his friend Carl Hutterstrasser, who continued to manage the company with verve and flair (despite being forced to relinquish Bösendorfer Hall for a construction project). World War I caused production to slump from 434 instruments a year in 1913 to 136 in 1919. Upon Ludwig's death that same year the City of Vienna honored him by naming the street to which the company had moved Bösendorferstrasse.

After the boom period of the mid to late 1920s, the world economic slump of the 1930s again saw production of Bösendorfer pianos fall from 310 per year in 1929 to only a little over 40 in 1933. Civil wars in Austria only added to the gloom, but two years later a decision by the British Broadcasting Corporation to equip its London music studios with Bösendorfer concert grands helped to lift production. But worse was to come.

Austria disappeared from the map in 1938 and the ensuing World War saw much of the company's reserves of wood destroyed. Finally, during heavy street fighting between Germans and Russians in 1945, the company's offices and showrooms were destroyed and the remaining pianos used for firewood. The employees either fled or were taken prisoner. From these ashes the company slowly arose, and a handful of workers managed to build 11 pianos during 1946 and 1947, rising to some 100 pianos a year from 1950 to 1966, at which time the firm became a publicly listed company.

Arnold H. Habig, head of the Jasper Corporation and subsequently president of Kimball International Inc., and whose ancestors emigrated to the US from Vienna, purchased Bösendorfer for his company in 1966. Habig's aim was to use Bösendorfer's expertise to help stimulate the Kimball range of pianos. Since its birth in 1949 Kimball had been primarily a woodworking company, and the purchase of Bösendorfer worked well for both companies. By Bösendorfer's 150th Anniversary in 1978 production had reached over 500 instruments a year, and the company had produced over 32,000 pianos in total. In that year alone Kimball made 54,800 pianos, which shows the scale of the Bösendorfer operation within Kimball.

Bösendorfer is affectionately known as the slowest piano manufacturer in the world: including the two-and-a-half years taken to season an instrument's wood, the total time taken to make a Bösendorfer grand is just over four years. The company also makes one of the world's largest commercial pianos, the 9ft 6in Imperial Concert Grand.

BOSTON

The Boston Piano Company was formed in 1991 by Steinway Musical Properties, owners of Steinway & Sons, with the aim of merging Steinway's traditional experience with modern machine production to produce affordable high-quality pianos. Although the companies share common ownership, Boston pianos have a unique design and there are no parts that are interchangeable with those used for the Steinway line.

BRADBURY

This long-established company was founded by William B. Bradbury in 1839 in Leominster, Massachusetts.

BRINSMEAD

Based in London, England, the company was founded by John Brinsmead in 1835. He succeeded in establishing a company that became highly respected and produced good quality instruments, and was granted several patents for work on the repetition action. In the 20th century the company continued to produce mostly upright instruments of above average quality. Brinsmead were appointed piano makers to King George V in 1911. The company is also known for its revolutionary although not especially successful 'top-tuner' mechanism (see p49). Brinsmead was taken over by Kemble in 1967.

BROADWOOD

This British-based company was arguably the most important piano manufacturer of the 18th and 19th centuries, but was in fact initiated by a Swiss cabinet maker, Burckhardt Tschudi, who first came to London seeking work around 1718. He joined the Flemish harpsichord maker Tabel and subsequently set up in business for himself in Great Pulteney Street in London in 1728.

Tschudi modified his name to Burkat Shudi. He continued to produce some of the finest harpsichords ever made in England, but was clever enough to realize that producing the best instrument wasn't necessarily the secret to succeeding in business. So he began to contact all the eminent musicians who came to London, including Haydn, Handel and their contemporaries, and marketed his instruments through famous and royal contacts.

John Broadwood was born in Cockburnspath, Scotland, in 1732. A joiner by trade, he moved to London around 1752 and found work with Shudi's company, proving to be a trusted and accomplished employee. He had grown fond of Shudi's daughter, Barbara, and in 1769 married her, from which time Shudi's harpsichords bore the name Burkat Shudi et Johannes Broadwood. During the 1760s the other great harpsichord manufacturer was Jacob Kirkman, and while his company was growing faster than Shudi's, Broadwood had been keeping a close eye on the development of the piano, especially as one of his fellow workers at Shudi's had been piano-maker Johannes Zumpe.

Shudi soon realized that Broadwood was more than competent to run the company, and in 1771 signed the business over to him. Two years later, at the age of 71, Shudi died. In 1774 Broadwood made his first square piano, and patented several major improvements in 1783. Broadwood was busily trying to keep pace with the demand for his square pianos, and by 1784 orders for pianos exceeded those for harpsichords. In that year the company sold over 130 pianos, and in 1793 produced their last harpsichord.

Broadwood was a great friend of Muzio Clementi, a prominent musician, piano-maker and entrepreneur who had arrived in England from Rome as a student at the age of 14. Clementi opened many doors for Broadwood, especially in Europe, and was quick to spot new developments in the piano world. He had warned Broadwood of the strengths of the Erard company, and the possible threat posed to his market, but luck was to come Broadwood's way in the form of the French Revolution. The Revolution closed down all the French industries serving the aristocracy, including the piano house of Erard which was forced to move to London, with the result that Broadwood's market was protected just at the most sensitive time of the company's expansion.

At first Broadwood's square pianos bore the name Johannes Broadwood, but in 1795 his son James joined the company and the name was duly changed to John Broadwood and Son. Another son, Thomas, joined in 1808 prompting a further change to James Broadwood and Sons. John Broadwood died in 1812, at which time James took control, and he furthered Broadwood's reputation as the greatest of all English piano manufacturers. The importance of piano-making within industry at the time is demonstrated by the fact that in 1842 Broadwood was recorded as the twelfth largest employer in London, although from the middle of the 19th century and into the 20th the company went into decline. Broadwood pianos are still in production today.

CHALLEN

Thomas Butcher opened a piano shop in London, England, in 1804, adding William Challen as a partner in 1816. In 1830 Challen took over, renamed the company with his own name, and continued to make pianos of above average quality. Challen was taken over in 1971 by the British firm, Barratt & Robinson. The company will be remembered for their 11ft 8in grand piano that was built in 1935 as the largest piano in the world, and for the fact that in the early 1930s it took on the large job of supplying the British Broadcasting Corporation with pianos.

CHAPPELL

Originally a firm of English music publishers founded by Samuel Chappell, Johann Baptist Cramer and Francis Tatton Latour in 1811, Chappell also built and sold pianos and other musical instruments. One famous instrument produced by the company was the three-octave pianino, or glass piano. Built around 1815 the instrument used glass rods as the vibrating medium, hit by down-striking hammers. In its heyday in the 1920s Chappell was producing over 1000 pianos a year.

CHICKERING

Benjamin Crehore was the founding father of the American piano industry. He made all manner of stringed instruments in workshops in Milton, near Boston, Massachusetts, from the 1790s to 1820. Among his apprentices were the Babcock brothers, the Bent brothers and John Osbourn. The latter set up his own workshop in Boston in 1815, and it was at that shop that Jonas Chickering was to develop his skills as a piano maker.

Chickering was born in Mason Village, New Hampshire, in 1798. He was apprenticed to a cabinet-maker, and it is said that in 1817 he saw a Ganer square piano reputedly owned by a European princess, Amelia. The story goes that the piano had been damaged on the sea-crossing to the US and also by the New Hampshire climate once it

arrived. No other carpenter was prepared to attempt repairs, so Chickering studied the instrument and managed to restore it to a playable condition. The satisfaction he derived from this accomplishment was apparently enough to sow the seed for his future career.

He left Mason soon after and moved to Boston where he found work at Osbourn's shop. There he remained for a further five years, learning every aspect of the piano industry. In 1823 he left to set up in business with James Stewart, a Scotsman who had also gone to work with Osbourn with a view to forming a partnership. But Stewart and Osbourn disagreed on many things, and so Stewart left to form Stewart & Chickering. But in 1826 Stewart left the company to return to Britain to work for Collard & Collard, and the House of Chickering was born.

Although Chickering's pianos were of a superb quality and design, he suffered at first from under-financing and poor marketing. But in 1830 Chickering had the good fortune to enter into partnership with Captain John Mackay, who had the talent, and opportunity, to get Chickering's piano known across North and South America. Not only would Mackay send his ship out with Chickering instruments aboard, but on the return he would bring back the finest rosewoods and mahogany for Chickering to use in construction. Alas Mackay perished at sea in a tropical storm off South America in 1841 leaving Chickering again sole owner of the business, however the company was now in a financially secure position.

Chickering had originally made square pianos, but in 1830 he made his first upright instrument – a bookcase piano. Chickering had studied Babcock's work on using a metal frame for his square pianos, and in 1840 he patented an improved metal frame. He also decided that this type of frame could be utilized in a grand piano. He built his first grand, which incorporated his concepts for a cast iron frame, in 1843. An improved version of this 1843 grand received unparalleled praise at the first International Exposition held in 1851 at Crystal Palace, London, winning the top awards.

In 1852 Jonas made his three sons Thomas E., C. Frank, and George H., partners in the firm, and the company's name was changed to Chickering & Sons.

Later that year tragedy was to strike – in December the Chickering factory in Boston was totally destroyed by fire with a resulting loss of $250,000. A year later Jonas Chickering died, no doubt partly as a result of the strain caused by the fire. However before he died he had set about building the new factory, which was to become the second largest building in America.

Thomas E. Chickering initially took control of the company, but his untimely death in 1871 meant that Frank had to take charge. Under Frank, the company flourished, and the quality of the instruments went from strength to strength. Chickering Hall is on Fifth Avenue, New York. It was opened in 1875, and it was here in the 2000-seater auditorium that many great performers of the time played. It was the showcase for the Chickering empire, and it was also the place that Frank developed new ideas for the instruments. George Chickering, meanwhile, following the wealth of experience his father had provided him with, successfully and efficiently supervised the production of the instruments in Boston, maintaining the high quality output that had been the company's trademark.

In 1867 following the great Paris Exposition of 1867 Frank Chickering had the Imperial Cross of the Legion of Honour, then one of the world's most prestigious non-military awards , bestowed upon him by Emperor Napoleon III for services to the art of music.

Frank Chickering died in 1891 and George in 1896. In 1900 financial pressures forced the sale of Chickering Hall, and in 1908 the company was purchased by the American Piano Company, which itself became part of the Aeolian Corporation. Chickering pianos continued to be made by Aeolian until 1982.

DECKER BROTHERS

David and John Decker established this company in 1862 in New York. The pioneering brothers filed many patents for improvements to piano design, and were keen to try unusual designs such as Paul von Janko's experimental keyboard which they incorporated into some of their instruments in the 1880s.

DUNHAM

The Dunham Piano Company was founded in 1827 in New York by John B. Dunham Jr..

ERARD

Sébastien Erard was born in Strasbourg, France, in 1752. He worked in Paris, firstly as an apprentice to a harpsichord-maker, but

as Zumpe's square pianos flooded into Paris he detected a trend and in 1777 set about building his own pianoforte, the first of which was a square, based on Zumpe's action. Despite protestations from the local harpsichord manufacturers, who realized that the piano threatened their livelihood, Erard continued to produce pianos. He subsequently evolved his own designs for which he won favor not only from French piano buyers but also from Louis XVI, and was granted a license to produce pianos.

Erard had set up an office in London and in 1792, in order to escape the ravages of the Revolution, he moved to London with his brother, Jean-Baptiste. They built their first grand piano there in 1796.

Erard was acutely aware of the importance of the action to the acceptance of his piano among the virtuoso players of the time. He patented an escapement action in 1808 which dramatically improved the performance of his instrument, and the double escapement (or repetition) mechanism, which was invented by Sébastien but patented by nephew Pierre Erard, became the mechanism on which virtually all modern actions are based. The invention was essential in the development of the modern instrument, and helped to put the Erard company at the forefront of piano-makers.

Sébastien died in 1831, leaving Pierre to run the business. In the 20th century the company produced pianos under several names, including those of Erard and Cie, Guichard et Cie, and Erard and Blondel, and in 1960 the company merged with the French firm of Gaveau before being taken over by Schimmel 11 years later.

ESTEY PIANO CORPORATION

Jacob Estey and his partner Levi K. Fuller started in business by making organs, but it was Fuller along with Jacob's son Julius who founded the Estey Piano company in 1869 and built a factory in New York. Estey was purchased in 1917 by George W. Gittens and later changed hands several times. In 1978 Jack Call purchased the rights to the Estey piano designs, and Call, originally a maker of piano and organ stools and also a retailer, was making around 1200 pianos a year, but in 1982 the factory was burned to the ground after being struck by lightning.

EVERETT PIANO COMPANY

Formed in Boston, Massachusetts, in 1883, the company was purchased by Yamaha in 1971. The factory was used to produce both Everett instruments and Yamaha uprights for the domestic market. Eventually Yamaha closed the Everett factory and moved production to Thomaston, Georgia.

FALCONE

Italian-born Santi Falcone came to the US at the age of 14 and began his working life as a piano tuner. He set up a piano store that sold, leased and renovated pianos, which quickly grew to a seven-store network, and Falcone set up his own company in 1984. Falcone imported pianos from Japan but wanted to establish a US manufacturing plant, and in 1985 he opened a facility in Haverhill, Massachusetts. Having sold some of his company to fund production, Falcone sold the balance of his shares to Bernard Greer in 1989, and left to pursue other interests.

FAZIOLI

The success of the Fazioli piano recalls the piano boom of the 19th century and also marks one of the most important contributions from Italy to the piano world since Bartolomeo Cristofori's instrument some 270 years earlier. Few piano manufacturers have achieved so much in such a short space of time. From the turn of the century the Fazioli family business had centered on the furniture business. With a view to diversification, Romano Fazioli experimented with some piano designs in the early 1930s. The political climate of Europe frustrated any plans to set up a piano manufacturing plant and it was left to Paolo, the youngest of Romano's six sons, to bring to fruition his father's plans some four decades later.

Paulo obtained a diploma in piano at the Conservatorio G. Rossini in Pesaro and also studied mechanical engineering at the University of Rome. Following a brief spell on the concert circuit he spent eight years in the family business, but with his musical background he did not find work in a furniture factory satisfying. He felt that there was a need for a truly top-class, hand-built instrument, and that despite the number of excellent instruments on the market he could do better. In 1977 he received backing from his family and set about designing what he considered the best piano in the world. The following year the Fabbrica di Pianoforti Fazioli swung into action, set in part of the family's furniture factory in Sacile, Italy.

In spite of the fact that it is a hand-built instrument, the Fazioli piano benefits from a good deal of technological input. Computerized mapping of the acoustic properties of the soundboard, for example, enable the instrument to be designed for optimum performance. Nonetheless, the use of the finest materials, and the skill and craftsmanship of the factory's select team of builders, has resulted in an instrument that is one of the best instruments currently in production.

Fazioli produces a range of different-sized grand pianos, from the smallest at 5ft 2in to the largest at a giant 10ft 3in, the longest piano currently being made. In 1993 Fazioli produced around 100 pianos and expects to increase this number to 200 each year by the turn of the century. Paolo Fazioli has said that to increase production beyond this figure would mean the loss of the personal touch.

FEURICH

This company based in Leipzig, Germany, was founded by Julius Feurich in 1851. By the turn of the century the company had a staff of 360 and was producing 600 grand pianos and 1200 uprights each year. During the World War II the factory was destroyed, but the firm survived and by 1950 Feurich was back making nearly 300 pianos a year.

FIRTH HALL & POND

The company was founded in 1833 in New York.

J.C. FISCHER

The New York firm of J.C. Fischer was founded in 1840 by two Italian brothers, John and Charles Fischer. The company was associated with William Nunns' company and together in 1847 they produced the eccentric Melodicon With Drums, a piano which played a set of tuned kettle drums in unison with certain strings of the piano. This was not a great success. J.C. Fischer continued in business until the early 20th century when the company became part of the American Piano Co..

AUGUST FÖRSTER

Established by F.A. Förster in Löbau, Germany, in 1859, this company has continued to produce instruments of above average quality. In the 1920s the company was among the first to experiment with quarter-tone pianos, and in the 1930s produced an electric piano known as an Elektrochord, at which time the company was making around 2000 instruments a year. August Förster continues to produce instruments today.

GABLER

Ernest Gabler was born in Silesia (a geographical area now divided between Poland, Germany and the Czech Republic) and emigrated to New York in 1851. He set up in business three years later, having learned about the American piano industry while working at the Chickering factory, and subsequently built good quality instruments at a very reasonable price, and as a result achieved a great deal of success.

GAVEAU

This maker of pianos and harpsichords was founded in Paris, France, in 1847. In 1960 the company merged with Erard, and the joint firm subsequently merged with Pleyel. The new company was taken over by Schimmel in 1971.

TIMOTHY GILBERT

The company was founded by Gilbert in 1829 in Boston, Massachusetts, and was best known for a square piano with built-in organ (known as a 'claviorganum').

GROTRIAN-STEINWEG

Both the Grotrian-Steinweg company and the Steinway & Sons company derive from Heinrich Engelhard Steinweg (Steinway) and the building of his first piano in 1835. In 1850, in order to escape political upheavals in Germany, Heinrich and most of his family emigrated to the US and settled in New York where they subsequently established Steinway & Sons. C.F. Theodor Steinweg, Heinrich's eldest son, was left in charge of the German operation.

Friedrich Grotrian, who was born in 1803 near Braunschweig, Germany, had for 25 years owned a thriving musical instrument store in Moscow, Russia. In 1855 he was left a substantial inheritance by an uncle and decided to sell up and return to his homeland, Germany. Soon afterwards he met up with C.F. Theodor Steinweg, and in 1858 Grotrian became a partner in the Steinweg company. Unfortunately Friedrich Grotrian died just two years later, but his son Wilhelm set about establishing the company as one of the great German piano houses.

The firm of Henry Steinway and Sons, which Theodor Steinweg's family had set up in the US, was growing rapidly, but in 1865 a series of deaths left the company reeling. Henry Steinway Jnr., Charles Steinway and Theodor Vogel, the factory superintendent, all died that same year, and C.F. Theodor was forced to sell his shares in the German operation and emigrate to America to help the family sort out the management problems. Wilhelm Grotrian along with Adolf Helfferich and H.O.W. Schulz bought all C.F. Theodor's shares and the company traded under the name C.F. Th. Steinweg Nachf. (1865). Four years later the name was changed to Grotrian, Helfferich, Schulz, Th. Steinweg Nachf. (nachfolger, or nachf., means successor).

Wilhelm Grotrian presided over a period of rapid growth, and by 1870 new premises were required. The company moved to the outskirts of Braunschweig, where it still produces instruments today, albeit in enlarged premises. In 1886 Wilhelm bought out his partners and took complete control of the operation. His sons joined the company in 1895, helping to maintain the technical excellence of the instruments. The company enjoyed rapid growth, particularly in the years between 1900 and 1910, with production rising from around 600 instruments to over 2,000 a year. The company registered and used several names between 1895 and 1926, including Steinweg Nachf., Steinweg Nachf. Grotrian Braunschweig, Grotrian-Steinweg Nachf., Grotrian, Steinweg, and Grotrian Steinweg.

Wilhelm Grotrian died in 1917, leaving his sons Willi and Kurt in control. They decided two years later that the family name should be changed to Grotrian Steinweg. The Depression of the 1920s hit all piano makers, and Grotrian-Steinweg (hyphenated from 1926), which was producing around 3,000 pianos per year in 1927, saw production fall to less than 700 in 1931. World War II caused production to be halted until 1948, but Grotrian-Steinweg soon re-established itself and continues to make pianos of the finest quality, and still under the auspices of the family. Current production is around 2,000 pianos a year.

GROVESTEEN

Established in Albany, New York, in 1844, this company produced instruments under its own name and also with several other companies. Brandnames include Grovesteen & Fuller, Grovesteen & Hale, Grovesteen & Ilsley, Grovesteen & Truslow and Townsend Grovesteen.

HAINES BROTHERS

Napoleon J. Haines was by all accounts a precocious child. He moved to America with his brother Francis in 1832, and in their teens the two brothers took up an apprenticeship at the New York Piano Manufacturing Company. Having mastered their craft, they set up in production in 1851 and within just a few years were producing 20 pianos a week. Napoleon J. Haines also founded the Union Dime Savings Bank of New York. The instrument business subsequently became part of the Aeolian American Piano Corporation.

WILLIAM HALL & CO

This company was founded in 1820 in New York by William Hall.

HALLET & CUMSTON

Part of the chain that formed part of the Hallet & Davis group, Hallet & Cumston was founded in 1849 in Boston, Massachusetts, by William Hallett.

HALLET & DAVIS

Originally the company was established in 1843 in Boston, Massachusetts, as Brown & Hallet, but on the retirement of Brown, George Davis took over the running of the firm. The company made both pianos and player pianos, the latter under the name of the Virtuola Player.

HARDMAN

This company was started in 1842 by Hugh Hardman in New York. In 1874 Hardman's son John joined the company and in 1890 Leopold Peck became a partner, at which time the name was changed to Hardman Peck and Co. The company became an important supplier in the US market and produced pianos, player pianos and electric pianos. The Hardman Peck operation was subsequently taken over by the Aeolian Corporation.

HAZELTON BROTHERS

Founded in 1849 in New York, the Hazelton Brothers were best known for their square pianos. In more recent times their upright pianos were made by Kohler & Campbell.

HOPKINSON

This English company was established in 1840 in Leeds. In 1846 founder John Hopkinson took on his brother James as a partner and moved the operation to London. The name was taken over in 1963 by Lowrey and Zender.

HULSKAMP

This small manufacturer was based in Troy, New York, where it had been established in 1840.

HUPFELD

Ludwig Hupfeld was born in 1864 and founded his company in 1880 in Leipzig, Germany. He became one of the pioneers of automatic or self-playing instruments, was probably the first to use an electric motor to drive a piano player, and produced a player called the Phonola which became extremely popular. By 1911 the company employed 1,300 and was producing all manner of automatic instruments. Demand was so high that Hupfeld would also fit his own player systems into instruments bought in from other manufacturers. He struck up a close working relationship with the Rönisch company and in 1918 the two companies merged (see Rönisch). Perhaps best known of all Hupfeld's instruments were their DEA and Triphonola reproducing piano systems.

IBACH

The Ibach company is the oldest surviving piano manufacturer in the world, and it has remained in the Ibach family's control since its establishment. Johannes Adolf Ibach (1766-1848) completed his education at the Beyenburg monastery in southern Germany and traveled around Germany to learn something of his country. During this period he learned about organ and piano manufacture from some of the best craftsmen, and returning to his home town obtained the contract to refurbish the great organ at Beyenburg. However his interest had been fired by the piano, and he felt that such an instrument had enormous potential. He subsequently set up a piano manufacturing workshop in 1794, primarily supplying local musicians who had also been won over by the new instrument.

The business flourished despite potential setbacks such as the Napoleonic Wars. However, in 1825 ill health forced Johannes to hand over the business to his eldest son Carl Rudolf Ibach who was then just 21. Carl Rudolf began to innovate in both the design and marketing of the instruments. In 1838 Ibach introduced possibly the first commercially produced upright piano, and later introduced cast iron frames. The reputation of the company soon spread across Europe, but Carl Rudolf, like his father, died young.

The company was taken over by Carl's son P.A. Rudolf Ibach, again at the relatively tender age of 20. Rudolf was largely responsible for making Ibach into a truly great company. He had charisma, foresight and intelligence coupled with a strategic business mind. He courted royalty and the best known musicians of the period, including Liszt, Wagner and Brahms. He sent his son Walter to study the manufacturing methods of the rest of the world's piano makers, and set up competitions with substantial cash prizes for the best art-case piano designs. He introduced a retail dealer network for the first time, and it was Rudolf who changed the name of the company to Rudolf Ibach Sohn, and the shortened form, Rud. Ibach Sohn, endures today.

A. Rudolf Ibach took the company through World War I, and J. Adolph Ibach through the 1939-45 war, the latter resulting in the complete destruction of the Ibach factory which prevented the company from producing instruments until 1952. The Ibach tradition continues with Rolf and Christian, the sixth generation, running the family business, while the next generation is being trained for the future. No other piano company can boast such a strong family heritage, and few instruments can match the enduring quality and craftsmanship of those that bear the Ibach name.

IRMLER

The company was founded in 1818 in Leipzig, Germany, and continued to produce pianos until the 1950s.

KAPS

This company was founded in 1858 in Dresden, Germany, by Ernest Kaps. Kaps is said to have built the first 5ft grand piano to employ overstringing.

KAWAI

It is said that at the age of just 12 Koichi Kawai was hired by Torakusu Yamaha to help him make pianos. Kawai, born in 1886, was the son of a maker of wagons and carts, and had successfully built himself a wooden bicycle that so impressed neighbor Yamaha that he enlisted Kawai's help in building Japan's first upright pianos.

Kawai continued to work with Yamaha until the latter's death in 1916. During that period he and Yamaha had introduced and established the piano in Japan. Kawai continued to work for the Nippon Gakki Co. Ltd (as Yamaha's company was called) for several years until in 1927, along with six associates, he established the Kawai Musical Instrument Research Laboratory, also in Hamamatsu, Japan.

By the end of the first year Kawai had designed and built a successful action, and the first instrument the company produced was a 64-note upright piano which sold for just 350 yen. In 1928 Kawai unveiled his first grand piano. The following year the company changed its name to Kawai Musical Instrument Manufacturing Company.

At that time demand for pianos in Japan was not strong. Kawai made barely 250 pianos a year, and the company had to rely on the production of harmonicas to supplement its piano-making activities. However, Kawai realized that he had to develop his own action in order to give the business a competitive edge. Until then all piano actions had been imported.

By 1935 Kawai was producing nearly 1000 upright pianos and over 100 grands a year, but then World War II intervened. The Kawai factory was required to switch from pianos to arms production and the facility was used to manufacture aircraft parts. In 1945 the city of Hamamatsu was bombed and most of the manufacturing base, including the Kawai factory, was destroyed.

Undaunted, Kawai and 57 former employees set about rebuilding the factory, and despite extreme hardship they managed to re-establish the company. By 1949 Kawai was back in production, making both grand and upright pianos. The company was considerably aided by the post-war US policy for Japan which encouraged the arts and led to music being put on the school curriculum. By 1953 the company was producing 1,500 pianos per annum.

Koichi Kawai died in 1955 and his son Shigeru became president of the company at the age of 33. The economic climate was most conducive to growth, and the company expanded rapidly, helped by aggressive sales techniques. In the 1960s salesmen would obtain lists of recent births and call on the new parents to exhort the benefits of a musical education. More recently Kawai has moved into the top league of instrument manufacturers, and the company continues to produce good quality instruments.

Kemble

This British firm was established in 1911 by Michael Kemble and Victor Jacobs. The company achieved considerable success in the 1930s and 1940s with their Minx range of small pianos. They took over the Brinsmead company in 1967, and 20 years later Kemble became Yamaha's manufacturing partner.

Kimball

W.W. Kimball and Co. was founded in 1857 when William Wallace Kimball, a business representative who came from a farming background in Oxford County, Maine, was drawn to the trading opportunities in Chicago, Illinois. He moved to the city and set up as a piano dealer, selling Chickering, Hallett & Davis and Emerson pianos. In 1871 the great fire of Chicago destroyed his complete stock of instruments, but he was soon back in business and subsequently became one of the largest piano retailers in America. Such was the stability of the company that one supplier, Joseph P. Hale, happily extended to the Kimball operation a $100,000 credit facility.

In order to expand his business, Kimball, with the help of Edwin Conway, set up dealerships across the western states. In the mid 1880s supply of organs and pianos became restricted and Kimball decided in 1886 to make his own instruments. With a ready made market, the manufacturing side of the company flourished, and Kimball was soon producing over 4,000 pianos a year. The Kimball company's main contribution to the evolution of the piano was in work on the improvement of the iron frame.

W.W. Kimball died in 1904. The company reached its peak in the 1910s, but the effects of the Depression and some poor decision making meant that the company never recaptured its former glory. In 1959 the company was purchased by the Jasper Corporation, a lumber and furniture company of Indiana. Under the Jasper Corporation the company grew and became known as Kimball International.

In 1966 Bösendorfer was purchased by Kimball, as were other important names in the industry including Krakauer (pianos) and Herrburger Brooks (piano actions). Today Kimball is best known for its lower-priced upright and console pianos, and the company produces various own-label brands for other dealers and distributors.

Knabe

William Knabe was born in Kreutzberg, Germany, where he was apprenticed to a piano-maker before emigrating to the US in 1833, where he settled in Baltimore, Maryland. After six years mastering the English language and learning how to do business in America, Knabe set up in partnership with another German piano-maker, Henry Gaehle, under the name Knabe & Gaehle. In 1854 Gaehle left the company, leaving Knabe with a free hand. It seems this was just what he wanted. Such was Knabe's business acumen that by 1860 he dominated the southern states. But the company suffered badly during the Civil War, and Knabe died in 1864, leaving the company in the hands of his sons.

The after-effects of the Civil War continued to affect the company badly, and Ernest Knabe decided that the only way out of their troubles was to sell the company's pianos in the northern and western states. Alfred Dolge in his book *Pianos And Their Makers* says that Knabe needed $20,000 to cover his expenses for a six-month sales trip into these areas, and went to his bank in Baltimore for a loan. The bank asked what security he had to offer. "Nothing but the name of Knabe," was his reply.

The bank rather ungenerously decided not to make the loan, and asked Knabe what he proposed to do. "I shall go down to my factory and tell my employees that I am compelled to discharge them all because your bank refused a loan to which I am entitled," he said, and left the bank. Before he could reach the factory gates, the president of the bank had sent a messenger to intercept Ernest with a letter agreeing to the loan in full. So Ernest set off on his sales trip, and within two months had sold enough pianos to keep the factory in full production – without having to draw on a single dollar of the loan.

Knabe pianos were very highly regarded by pianists such as Camille Saint-Saëns, an enthusiastic user, and by the turn of the century the company was making around 2,000 instruments each year. In 1908 Knabe became part of the American Piano Co..

Knight

A well respected English company founded in 1935 by Alfred Knight, the company had the reputation of producing some of the best upright pianos in England in recent times. They also produced specially-strengthened pianos for use in entertaining British troops during World War II. Nine such pianos went ashore during the Normandy landings in 1944.

Kohler & Campbell

Charles Kohler and J.C. Campbell founded this leading piano and player piano manufacturing company in 1896 in New York City. In 1954 the company moved to North Carolina where it continued to produce pianos until 1985.

Krakauer Bros

Violinist and conductor Simon Krakauer was born in Kissingen, Germany, in 1816, and emigrated to the US in 1854 where he founded the company with his son David in 1869. It remained in family control until 1977. Originally the company made upright pianos of a superior quality, but like many such companies Krakauer decided that they could become more profitable by making cheaper pianos and thereby selling more instruments. Howard Graves was the new owner of the company, and he moved the factory from New York City to the Amish town of Berlin, Ohio. This did not prove to be a success and Graves sold the company to Kimball in 1980, who in turn closed the factory in 1985, over one hundred years since the company's origins.

Kranich & Bach

Founded in 1864 in New York, this company which produced good quality instruments was subsequently taken over by the Aeolian Corporation.

Lemuel Gilbert

This firm was founded in 1839 in Boston, Massachusetts.

Lighte & Newton

This company was founded in 1848 in New York. Newton left the company in 1853 and William Bradbury then took an active part until his death in 1867. The company was subsequently renamed Lighte & Bradbury.

Lindemann

Famed for their curved grand and square pianos with three legs, the company was founded in 1836 in New York, and was subsequently taken over by the American Piano Company.

Luther

This company was founded by John Frederik Luther in 1843 in New York.

Mannborg

This firm, founded in 1889 in Leipzig, Germany, continued to produce pianos into the 1960s.

Marshall & Mittauer

This company, founded in 1867 on Long Island, New York, was taken over by Hugo Sohmer in 1872.

Mason & Hamlin

This Boston, Massachusetts, firm was founded in 1854 by Henry Mason and Emmons Hamlin. Originally they made reed organs, but it was their American Cabinet Organ that won them great acclaim, and the success of this instrument in 1881 led the company to produce pianos. The company's instruments were of an extremely high quality and soon Mason & Hamlin became one of the most prestigious US brands, although at the turn of the century its output of around 700 instruments a year was not large by American standards. As a result of the Depression in the 1930s the company became part of the Aeolian American Corporation.

Meyer

Conrad Meyer founded this company in 1824 in Philadelphia, Pennsylvania. It is said that Meyer produced a complete iron frame in 1833, which would mean that he was one of the first to do so.

Neumeyer

This company was founded in 1861 in Berlin, Germany.

Niendorf

This firm was founded in 1896 in Luckenwald, Germany, and Niendorf continued to make pianos into the 1970s.

Nunns & Clark

The New York company was founded in 1823 by two immigrants from London, England. Robert and William Nunns were joined some ten years later by another Englishman, John Clark, and the company was best known for its square pianos. William Nunns subsequently left Nunns & Clark and went to work for J.C. Fischer.

Pape

Jean-Henri Pape was probably the most inventive figure in the world of the 19th century piano, and constantly developed new concepts and ideas in manufacturing and design. Many of his ideas were too extreme to gain general acceptance, especially some of the odd-shaped instruments that he produced or, for example, his design of 1850 for a piano with six strings per note. But among the 120 or more patents that he filed there were some revolutionary ideas that were to prove most beneficial in the evolution of the piano.

Pape was born in Sarstedt, Germany, in 1789. He moved to Paris in 1809 but almost immediately left to spend a few years in London studying piano manufacturing techniques. On his return he became foreman at the Pleyel factory where he put into effect much of what he had learned in London. In 1817 he set up his own workshop and this gave him the freedom to experiment – which he most certainly did.

He is best known for the elegant design of his instruments, as can be seen in his square and console instruments shown within this book. His main technological contributions include what became known as the French down-striking action (inspired by Wornum's and Streicher's designs), the use of felt to cover hammers, his console pianos, and his use of tempered steel wire for strings.

At one point Pape ran the largest piano factory in Paris, employing over 300 workers. He also sponsored a comprehensive training program that attracted students from all over the world, the most famous of whom was Carl Bechstein. And yet despite all these achievements and apparent success, Pape died in 1842 a relatively poor man.

Perzina

Founded by Paul Perzina in 1871 in Schwerin, Germany, Perzina was a medium sized manufacturer producing average quality pianos. The company is best known for its pioneering work on the mechanics of the keyboard action, with Paul Perzina reworking the Janko keyboard design to make it more playable.

Petrof

The Petrof company was founded by Antonin Petrof in 1864 in a

Bohemian town called Hradec Králové (now in the Czech Republic). Antonin was born in 1839, and while a woodworking apprentice was sent by his father Jan Petrof to the home of a choirmaster to repair a piece of furniture. While he was there Antonin noticed a piano in the middle of the room and became fascinated by its appearance and sound. The choirmaster explained the history of the instrument, and expressed some regret that such instruments had to be imported from Vienna as there was no domestic piano-maker in Bohemia.

Prompted by these comments, Petrof expressed an interest to stay with his uncle, Jan Heitzmann, a piano-maker based in Vienna, to learn more of the instrument. He studied in Vienna for four years and subsequently went to work for Ehrbar and Schweighofer where he studied piano tuning, voicing and regulation.

He returned to Hradec Králové at a time when Bohemia was undergoing a period of economic and cultural growth. With the aid of his father and four co-workers, Antonin produced four pianos which were received with great acclaim. This led to a rapid expansion in the company's output, hindered only by the Austrian-Prussian War, the main battle of which was fought just a few miles away at Sadová. This led to a local outbreak of cholera, in which Antonin's father died. Antonin had to register a new company in 1865. He married in 1869, and with the dowry expanded the business. In 1874 he bought a local inn and turned it into a workshop, and when he brought in steam engines in 1876 this made the Petrof factory the first facility in Bohemia with such equipment. By the turn of the century Petrof was making grand and upright pianos and other keyboard instruments, and the company continued to grow with the aid of his son Antonin Petrof Jr. In 1908 Petrof began producing player pianos and took over various allied companies, mostly in Vienna.

The company's 50th anniversary fell during World War I, which was not a positive time for the company as the two eldest Petrof sons had to fight for their country, and a year later, in 1915, Antonin Petrof senior died. By 1928 355 people were employed at Petrof, producing 2,300 pianos a year, and although the slump of the 1930s affected the company, its structure was sufficiently sound to withstand the adverse economic conditions. Two of the family's next generation, Ivan and Dimitrij Petrof, were sent to work at the Steinberg and Bechstein factories to gain experience, and subsequently Bechstein had its Neo Bechstein electric grand pianos made at the Petrof factory in Hradec Králové.

Petrof also managed to function through World War II, albeit with a reduced workforce of 90 employees. The company had to manufacture ammunition boxes for the war effort, but their construction was so easy that it was possible still to make some pianos. One of the limitations on piano manufacture during the war was that bass strings could not be wound with copper.

In 1948 the company became state-owned, and the period of family ownership that had lasted three generation was at an end. At first production fell, but by 1955 output had started to increase again, and in 1963 the company, which still used the Petrof brandname, produced its 100,000th instrument, while in 1964 800 grand pianos and some 3,000 uprights were produced. At present the company produces over 25,000 pianos a year.

PFEIFFER

Stuttgart, Germany, has always been the home of the Carl A. Pfeiffer company. It was founded in 1862 by Joseph Anton Pfeiffer, and this small company has been responsible for producing instruments of high quality. The company bears the full name of Carl Anton Pfeiffer, Joseph's son, who learnt his craft while working at the Steinway and Brinsmead companies. Pfeiffer was once the world's leading manufacturer of pedal pianos, producing systems for both upright and grand pianos. These were used primarily to enable organists to practice their skills on the piano, although the instruments were also used in their own right. Mendelssohn and Schumann both owned pedal pianos, and Schumann composed several works for the instrument.

PIRSSON

The company was founded by James Pirsson in 1829 in New York. One notable patent held by Pirsson was for a duoclave or double piano, which dates from 1850. This instrument had two keyboards – the players had to sit facing one another – and the frame, for which the patent was issued, supports two sets of strings. The company continued until 1857.

PLEYEL

One of the most important French piano houses was that of Pleyel, founded in 1807 by Ignace Pleyel who was trained as a composer by Haydn. In 1789, at the start of what was to become the French Revolution, Pleyel had been accused of favoring the nobility. To prove his allegiance to the Revolution he was ordered to write a score for a Republican drama. Fortunately the work was well received and Pleyel's politics were no longer doubted, but the experience was enough for him to move, temporarily, to England, where he became acquainted with the burgeoning piano industry.

On his return to Paris, Pleyel set up a piano factory in 1807 and three years later was granted an important patent for the tempering of brass and steel piano strings. The company became best known for their pianinos, which were based on designs produced by Robert Wornum in England. Henri Pape, then foreman at the Pleyel factory, developed this type of upright instrument which became so popular in France that there was little subsequent demand for the square piano.

Pleyel also developed a range of grand pianos based on the Broadwood grand action. Ignace himself became a close friend of Frédéric Chopin, who was a devoted user of Pleyel pianos. Ignace handed the company over to his eldest son, Camille, in 1824. He successfully developed the business, and helped to establish the Bord piano company in 1840. Camille died in 1855 at which point his partner Auguste Wolff took control. With non-family members running the company the name changed to Pleyel, Wolff & Cie and then to Pleyel, Lyon & Co. (1887). The company purchased Bord in 1934, but following a merger with Erard-Gaveau in 1961 the company subsequently became owned by Schimmel.

QRS

QRS Music Rolls Inc. was established in 1900 and is one of the few survivors in this marketplace. The company was founded by Melville Clark, of Story and Clark, who was instrumental in the success of the pneumatic player piano. The invention of the Marking Piano was the key to QRS success. This device enabled QRS to produce 'Hand Played' rolls, which meant that great pianists could produce master rolls as they played. The first such commercially successful roll was 'Pretty Baby' played by ragtime pianist Charlie Straight and released in 1912.

Under the auspices of Thomas M. Pletcher the company grew, and was associated with many famous players and artists such as Fats Waller and James P. Johnson, both of whom cut QRS rolls. Sales in 1926 amounted to a staggering 11 million rolls, but the Depression and the arrival of other entertainment media hit QRS badly over the following decades, and by the 1950s only about 20,000 rolls a year were being sold. However, a resurgence in the market during the 1960s saw the company's sales start to improve once more. The Marking Piano was dusted off and artists such as Liberace, Peter Nero and Roger Williams all cut new rolls. The fact that so many player pianos still survive ensures the continuing existence of the company, coupled with the fact that QRS and the Story & Clark Piano Co. joined forces in 1993 and now produce several new player pianos and Nickelodeons for the world market.

RÖNISCH

In 1845 Carl Rönisch, in his early 30s and with virtually no money, managed to establish his piano making company in Dresden, the cultural center of Saxony (later part of East Germany). The grand pianos and uprights that Rönisch built were very good and became extremely popular on the German market. Rönisch also knew how to sell abroad, and such was his success in Russia that he built a factory in St. Petersburg. Rönisch was personally honored for his achievements and was appointed purveyor of the court of Saxony, which led to the company bearing the title 'Carl Rönisch Court Piano Factories Dresden'.

Rönisch died in 1893, and his sons Albert and Hermann took over the running of the company. Rönisch was later sub-contracted to make pianos for Ludwig Hupfeld's self-playing instrument company. Eventually it was clear that a merger between the companies would be sensible, and this happened in 1918. Together they produced a line of pianos and a collection of different automatic instruments, including the Phonoliszt-Violina (a self-playing piano with violins, see p58) and many Orchestrions (self-playing instruments containing most of the instruments of a small dance orchestra).

With the advent of radio and the gramophone, along with the decline in demand for automatic instruments, the company concentrated its efforts on grand pianos, and despite difficulties throughout World War II the company survived. In 1947 it became known as Leipziger Pianofortefabrik, but under state control became the Deutsche Piano-Union Leipzig. Following re-unification the Leipziger Pianofortefabrik name was reinstated, and today the company produces a full range of upright and grand pianos.

ROTH & JUNIUS

This company was founded in 1889 in Hagen, Germany.

SAMICK

In 1958 Hyo Ick Lee established the Samick Musical Instrument Co. Ltd. in Incheon, South Korea. Korea had suffered from the effects of recent war, but the company rapidly grew as the country's economy began to heal. Indeed, the growth that Samick enjoyed was phenomenal, and in 30 years it became one of the world's largest piano-makers, with over 10,000 employees. Samick produces pianos for other distributors, including Hyundai and Schumann, and in addition claims to produce more fretted instruments than any other company in the world.

SAUTER

Johann Grimm, a carpenter, left his home town of Spraichingen, Bavaria, in 1813 and traveled to Vienna where he settled and began to learn the business of piano-making. He was apprenticed at the Streicher workshop for six years, after which he decided to return home. In 1819 he built six square pianos with the assistance of his adopted step-son Carl Sauter, and together they subsequently assembled a team of craftsmen to produce further instruments. So began another important piano house whose control has remained in the same family through six generations. Sauter continues to build pianos of a very high quality, and concentrates on producing instruments that sell at the higher-priced end of the market.

SCHIEDMAYER

The company of J. & C. Schiedmayer was founded in 1853 in Stuttgart, Germany, by Julius and Paul Schiedmayer, grandsons of Johan David Shiedmayer who had worked with Johann Andreas Stein. The company originally produced harmoniums, but was forced into the piano market by the increasing dominance of the instrument. The name is now used by Kawai for a line of their pianos.

SCHILLER

This company was founded in 1884 in Berlin, Germany, by J. Schiller.

SCHIMMEL

At the age of 16 Wilhelm Schimmel, the son of a schoolmaster, started his apprenticeship as a cabinet maker. The year was 1870, and part of his instruction included the manufacture of accordions and violins. His interest in musical instruments was kindled, but after finishing his apprenticeship he soon rose to become supervisor of the local cabinet-making firm. Then Schimmel heard that Stichel Pianofortefabrik in Leipzig had a vacancy for an apprentice piano-maker, and in 1876 without hesitation he left his supervisor's job to start again as an apprentice. Here he worked for some eight years before being tempted to set up in business on his own.

Schimmel started on his own in 1885 and set about producing instruments from a tiny building in Neuschönefeld, near Leipzig. In less than nine years Schimmel made over 1,000 instruments, and just four years later the company produced their 2,500th piano.

Wilhelm Schimmel finally retired from the company in 1927 at the age of 73. His legacy to his son, Wilhelm Arno, was a highly profitable company, a prestigious brandname and a line of pianos with an excellent reputation for good quality and value for money. Unfortunately Wilhelm Arno had taken control of the company at a time when the world's economies were in decline and the demand for pianos was being eroded by the arrival of the gramophone and radio. Schimmel and several other German piano makers consolidated their positions by pooling resources, and this loose merger was known as the Deutsche Piano Works. The company's manufacturing base was moved to Brunswick.

After a few years it became clear that Schimmel's interests would be best served by leaving the co-operative, and in 1931 Wilhelm Arno made his company independent once again, renaming it Wilhelm Schimmel Pianofortefabrik GmbH and providing a now permanent base in Brunswick. Unlike most of the established piano-makers Schimmel was ready to respond to the demands of the new generation of piano buyers, and concentrated its production on instruments with the contemporary 'console' styling. Their Golden Jubilee model of 1935 was the precursor to the Mini-Royal, which was licensed to Eavestaff with great success. In 1944, toward the end of World War II, the factory was virtually destroyed, but a modest facility for the repair and renovation of instruments was rebuilt by the end of 1945 and by 1947 production had resumed.

In 1973 the company was under the auspices of Nicholas Wilhelm Schimmel, and moved to new, larger premises on the outskirts of

Brunswick that enabled production to grow to approximately 9,000 grands and uprights a year, making it the largest piano manufacturer in western Europe. Schimmel pioneered the use of acrylic for piano construction and it is probably the only company to offer this 'finish' as a standard option for a new instrument. One such instrument is to be found on board the Queen Elizabeth II (QE2) cruise liner.

SCHMIDT-FLOHR

Founded in Berne, Switzerland, in 1833 by A. Schmidt, the company produced good quality pianos and is best known for building the prototype of Emanuel Moór's two-manual keyboard action in 1921.

SEILER

In the early 1920s Seiler was the largest piano-maker in Eastern Europe, producing some 3,000 instruments a year. It was founded in 1849 by Eduard Seiler, who originally made pianos in Liegnitz, Silesia (then part of Germany; now divided between Poland, Germany and the Czech Republic). By the 1860s the company was making over 100 pianos a year, and received international acclaim for its instruments. Eduard died in 1875, and the business was taken over by his son Johannes. The company continued to grow, producing around 1,300 pianos a year by the turn of the century, and the 25,000th Seiler piano was made in 1898.

The end of World War II saw the company in complete disarray. Liegnitz had become part of Poland, and the family home and factory had been destroyed. Political upheaval had yet again affected a famous piano house. Steffen Seiler, a member of the fourth generation of the Seiler family, moved to Denmark and began producing pianos based on an earlier design of the Brødr Jørgensen company. Barely 200 pianos were built between 1945 and 1952, but gradually the situation improved and in 1957 the company was able to move back to Germany and set up a factory in Kitzingen, where annual production is now around 5,000 pianos.

The Seiler company produces high quality instruments and is not adverse to experimentation and new ideas. Their Membrator soundboard, patented in 1983, features a groove around its edge that gives the soundboard greater flexibility. Seiler claims that this particular feature enables smaller pianos to produce a sound comparable in tone and volume to larger instruments with traditional soundboards.

Seiler also produces its unique Showmaster grand and upright pianos which incorporate electro-magnetic pickups and MIDI sensors for synthesizer linking, and all in a highly stylized case (see p78). The company also recently developed a magnetic piano action which serves to provide additional force on the jack that will relocate it after a note has been played. This enables a faster repetition of the note and dispenses with the necessity for the key to be released so much before the note can be replayed.

F.G. SMITH

Freeborn Garrettson Smith worked in the Chickering factory before becoming foreman at the Bradbury piano factory in Leominster, Massachusetts, which he bought after Bradbury's death. Smith's company was established in 1866 and he made a considerable fortune by developing piano 'warehouses' in larger cities that enabled him to sell instruments directly to the public.

SOHMER

Hugo Sohmer, born in Germany's Black Forest region in 1846, moved to New York at the age of 16. In 1872 he took over the Marshall & Mittauer piano business and founded the American piano-maker Sohmer & Co. in partnership with K. Kuder. The pianos made by Sohmer were of an extremely high quality, and it is believed that Hugo had close liaisons with Steinway & Sons, sharing ideas and work practices.

The business remained in the control of the family until 1982, when the founder's grandsons, Harry and Robert Sohmer, sold the company to the American piano key manufacturer Pratt, Read and Co. who moved the business to the aptly named Ivoryton, Connecticut. However, in 1986 Pratt, Read and Co. sold the business to Robert McNeil, who in turn sold the company and its related brandnames to Bernard Greer, owner of the Falcone Piano Co. The company continues to produce instruments of a high standard of craftsmanship.

STECK

George Steck established this successful company in 1857 in New York. Steck came from Cassel, Germany, and is best known for producing scales for both upright and grand pianos. These have subsequently been copied by many of the great piano houses. Because of the high quality and durability of Steck's pianos, they were used in schools across America at the turn of the century. Steck is also notable as one of the first company owners to introduce an employee share scheme.

STEINGRAEBER & SÖHNE

Eduard Steingraeber, born in 1823, founded this small but prestigious company in 1852 in Bayreuth, Germany, the same year that he passed his master craftsman's examination. His family had its roots in harpsichord manufacturing in the 18th century; Eduard's father Christian, for example, had spent some time working at his uncle Gottlieb's harpsichord works in Neustadt an der Orla, Thuringia.

The quality of Eduard's pianos became famous, and in 1874 Richard Wagner asked Eduard to build a special piano with a carillon for use in the temple scenes of 'Parsifal', a piece of music described by the composer as his 'sacred festival drama'.

The company is still run today by the Schmidt-Steingraeber family. Worthy of note is the fact that this is one of the few piano-makers to provide options for the disabled: the sustain and damper pedals are activated by switches which may be located in positions that suit the player's disability. The company also makes what is claimed to be the largest commercially available upright piano, the Model 138.

STEINWAY & SONS

The world's best known piano manufacturer owes its existence to strike action in 1853 at the factory of Bacon & Raven, then New York's largest piano manufacturer. Some three years earlier Heinrich Engelhard Steinweg Snr, his wife and five of their seven children had left their hometown of Seesen in the Province of Brunswick, Germany, to set up a new home in the US. (This emigration of key figures in the piano world to an economically more favorable climate has been a key element in the evolution of the piano, right from the time of the legendary Twelve Apostles' move to London in the 1760s.)

Steinweg was originally a cabinet maker by trade, but had shown great interest in musical instruments. He made his first piano in 1836 at the age of 39. The Steinweg family had subsequently run a small musical instrument shop in Seesen where they had also made many types of instruments, among which were included up to 10 pianos a year.

A political revolution occurred in Germany in 1848, and many businesses had been forced to close or suffered great hardship. Heinrich decided he had to leave Germany, and he and his family, with the exception of his eldest son C.F. Theodor Steinweg, emigrated to America. On arriving, the family decided to Americanize their surname from the German 'Steinweg' to the more American-sounding 'Steinway'. Henry E. Steinway Snr. found work at Laucht, a company that made soundboards, his sons Henry Jnr. and Albert joined Charles Steinway (who had been in America since 1849) at the Bacon & Raven Company, and William Steinway (then aged just 14) went to work at William Nuns & Co., another piano manufacturer.

By 1853 Henry Snr. and his brothers had assimilated the workings of the American piano industry, and a strike at Bacon & Raven was the trigger for them to start up their own business. They did this with the capital they had brought with them from Germany together with the savings the Steinweg brothers had amassed from their American employment. Within ten years they were running the world's largest piano factory.

The Steinways originally began working in a rented loft at 85 Varick Street, New York City, building one piano a week, but as the business grew they moved to 82-84 Walker Street (1854), and by 1860 had acquired their own factory and lumber yard that took up a whole block between 52nd and 53rd Streets and what is now Park Avenue, the present site of the Seagram Building.

When the Steinways set up their new facility they took the opportunity to introduce completely new designs and working methods, and became truly innovative in their approach to piano construction. However, their first instrument had been a conventional square piano. At that time, as William Steinway wrote, "The sale of grand pianos were about as scarce as angels' visits." Although the first instruments of 1853 featured no notable innovations, they were built to a remarkably high standard of workmanship.

Theodor Steinweg in Germany moved in 1855 from Seesen to Wolfenbuttl, and again in 1860 to Braunschweig where he began manufacturing pianos under the Steinweg name. Henry Jnr. in the US and Theodor in Germany exchanged many letters back and forth, bouncing ideas as to how the design and manufacture of pianos might be improved.

Their first major innovation was to introduce cross-stringing to their square piano in 1855. Cross-stringing involves the running of the bass strings over the top of the treble strings, enabling the use of much longer strings which consequently makes the instrument louder. They also introduced at the same time a cast iron frame (or plate). Steinway was one of the few companies to realize the value of exhibiting at fairs, and it was at the 1855 World Fair that the company's new square piano received universal acclaim, putting the name of Steinway clearly on the map.

In 1860 the company produced the piano that was to be the basis for the modern grand piano. This was the overstrung grand, the forerunner to the modern concert grand. It received wide praise. However, five years later the Steinway company was badly shaken by the deaths of Henry Jnr., aged just 34, Charles, and Theodor Vogel (husband of Wihelmine Steinway) who had become a superintendent at the factory. Coupled with the loss of Albert Steinway to the Union Army for the period of the Civil War, this meant Steinway was suddenly drastically lacking senior management.

C.F. Theodor immediately sold the German business, now known as Grotrian-Steinweg, and moved to America to look after the design and constructional side of the operation. Theodor had a strong scientific background and worked in conjunction with many scientists and engineers in the development of the instrument. Most notably he had a close relationship with Hermann von Helmholtz, the physicist and acoustic engineer who had been specializing in the study of and research into the harmonic structure of various musical instruments.

Theodor's legacy to the piano world was immense. When he was in charge of design the company introduced, among many other things, the one-piece piano rim, produced using 18 laminations of wood. This gave the instrument greater strength, which meant higher potential string tensions and consequently an increased volume. The 88-note 8ft 9in Centennial grand of 1876 could handle 60,000lbs of string tension, and is remarkably similar to the Steinway grand of today. By the time of his death in 1889 at the age of 63, Theodor Steinway had to his credit 45 essential patents relating to the design and construction of the piano, most of which have been adopted by other piano makers.

The Steinway company was not only adept in matters concerning design, but also in the field of marketing. William Steinway inaugurated the 2,000-seater Steinway Hall which opened in 1866. Until the opening of Carnegie Hall in 1891 this was the cultural center for all New Yorkers, and the focal point of the Steinway company. With all the great virtuosi of the era playing there, the Steinway Hall was a living advertisement for the piano that shares its name. William Steinway also linked the Steinway name with great players such as Anton Rubinstein and Ignace Jan Paderewski (whom he brought to the US from Poland), associations that were to help establish the Steinway piano as the world's finest.

Building upon this international fame, in 1880 William instigated the opening of a factory in Hamburg, Germany, in order to challenge the European dominance by companies such as Bechstein, Blüthner and Ibach. Another Steinway Hall was opened in London.

Steinway & Sons began to realize that central Manhattan was not necessarily the best location for heavy industry, and so the company purchased 400 acres of land on Bowery Bay, Long Island (now in the borough of Queens) in order to set up a foundry and wood mill. Continuing labor troubles in Manhattan led to William Steinway moving more and more of the Steinway operation out to Long Island, where he effectively set up an entire Steinway village. In 1910 the city of New York council passed an ordnance forbidding the operation of a factory on Park Avenue, and the whole production operation was moved to Long Island.

The Depression of the 1930s saw Steinway's output fall from 280,000 pianos in 1927 to 50,000 by 1931. Steinway survived but had to introduce less expensive models. The market had picked up by 1940, but the advent of World War II meant that Steinway was not allowed to make pianos for the consumer market, and instead the company was required to help the war effort. Its expertise in laminate technology meant that the company was ideally suited to produce aircraft parts, in particular for the CG-4A troop transport gliders. Steinway was also commissioned to produce portable pianos called the Victory Verticals for the forces overseas – these became known as 'G.I. pianos' and around 3,000 were built. The Hamburg factory was declared enemy property and, taken over by the Nazi government, was used to make dummy airplanes, beds and rifle butts.

In 1972 the Steinway company was sold to the Musical

Instrument Division of Columbia Broadcasting System (CBS). John Steinway stated, "The ownership change was dictated by the classic problem of taxes on estates. It's tough to run a family business over many generations because of inheritance taxes, and because ownership had become spread out in the family to cousins who had nothing to do with the business, but who owned a piece of it and who were not willing to reinvest. So selling to CBS seemed to be the obvious solution."

CBS managed the company until 1985 when corporate policy led the company to divest itself of 'non-core' operations. The company was sold to a group of Boston businessmen, John P. and Robert M. Birmingham and Bruce A. Stevens, who hold the company under the name Steinway Musical Properties Inc.. The name found on the instruments is still Steinway & Sons.

STODART & MORRIS

This company was founded in 1856 in New York.

STORY & CLARK

Hampton Story, his son Edward, and Melville Clark founded this company in 1884 for the purpose of making reed organs. Hampton Story had been in the American musical instrument industry for many years as a wholesaler and retailer, but he saw his future as a manufacturer. In 1895 the firm started to make pianos, but in 1900 Melville Clark left. Later the company introduced an electric piano, the Storytone, which incorporated a record player and radio. In the 1970s the company became part of Lowrey, but in 1993 the story turned full circle as Story & Clark joined up with QRS, the company originally founded by Melville Clark in 1900 to produce a new range of automatic instruments.

STREICHER

This Austrian firm was established in 1802 by Johann Andreas Stein's daughter, Nannette, and her husband Johann Andreas Streicher. This followed the dissolution of the Stein company that Nannette and her brother Matthäus Stein had been running. The company remained under family control until 1896.

STROHMENGER

Established in London, England, in 1835 by John Strohmenger, the company was bought by Chappell in 1938.

THÜRMER

Thürmer are an important German manufacturer, founded in 1834 by Ferdinand Thürmer in Meissen, Saxony (later part of East Germany). The company achieved an output of 2,800 pianos a year in 1908, making it the fourth largest producer in Germany at the time. The company carries on today, run by the fifth generation of the Thürmer family, and continues to make high quality instruments. The present Thürmer factory, located in Bochum, Germany, incorporates a 450-seat theater which is regularly used for piano concerts and, since 1984, an annual piano festival.

UEBEL & LECHLEITNER

Founded in 1871 in Heilbronn, Germany, this company is a medium-size manufacturer which continued to make pianos into the 1980s.

WEBER

Albert Weber, a German immigrant to the US, founded this high-quality manufacturing company in 1852 in Rochester, New York. Weber was instrumental in persuading famous players to promote their instruments, courting such artists as Hofmann and Paderewski. In 1903 the company became part of the Aeolian Corporation, and in 1986 the name was purchased by Young Chang, who subsequently sold it to Samsung (although Young Chang continue to manufacture the pianos).

WHELPDALE MAXWELL & CODD

Originally the company was formed in 1876 to act as British agents for the German piano-maker Blüthner. However, just before World War II a fire at the Squire & Longson factory meant that a fully trained piano-manufacturing workforce became unemployed. Company directors Whelpdale and Maxwell decided then to launch their own range of pianos using this skilled team of craftspeople, and has produced the Welmar range of pianos. The company subsequently purchased Marshall & Rose, and more recently has taken over the Rogers, Hopkinson and Knight brands. The company also produces Broadwood upright pianos under license.

WOODWARD & BROWN

This firm was established in 1843 in Boston, Massachusetts.

WORCESTER

This company was founded by Horatio Worcester in 1836 in New York, and Worcester subsequently joined forces with William Stodart.

WORNUM

Robert Wornum Jr. was born in England in 1780, the son of a music publisher. He set up in partnership with George Wilkinson in 1811, with whom he worked for two years, but the death of Robert's father required Wornum to take over the family business, and he thus severed all links with Wilkinson.

Wornum contributed more to the development of the upright piano than any other manufacturer. It was his design of 1811 with diagonal stringing, later to be known as a 'cottage piano', that marked an enormously important step forward in piano design. He also produced several highly important actions, including his 1826 upright design which is the blueprint for the action of the modern upright, and the tape-check action which also is used with only minor modifications to the present day.

Nevertheless, Wornum's upright designs were generally rather delicate and lacking in power and volume. This lack of power is puzzling, especially when comparisons are made with Wornum's grand pianos, although it is most likely due to his decision not to use any form of metal strengthening in his frames. Consequently Wornum's uprights did not fulfill their potential, and exploitation of the general design was left to other manufacturers, most notably the French houses of the period. Robert Wornum died in 1852, although the company continued to produce pianos until about 1878.

WURLITZER

In 1853 the 22-year-old Franz Rudolph Wurlitzer arrived penniless in Hoboken, New Jersey. He had left his home in Saxony (later part of East Germany) intending to take advantage of the opportunities that he had heard America offered. On arrival he took clerical jobs, including working for a bank. Next to the bank was a music shop, and Wurlitzer noticed that European musical instruments on display were being sold for disproportionately high prices. He discovered that this was because the imported goods had to pass through so many intermediaries. He saved $700 which he sent to his father with the instructions that he should purchase certain musical instruments and ship these to him in New York. This he did, and Franz was able to sell them at a fraction of the cost that they previously commanded in America. This marked the inception of the Wurlitzer Co. in 1856.

The company continued to wholesale instruments until Wurlitzer had enough money to set up a manufacturing plant in Cincinnati, Ohio, in 1861. Four years later he opened a retail shop and expanded the distribution business across the US. In 1880 Wurlitzer started to make pianos, and the company grew and became particularly well known for military and mechanical instruments. Franz Rudolph Wurlitzer died in 1914, but the company continued and managed to survive the age of the gramophone by introducing the first automatic jukebox, the Wurlitzer Simplex, in 1934. Wurlitzer was also known for its pipe and theater organs, and in 1954 it introduced an influential electric piano, the Model 100.

YAMAHA

Yamaha is at the time of writing one of the world's two largest piano makers, producing around 130,000 instruments a year. This is a vast number when compared to the output of the other major piano houses.

Torakusu Yamaha was born in 1851, the son of a samurai of the Tokugawa Shogunate. His father was an astronomer and a surveyor, and ensured that Torakusu received a good education. Following the Meiji Restoration of 1868, when a more liberal attitude swept Japan, Yamaha went to Nagasaki to study horology under a British engineer. At the time, all the wristwatches available in Japan were imported, and so Yamaha, who had used such timepieces when helping his father, reflected that the skilled workmanship needed to make such objects would be in great demand in the new Japan. Though he studied hard and did become a proficient watchmaker, Yamaha's lack of funds prevented him from setting up his own watchmaking company. His mechanical skills were to serve him well, however, and subsequent employment brought him to Hamamatsu, a remote town of some 17,000 inhabitants, where he worked as a mechanical engineer.

In 1887 Yamaha was called to a local Hamamatsu school to repair an American reed organ. These instruments were extremely rare in Japan at the time, and the organ was highly prized. Through studying the workings of the organ, Yamaha became fascinated by this new musical technology and decided to build his own instrument. Having little money, he had to improvise using everyday items to fabricate the components. Thus in 1887 the first Yamaha organ was made. The device was a great success and Yamaha used it to generate enough investment to allow him to set up the Yamaha Organ Mfg. Co. in Hamamatsu in 1889. That first year he sold 250 organs.

In 1897 the company changed its name to Nippon Gakki Seizo Kabushiki Kwaisha (Japanese Musical Instrument Manufacturing Company) or Nippon Gakki Co. Ltd. The change of name enabled the company to develop other types of musical instrument. Two years later, Yamaha received a commission from the Japanese Ministry of Education to tour the US to study piano manufacturing and to acquire the necessary knowledge and machinery to set up a Japanese piano facility.

Having accomplished his mission he returned to Japan, followed shortly by all the machinery and materials required to start manufacture. No sooner had this essential equipment arrived than Yamaha and his team started to produce instruments, and in 1900 at his Hamamatsu factory he built the first Yamaha upright pianos, followed two years later by the company's first grand pianos.

The company began to win many awards for its pianos at various international expositions. Until 1907 Yamaha had used imported actions in his pianos, but in that year he developed his own action which evolved to become the Yamaha action of today. The company grew rapidly and started to make other instruments, including harmonicas, xylophones, toy pianos and much more.

Torakusu Yamaha died in 1916, at the age of 64. Despite the 1920s recession, the company did not suffer any long term damage from the economic crisis, but fires at Yamaha's recently built Nakazawa Plant in 1922 and at the main Itaya-machi plant the following year, as well as a major earthquake that destroyed the Tokyo branch office and Yokohama plant, and a 105-day strike in 1926 all served to confound the company's operations. A complete restructuring led to a greater emphasis on research, and in 1930 Yamaha made the bold move of setting up an acoustics laboratory which was allied to the piano design and manufacturing plant.

During World War II the company was made to produce munitions, and mainly built propellers and wings for aircraft. In 1944 demand from the military was such that Yamaha had to cease production of instruments completely. By 1947 the company had started to make pianos again, and the company grew rapidly, in 1953 opening the Yamaha Hall complex in Ginza, Tokyo's up-market shopping area.

Nippon Gakki Co. Ltd changed its name in its centennial year, 1987, to Yamaha Corporation. Today Yamaha is the largest musical instrument manufacturer in the world. Not only does the company make pianos and other acoustic and electronic musical instruments, but products such as hi-fi, P.A. equipment, golf clubs, tennis rackets and skis, furniture, kitchen equipment and components for the electronics industry, as well as motorcycles and yachts which are produced by a sister company, Yamaha Motors Co. Ltd.

YOUNG CHANG

The South Korean company Young Chang is one of the world's largest piano manufacturers, and this has been achieved in a little over 30 years. The company was formed by the three Kim brothers in 1956. They had a contract to sell Yamaha pianos in Korea, but by 1964 tariff controls on imports meant that it was too expensive to continue these imports. However, by bringing in semi-completed units and assembling them in Korea, the tariff regulations could be side-stepped. Yamaha subsequently helped Young Chang to tool-up for full production, although in 1975 the two companies decided to part.

Young Chang, in common with many other South Korean enterprises, grew very rapidly, and now it challenges Yamaha in many instrument markets. Kawai's pianos are currently some of the best to come out of South Korea.

ZIMMERMANN

Two brothers, Max and Richard Zimmermann, founded this company in Leipzig, Germany, in 1884, intending to produce instruments only for use in the home. The company grew, and at the beginning of the 20th century claimed to have become the biggest piano-maker in Europe. But two world wars and state ownership took their toll, and during the period of state ownership the entire production was devoted to one small piano model designed to fit into post-war apartments. Following the reunification of Germany the company became part of the Bechstein group and uses much of Bechstein's design expertise to produce consumer-oriented instruments.

PIANOS ON RECORD

This discography includes a selection of recordings of notable pianos, some of which are pictured in this book. Discs are numbered in the main list (right) to allow cross-referencing from the Disc column in the Featured Pianos list and from entries in the Composers & Performers list.

FEATURED PIANOS

This chart lists all the pianos recorded on the selected discs. Where the actual piano is pictured in this book, a page number reference in given. The number in the far right-hand column indicates the disc(s) on which the piano appears.

Page	Maker	Type	Year	Disc
	Antonelli street piano	barrel	c1890	30
	Astor	square	c1800	14
	Broadwood	cabinet	c1850	35
	Broadwood	grand	1801	5, 6
	Broadwood	grand	1805	28
37-38	Broadwood ('Beethoven')	grand	1817	9
	Broadwood	grand	c1820	35
	Broadwood	grand	1823	5
33-34	Broadwood	grand	1848	5
35	Broadwood ('Chopin')	grand	1848	11
	Broadwood	grand	c1850	35
	Broadwood	grand	1850	19
	Broadwood	grand	c1900	35
	Broadwood	square	c1791	35
19	Broadwood	square	1795	6
	Broadwood	square	1789	14, 16
	Broadwood	square	c1815	35
	Broadwood	square	1823	15
	Broadwood	square	c1830	35
38	Broadwood	square	1844	29
	Brodmann	V. grand	1820	12
	Clarke after Fritz c1818	V. grand (r)	1981	25, 26
	Clarke after Walter c1790	V. grand (r)	1989	21
	Clarke after Walter c1792	V. grand (r)	1982	22
	Clarke after Walter c1795	V. grand (r)	1986	23
30-31	Clementi	grand	1822	5, 6, 7
	Clementi	cabinet	c1822	6
	Clementi	square	1832	17, 18
	Clementi	upright	c1825	5
31	Collard & Collard	grand	c1835	6
13	Cristofori	grand	1726	34
	D'Almaine	square	c1835	15, 16
48	Erard	grand	1866	5, 19
	Erard	grand	1889	3
26-27	Fritz	V. grand	1814	6, 8
	Fritz	V. grand	c1825	27
27	Graf	V. grand	1826	5, 6, 19
	Graf	V. grand	c1830	2
24	Heilmann	grand	c1790	1
	Henschker	V. grand	c1840	10, 11
79	Klavins Model 370	U. grand	1989	33
	Longman & Broderip	square	1787	14
	Longman & Broderip	square	1823	16
	May after Walter 1791	V. grand (r)	c1980s	20
	McNulty after Stein	V. grand (r)	c1980s	4
	Pasquale street piano	barrel	c1900	30
25	Rosenberger	V. grand	1800-05	5, 6
	Stodart	square	1823	14, 15, 16
	Streicher	V. grand	1800	34
	Streicher	V. grand	1839	24
	Tomasso street piano	barrel	c1900	30
	Unknown	repro.	1929	31
	Unknown cylinder piano	barrel	1846	30
22	Walter	square	c1803	5, 6
	Walter	V. grand	1790	13

repro. = reproducing, V. grand + Viennese grand, U. grand = Upright grand, (r) = reconstruction.

DISCS A number is given first to enable cross-referencing from the Featured Pianos list and from the Composers & Performers list. In most cases the first line of the entry gives the composer in bold type, the title(s) of the piece(s), and the pianist in italic type, but where relevant the title of the disc is given. The piano(s) used and the record label of the disc are also shown. Please note that in some countries the recordings may appear on labels other than those listed.

1 **J.C. Bach:** Six Sonatas Op 17, *Robert Woolley*
Piano: Heilmann.
Label: Chandos.
In 1766 Bach published the Opus 5 sonatas for Piano Forte or Harpsichord, the earliest known pieces of piano music to be published in England, just as Zumpe produced the first of his square pianos. The Six Sonatas recorded on this disc were written in 1774 and are considered to be far more mature than the earlier Opus 5 works.

2 **Beethoven:** Op.109, 110, 111, *Paul Komen*
Piano: Graf c1830.
Label: Globe.

3 **Liszt:** Sonata in B Minor, Prelude and Fugue, Csárdás Macabre, Norma Fantasy, *Alexei Orlowetsky*
Piano: 1889 Erard concert grand.
Label: Globe.

4 **Mozart:** Six Violin Sonatas, K.301-6, *Rumiko Harada*
Piano: Paul McNulty after Johann Andreas Stein.
Label: Globe.

5 **'Richard Burnett's Musical Tour'**, *Richard Burnett*
Pianos/pieces: Broadwood grand 1801/*Haydn*: Sonata in D; Broadwood grand 1823/*Mendelssohn*: Venetian Gondola Song; Broadwood grand 1848/*Walmisley*: Sonatina no.2 in G; Clementi grand 1822/*Clementi*: Monferrinas; Clementi upright c1825/*Field* Nocturne No.12 in G; Erard grand 1866/*Gottschalk*: La Savane. Graf grand 1826/*Beethoven*: Sonata for Piano and Violin, Op.24, *Chopin*: Nocturnes in E minor and C sharp minor, *Schumann*: Piano Quintet in E flat major, op.44, *Weber*: Sonata in D; Rosenberger grand c1800/*Beethoven*: Songs, Der Kuss Op.128, *Hummel*: Sonata in C Op.37, *Vanhal*: Adagio Cantabile; Walter traveling square 1805/*Haydn*: Sonata in A.
Label: Amon-Ra.

6 **'Keyboard Collection'**, *Richard Burnett*
Pianos/pieces: Broadwood square 1795/*J.C. Bach*: Sonata op5.no.5; Broadwood grand, 1801/*Dussek*: Sonata in Bflat op.23; Clementi grand 1822/*Clementi*: Sonata in D op.16**; Clementi cabinet piano c1822/*Field*: Nocturne in E minor; Collard & Collard grand c1840/ *Mendelssohn*: Venetian Gondola Song in F sharp; Fritz grand c1814/ *Schubert*: German Dances*, *Mozart*: Turkish Rondo*; Graf grand 1826/ *Chopin*: Waltz in A flat op.42; Rosenberger grand c1800/ *Beethoven*: Bagatelle in C op.119 no.2; Walter square piano c1800/*Mozart*: Adagio for Glass Harmonica.
Label: Amon-Ra.
*The tracks marked * feature a bassoon stop and Janissary music; the track marked ** features a harmonic swell pedal.*

7 **Clementi:** Late Piano Works, *Richard Burnett*
Piano: Clementi grand 1822.
Label: Amon-Ra.
The instrument features a harmonic swell pedal.

8 **Schubert:** Sonatas, *Howard Shelley*
Piano: Fritz grand 1814.
Label: Amon Ra.

9 **'The Beethoven Broadwood Fortepiano'**, *Melvyn Tan*
Piano: Beethoven's Broadwood grand 1817.
Label: EMI Classics.

10 **Mendelssohn:** Symphony No,4 'Italian' Piano Concerto No.1, Violin Concerto, *Christopher Kite*
Piano: Henschker grand c1840.
Label: Nimbus.

11 **Chopin:** Piano Concerto No.1, *Weber:* Konzertstück in F Minor, *Christopher Kite*
Pianos: Chopin's Broadwood grand 1848, Henschker grand c1840.
Label: Nimbus.

12 **Schubert:** Tänze, *Jörg Ewald Dähler*
Piano: Brodmann Viennese grand 1820.
Label: Claves.
Track 3, '12 Deutsches sammt Coda op. post 127', illustrates the use of the instrument's bassoon stop.

13 **Haydn:** Divertimenti und Concertini für Clavier und Streicher, *Jörg Ewald Dähler*
Piano: Walter Viennese grand 1790.
Label: Claves.

14 **Haydn:** Variations in F minor, Three Sonatas, *Joanna Leach*
Pianos/pieces: Astor square c1800/Sonata in E flat; Broadwood square 1789/Sonata in C major; Longman & Broderip square 1787/Sonata in C minor; Stodart square 1823/Variations in F minor.
Label: Athene.

15 **'Three Square'** Field: Nocturnes, *Joanna Leach*
Pianos: Broadwood square 1823; D'Almaine square c1835; Stodart square c1823.
Label: Athene.

16 **'Four Square'**, *Joanna Leach*
Pianos: Broadwood square 1789; D'Almaine square c1835; Longman & Broderip square c1823; Stodart square 1823.
Label: Athene
Includes a selection of 18th & 19th century piano works by Soler, Haydn, J.S. Bach, Mozart, Schubert and Mendelssohn.

17 **'Clementi on Clementi'** Clementi: Sonatas, *Peter Katin*
Piano: Clementi square 1832.
Label: Athene.

18 **Schubert:** Impromptus D899 and D935, *Peter Katin*
Piano: Clementi square 1832.
Label: Athene.

19 **Gottschalk:** Piano Music, *Richard Burnett*
Pianos: Broadwood grand 1850; Erard grand 1866; Graf grand 1826.
Label: Amon-Ra.

20 **C.P.E. Bach:** Chamber Music, Les Adieux, *Andreas Staier*
Piano: May after Walter 1791.
Label: Deutsche Harmonia Mundi.

21 **Haydn:** Sonatas for Fortepiano (Hob.XVI/48-52), *Andreas Staier*
Piano: Clarke 1989 after Walter c1790.
Label: Deutsche Harmonia Mundi.

22 **Haydn:** Variations and Sonatas for Fortepiano, *Andreas Staier*
Piano: Clarke 1982 after Walter c1792.
Label: Deutsche Harmonia Mundi.

23 **Haydn:** Sonatas for Fortepiano (Hob.XVI/35-39 & 20), *Andreas Staier*
Piano: Clarke 1986 after Walter c1795.
Label: Deutsche Harmonia Mundi.

24 **Mendelssohn:** Works for Cello & Piano, *Melvyn Tan*
Piano: Streicher grand 1839.
Label: RCA Victor Red Seal.

25 **Schubert:** Fair Maid of the Mill, *Andreas Staier*
Piano: Clarke 1981 after Fritz c1818.
Label: Deutsche Harmonia Mundi.

26 **Schubert:** Songs to Poems by Friedrich Schiller, *Andreas Staier*
Piano: Clarke 1981 after Fritz c1815.
Label: Deutsche Harmonia Mundi.

27 **Bartholdy/Mendelssohn/Schubert/Schumann:** Songs to Poems by Heinrich Heine, *Andreas Staier*
Piano: Fritz grand c1825.
Label: Deutsche Harmonia Mundi.

28 **Dussek:** Sonatas, *Andreas Staier*
Piano: Broadwood grand 1805.
Label: Deutsche Harmonia Mundi.

29 Elgar: 'His music performed on his piano', *Anthony Goldstone*
Piano: Broadwood square 1844.
Label: Cobbe Foundation.
Includes 'Enigma Variations'. This CD only available directly from The Cobbe Foundation, Hatchlands Park, East Clandon, Surrey, GU4 7RT, England.

30 'Music of the Street'
Pianos: Various barrel types.
Label: Saydisc.
A collection of street instruments playing period tunes.

31 Nancarrow: 'Studies for Player Piano Vol. I & II'
Piano: Ampico reproducing piano 1927.
Label: Wergo.
Conlon Nancarrow's unique works were produced by direct cutting to piano rolls. Volumes III to V are also available.

32 Nancarrow: Studies, Ensemble Modern (arr. Ingo Metzmacher), *Ueli Wiget, Hermann Kretzschmar*
Piano: modern instrument.
Label: RCA Victor Red Seal.
This recording features some of Nancarrow's Studies arranged for chamber ensemble, with the instrumentation he originally had in mind. It is interesting to compare this with Disc 31, where the Studies are realized on player piano.

33 Mussorgsky/Chopin/Liszt: 'Michael Ponti live on Klavins Model 370', *Michael Ponti*
Piano: Klavins Model 370.
Label: Klavins Music.
An interesting recording using the huge Klavins piano. Available from Klavins Music, Bergstr. 27A, 5210 Tdf. Bergheim, Germany.

34 'Historische Tasteninstrumente aus dem Musikinstrumenten Museum der Universität Leipzig', *Walter Heinz Bernstein, Christine Schornsheim*
Pianos/pieces: Cristofori grand 1726/*Paladini:* Divertimento; Streicher 1800/*Beethoven:* Sonate Op.10 No.1.
Label: Verlag K.-J. Kamprad.
A collection of recordings featuring the instruments of the musical instrument museum at the University of Leipzig.

35 'Seven Broadwoods: the Evolution of the English Piano', *Richard Burnett*
Pianos (all Broadwoods)/pieces: square c1791/*J.C. Bach:* Sonata in C minor Op.17 No.2; square c1815/ *Field:* Nocturnes No.2 in C minor & No.5 in Bflat; square c1830/*Mendelssohn:* from Lieder Ohne Worte; grand c1820/*Beethoven:* Sonata für Klavier No.27 in E minor Op.90; cabinet c1850/*Schumann:* from Kinderszenen Op.15; grand c1850/*Chopin:* Valse in E minor, Berceuse in Dflat Op.57; grand c1900/*Debussy:* La cathédrale engloutie, La sérénade interrompue, Clair de lune.
Label: Sonic Culture Design.
Features a collection of Broadwood pianos which clearly illustrate the evolution of the company's instruments.

COMPOSERS AND PERFORMERS

The number in bold after the Composer/Performers name refers to the disc on which the music can be found.

C.P.E. Bach **20**	Joanna Leach **14, 15, 16**
J.C. Bach **1, 5, 35**	Franz Liszt **3, 33**
J.S. Bach **16**	Felix Mendelssohn **5, 6, 10, 16, 24,**
Ludwig van Beethoven **2, 5, 6, 9,**	**27, 35**
34, 35	Wolfgang Amadeus Mozart **4, 6, 16**
Walter Heinz Bernstein **34**	Modest Mussorgsky **33**
Richard Burnett **5, 6, 7, 19, 35**	Conlon Nancarrow **31, 32**
Frédéric Chopin **5, 6, 11, 33, 35**	Alexei Orlowetsky **3**
Muzio Clementi **5, 6, 7, 17**	Giuseppe Paladini **34**
Jörg Ewald Dähler **12, 13**	Michael Ponti **33**
Claude Debussy **35**	Christine Schornsheim **34**
Jan Ladislav Dussek **6, 28**	Franz Schubert **6, 8, 12, 16, 18,**
Edward Elgar **29**	**25, 26, 27**
John Field **5, 6, 15, 35**	Robert Schumann **5, 27, 35**
Anthony Goldstone **29**	Howard Shelley **8**
Louis Gottschalk **5, 19**	Vicente Soler **16**
Rumiko Harada **4**	Andreas Staier **20, 21, 22, 23, 25,**
Josef Haydn **5, 13, 14, 16, 21, 22,**	**26, 28**
23	Melvyn Tan **9, 24**
Johann Hummel **5**	Jan Vanhal **5**
Peter Katin **17, 18**	Thomas Walmisley **5**
Christopher Kite **10, 11**	Carl Maria von Weber **5, 11**
Paul Komen **2**	Ueli Wiget **32**
Hermann Kretzschmar **32**	Robert Woolley **1**

Alternative words are shown in brackets following the key word. Foreign expressions are marked with an abbreviation indicating their origin: *Eur.* = European; *Fr.* = French; *Ger.* = German; *It.* = Italian.

action The mechanism that translates the downward pressure of fingers on keys into a movement of the hammers toward the strings.
action centers The points around which various parts of the action pivot.
aeolian piano A piano that features a mechanism that blows air over the strings to sustain their vibrations.
agraffe A brass stud through which one, two or three strings pass. It serves to anchor and space the strings and to define one end of their speaking length.
aliquot bars Small, movable bridges under the free portion of duplex strings that are used to tune that section of the string.
aliquot scaling/strings An extra set of treble strings, unstruck and undamped, sometimes used to strengthen the piano's tonal quality.
artist rolls Piano rolls 'cut' by famous composers, pianists or performers.
attack The instantaneous sound that the hammer makes as it strikes the string.
Auslöser *Ger.* The escapement of the Viennese action, evolved from the Prelleiste.
baby grand A small grand piano, typically between 4ft 6ins and 5ft 6ins long.
back pin The latter of the two bridge pins. It guides the non-speaking length of the string to the hitch pin.
backstring The non-speaking length of a string.
balance pin The pin at the fulcrum point on which the key pivots.
balance rail The length of wood on which the balance pins are mounted.
banding Decorative strips of veneer 'outlining' the casework.
barrel piano A mechanical piano that uses a rotating, pinned drum or cylinder to trigger the action and hammers and play a predetermined set of tunes.
bass The lower-pitched notes, activated by the keys at the bottom end (left) of the keyboard.
bassoon stop A roll of parchment lowered on to the bass strings to produce a buzzing, bassoon-like effect.
bat pin The guide pin located under the front of a key.
beak In German and Viennese actions, the part of the hammer shank that catches on the Auslöser and flicks the hammer toward the string.
bearing The pressure that the string applies to parts of the piano with which it comes into contact.
belly rail The heavy-duty timber that supports the front edge of the soundboard on a grand piano. Sometimes upper and lower belly rails are used.
bent side (bent side) The curved side of a grand piano.
bichord (double-strung) Two strings for each note.
birdcage action A type of overdamped upright action where the assembled damper wires resemble the bars of a birdcage.
bluing The oxidation of tuning pins to aid their grip on the pin block. (The term derives from the blue tinge that the oxidation process tends to produce in treated metals.)
bookcase piano See cabinet piano.
bottom brace A structural member under the soundboard that connects the bentside to the spine.
bottom door The removable panel located beneath the keyboard of an upright piano.
bracing A strengthening element used to withstand the forces exerted by the strings on the frame.
bridge A long strip of curved hardwood against which the strings press. It conducts the sound energy of the vibrating strings to the soundboard.
bridge cap A thin top layer sometimes applied to the bridge to prevent splitting and to ensure good contact between string and bridge.
bridge pins Small metal pins inserted in the bridge to guide the strings over the bridge and to ensure good energy transfer between string and bridge. Early instruments had just one pin per string; later pianos have two.

---

bridle (bridle strap) In a tape-check action, the piece of tape that aids the return of the hammer.
bridle strap See bridle.
bridle wire The element that attaches the bridle strap to the wippen.
buff stop A rail covered with damping material (made from buffalo leather) that is pushed against strings to provide a muting effect. It is found mostly on early square pianos.
cabinet grand See cabinet piano.
cabinet piano (cabinet grand, bookcase piano) A grand piano (typically 70-100in high) with strings running vertically up from the keyboard. Later, the strings were extended down to the floor.
capo d'astro *It.* A metal bar used instead of a nut to press down on the strings, developed by Antoine Bord in 1843.
capstan screw The part of the piano key action that links directly with the action.
celeste pedal In an upright piano, a strip of felt that is positioned between the hammers and strings, usually by the action of a pedal.
cembalo *It.* A harpsichord.
cembalo stop (harpsichord stop) Imitates the sound of a harpsichord.
check A leather pad mounted on a wire that catches the hammer after it strikes the string, thus preventing it from re-striking the string.
check rail In Viennese pianos, a wooden rail that catches the hammers after they have hit the string.
clavecin *Fr.* A harpsichord.
clavecin royal *Fr.* An early type of square piano with bare wooden hammers.
clavecin à maillet *Fr.* A harpsichord with hammers made by Jean Marius in 1716.
clavichord *Fr. clavicorde; Ger. Clavichord, Clavier; It. clavicordio* An early keyboard instrument with the strings running parallel to the keyboard and with a tangent action.
clavicytherium A harpsichord with vertical strings.
clavier A keyboard.
Clavinet An electric clavichord, the normal soundboard of which is replaced by electromagnetic pickups.
claviharp A keyed harp.
claviorganum A keyed stringed instrument (virginal, harpsichord or piano) combined with an organ.
close-wound string A string consisting of a core around which is tightly wound a single-layer covering such that each winding touches its neighbor. *See also* open-wound string.
compensating frame A type of frame designed to correct movement caused by climatic changes and used mostly in the early 19th century.
conductor's piano A small portable piano.
console piano *Eur.* An early upright piano with no upper section. When the lid is closed the instrument is virtually flat-topped, giving something of the appearance of a desk.
console piano A small modern upright piano (typically 38-43in high) with a drop action.
cottage grand piano A small grand piano.
cottage piano Typically a rather small, upright, straight-strung piano (around 40in high) with a wooden or three-quarter iron frame. It was especially popular toward the end of the 19th century.
cross-stringing *Eur.* A system where the bass (longer) strings are set at an angle over the treble strings in order to make the best use of available space.
crossbanding Thin, decorative strips, 'outlining' the casework, the grain of which runs perpendicular to the strip.
crown The curvature of the soundboard that helps to press the bridge firmly against the strings.
damper Part of the action mechanism that is lowered or pressed against the strings to prevent them from oscillating.
damper pedal See sustain pedal.
decay The period after the string has been struck during which the vibrations gradually die away.
desk See music desk.
digital piano An electronic musical instrument that produces piano sounds from data stored as numbers in its computer memory.
direct blow action An upright action positioned above the level of the keys.

Ditanaklasis *Ger.* One of the earliest upright pianos, invented by Matthias Müller in 1800.

dolly A small four-wheeled frame used for moving pianos.

dolly damper A type of damper found in square pianos that resembles a doll's head.

Doppelflügel *Ger.* A piano with two keyboards.

double-strung (bichord) Two strings for each note.

downbearing The downward pressure that the string applies to parts of the piano with which it comes into contact.

down-striking action A grand piano action where the hammers are positioned above the strings.

drop action *See* indirect blow action.

due corde The effect of moving the hammers so that they strike only two strings instead of three. *See also* una corda.

due corde pedal The pedal that moves the hammers to the due corde position.

Duo-Art A type of mechanism for a reproducing piano.

duoclave A piano with two keyboards (typically two grand pianos housed in a single case, providing a keyboard at each end).

duplex scaling/strings A method of tuning the non-speaking length of the strings to produce additional sympathetic harmonics. *See also* aliquot bars.

dust cover A thin, removable, wooden board found on early square pianos (and sometimes on early grands) that covers the action, pin block and tuning pins.

electric piano An instrument designed to produce a sound like that of an acoustic piano but using pickups to amplify a vibrating medium that has been struck. The vibrating medium in an electric piano is not necessarily a string.

electronic piano An instrument that uses electronic circuitry to recreate the sound of a piano. Unlike the electric piano, the electronic piano has no mechanically vibrating medium, instead producing oscillations from electronic circuitry.

end blocks (keyblocks) The pieces that fill the space between the keyboard and the end cheeks.

end cheeks *See* key cheeks.

English double action *Ger. Stossmechanik* An action used in the 18th and 19th centuries that had an intermediate lever and escapement. It was used primarily for English and American square pianos.

English grand action An action used in the late 18th and 19th centuries that had an escapement in which the jack acts directly on to the hammer butt. It was used primarily for English grand pianos.

English single action An action used for the English square piano in the mid to late 1700s.

escapement Part of the action that enables the hammer assembly to disengage from the rest of the action so that the hammer is free to fall back away from the string after it has hit the string.

expression piano A type of player piano that has a limited amount of expression encoded in its piano rolls.

fall board (fallboard) A hinged cover that protects the keyboard. When open, it displays the manufacturer's name. *See also* nameboard.

Flügel *Ger. 'wing'* A grand piano (originally used to describe a harpsichord).

fortepiano An arbitrary term used to describe: (1) a piano made before about 1850; (2) a Viennese piano; or (3) a piano of historical importance. It is also often used to distinguish an early piano from a modern instrument.

frame *Eur.* The supporting structure that is designed to withstand the tension of the strings.

fundamental The establishing tone produced by a string that provides its pitch.

French grand action A term often used to describe a down-striking action.

fretted clavichord A clavichord that shares some strings with more than one note. The point at which the tangent strikes the string defines the speaking length of the string. *See also* unfretted clavichord.

gap The space between the pin block and the soundboard through which the hammer strikes the string.

gap spacer A structural element located between the pin block and the belly rail, more recently made of iron and designed to strengthen the frame.

genouillère *Fr.* A knee lever.

giraffe piano An upright grand piano popular in the early 19th century with a straight, vertical bass side and the treble inclined, often adorned with a scroll motif.

glasschord *See* pianino.

grand piano A wing-shaped piano with horizontal strings running away from the keyboard.

grasshopper action An early and influential action used for square and upright pianos, developed by John Geib, and from which comes the term hopper (*see* jack).

gravicembalo A harpsichord.

guide pins Pins placed on the bridge (and sometimes the nut) that fix the positions of the strings.

half-pedaling Using the mid position of a pedal to obtain a finer degree of control.

hammer The part of the action that strikes the string.

hammer molding The central wooden part of the hammer around which is fixed a felt covering.

hammer rail In an English action, the rail to which the hammers' shanks are hinged.

hammer stroke The distance that the hammer head has to travel from rest to the point where it strikes the string.

Hammerflügel *Ger. See* fortepiano.

Hammerklavier *Ger.* An early stringed keyboard instrument with hammer action or tangent action.

hand stop (stop) A knob controlling a lever mechanism and used to modify in various ways the sound produced by a piano.

harmonic series A series of pitches that are whole number multiples of the fundamental.

harmonic A tone whose frequency is a whole number multiple of the fundamental.

harpsichord *Fr. claveçin; Ger. Klavizimbel, Flügel; It. clavicembalo, gravicembalo, cembalo, arpicordo* A large wing-shaped stringed keyboard instrument in which the strings are plucked by a plectrum action. The strings run parallel to the floor and perpendicular to the keyboard.

harpsichord stop *See* cembalo stop.

heel *See* tail.

high-tension scale A scaling where strings are held under a greater tension than normal. They produce a brighter sound but require a stronger frame, leading to a risk of string breakage.

hitch pin (hitchpin) A metal pin around which treble and tenor strings are looped. In the case of wound bass strings, it is the point at which the string is attached to the frame.

hitch pin plank In early pianos, the solid piece of wood into which the hitch pins are driven.

hitch pin plate In later instruments, the metal part of the frame that holds the hitch pins.

hopper *See* jack.

indirect blow action An upright action positioned below the level of the keys and found in smaller pianos.

inharmonicity A phenomenon where the harmonics of a thicker string deviate from their theoretical value because of the stiffness of the string.

Irish damper In early square pianos, a dolly damper that operates directly from the back end of the key and sits on the string.

jack (hopper) The part of the action that transmits the upward motion of the rear end of the key to the hammer assembly. The jack is free to pivot, and this means that it can escape from the hammer assembly.

Janissary stop Percussion devices (bells, drums etc) that extended the sound-producing repertoire of some southern European pianos in the early 19th century.

Kapsel *Ger.* In a German or Viennese action, the fork-shaped element attached to the key into which the hammer shank sits and is able to rotate.

key blocks *See* end blocks.

key cheeks The vertical side pieces of the case located at either end of the keyboard.

key dip The maximum distance that the front of the key may travel.

key frame An assembly consisting of the balance rail, back rail, treble and bass rails, and (normally) the front rail.

keyblocks (end blocks) The pieces that fill the space between the keyboard and the key cheeks.

keyboard The set of levers, consisting of naturals and accidentals, that trigger the action.

keyboard references Throughout this book when referring to a specific key or keys on the piano keyboard we have used the standard reference system, as shown in the diagram at the foot of this page.

keyboard shift A sideways movement of the keyboard action, or part of action that aligns the hammers with only two strings (due corde) or one string (una corda).

keyslip The rail that runs in front of the keys.

keywell The nameboard and inner sides of the key cheeks.

knee lever *Fr. genouillère* A lever mechanism positioned under the keyboard that activates various stops.

liner A wooden frame forming part of the back of an upright piano, and to which the soundboard is attached.

listing cloth Material that prevents the backstring from ringing and producing unwanted harmonics and overtones.

loop stringing The formation of two speaking lengths from one string by running it from the tuning pin around the hitch pin and back to the adjacent tuning pin. It is not used for wound strings.

Lyraflügel *Ger.* A lyre piano.

lyre The mechanical assembly that houses the pedals and lower trapwork of a grand piano.

lyre piano A type of pyramid piano shaped like a lyre.

machine A mechanism found on harpsichords that links a series of stops to a footpedal.

MIDI (Musical Instrument Digital Interface) A connection that enables electronic musical instruments to communicate with one another. It allows one keyboard, for example, to be used to play several other instruments simultaneously.

minipiano A small piano popular in the 1930s and 1940s with the action below the keyboard.

moderator stop (muffler pedal) A lever or hand stop that moves a rail to which are connected strips of leather or cloth. These slip between the hammer and strings to reduce the force of the hammer and produce a softer tone. Some modern upright pianos use a third (middle) pedal to control this effect.

mopstick *See* dolly damper.

muffler pedal *See* moderator stop.

music roll *See* piano roll.

nameboard The board immediately behind the playing surface of the keys on which may be the maker's inscription or a name plaque.

name plaque A small wooden plate (ceramic in older instruments) on which is inscribed the manufacturer's details.

name plate A metal name plate.

nut In early instruments, a piece of hardwood attached to the pin block that defines one end of the string's speaking length. (The other end is defined by the bridge.)

open-wound string A type of string used on some early square pianos where the winding is spaced out. *See also* close-wound string.

organ-piano A piano to which organ pipes have been added, the whole housed in a single case. It is played either from one keyboard or from a keyboard for each section. *See also* claviorganum.

organistrum A hurdy-gurdy.

* Middle C is referred to as c¹

overdamper In an upright piano, dampers positioned above the hammers.

overspun string A string around which is wrapped an additional string in order to increase its mass. *See also* open-wound string *and* close-wound string.

overstrung *See* cross-stringing.

pantaleon A multi-stringed dulcimer invented by Pantaleon Hebenstreit.

partials A constituent part of a musical note. *See also* harmonics.

pedal piano There are three types of pedal piano: (1) a piano with a pedalboard that plays the strings contained within the piano; (2) a piano to which is attached a second soundboard and separate strings which are struck by hammers activated by a pedalboard; and (3) a separate piano unit with a pedalboard rather than a keyboard.

pedal A foot-operated lever used to modify the sound of a piano.

Pianet An electric piano-type instrument that uses vibrating reeds rather than strings.

pianino *It. 'small piano'* A term used on the European mainland until about 1840 to describe small, vertically-strung pianos. After 1840 it was used when referring to small and very small obliquely-strung instruments. The term is also used to describe a glasschord, a small three-octave keyboard with percussive action that employs glass rods rather than strings as its vibrating medium.

piano à claviers renversés *Fr.* A hybrid piano with two keyboards, the upper module reversed so that the bass notes are played with the treble keys.

piano à queue *Fr.* A grand piano.

piano attachment A small electronic keyboard popular in the 1940s and 1950s that fixed to the underside of a piano to provide a range of solo voices to complement the normal sounds.

piano carré *Fr.* A square piano.

piano droit *Fr.* An upright piano.

piano player A box fitted with mechanical 'fingers' positioned over the keys of a normal piano. The fingers 'play' the piano in accordance with the musical information that has been stored on a piano roll.

piano roll (music roll) A punched paper roll on which is stored music in a form that can be understood and 'played back' by the mechanism of an automatic piano player or player piano.

pianoforte The original English name for the piano.

pianola A piano player developed by the Aeolian company.

pin block Wooden panel into which tuning pins are driven.

pitch The position of a note in the musical spectrum, high (treble) or low (bass), related to the note's frequency of vibration.

plain-sawn A simple method of cutting the trunk of a tree into vertical planks that run the length of the trunk.

plate *See* frame.

player piano A piano into which has been fitted a player mechanism, enabling the piano to play music automatically from piano rolls.

Prelleiste *Ger. 'rebound rail'* In a German action, a fixed rail on which the rear end of the hammer engages.

Prellmechanik action An early German piano action, with hammer heads lying nearest the keyboard, and no escapement.

Prellzungenmechanik action This is a Prellmechanik action with escapement (which subsequently became the Viennese action).

prop stick (propstick) The support that holds open the lid of a grand piano.

pyramid piano An early form of upright piano with oblique stringing that allows the case to be symmetrical.

quad-strung Four strings for each note.

quarter-sawn A method of cutting the trunk of a tree into quarter segments and then into planks that maximizes the integrity of the resulting timber.

Querflügel *Ger.* A wing-shaped bentside piano with the strings running obliquely to the right.

ravalement *Fr.* A major overhaul of a piano.

recumbent harp A type of piano, the shape of which resembles a harp lying on its side.

register In a harpsichord, a set of jacks controlled by a stop.

regulating The process of adjusting the action of a piano to provide the desired touch-response and to ensure conformity across the entire compass.

repetition The method of repeating a note. In a 'repetitive' action a note can be replayed without having to fully release the key.

reproducing piano A mechanical piano driven by a piano roll that can capture virtually every nuance of the original performance, including note dynamics and pedaling.

rib A reinforcing bar glued to the underside of the soundboard. The rib also helps to distribute the sound energy over the entire surface of the soundboard.

rose In the soundboard, a decorative hole or semblance of a hole that is usually circular in shape.

sampling piano A digital piano that replays digital recordings of pianos from a computer memory store when notes are played. The system emulates quite successfully the sound of the acoustic instrument, but cannot reproduce the feel of an acoustic piano nor the interaction between the strings.

scale design The design of all elements relating to the strings and frame.

Schnabel *Ger.* In a Viennese action, the protruding 'beak' at the far end of the hammer that catches on the Auslöser and flicks the hammer towards the string.

sharp A black key on a modern keyboard, an 'accidental' note.

shims Small pieces of wood used to fill up cracks in the soundboard.

short octave An arrangement of the notes in the bottom octave that omits the less commonly used 'accidental' keys.

sidebearing The sideways pressure that the string applies to the bridge pins, ensuring a good 'connection' between bridge and string.

sostenente piano Various types of piano that incorporated a mechanism to prolong the oscillations of the strings after a note had been played. The mechanisms used currents of air, magnetic fields, bows, vibrating rods, and so on.

sostenuto pedal An extra middle pedal on more expensive grand pianos and occasionally on better uprights. It sustains only those notes that are being held when the pedal is depressed.

soundboard A thin wooden sheet that amplifies the oscillations of the strings.

speaking length The part of the string that is hit by the hammer and oscillates to provide the required note.

spine *See* straight side.

spinet A plucked-string instrument of the harpsichord family that has strings running obliquely away from the keyboard. Spinets are usually wing- or triangular-shaped.

spinet piano A small, modern upright piano (typically 36-38in high) with a drop action.

square piano A rectangular-shaped instrument descended from the clavichord that has strings running parallel to the keyboard.

stencil piano A piano made by a large manufacturer to which a dealer or distributor has attached his or her company's name or brandname.

sticker In some early and larger upright piano actions, a long wooden rod that connects the hammer assembly with the rest of the action.

sticker action In early upright pianos, an action that uses stickers (wooden rods) to enable the hammers to be positioned at the correct point along the string.

stop *See* handstop.

straight side (spine) The long, bass side of a grand piano or harpsichord.

straight-strung With strings running parallel to one another and perpendicular to the keyboard.

strike line An imaginary line drawn across the strings and denoting the strike point for each note.

strike point The point at which the hammer strikes the string.

stringing Apart from the obvious reference to strings, this term is also used to describe a decorative line of inlaid wood or metal.

strut In German and Viennese instruments, a piece of metal used to brace the gap between the belly rail and the pin block.

sustain pedal (damper pedal) The pedal on the player's right that lifts all the dampers from the strings simultaneously.

swell A pedal that raises the lid of a square piano to control the overall volume and timbre of the instrument.

sympathetic strings Unstruck strings, the vibrations of which are used to enhance the overall tone of the piano. *See also* aliquot strings.

tail (heel) The far end of a grand piano.

tangent A jack fixed to the key of a clavichord so that when the key is played the tangent simultaneously impinges on the string, sets it into vibration and defines its speaking length. In the action of a tangent piano, the jack is not fixed to the key but is free to be 'thrown' at the string.

tape-check action An early upright piano action that incorporated a bridle strap (or tape) to assist in the return of the hammer from the string. The tape-check action provided the basis of the modern upright action.

tenor The strings that form the middle octaves of a piano.

tine A vibrating metal rod used in the Rhodes electric piano.

top door The removable panel located above the keyboard of an upright piano.

touch weight The force required by the player to lower the key of a piano.

transposing keyboard A piano usually with a keyboard that can be made to slide to the left or right so that the hammers of a given key will strike strings of a different pitch.

transverse grand A small, horizontal bentside piano.

trapwork The pedal or knee mechanism.

treble The higher-pitched notes, activated by the keys at the top end (right) of the keyboard.

trichord Three strings for each note.

tuning A slight alteration to the tension in the strings, made by rotating the tuning pins, which raises or lowers the pitch so that each string can be set to produce precisely the desired pitch. The accurate tuning of a piano is a highly skilled job.

tuning pin A small steel pin driven into the pin block and around which one end of a string is coiled. By turning the tuning pin using a tuning key or hammer the tensioning of the strings can be adjusted and tuned to the desired pitch.

'Turkish music' *See* Janissary stop.

una corda The effect of moving the hammers so that they strike only one string instead of two or three. *See* due corde.

underdamper In an upright piano, dampers positioned below the hammers. Most modern pianos have underdampers.

unfretted clavichord A clavichord with one or more strings for each note. *See also* fretted clavichord.

unichord One string for each note.

unison Two, three or more strings tuned to the same pitch.

upbearing The upward pressure that the string applies to parts of the piano with which it comes into contact.

upright grand piano A grand piano from the 18th or early 19th century in which the string, frame and soundboard have been rotated up to the vertical plane.

upright piano A piano with strings running vertically so that the keyboard bisects the strings at some point. The broad end (where the tuning pin is located) is positioned at the same level as, or above, the keyboard.

veneer A thin surface layer of finely grained wood, glued to a base (which may be of an inferior material).

Venetian swell A set of slats or louvers that cover the soundboard and strings and that can be used to control the overall volume of a piano or harpsichord.

verre églomisé *Fr.* A painting on the back of a piece of glass, designed to be viewed from the front, often with gilding, and to be found on some decorated pianos.

vertical piano Any piano with strings that run perpendicular to the floor.

Viennese action An evolution of the German action with escapement. This type of action began to appear at the start of the 19th century.

virginal A plucked-string instrument, generally rectangular or sometimes polygonal in shape, the keyboard of which runs parallel to the strings.

vis à vis *Fr. 'face to face'* A grand piano or harpsichord with a keyboard at each end.

voicing The process of adjusting the hammers of the piano to produce the desired timbre. It is achieved by softening the hammer felt with a set of 'voicing needles'.

wippen A lever that rises as the key is depressed. It is the principle element of the upright action.

Page numbers in **bold** refer to illustrations.
Keyboard/note abbreviations used throughout the book (for example AAA, e¹, g⁴ and so on) are detailed on p106.
Family members are listed before their company and instruments; for example Carl Bechstein precedes entries for Bechstein and for Bechstein grand piano.

Accelerated Action (Steinway) **60**
Acoustigrand 96
Acousti-Lectric 75
acrylic 73, 84, 101
action 14, 92, 105
  Accelerated **60**
  Anglo-German 17
  birdcage 105
  centers 105
  Cristofori **13/14**, 14, 18
  clavichord **8**
  direct blow 105
  double escapement 30, 31, 34, 60
  down-striking 106
  drop 71, 80
  Englische Mechanik 17
  English 17, 18, 20, 24, 27
  English double **18**, 20
  English down-striking 72
  English grand 28, 34
  English single **18**
  French action see tape check action
  German 17, 24
  grand 20, **29**
  grand, modern **93**
  grasshopper 106
  hanging German 39, 40
  hanging Viennese see hanging German
  indirect blow 106
  modern grand **93**
  modern underdamped upright **94**
  modern upright **80/81**
  overdamped **49**
  plastic **79**
  Prellmechanik 17
  Prellzungenmechanik 17, 24
  repetition see double escapement
  spinet piano **94**
  sticker **41**, 43, 44, 107
  Stossmechanik 17
  Stosszungenmechanik 17
  tape check 43, 44, 45, **49**, 107
  underdamped upright, modern **94**
  upright, modern **80/81**
  Viennese 17, 24, **25**, 26, 27, 107
Adam, Christian 86
Adam, Robert 65
Adiaphon 72
Adlam & Burnett harpsichord **10**
Aeolian Co. 54, 56, 57, 96, 99, 100, 103
aeolian piano 105
agraffe 30, 34, 90, 91, 105
air compression 87
Air Corps Piano see Rhodes
air rarefaction 87
Albrecht, Charles 20
Albrecht square piano **20**
aliquot bars 105
aliquot scaling/strings 91, 97, 105
Allen & Thom 34
Alma-Tadema, Sir Lawrence 65
American piano 49
American Fotoplayer Model-20 **58**
American Piano Co. 57, 96, 99, 100
Ampico 56, 57, 96
amplifier 72, 74, 75
Anglo-German action 17

Ansley, Arthur C. 75
anti-node 95
Antonelli street piano 104
Appleton, Thomas 96
armonie 6
art-case piano 48, 63-67
art deco style 67
art nouveau style 67
artist rolls 105
Arts & Crafts style 67
Ashbee, C.R. 67
Ashkenazy, Vladimir 59
Astin, Ray 96
Astin-Weight 96
  upright piano **79**
Astor square piano 104
attack 105
Audiograph 56
Audion Piano 75
Aurore see Rameau
Auslöser 105
automata 55
Automatic Music Paper Co. 96
automatic piano 52-58
Ayuso, Jean 66

Babcock, Alpheus 20, 21, 96
  and cast iron frame 96
Babcock, Lewis 96
Babcock 96, 98
baby grand piano 59, 105
Bach, C.P.E. 36, 69, 105
Bach, J.C. 18, 20, 24, 35, 105
  Zumpe piano **35**
Bach, J.S. 9, 15, 17, 36, 105
back pin 105
Backers, Americus 18, 20, 28, 29, 34, 35
backframe see backpost
backpost 90, 91
backstring 105
Bacon, George 96
Bacon & Raven 96, 102
Baillie Scott, M.H. 67
Bain 55
balance pin 92, 105
balance rail 105
Baldwin, Dwight Hamilton 96
Baldwin 96
  and Bechstein 66, 97
  and Liberace 84, 96
  SD-10 grand piano **84**
banding 105
baroque style 64
Barratt & Robinson 96, 98
barrel piano 52-53, 105
bassoon stop 26, 105
bat pin 92, 105
Bauhaus style 67
BBC see British Broadcasting Corporation
beak 105
Beale euphonicon **51**
bearing 105
bebung 8
Bechstein, Carl Jr. 97
Bechstein, Carl Sr. 44, 66, 96-97, 100
  and Kriegelstein 97
  and Pape 97
Bechstein, Edwin 97
Bechstein, Helene 97
Bechstein, Johann 97
Bechstein 66, 96-97, 103
  art-case piano **66**
  and Baldwin 66, 97
  electric grand piano **75**
  Empire grand piano 66
  grand piano **66**
  Lilliput grand piano 97
  Neo-Bechstein 75, 101

similar brandnames 96
Beck, Dunbar 83
Beck, Frederick 18
van Beethoven, Ludwig 32, 35, 36, 37, 105
  Broadwood piano **37/38**
  Graf piano **36**
Behrent, Johann 20
Beier 75
Beleton 75
belly bars 88
belly rail 105
Bent 96, 98
bentside 105
Berlin, Irving 69
Bernhardt Electronic Piano 75
Bernstein, Leonard 84
Bernstein, Walter Heinz 105
Béthenod, Joseph 75
Beyer, Adam 18, 19
  Beyer square piano **18/19**
bichord 91, 105
Bidermann, Samuel 52
Bienfort 16, 17
birdcage action 105
Birmingham, John P. 103
Birmingham, Robert M. 103
Blanchet et Roller 42, 44
bluing 105
Blüthner, Bruno 97
Blüthner, Julius 91, 97
  and aliquot scaling 97
Blüthner, Max 97
Blüthner, Robert 97
Blüthner 68, 72, 97, 103
Boardman, William G. 97
Boardman & Gray 97
Bode, Harald 77
Bononiensis, Hieronymus 9
bookcase piano see cabinet piano
Bord, Antonie 91, 105
Bord 101
Bösendorfer, Ignaz 25, 34, 65, 97
Bösendorfer, Ludwig 47, 65, 97
Bösendorfer 65, 97
  art-case piano **65**, **85**
  and BBC 70, 97
  and Carl Hutterstrasser 65. 97
  Empress Eugénie piano **65**
  grand piano 47, **65**, **82**, **85**
  Half Concert Grand piano 59
  Imperial Concert grand piano 59, 65, **82**, 97
  and Kimball 65, 97
  and Liszt 33
  Mignon Grand piano 59
  Model-120 upright piano 81
  Model-130 upright piano **80/81/82**
  modern upright action **80/81**
  Parlour Grand piano 59
  97-key keyboard **82**
Boston Piano Co. 97
bottom door 105
bracing 105
Bradbury, William B. 97, 100
Bradbury 97, 102
Brahms, Johannes 99
Brasted, Percy 70, 71
Bretzfelder, Maurice K. 75
bridge 59, 88-89, 90, 105
  cap 105
  overhanging 89
  pin 89, 90, 105
  'of reverberation' 31
bridle 105
Brinsmead, John 97
Brinsmead 97, 100
  top tuner **49**, 97
British Broadcasting Corporation (BBC) 70, 97, 98
Broadwood, James 28, 37, 98

Broadwood, John 19, 20, 28, 98
Broadwood, Thomas 28, 37, 98
  and Beethoven 37
Broadwood 19, 20, 28, 31, 52, 97-98, 103
  art-case piano **63**, **64**, **67**
  and Beethoven 37, 104
  bridge split 28, 29
  cabinet grand piano **52**, 104
  and Chopin 35, 104
  and Clementi 98
  and Elgar 38
  first grand piano 28, 34
  grand piano 29, **33/34**, 35, **37/38**, **63**, **64**, 104
  harpsichord 28
  and iron frame 32, 33, 34
  and iron hitch pin plate 20
  with Jankó keyboard **68**
  nameboard changes **28**
  scientific experiments 28, 34
  short grand piano 64
  six-octave piano 34
  square grand piano **67**
  square piano **19**, 20, **21**, **38**, 104
  upright transposing piano **68/69**
  use of metal 32
Brodmann, Joseph 25, 97
Brodmann grand piano 104
Brodr Jorgensen 102
broken bass octave 6
Brown & Hallet 99
Brunenhausen 64
buff stop 105
von Bülow, Hans 66, 97
Buntebart, Gabriel 18
Burne-Jones, Edward 63
Burnett, Richard 105
Burney, Charles 18, 19
Busoni, Ferruccio 82
Butcher, Thomas 98

cabinet grand piano 52
cabinet piano 39, 40, 43, 44, 52, 105
cabinet upright grand piano 39
Call, Jack 98
Campbell, J.C. 100
capo d'astro 90, 91, 105
capstan screw 105
carillon 102
Carpenter, Richard 74
Castle, Wendell 67, 83, 86
Cavallo, Sr. Tiberius 28, 34
CBS see Columbia Broadcasting System
celeste pedal 105
cembalo 105
Challen, William 98
Challen 98
  and BBC 70, 98
  Giant horizontal grand piano **71**
Chappell, Samuel 98
Chappell 98
  and Strohmenger 67, 103
  upright yacht piano **73**
check 105
check mechanism 17
Chickering C. Frank 98
Chickering George H. 98
Chickering, Jonas 20, 21, 34, 96
Chickering, Thomas E. 98
Chickering 98
  and Aeolian 96, 98
  and American Piano Co. 96, 98
  and Baldwin 96
  and iron frame 34, 98
Chopin, Frédéric 35, 36, 43, 101, 105
  Broadwood piano 35
chromatic keys 6
Clark, John 100

Clark, Melville 55, 101, 103
Clarke 104
claveçin 105
claveçin à maillets 15, 105
clavicembalum 9
clavichord 7, **8**, 11, 14, 15, 18, 76, 105
  electric 76
  fretted 8, 106
  unfretted 8, 107
clavicordium 9
clavicytherium 9, 10, 105
Clavier (model) 75
clavier (term) 15, 105
claviharp 105
Clavinet see Hohner
Clavioline 77
claviorganum 17, 50, 105
Clementi, Muzio 28, 31, 98, 105
Clementi 31
  cabinet piano 104
  grand piano **30/31**, 104
  harmonic swell 31
  renamed Collard & Collard 31
  square piano 20, 104
  upright piano 104
  upright grand piano **39**
Clementi Collard & Collard 31
Clemm, Johann 9
close-wound string 105
Cludsam 68
Collard, Frederick 31, 44
Collard & Collard 31, 47, 98
  grand piano **31**, 104
Columbia Broadcasting System (CBS) 103
Combichord 77
compensating frame 34, 105
computer 78, 83, 98
concert grand piano 59
conductor's piano 22, 105
console piano 43, 44, 80, 105
Conway, Edwin 100
Cooper, Simon 75
Corri, Domenico 22
cottage piano 43, 44, 103, 105
Couchet, Jan 9
Cramer, Johann Baptist 98
Crea-Tone 75
Crehore, Benjamin 96, 98
Cristofali see Cristofori
Cristofori, Bartolomeo 9, 11-14
  earliest instruments 13
  and Scipione Maffei 13, 15
  and Prince Ferdinand de' Medici 11, 13
Cristofori
  action **13/14**, 14, 18
  cello **14**
  grand piano **11**, **11/12**, **13**, 104
  harpsichord 13
  other stringed instruments 14
crossbanding 105
cross-stringing 48, 102, 105
crown 88, 105
Cuel 64
Cuisinié 15
cycles per second see Hertz
cylinder piano 104

Dähler, Jörg Ewald 105
D'Almaine square piano 104
damper 92, 105
damper pedal 36, 105
Davis, George 99
Davis, Samuel 34
DEA see Hupfeld
Debain, Alexandre 53
Debain planchette piano 53
Debussy, Claude 57, 105
decay 105

Decker, David 98
Decker, John 98
Decker 98
   piano with Jankó keyboard **68**
decorative styles 64-65
desk *see* music desk
Deutsche Piano-Union 101
Deutsche Piano Works 101
Dewing, Thomas 66
digital piano 78, 105
digitorium **51**
diode tube 74
direct blow action 105
Disklavier *see* Yamaha
Ditanaklasis 25, 42, 69, 106
dog kennel piano 42
Dohnal, Joseph 23
Dohnal orphica **23**
Dolge, Alfred 45
dolly 106
Doppelflügel 106
double escapement action 30, 31, 34
double giraffe piano 40
double grand piano 69
double-strung 106
downbearing 106
down-striking action 106
von Dräger 75
drop action 71, 80, 106
due corde 30, 94, 105
dulcimer **4**, 5, 7, 15
Dulcitone *see* Machell
Dunham, John B. Jr. 98
Dunham 98
Duo-Art reproducing system 56, 57, 96, 106
duoclave 69, 101, 106
duplex scaling/strings 91, 106
Dussek, Jan Ladislav 105
dust cover 106
Dynatone 75

ear, function of 87
Eavestaff 101
   De Luxe Minipiano **70**, 71
Ehrbar 101
Eisenmann, Richard 75
Electone 75
electric grand piano 75, 76, 77
electric piano 72, 74-77, 106
electric pickup *see* pickup
electric reed piano 76
electric upright piano 79
electronic piano 76-77, 78, 106
'Electronic Piano' (model) *see* Miessner
electrostatic pickup 74
Elektrochord 75, 99
Elektrophonisches Klavier 75
Elgar, Edward 105
Empire grand piano *see* Bechstein
Empire style 65
end block 106
end cheek 106
Englische Mechanik action 17
English action 17, 18, 20, 24, 27, 106
English down-striking action 72
English grand action 28, 34, 106
English piano 27, 31, 32
Engramelle, Fr. Marie-Dominique Joseph 52
equal temperament 69
Erard, Jean-Baptiste 30, 98
Erard, Pierre 30, 34, 37, 43, 98
Erard, Sébastien 28, 30, 31, 34, 36, 92, 98
Erard 20, 28, 37, 49, 59, 98, 99, 101
   and agraffe 30, 34, 91
   art-case piano **63**, **67**
   and double escapement action 30, 60, 98

grand piano 30, **37**, **48**, **63**, **67**, 104
   and pedal mechanism 34
   square piano **36**
   transposing piano 69
   two-keyboard piano 69
Erard & Blondel 98
escapement 14, 17, 20, 30, 106
Estey, Jacob 98
Estey 98
euphonicon 51
Euphonium 72
Everett 75, 98
expression piano 106

Falcone, Santi 98, 102
Falcone 96, 98
fall board 106
Faner, Tim 83
Fazioli, Paolo 98-99
Fazioli, Romano 98
Fazioli 98-99
   F308 grand piano **86**
Fender, Leo 77
Fender-Rhodes 77
Ferrini, Giovanni 14
Feurich, Julius 99
Feurich 71, 99
Field, John 105
Firth Hall & Pond 99
Fischer, Charles 99
Fischer, J.C. 96, 99, 100
Fischer, John 99
Fleming, Sir John 74
Flügel 106
de Forest, Lee 74
Förster, August 75, 99
Förster, F.A. 99
fortepiano 4, 106
Fotoplayer *see* American
Fourneaux, J.L.N. 55, 57
frame 90, 106
   cast iron 32, 34, 48, 59, 90, 96
   compensating 34
   developments 21, 32, 34, 79, 90-91
   grand piano assembly 90
   upright piano assembly 90
French action *see* tape check action
French piano 27, 43
frequency 95
Friederici, Christian Ernst 16, 17, 39, 44
Friederici pyramid piano **16**
Fritz, Johann 26
Fritz grand piano **26**, 104
fuerte-piano 4
Fuller, Levi K. 98
fundamental pitch 95, 106

Gabler, Ernest 99
Gabler 99
Gaehle, Henry 100
Ganer 98
gap 106
Gaveau 66, 71, 98, 99
Geib, John 18, 20, 41, 106
geigenwerck **6**, 7, 11, 15
genouillère 106
German action 17, 24, 39
Gernsback, Hugo 75
Giant *see* Challen
Gibson 77
giraffe piano 39, **40**, 44, 106
Giraffenflügel 40
Gittens, George W. 98
Giustini, Lodovico 15
glasschord *see* pianino
Gleitz, Johann 97
gloves, weighted players' **51**
Gluck 19

Goldstone, Anthony 105
Goodrich, William 96
Gothic revivalist style 65
Gottschalk, Louis 105
Graf, Conrad 25, 36, 40
Graf
   grand piano **27**, **35**, 104
   quad-strung grand piano **36**
   upright grand piano **40**
grand piano action 20, **29**
grand piano 11-14, 15, 17, 24-34, 35, 36, 37, 46, 47, 48, 59-62, 63, 64, 65, 66, 67, 73, 75, 76, 77, 82, 84, 85, 86, 106
Granfeldt, Olof 68
Granfeldt square piano **68**
grasshopper action 106
Graves, Howard 100
gravicembalo 106
Gray, Dr Edward 28, 34
Gray, James A. 97
Great Exhibition London **46**, 69
Greer, Bernard 96, 98, 102
Gretschel, H. 97
Grimm, Johann 101
Grotrian, Friedrich 99
Grotrian, Kurt 99
Grotrian, Wilhelm 99
Grotrian, Willi 99
Grotrian-Steinweg 99, 102
   reproducing piano **57**
Guarracino virginal **9/10**
Gugler, Eric 83
Guichard 98
guide pins 106
Guido of Arezzo 5

Habig, Arnold H. 65, 97
Haiden, Hans 15
Haines, Francis 99
Haines, Napoleon J. 99
Haines Bros. 96, 99
Hale, Joseph P. 100
half blow pedal *see* soft pedal
half-pedaling 106
Hall, William 99
Hallet, William 99
Hallet & Cumston 99
Hallet & Davis 99
Hamlin, Emmons 100
hammer 92, 95, 100, 106
Hammerflügel 106
Hammerklavier 106
Hammond 77
Hancock, John Crang 28
Hancock transverse grand piano **28**
hand stop *see* stop
Handel, George Frederick 36, 98
hanging German action 39, 40
hanging Viennese action *see* hanging German action
von Hansen, Theophil 47
Harada, Rumiko 105
Hardman, Hugh 99
Hardman, John 99
Hardman 99
Hardman Peck 99
   and Aeolian 96, 99
   Minipiano 71
   Minipiano (electric) **74**, 75
harmonic 95, 105
harmonic envelope 95
harmonic series 95, 106
harmonic swell 31
harmonium-piano 50
harp piano 49
Harper player piano **55**
harpsichord 7, 8, 9, **10**, 11, 13, 14, 15, 17, 18, **29**, 36, 106

harpsichord-piano 14, 28, 50
Haschka, Georg grand piano **26/27**
Hawkins, John Isaac 42, 44
Hawkins portable upright piano **42**
Haydn, Josef 36, 98, 101, 105
Hayt 96
Hazelton Brothers 99
Hebenstreit, Pantaleon 7, 15
Heilmann, Matthäus 24
Heilmann grand piano **24**, 104
Heitzmann, Jan 101
Helberger, Bruno 74
Helfferich, Adolf 99
Hellertion 74
von Helmholtz, Hermann 40, 68, 91, 102
Hemch, Henri 10
Henderson cabinet grand piano **52**
Henfling, Conrad 68
Henschker grand piano 104
Herce, Auguste 50
Herce Tribune piano **50**
Herrburger Brooks 93, 100
Hertz (Hz) 95
Herz, Henri 31, 34, 92
Hewitt, Daniel 50
Hicks cylinder piano 52
high-tension scale 106
Hiller 75
Hindenburg airship 72
hitch pin 88, 106
hitch pin plate, iron 20
Hofmann, Ferdinand 25, 103
Hofmann grand piano **25**
Hohner
   Cembalet 76
   Clavinet D6 76
   Clavinet I **76**
   Pianet L electric reed piano **76**
   Pianet T 76
Hollein, Hans 85
Hopkinson, James 99
Hopkinson, John 99
Hopkinson 68, 99, 103
hopper *see* jack
horizontal grand piano 71
Horn, Rebecca 78
Horsburgh, Richard 22
Horsburgh portable upright piano **22**
Horse Race piano *see* Mills
Hulskamp 99
Hummel, Johann 105
Hunt, R.D. & J.H. 66
Hupfeld, Ludwig 58
Hupfeld 99, 101
   DEA reproducing system 57, 58
   Orchestrion 58, 101
   Phonola (Solo/Duo/Trio) 57, 58, 99
   Phonoliszt-Violina **58**, 101
   and Rönisch 101
   Vorsetzer piano player **54**
hurdy-gurdy 6, **7**, 15
Hutterstrasser, Carl 65, 97
hydraulis 6
Hyundai 101

Ibach family 99
Ibach, Johannes Adolf 99
Ibach 68, 99
indirect blow action 106
inharmonicity 106
International Standard Pitch 95
Irish damper 106
Irmler 99
Ishermann, J.C.L. 34
Italian piano 13
Ivers & Pond 96
ivory 86, 92

jack 106
Jacobs, Victor 100
Jacquard, Joseph Marie 53, 55, 57
James, Round & Co cabinet upright grand piano **39**
Janissary music 26, 28, 34, 106
von Jankó, Paul 68
Jankó keyboard 68, 98, 100
Jansen 67
Jarrett, Keith 62
Jasper 65, 97, 100
Johnson, James P. 101

Kaps, Ernest 99
Kaps 68, 99
Kapsel 106
Katin, Peter 105
Kawai, Koichi 99-100
Kawai, Shigeru 100
Kawai 99-100
   CR-40N transparent grand piano **84**
   EP-308s electric grand piano **76**
   and Schiedmayer
   Semi-Concert Grand piano 59
Kemble, Michael 100
Kemble 97, 100
   Minx Miniature piano **71**, 100
   and Yamaha 100
key 92, 106
   abbreviations ('keyboard reference') 106
   bed 61, 91
   cheek 106
   chromatic 6
   construction 92
   dip 92, 106
   frame 92, 106
   reversed color 24
   'skunk's tail' 8
   specifications 92
   weight 92
keyboard 92, 106
   abbreviations ('keyboard reference') 106
   Cludsam 68
   curved keyboard 68
   early types **6**, **7**
   evolution 6-7
   Granfeldt 68
   Henfling 68
   instruments, early 6
   Jankó 68, 98, 100
   Lunn 68
   Moór 69, 97, 102
   reference 106
   Rohleder 68
   shift 30, 32, 106
   slip 106
   transposing 69
   two 50, 68, 69
   variations 68-69
   well 106
   97-key 82
Kim brothers 103
Kimball, William Wallace 100
Kimball 65, 97, 100
   and Bösendorfer 100
Kirkman, Jacob 29
Kirkman, Joseph 29
Kirkman grand piano **29**
Kite, Christopher 105
Klavins Model 370 upright piano **79**, 104
Klemm 96
Knabe, Ernest 100
Knabe, William 100
Knabe 96, 100
Knabe & Gaehle 100
knee lever 106
Knight, Alfred 100

Knight 100, 103
Kohler, Charles 100
Kohler & Campbell 99, 100
Komen, Paul 105
Komoro, Tetsuya 85
Kopf, Silas 83
koretzug 17
Korg C303 digital home piano **78**
koto **5**
Kranich & Bach 100
Krakauer, David 100
Krakauer, Simon 100
Krakauer 75, 100
Kretzschmar, Hermann 105
Kriegelstein 66, 97
Kuder, K. 102
Kuhn & Ridgeway harp piano **49**
Kurka 68

Lambert upright piano **47**
Landreth, John 41, 44
Latour, Francis Tatton 98
Laucht 102
Lautsprecherklavier 75
Leach, Joanna 105
Lee, Hyo Ick 101
legato playing 36
LeGrain, Pierre 84
Leipziger Pianofortefabrik 101
Lemuel Gilbert 100
Lengerer, Sebastian 25
Lengerer grand piano **25**
Liberace 84, 96, 101
Lichtenthal, Herman 44, 45
lid swell 19
Lighte & Bradbury 100
Lighte & Newton 100
Lilliput see Bechstein
Lindemann 100
Linke, François 67
Linley, David 86
Linley upright piano **86**
listing cloth 106
Liszt, Franz 27, 32, 33, 36, 37, 43, 49,
   65, 66, 97, 99, 105
Loar, Lloyd 75
London 31
Longman & Broderip square piano 104
loop stringing 34, 48, 91, 106
Loud, Thomas 42, 44
Loud Brothers 34
Lowrey 99, 103
Lunn, William 68
Luther, John Frederik 100
Luther 100
lying giraffe piano 40
lying harp piano 22
Lyraflügel 41, 106
lyre 106
lyre piano 39, **41**, 70, 106

Machell, Thomas 72
Machell Dulcitone **72**
machine 106
Mackay, John 98
Maffei, Scipione 13, 15
Mahler, Gustav 35, 57
   Graf piano **35**
Mahoon bentside spinet **8**
Maitre & Martin 75
manichord(ian) 5
Mannborg 100
manufacturer listing see piano houses
Manxman piano 67
Manzarek, Ray 77
Marius, Jean 15
Markham, Richard 69
Marking piano 101
Marshall & Mittauer 100, 102

Marshall & Rose 103
Martin, Constant 77
Mason, Henry 100
Mason & Hamlin 96, 100
mass production 65
May 104
McNeil, Robert 102
McNulty grand piano 104
McTammany, John 55
Mechanical Orguinette Co. 57, 96
mechanized piano 52-58
de' Medici
   family 12
   Prince Ferdinand 11, 13, 14
medium grand piano 59
melodicon with drums 99
Melodigrand 96
melody piano 55
Mendelssohn, Felix 37, 101, 105
Mercier, Sébastien 42
Mercier upright piano **42/43**
Merlin, John Joseph 50
Merlin claviorganum **50**
Metropolitan Museum of Art 65
Metrostyle 56
Meyer, Conrad 100
Meyer 100
micro-tonal music 69
middle-C 106
MIDI see Musical Instrument Digital
   Interface
Miessner, Benjamin Franklin 74
Miessner 74, 75
   'Electronic Piano' 74, 75
   and Hardman Peck 74
   'stringless' piano 74, 75
   and Wurlitzer 74
Mills
   Horse Race Piano **58**
   Violano-Virtuoso **57**
Milner pedal piano **68**
miniature piano 23, 70-71
Minipiano (model) see Eavestaff, and
   Hardman Peck
Mini-Royal see Schimmel
Minstrelle 71, 96
Minx Miniature piano see Kemble
moderator stop 106
monochord **5**, 7
Montanini barrel piano **52**
Moór, Emanuel 69, 97, 102
Morley
   orchestral upright grand piano 70
   symmetrical grand piano 70
Mozart, Leopold 52
Mozart, Wolgang Amadeus **16/17**, 24,
   26, 36, 52, 105
Müller, L.W., upright piano **47**
Müller, Matthias 25, 42, 44, 69, 106
music roll see piano roll
Musical Instrument Digital Interface
   (MIDI) 78, 79, 85, 106
Mussorgsky, Modest 105

name plaque 106
name plate 106
nameboard 106
Nancarrow, Conlon 57, 105
Needham 57
Neo-Bechstein see Bechstein electric
   grand piano
neo-classical style 64-65
Nernst, Dr Walther 75
Nero, Peter 101
Nettle, David 69
Neumeyer 100
New York Exhibition 46
New York Piano Manufacturing Co. 99
Nickelodeon 101
Niendorf 100

Nippon Gakki 100, 103
node 95
note abbreviations ('keyboard
   reference') 106
Nunns, Robert 100
Nunns, William 99, 100, 102
Nunns & Clark 100
nut 106

octave span 23
octave stop 29
Oeben, Jean François 67
open-wound string 106
orchestral instruments, emulation of 26
orchestral upright grand piano 70
Orchestrelle Pianola piano player **54**
Orchestrion see Hupfeld
organ 11
   Aeolian 96
   American Cabinet 100
   two-octave 6
   water 6
organ-piano 17, 50, 106
organist's piano 68
organistrum 6, 7, 106
Orlowetsky, Alexei 105
ormolu 67
orphica 23
Osbourn, John 98
ottavina 22
overdamped 92, 107
overdamped action **49**
overspun string 107
overstringing 32, 34, 44, 48

Paderewski, Jan 57, 102, 103
Paine, R.W. 57
Paladini, Giuseppe 12, 105
pantaleon 7, 15, 107
Pape, Camille 101
Pape, Jean-Henri 34, 43, 44, 100, 101
Pape 43, 44, 55, 66, 97, 100
   console piano **44**
   eight-octave piano 34
   and French down-striking action 100
   square piano **21**
   upright console piano **44**
Paris Exposition 46, 63, 65, 66
partial 107
Pasquale barrel piano **52**, 104
peacock dampers 19
Peck, Leopold 99
pedal 94, 107
   bass sustain 94
   celeste 105
   damper 36, 81, 94, 105
   due corde 106
   half blow (soft) 81, 94
   mechanism 34
   muffler see practice
   practice (muffler) 94
   soft 86, 94
   sostenuto 92, 94, 107
   sustain see damper
pedal piano 68, 107
Perau 97
Percival, Henry 57
Percival perpendicular piano **50**
Perez, Peter 96
perpendicular piano 50, 70
Perzina, Paul 100
Perzina 100
Petrof, Antonin Sr. 100-101
Petrof family 101
Petrof 100-101
Pfeiffer, Carl Anton 101
Pfeiffer, Joseph Anton 101
Pfeiffer 101
Phonola see Hupfeld

Phonoliszt-Violina see Hupfeld
physical modeling 78
Pianet see Hohner
pianino 42, 43, 44, 107
Pianista 55, 57
piano à claviers renversés 107
piano à queue 107
piano attachment 107
piano carré 107
piano droit 42, 43, 107
Piano Électrique 75
piano harpsichord see harpsichord-
   piano
piano houses
   chronology 96
   listing 96-103
piano manufacturers see piano houses
Piano Melodica see Racca
piano music, early 15, 35
piano-organ see organ-piano
piano player 54-57, 107
piano roll 54-58, **56**, 107
piano trio 36, 37
pianoforte 4, 107
Pianoforte magazine 34
Pianola 54, 57, 96, 107
Pianophon 75
Pianor 75
Pianorad 75
Pianotron 75
piccolo piano 43, 49
pickup 74, 84
pin block 14, 20, 62, 88, 90-91, 107
Pirsson, James 69, 101
Pirsson 101
pitch 107
plain-sawn 107
planchette piano 53
plastic action 79
plate see frame
player piano 55-57, 107
Pletcher, Thomas M, 101
Pleyel, Camille 35, 43
Pleyel, Ignace 43, 101
Pleyel 35, 37, 42, 43, 44, 99, 100, 101
   Duoclave 69
   Elite miniature piano 71
   pianino **43**
pocket grand piano 32
Pohlmann, Johannes 18, 19
Pohlmann 19
   square piano **19**
Pollak-Rudin 75
polychord 5, 7, 8
Ponti, Michael 105
portable grand piano 42
portable piano 22/23, 42, 72-73
portable square piano 22
portable upright piano 22, 42
de Portalupsis, Franciscus 9
Pottier & Stymus 63
Poynter, Sir Edward 65
Praetorius, Michael 7
Pratt Read & Co. 102
Prelleiste 17, 107
Prellmechanik action 17, 107
Prellzungenmechanik action 17, 24,
   107
pressure bar 34, 90, 91
prop stick 107
psaltery 5, 8
Pugin, Augustus Welby Northmore 46
Pugin upright piano **46**
pyramid piano 16, 39, 44, 70, 107
Pyramidenflügel 39
Pythagoras 5

qanum 5
QE2 see Queen Elizabeth II
QRS 55, 101, 103

quad-strung 107
quanum 5
quarter-sawn 107
quarter-tone piano 69
Queen Elizabeth II cruise liner 73
Querflügel 28, 107
Querspinett **8**

Racca, Giovanni 55
Racca Piano Melodica **54/55**
Rachmaninov 57
radio 74
Radiopiano 75
Rameau Aurore upright piano **86**
ravalement 107
Raven, Richard 96
Raven, Thomas 96
recumbent harp piano **22**, 107
reed 72, 74
Regency style 65
register 107
regulating 107
Renaissance revivalist style 65
Renner 80
repetition 107
reproducing piano 56-58, 104, 107
Rhea, Tom 74
Rhodes, Harold 72, 75, 77
Rhodes
   Air Corps Piano 77
   Piano 75
   Pre-Piano 77
   Stage-54 electric piano **77**
rib 88, 107
Riesiner, Jean-Henri 67
rim 59, 90, 102
rim, inner 90, 91
rim-bending 59
RMI see Rocky Mount Instruments
Rocky Mount Instruments 77
rococo style 64
rococo revivalist style 65
Rogers 103
   organist's piano **68**
Rohleder, Johann 68
Roland RD-500 digital stage piano **78**
Rolfe, William 34, 39
Römantic music 32, 36
Röllig, Carl 23
Rönisch, Albert 101
Rönisch, Carl 101
Rönisch, Hermann 101
Rönisch 99, 101
rose 107
Rosenberger, Michael 25
Rosenberger grand piano **25**, 104
Rossini, Gioacchino 42
Roth & Junius 101
Rubinstein, Artur 57, 62
Ruckers, Andreas 10
Ruckers, Hans 91
Ruckers, Johannes 9
Ruckers 9, 10, 64
Ruhlmann, Emile-Jacques 66
Ruhlmann/Gaveau grand piano **66**
Russian piano 20
Ryley, Edward 69

Saint-Saëns, Camille 100
Samick 101
samples, digital 78
sampling piano 107
Samsung 103
Sandell, Henry Conrad 57, 58
Sassmann
   grand piano **24**
   harpsichord **10**
   virginal **9**
Sauer, Leopold 39

Sauer pyramid piano **39**
Sauter, Carl 101
Sauter 101
scale design 107
Schantz, Johann 25
Schiedmayer family 101
Schiedmayer, Johann David 24
Schiedmayer 101
Schiller, J. 101
Schiller 101
Schimmel, Nicholas Wilhelm 101-102
Schimmel, Wilhelm 101
Schimmel, Wilhelm Arno 101
Schimmel 98, 99, 101-102
    Golden Jubilee model 101
    Mini-Royal 101
    transparent grand piano **73**, 84
Schleip, Johann 41
Schleip lyre piano **41**
Schmahl, Johann Matthäus 22
Schmahl
    fretted clavichord **8**
    recumbent harp piano **22/23**
Schmidt, A. 102
Schmidt-Flohr 102
Schnabel 107
Schneider grand piano **46/47**
Schoenberg miniature piano **71**
Schöffstoss, Franz 22
Schöffstoss, Joseph 22, 25
School of Stein grand piano **24**
Schornsheim, Christine 105
Schröter, Gottlieb 11, 15
Schubert, Franz 105
Schulz, H.O.W. 99
Schulze, Karl 66, 97
Schumann, Robert 36, 101, 105
Schumann (manufacturer) 101
Schweighofer 101
Seiler, Eduard 102
Seiler, Johannes 102
Seiler, Steffen 102
Seiler 102
    Membrator soundboard 102
    Showmaster SM-180 grand piano **84**
    Showmaster Junior-114 electric
        upright piano **78/79**
Selmer
    Clavioline **77**
    Pianotron 75
Sequential Circuits 78
Seuffert, Franz 40, 44
sewing box piano **23**
Seytre 53, 55
sharp 107
Shearing, George 84
Shelley, Howard 105
Sheraton, Thomas 65
shims 107
ship piano 73
short (bass) octave **6**, 107
Shudi, Barbara 98
Shudi, Burkat 10, 28, 29, 97
Shudi-Broadwood harpsichord **10**, 29
sidebearing 107
Siemens 75
Silbermann, Gottlieb 11, 15, 17, 18
Silbermann grand piano **15**
Simoni, Gaetano
Simoni barrel piano **53**
Simonnet, Lucien 64
Singer, Eugene 75
sloping upright square piano 41
Smart, Sir George 22
Smith, Freeborn Garrettson 102
Smith 102
Socher, Johannes 18
soft pedal 86
Sohmer family 102
Sohmer, Hugo 100, 102
Sohmer 69, 96, 102

Soler, Vicente 105
Solovox 77
sonata 36
sostenente piano 74, 107
sostenuto pedal 92, 107
sound module 78, 79
sound theory 87
soundboard 59, 72, 74, 88, 89, 102,
    107
soundwaves 87
Southwell, William 41, 43, 44
Southwell upright square piano **41**
speaking length 107
Spielmann, Emerick 75
spine 107
spinet 8, 9, 11, 107
    bentside 9
    octave 9
spinet piano 50, 80, 107
spinet piano action 94
square piano 18-21, 22, 35, 36, 38, 43,
    50, 68, 107
Squire & Longson 103
Staier, Andreas 105
Steck, George 56, 96, 102
Steck 102
    reproducing piano **56**
Stein, Carl 36
Stein, Johann Andreas 17, 23, 24, 50,
    101, 103
Stein, Matthäus Andreas (André) 24,
    36, 103
Stein, Nannette 24, 103
Stein 103
    double manual organ-grand **17**
Steingraeber, Eduard 102
Steingraeber 102
Steinway, Albert 102
Steinway, C.F. Theodor 48, 91, 99, 102
Steinway, Charles 99, 102
Steinway, Heinrich (Henry) Engelhard
    Sr. 48, 99, 102
Steinway, Henry Jr. 32, 34, 99, 102
Steinway, John 103
Steinway, Wihelmine 102
Steinway, William 102
Steinway 48, 99, 102-103
    Accelerated Action **60**
    art-case piano 48, **63**, **63/64**, **65**, **66**,
        83, **86**
    and BBC 70
    and Boston Piano Co. 97
    Boudoir Grand piano 59
    and cast-iron frame 48
    and CBS 103
    Centennial Grand piano 63, 102
    and cross-stringing 48, 102
    factory locations 102
    first piano 48, 102
    German vs. US manufacture 61
    'G.I.' piano 102
    grand piano **48**, **59/60/61/62**, **63**,
        63/64, **65**, **66**, **83**
    Miniature Grand piano 59
    Model C grand piano **63/64**
    Model D grand piano **59/60/61/62**,
        65
    Model L grand piano **83**
    and one-piece piano rim 102
    overstrung grand piano 48, 102
    overstrung square piano 20
    parlor grand piano 64
    sale of company 1985 103
    and sostenuto pedal 20
    square piano **21**
    upright piano **86**
    White House piano **66**, **83**
    300,000th piano 83
    500,000th piano 83
Steinweg 48, 99, 102 see also
    Grotrian-Steinweg

Steinweg family members see also
    under Steinway
stencil piano 96, 107
Stevens, Bruce A. 103
Steward, John 51
Stewart, Albert 83
Stewart, James 34, 98
Stichel 101
sticker action **41**, 43, 44, 107
Stodart, Matthew 20
Stodart, Robert 20, 28, 29, 34
Stodart, William 20, 44, 103
Stodart square piano **20**, 104
Stodart & Morris 103
stop 10, 23, 26, 28, 29, 107
Story, Edward 103
Story, Hampton 103
Story & Clark 55, 75, 101, 103
Storytone 75, 103
Stossmechanik action 17
Stosszungenmechanik action 17
Straight, Charlie 101
straight side 107
straight-strung 107
Strauss, Richard 57
street piano 52-53
Streicher, Johann Andreas 25, 44, 103
Streicher 101, 103
    grand piano **104**
strengthening 32, 45
strike line 107
strike point 95, 107
stringing (decoration) 107
'stringless' piano 74
strings 4, 5, 10, 14, 20, 21, 29, 32, 34,
    36, 42, 43, 44, 45, 48, 50, 59, 62,
    82, 87-88, 90, 91, 95, 100
Strohmenger, John 103
Strohmenger 103
    upright piano **67**
strut 107
stud see agraffe
studio piano 80
Superpiano 75
Supertramp 74
sustain pedal see damper pedal
swell 107
Swift 96
Sylig 41
symmetrical grand piano 70
sympathetic strings 107
symphonie 6
symphony 36
synthesizer 76, 78

Tabel 29, 97
table piano 18, 44, 50
Tafelklavier 18
tail 107
Tan, Melvyn 105
tangent 107
tape check action 43, 44, 45, **49**, 107
tenor 107
Thermodist 56
Thomas, Michael Tilson 84
three year plan 49
Thürmer, Ferdinand 103
Thürmer 103
Tiffany, Joseph Burr 66
tine 72, 77, 107
Tomasso street piano **53**, 104
Tompkinson, Thomas 30
Tompkinson 31
    grand piano **30**
toning 95
toning needle 95
top door 107
top tuner 49
touch weight 107

Townsend Groovesteen 99
toy piano 23
transient 95
transparent grand piano 73, 84
transposing keyboard 107
transverse grand piano 28, 107
trapwork 107
travel piano 72-73
Tremaine, Harry B. 96
Tremaine, William B. 57, 96
Tribune piano 50
trichord 91, 107
Trimpin MIDI-controlled prepared
    piano **79**
triode tube 74
Tschudi, Burckhardt see Shudi, Burkat
tuning 69, 78, 88, 90-91, 95, 107
tuning-fork piano 72
tuning pin 88, 90-91, 107
Turkish music see Janissary
'Twelve apostles' 18, 20, 102
Typophone 72

Uebel & Lechleitner 103
una corda 11, 13, 14, 30, 43, 94, 107
underdamped 92, 107
unichord 107
unison 91, 107
United States piano see American
    piano
Univox 77
upbearing 107
upright console piano 44
upright grand piano 39, 40, 41, 44,
    107
upright piano 17, 42-45, 46, 47, 49,
    67, 73, 74, 79, 80-82, 86, 107
upright piano with electronics 74
upright square piano 41, 44
upright transposing piano 68/69
upright yacht piano 73

Vanhal, Jan 105
Variachord 75
Vatter, Antoine 10
Vaucanson 55
veneer 107
Venetian swell 10, 42, 107
Verel, Ludovicus 22
Verel portable square piano **22**
verre églomisé 30, 107
vertical piano 107
Vienna 24, 25
Viennese action 17, 24, **25**, 26, 27,
    107
Viennese piano 24/25, 26/27, 32
Viennese swell 29
Vierling, Oskar 75
da Vinci, Leonardo 6
viola organista 6
Violano-Virtuoso see Mills
virginal 8, **9**, 11, 22, 52, 107
Virtuola Player 99
vis à vis 107
Vivi-Tone 75
Vogel, Theodor 99, 102
voicing 95, 107
Vorsetzer see Hupfeld
Vose 96
Votey, Edwin 54, 57, 96

Wachtl, Joseph 40, 44
Wagner, Richard 99, 102
wall piano 50
Waller, Fats 57, 101
Walmisley, Thomas 105
Walsh, Frank 62
Walter, Anton 22, 25

Walter
    grand piano 104
    portable square piano **22**
    square piano 104
water organ see organ, water
Weber, Albert 103
Weber 96, 103
von Weber, Carl Maria 105
weekend piano 23
Weight, Don 96
Welmar 73
Welte, Edwin 55, 56, 57
Welte 97
    Green 57
    Red 54, 57, 58
Whelpdale Maxwell & Codd 103
White House piano see Steinway
Wiget, Ueli 105
Wilkinson, George 45, 103
Williams, Roger 101
Winwood, Steve 77
wippen 107
Woodward & Brown 103
Woolf, Auguste 43, 101
Woolley, Robert 105
Worcester, Horatio 103
Worcester 103
World's Fair 46, 102
Wornum, Robert 32, 43, 44, 45, 49,
    50, 103
    and tape check action 43, 44, 45, 103
    and upright action 43, 44, 103
Wornum 103
    Albion square piano **50**
    and cottage piano 103
    piccolo piano **45**
    pocket grand piano **32**
    upright piano 43, 44, **49**
wrest pin see tuning pin
wrest plank see pin block
Wulsin, Lucien 96
Wurlitzer, Franz Rudolph 103
Wurlitzer 103
    and Aeolian 96
    and Baldwin 96
    EP-100 electric piano **74**, 103
    EP-200 electric piano 74
    jukebox 103
    upright piano with electronics 74

yacht piano 73
Yamaha, Torakusu 84, 99-100, 103
Yamaha 98, 100, 103
    Centenary grand piano **84**
    CP-70/CP-80 electric grand piano 77
    Disklavier 85
    electric grand piano **76/77**
    factory locations 103
    first piano 103
    first reed organ 103
    'Moon & Piano' grand piano **84/85/**
        86
    Nippon Gakki name change 103
Young Chang 96, 103

Zacharias, Ernst 76
Zender 99
Zenti, Girolamo 9
Zimmermann, Max 103
Zimmermann, Richard 103
Zimmermann 103
zither 4, 5
Zumpe, Johannes 18, 19, 20, 28
Zumpe 30, 98
    square piano **18**, **35**

OWNERS' CREDITS
Instruments photographed especially for this book came from the following individuals, organizations and collections, and we are most grateful for their help. The owners are listed here in the alphabetical order of the code used to identify their instruments in the Key To Commissioned Photographs below.
Addington Palace **AP**; Bösendorfer London **BL**; Colt Clavier Collection **CC**; Finchcocks **FC**; Goodwood House **GH**; The Musical Museum (Brentford) **MB**; The Musical Museum (Holdenby House) **MH**; HRH Princess Firyal **PF**; Royal National College for the Blind **RN**; Steinway & Sons London **SS**.

KEY TO COMMISSIONED PHOTOGRAPHS
The following key is designed to identify the owners of instruments specially photographed for this book. After the relevant page number (*in italic type*) we list: the maker, model or other identifier, followed by the owner's initials in **bold type** (see Owners' Credits above). For example, '*4* dulcimer **RN**' means that the dulcimer shown on page 4 was owned by the Royal National College for the Blind.
4 dulcimer **RN**; *5* monochord **CC**; *6* spinet keyboard **FC**; *8* Schmahl **FC**, Mahoon **FC**; *9* Guarracino **FC**; *10* Adlam **FC**; *18/19* Beyer **FC**; *18* Zumpe **FC**; *19* Broadwood **FC**; *20* Stodart **FC**; *20/21* Pape **CC**; *21* Broadwood **FC**, Steinway **CC**; *22* Verel **CC**, Horsburgh **GH**, Walter **FC**; *24* School of Stein **CC**, Heilmann c1790 **CC**; *25* Lengerer **FC**, Hoffmann **CC**, Rosenberger **FC**; *26/27* Haschka **CC**; *26* Fritz **FC**; *27* Graf 1826 **FC**, Graf c1830 **CC**; *28/29* Broadwood **CC**; *28* Hancock **FC**, Broadwood nameboards **CC**; *29* Shudi **CC**, Kirkman **CC**; *30/31* Clementi **FC**; *30* Erard agraffes **CC**, Tompkinson **CC**; *31* Collard **FC**; *32* Wornum **CC**; *33* Broadwood **FC**; *39* Sauer **FC**, Jones **FC**, Clementi **CC**; *40* unknown **CC**; *41* unknown **FC**, Schleip **CC**, Southwell **FC**; *42/43* Mercier **FC**; *43* Pleyel **FC**; *44* Pape 1841 **FC**, Pape 1840 **CC**; *45* Wornum **CC**; *46/47* Schneider **CC**; *47* Müller **MH**, Lambert **MH**; *48* Erard **FC**; *49* Wornum **MH**, Brinsmead **RN**; *50* Merlin **CC**, Wornum **CC**, Percival **MH**; *51* gloves **MB**, digitorium **FC**; *52* Henderson **CC**, Pasquale **MB**; *53* Tomasso **MB**, Debain **MB**; *54/55* Racca **MB**; *54* Hupfeld **MB**, Orchestrelle **MB**; *55* Harper **MB**; *56/57* Steck **MB**; *56* piano rolls **MB**; *57* Grotrian-Steinweg **MB**, Mills **MB**; *58* Mills **MB**, American Photo **MB**, Hupfeld **MB**; *59/60/61/62* Steinway **SS**; *65* Bösendorfer **PF**; *68/69* Broadwood transposing **MH**; *68* Rogers **RN**, Milner AP; *70* Eavestaff **RN**, Morley orchestral **RN**, Morley symmetrical **RN**; *72* Machell **FC**; *73* Chappel **MH**; *74* Hardman **MH**; *76* Hohner **MB**; *77* Selmer **MB**; *81/82* Bösendorfer 130 **BL**.

Principal commissioned photography was by Nigel Bradley of Visuel 7. Additional photographs were taken by Will Taylor (Visuel 7), Miki Slingsby and the author.

OTHER ILLUSTRATIONS
Existing photographs of instruments were kindly supplied by Astin-Weight, Salt Lake City, US (*Astin-Weight frame p79*); H. Blairman & Sons Ltd, London, UK (*Pugin p46*); Bösendorfer, Vienna, Austria (*Bösendorfers p47, p82, p85*); The Broadwood Trust, Surrey, UK (*Shudi p10, Broadwoods p63, p67*); Calderdale Leisure Services, Halifax, UK (*Pohlman p19*); The Cobbe Foundation, Hatchlands, Surrey, UK (*Zumpe p35, Broadwood p35, Grafs p35, p36, Erards p36, p37, Broadwood p38*); Collezione Marino Marini, Ravenna, Italy (*Montanini p52, Simoni p53*); Fazioli, Sacile, Italy (*Fazioli p86*); John Dilworth, Twickenham, UK (*Cristofori violoncello p14*); Haags Gemeentemuseum, The Hague, Netherlands (*Stein p17, Unknown recumbent harp piano p22, Erard p30, Graf p40, Bechstein p74/75*); Handel-Häus, Halle, Germany (*Dohnal p23*); Bruce Hayes, Reading, UK (*Schoenberg p71*); Stefan Jakubowski, London, UK (*Strohmenger p67*); Kawai Musical, Hamamatsu, Japan (*Kawais p76, p84*); Kemble & Co., Milton Keynes, UK (*Kemble p71*); Klavins Music, Bonn, Germany (*Klavins p79*); Korg UK Ltd, London, UK (*Korg p78*); The Liberace Museum, Las Vegas, US (*Baldwin p84*); David Linley Furniture, London, UK (*Linley p86*); Maximiliaan's House of Pianos, New York, US (*Erard p63, Steinway 1877 p63, Steinway 1897 p63/64, Broadwood p64, Bechstein 1898 p66, Ruhlmann p66, Erards p67*); Metropolitan Museum of Art, New York, US (*Cristofori p12*); Musée Instrumental Bruxelles, Belgium (*geigenwerck p6, Friederici p16*); Museo degli Strumenti Musicali, Rome, Italy (*Cristofori p11*); Musikinstrumenten-Museum der Universität Leipzig, Germany (*Cristofori p13, Schmahl p22-23*); National Museums & Galleries on Merseyside, UK (*Unknown 'sewing box' p23*); Nettle & Markham, London, UK (*Pleyel p69 pic Julian Easten*); Phillips, London, UK (*Beale p51*); Rameau, Paris, France (*Rameau p86*); Roland UK Ltd, Swansea, UK (*Roland p78*); Russell Collection, University of Edinburgh, UK (*Backers p29*); Sassmann GmbH, Hückeswagen, Germany (*Sassmanns p9, p10, Heilmann reconstruction p24*); Schimmel Pianos, Braunschweig, Germany (*Schimmel p73*); Schloss Sanssouci, Potsdam, Germany (*Silbermann p15*); Seiler, Kitzingen, Germany (*Seilers p78/79, p84*); Sibeliusmuseum, Åbo, Finland (*Granfeldt p68*); Smithsonian Institution, Washington DC, US (*Albrecht p20 #56364, Hawkins p42 #56414, Kuhn p49 #56385A, Decker Janko p68 #56378*); Steinway & Sons, New York, US (*Steinways p48, p65, p66, 1987 p83, 1990 p83*); Thorn EMI, London, UK (*Broadwood Beethoven p37/38 pic Sheila Rock*); Trimpin, Seattle, US (*Trimpin p79*); David Wainwright, Surrey, UK (*Broadwood Janko p68*); Wendell Castle, New York, US (*Steinway p86*); White House, Washington, US (*Steinway 1938 p83*); Wurlitzer Co., Ohio, US (*Wurlitzer EP-100 p74*); Yamaha Corporation, Hamamatsu, Japan (*Yamahas p76, p84, p85/86*).

Piano actions photographed for this book were kindly supplied by the Royal National College for the Blind, Hereford, UK, with the exception of those on p60 (Steinway & Sons London), p79/80 (Bösendorfer London), and p93/94 (Herrburger Brooks).

Illustrations of piano details in *How A Piano Works*, pp87-95, were kindly supplied by Blüthner (London, UK), Schimmel Pianos (Braunschweig, Germany) and Yamaha Corporation (Hamamatsu, Japan).

Memorabilia illustrated in this book, including catalogs, brochures, magazines, disc sleeves, paintings, engravings and photographs, are reproduced with thanks to Amon-Ra, Athene, Blüthner, Bösendorfer, Musical Museum (Brentford), The British Museum, The Broadwood Trust, Chandos, Claves, The Cobbe Foundation, Cunard, Deutsche Harmonia Mundi, ECM, EMI Classics, Finchcocks, Globe, John Glyn, Keith Hamshere (Majestic Films), Mark Heathcote, Kemble Pianos, Klavins Music, Marcus Leith, The Liberace Museum, *The Music Trades* magazine, *Music Trades Review* magazine, Nimbus, *Piano Maker* magazine, RCA Victor Red Seal, Saydisc, Steinway & Sons, Verlag K.-J. Kamprad, Wergo, Whelpdale Maxwell & Codd.

IN ADDITION
As well as those named in OWNERS' CREDITS and OTHER ILLUSTRATIONS we would like to thank: Gwen Alexander; William G Allman (The White House, Washington, US); John Andrews (Bell & Crane Music, Surbiton, UK); Barbara Ascherfeld (Steinway & Sons, Hamburg, Germany); Ray Astin (Astin-Weight, Salt Lake City, US); Janice Morelock Bearden (Morelock Organs, Mississippi, US); Simon Beck; Michael Benson (Addington Palace, UK); Steve Beresford; Tony Bingham; Margaret Birley (Horniman Museum, London, UK); David Blake (Harmonia Mundi, London, UK); Bob Brown (Kemble & Co., Milton Keynes, UK); Nigel Brown (The Music Studios, London, UK); Barbara Brooker (Holdenby House, Northants, UK); Ray Burford (Sony Music, London, UK); Gwyneth Campling (Royal Collection Enterprises, Windsor, UK); Laurence Casserley (Royal College of Music, London, UK); Robert Castle (Korg, London, UK); Trevor Chriss (A.C. Cooper Fine Art Photographers, London, UK); Trevor Clarke; Martha Novak Clinkscale (University of California, US); Alexander Cobbe (The Cobbe Foundation, Hatchlands, UK); Michael Cole; Sarah Crombie; Flora Crossthwaite (David Linley Furniture Ltd, London, UK); Ian Cullen (Roland UK, Swansea, UK); Sue D'Arcy (Majestic Films, London, UK); Hugh Davies; Michael Deacon (RCA Records, London, UK); Bob Doerschuk (*Keyboard* magazine, California, US); Alastair Duncan (J. Alastair Duncan Ltd, New York, US); Henrietta Edwards (Royal Collection Enterprises, Windsor, UK); Heidrun Eichler (Musikinstrumenten-Museum, Markneukirchen, Germany); Alun Evans; Paulo Fazioli (Fazioli Pianoforti srl, Sacile, Italy); Craig Ferguson (Allen Organ Co, Pennsylvania, US); HRH Princess Firyal; David Flanders (Royal Academy of Music, London, UK); Eric Flounders (Cunard, Southampton, UK); Henry Ford Museum, Michigan, US; August Förster GmbH, Löbau, Germany; Waltraud Fricke (Museum für Verkehr und Technik, Berlin, Germany); Ken George; John Glyn; Robert Glazebrook (Steinway & Sons, London, UK); John Gould (Sound Instruments, Uckfield, UK); Göran Grahn (Stiftelsen Musikkulturens Främjande, Sweden); David Grover (Bentley Piano Co Ltd, Stroud, UK); Knut Grotrian-Steinweg (Grotrian-Steinweg, Braunschweig, Germany); Sumi Gunji (Kunitachi College of Music, Tokyo, Japan); Christine Harris (Cunard, Southampton, UK); Bruce Hayes; Mary Jane Hayward (State Museum of Pennsylvania, US); Dr Birgit Heise (Musikinstrumenten-Museum der Universität, Leipzig, Germany); Dr Hubert Henkel (Deutsches Museum, Munich, Germany); Peter Holman (Hyperion Records, London, UK); Rebecca Horn; Simon Howe (Cambridge Pianoforte Centre, UK); Colin Hunt (Steinway & Sons, London, UK); David Hunt; Mark Hunter (Baldwin Piano & Organ Co., Ohio, US); Tim Ingles (Sothebys, London, UK); Adam Johnston (Broadwood Trust, Surrey, UK); Yutaka Kasahara (Kawai Musical Inst Mfg Co Ltd, Hamamatsu, Japan); Roy Kemble (Yamaha-Kemble Music UK Ltd, Milton Keynes, UK); Philip Kennedy (Royal National College for the Blind, Hereford, UK); John Koster (Shrine to Music Museum, Vermillion, US); Cornelia Krumbiegel (Bach-Archiv, Leipzig, Germany); Berenice Küpper (C Bechstein Pianofortefabrik GmbH, Berlin, Germany); Janice Lane (Liberace Museum, Las Vegas, US); Alastair Laurence; David Lay; Joanne Leach (Athene Records, London, UK); David Legg-Willis (Goodwood House, Chichester, UK); Martin P. Levy (H. Blairman & Sons, London, UK); Jeff Lincoln (World of Pianos, London, UK); James Lowther (Holdenby House, Northants, UK); Werner Maas (Seiler, Kitzingen, Germany); Brian Majeski (*The Music Trades* magazine, New Jersey, US); Donald E Mannino (Young Chang, California, US); Marino Marini (Collection of Mechanical Musical Instruments, Ravenna, Italy); Richard Markham; David Martin (Herrburger Brooks, Nottingham, UK); Nicolas Meeùs (Musée Instrumental, Bruxelles, Belgium); Dominic Milano (*Keyboard* magazine, California, US); Helen Moore (Complete Record Co, London, UK); John Morley; Museo Degli Strumenti Musicali, Rome; Arnold Myers (Edinburgh University, UK); Hiroaki Nakata (Yamaha Corporation, Hamamatsu, Japan); David Nettles; Sally O'Grady (Thorn-EMI, London, UK); Frances Palmer (Horniman Museum, London, UK); Guy Pearson; Petrof, Hradec Králové, Czech Republic; Elizabeth Pilwachs (Bösendorfer, Vienna, Austria); Karen Pitchford (Kotch International, London, UK); Ian Pleeth; Laurie Prior; Eugene Quills (Balham Piano Preservation Society, UK); Don Randall (Randall Instruments, Santa Ana, US); Dr Bruce Reader (Altarus Records, Bath, UK); Gordon Read; Richard Reason (Phillips, London, UK); Konstantin Restle (Staatliches Institut für Musikforschung, Berlin, Germany); Christiane Rieche (Händel-Haus, Halle, Germany); Véronique Rigaud-Költzsch (Technik Museum, Sinsheim, Germany); Marcie M Rowan (Wurlitzer, Ohio, US); Pauline Rushton (National Museums & Galleries on Merseyside, UK); Max Rutten (Maximiliaan's House of Pianos, New York, US); Christian Sabisch (Rud. Ibach-Sohn, Schwelm, Germany); Roy Saer (National Folk Museum of Wales, UK); Saydisc, Wooton-Under-Edge, UK; Nikolaus Schimmel (Schimmel Pianos, Braunschweig, Germany); Ursula Seiler (Seiler, Kitzingen, Germany); Dane Sinclair; Pam Skerry (Blüthner, London, UK); John Sladden (Goodwood House, Chichester, UK); Andrew Smith (Horsham Piano Centre, UK); Leo Spellman (Steinway & Sons, New York, US); W. Spiers (Colt Clavier Collection, Bethesden, UK); Staatliche Schlösser und Garten, Potsdam, Germany; Tate Gallery Press Office, London, UK; Ilpo Tolvas (Sibeliusmuseum, Åbo, Finland); Tessa Trethowan (Christies Images, London, UK); Elizabeth Tye (TradeLink Associates, Boston, UK); David Wainwright; Martin Weedon (Piano Workshop, London, UK); Roger H. Weisensteiner (Kimball Piano, Indiana, US); Rosalind Westwood (Shibden Hall, Halifax, UK); Mark Wiggins (*Gramophone* magazine, London, UK); Lucy Wood (National Museums & Galleries on Merseyside, UK); Markus Worm (Sassmann GmbH, Hückeswagen, Germany); Erica Worth (EMI Records, London, UK); James Yorke (Victoria & Albert Museum, London, UK); Jan Younghusband; Jane Zenner (Museum of London, UK).

BIBLIOGRAPHY
G. Armbruster (ed) *The Art Of Electronic Music* (Quill 1984); T. Bacon (ed) *Rock Hardware* (Blandford 1981); M.N. Clinkscale *Makers Of The Piano 1700-1820* (Oxford University Press 1993); C.F. Colt *The Early Piano* (Stainer & Bell 1981); C. Ehrlich *The Piano: A History* (Clarendon 1990); L. Fine *The Piano Book* (Brookside 1987); P. Forrest *The A-Z Of Analogue Synthesisers Part One: A-M* (Susurreal 1994); D. Gill (ed) *The Book Of The PIano* (Phaidon 1981); Dr R.E.E. Harding *The Piano-Forte, Its History Traced To The Great Exhibition Of 1851* (Gresham 1978); J. Koster *Keyboard Musical Instruments In The Museum Of Fine Arts, Boston* (Northeastern University Press 1994); L. Libin *Keyboard Instruments, The Metropolitan Museum Of Art* (Metropolitan Museum of Art 1989); S. Marcuse *A Survey Of Musical Instruments* (David & Charles 1975); M. Matthias *Steinway Service Manual* (Verlag Erwin Bochinsky 1990); J. Meffen *A Guide To Tuning Musical Instruments* (David & Charles 1982); B. Pierce *Pierce Piano Atlas 9th Edition* (Bob Pierce 1990); R. V. Ratcliffe *Steinway* (Chronicle 1989); H. R. Rice *The Piano* (David & Charles 1975); P. Rushton, (ed) *European Musical Instruments In Liverpool Museum* (NMGM 1994); S. Sadie (ed) *The New Grove Dictionary Of Musical Instruments* (Macmillan 1984); H. Shead *The Anatomy Of The Piano* (Gresham 1978); E. Smith *Pianos In Practice* (Scholar 1978); W. S. Sumner *The Pianoforte* (Macdonald 1966); K. Van Barthold & D. Buckton *The Story Of The Piano* (BBC 1975); D. Wainwright *Broadwood By Appointment* (Quiller 1982); D. Wainwright *The Piano Makers* (Hutchinson 1975); D. Wicks *The Family Piano Doctor* (Batsford 1991).